WHATEVER

HAPPENED

TO THE

WORLD

OF

TOMORROW?

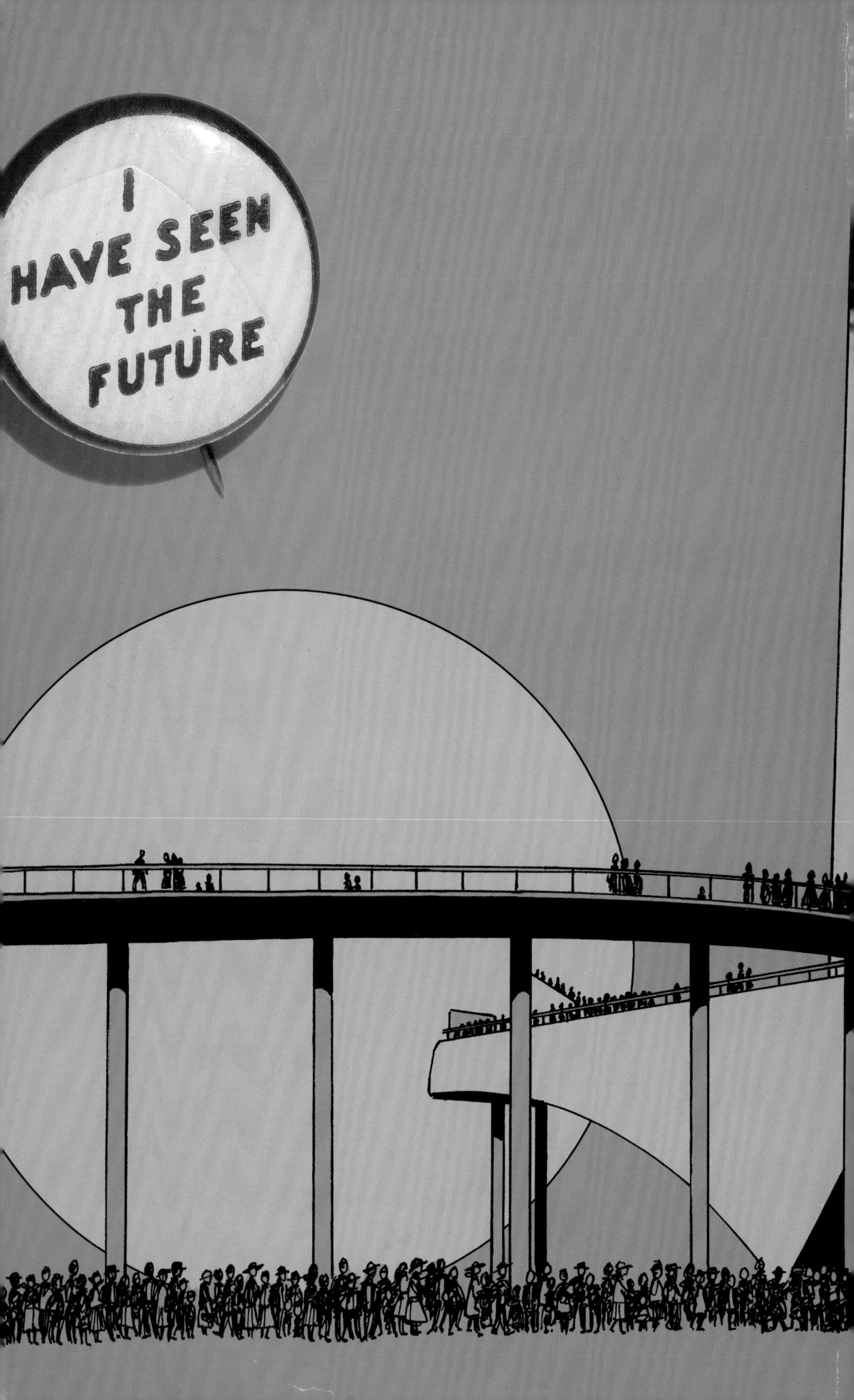
I HAVE SEEN THE FUTURE

# WHATEVER HAPPENED TO
# the WORLD OF TOMORROW?

## BRIAN FIES

SCHOLASTIC INC.

NEW YORK   TORONTO   LONDON   AUCKLAND
SYDNEY   NEW DELHI   HONG KONG

To Robin and Laura, my future


## ACKNOWLEDGMENTS

I wouldn't have finished this book on time or within the decade without the assistance of four talented young women: Laura Fies, Robin Fies, Kelly Swenson, and Kristen Swenson. All are terrific artists much more adept with digital media than I am. They will surely go on to do great things, and I was lucky to hire them while I could still afford their rates.

Several friends and colleagues reviewed early drafts of this book and provided invaluable criticism, including Mike Peterson, Sherwood Harrington, Ronnie Pardy, F. Bruce Oliver, Marion Deeds, Otis Frampton, and Mike Lynch. In addition, my best sounding board and critic is always my wife, Karen Fies. I did not take all of their advice, so don't blame them.

Many dedicated people at Harry N. Abrams worked very hard to make this book special in content and form, including president and CEO Michael Jacobs, publisher Steve Tager, executive managing editor Andrea Colvin, production V.P. Anet Sirna-Bruder, art director Michelle Ishay, designer Neil Egan, and assistant editor Sofia Gutiérrez. Executive editor Charlie Kochman, my friend and collaborator, contributed more to this book than either of us will ever admit.

My sincere thanks to them all.

Cover design by Sara Corbett.
Book design by Neil Egan.

Additional photography on pages ii and v by Geoff Spear.





Printed in China.

ISBN-13: 978-0-545-65628-3
ISBN-10: 0-545-65628-1





5 6 7 8 9 10 38 23 22 21 20 19 18 17 16 15

CONTENTS



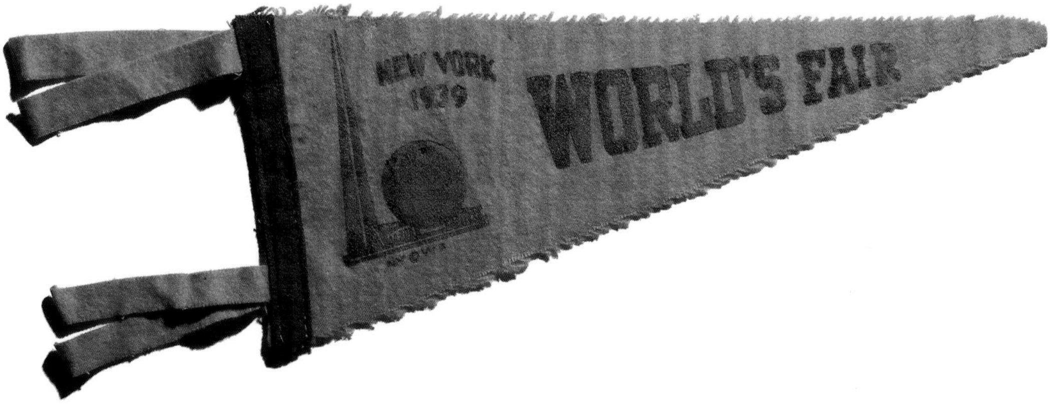

NEW YORK
1939
WORLD'S FAIR

*Ad astra per aspera.*
"Through hardships to the stars."

## AUTHOR'S NOTE

Predictably relative in space, time is chaotically fluid in the comics. It can advance slowly, stop entirely, or leap centuries in the gaps between panels. It preserves Batman as a prime physical specimen for seven decades and allows Dennis the Menace to celebrate his sixth birthday every year, only to awaken the next day as five again. Comics Time is a kind of magical realism almost unique to the realm of graphic fiction. It begins on the next page with a boy and his father, for whom time passes at a pace that serves their story.

I was born in Real Time near the beginning of the Space Age. My peers and I are just about the youngest cohort that will know the Apollo lunar landings as personal memories rather than impersonal history. We grew up expecting the future to be ours. An older generation born before the invention of the lightbulb had lived to see men walk on the moon; surely that trend of breathtaking technological progress would continue. We would conquer the lands of the Earth, the floors of the oceans, the surfaces of the planets. We would feed the hungry, enrich the poor, and free the enslaved. Certainly a golden age, if not outright utopia, was just around the corner.

We were wrong.

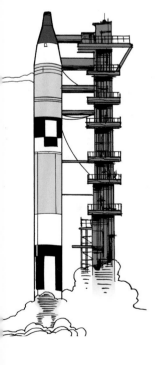

The millennial complaint "Where's my flying car and jetpack?" was a joke, but one that hinted at the hurt of a broken promise. Somewhere along the way, we lost something more important and profound than personal light aircraft. As the World of Tomorrow's dark and unintended consequences emerged, the very idea of a hopeful future worth working toward became old-fashioned and naïve. Onetime heroes became villains. Optimism was for saps; dystopian doom was where all the smart, cool, cynical people placed their bets.

I disagree. *Whatever Happened to the World of Tomorrow?* is an appreciation of, and an argument for, an increasingly rare way of thinking, creating, working, and living that has value. There was a time when building the future was inspirational. Ambitious. Romantic. Even ennobling. I think it can be again.

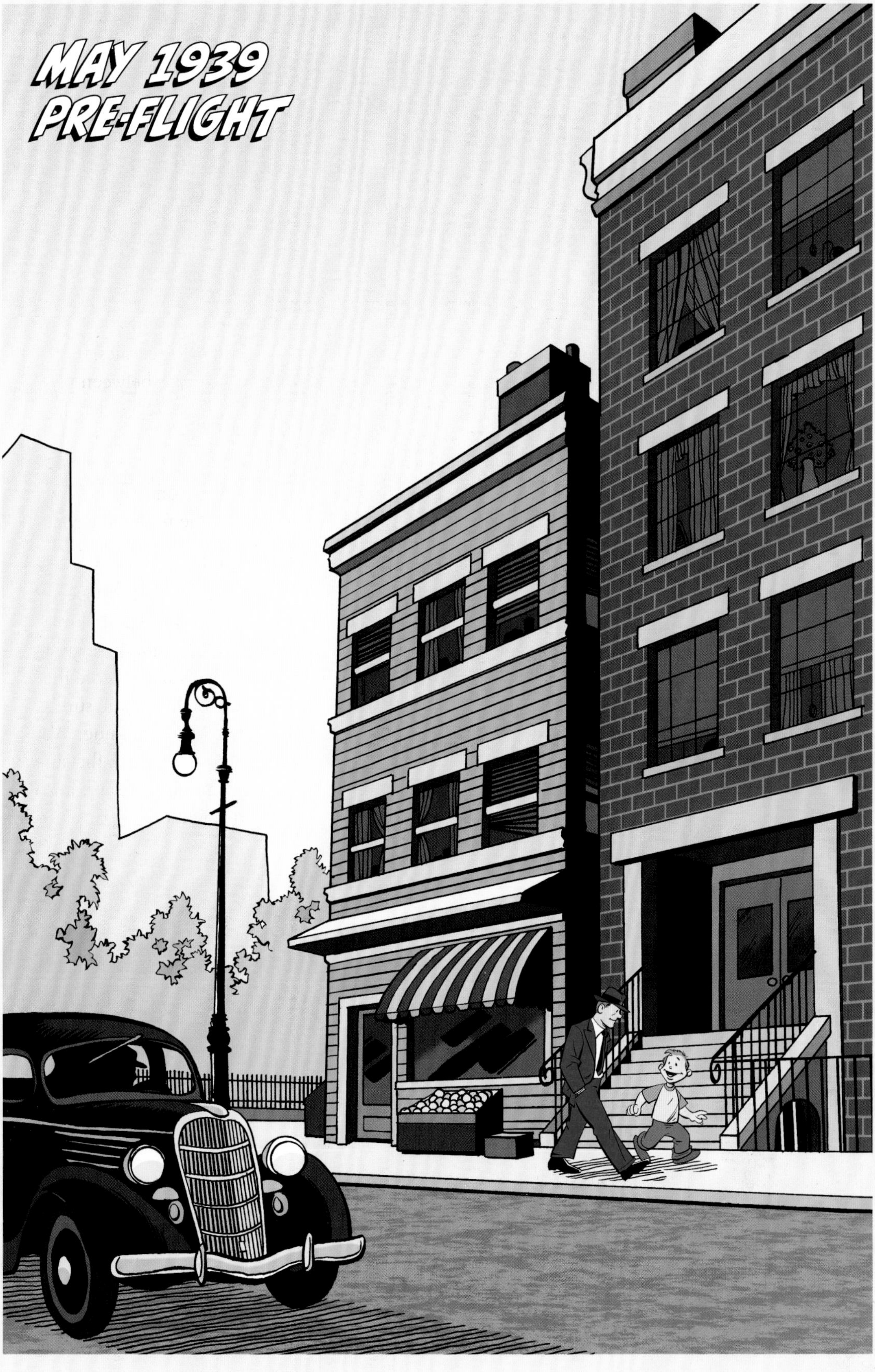
MAY 1939
PRE-FLIGHT

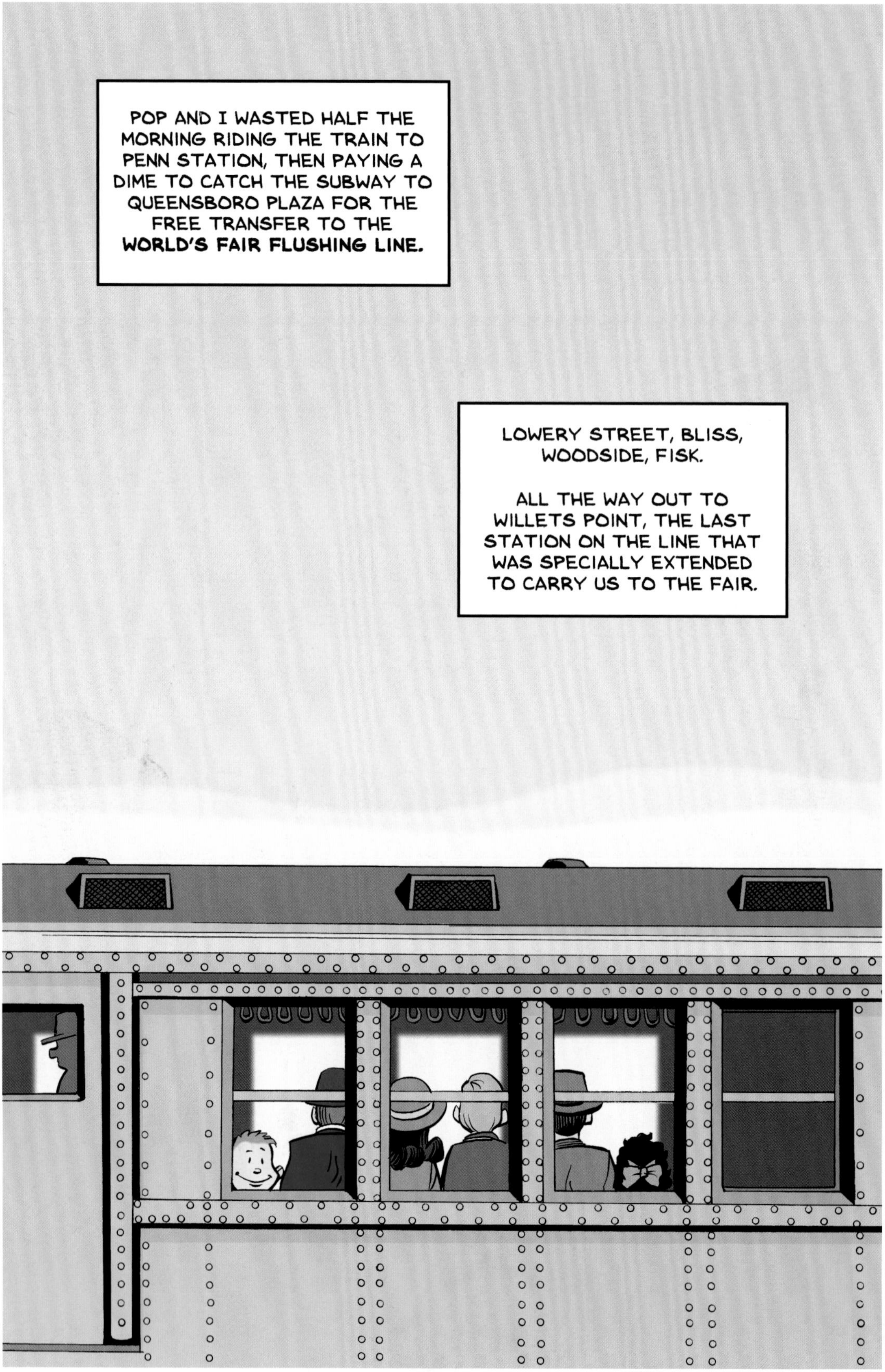
POP AND I WASTED HALF THE MORNING RIDING THE TRAIN TO PENN STATION, THEN PAYING A DIME TO CATCH THE SUBWAY TO QUEENSBORO PLAZA FOR THE FREE TRANSFER TO THE **WORLD'S FAIR FLUSHING LINE.**
LOWERY STREET, BLISS, WOODSIDE, FISK.
ALL THE WAY OUT TO WILLETS POINT, THE LAST STATION ON THE LINE THAT WAS SPECIALLY EXTENDED TO CARRY US TO THE FAIR.

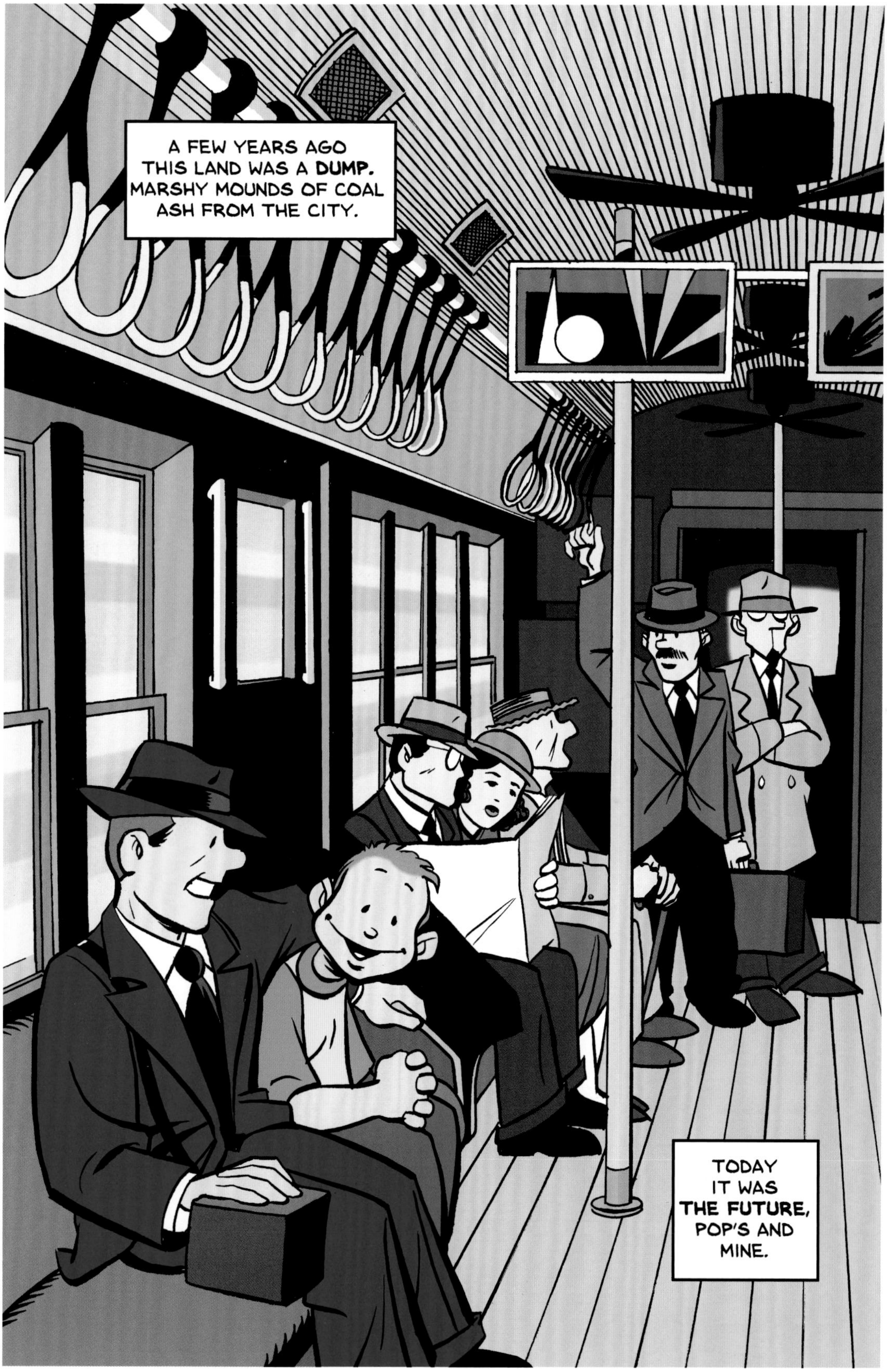
A FEW YEARS AGO THIS LAND WAS A **DUMP.** MARSHY MOUNDS OF COAL ASH FROM THE CITY.
TODAY IT WAS **THE FUTURE,** POP'S AND MINE.

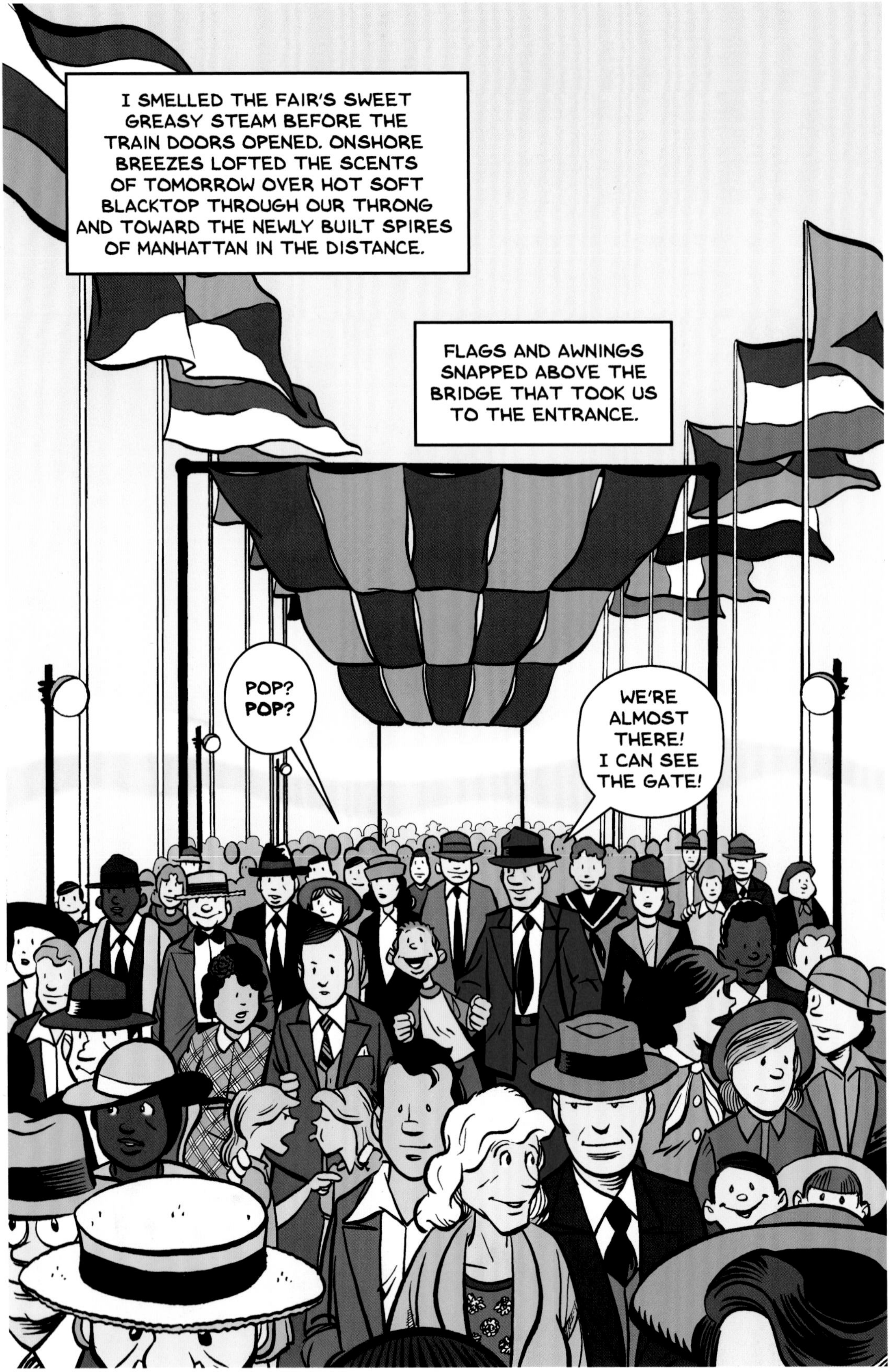
I SMELLED THE FAIR'S SWEET GREASY STEAM BEFORE THE TRAIN DOORS OPENED. ONSHORE BREEZES LOFTED THE SCENTS OF TOMORROW OVER HOT SOFT BLACKTOP THROUGH OUR THRONG AND TOWARD THE NEWLY BUILT SPIRES OF MANHATTAN IN THE DISTANCE.
FLAGS AND AWNINGS SNAPPED ABOVE THE BRIDGE THAT TOOK US TO THE ENTRANCE.
POP? POP?
WE'RE ALMOST THERE! I CAN SEE THE GATE!

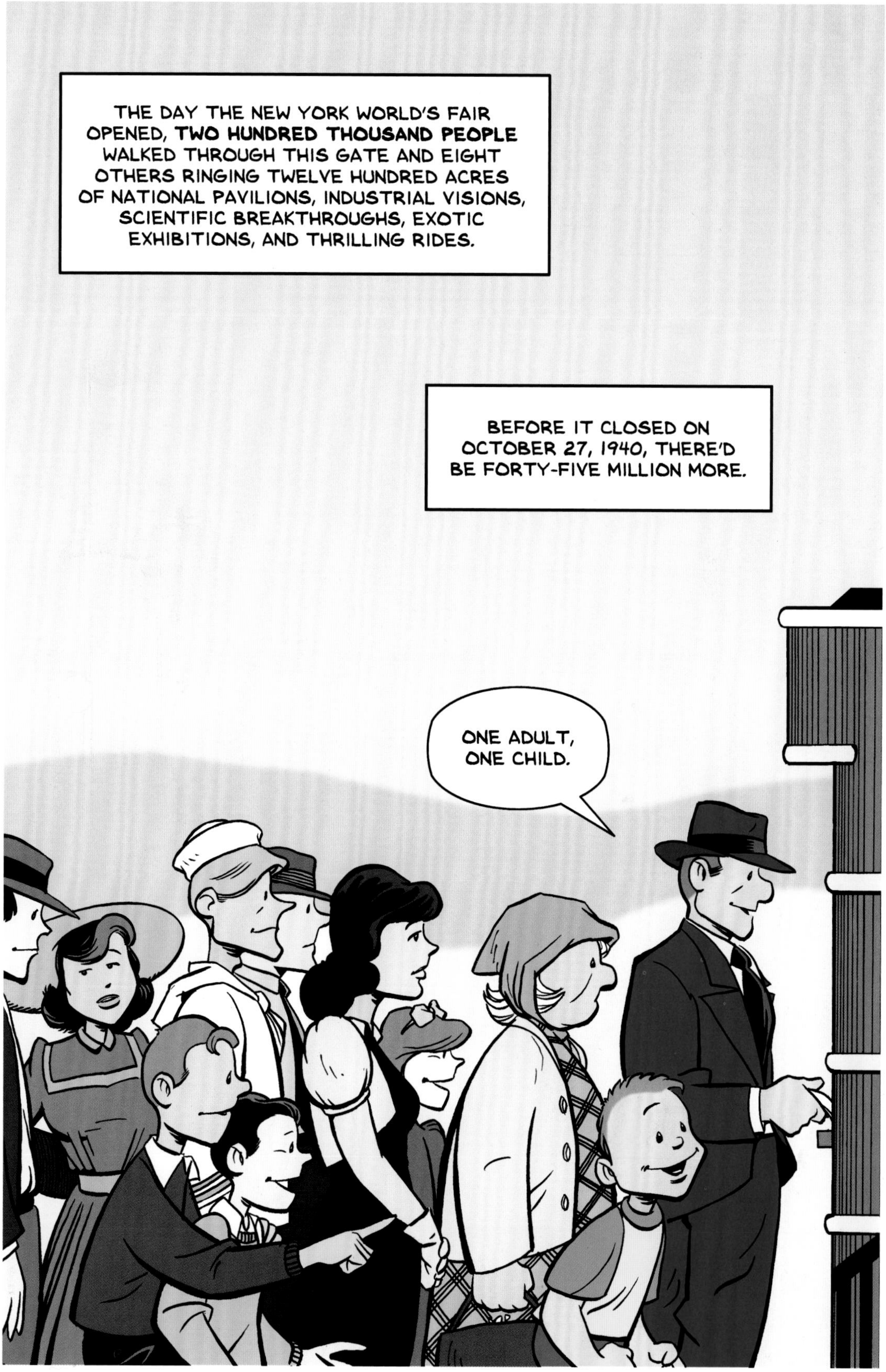
THE DAY THE NEW YORK WORLD'S FAIR OPENED, **TWO HUNDRED THOUSAND PEOPLE** WALKED THROUGH THIS GATE AND EIGHT OTHERS RINGING TWELVE HUNDRED ACRES OF NATIONAL PAVILIONS, INDUSTRIAL VISIONS, SCIENTIFIC BREAKTHROUGHS, EXOTIC EXHIBITIONS, AND THRILLING RIDES.
BEFORE IT CLOSED ON OCTOBER 27, 1940, THERE'D BE FORTY-FIVE MILLION MORE.
ONE ADULT, ONE CHILD.

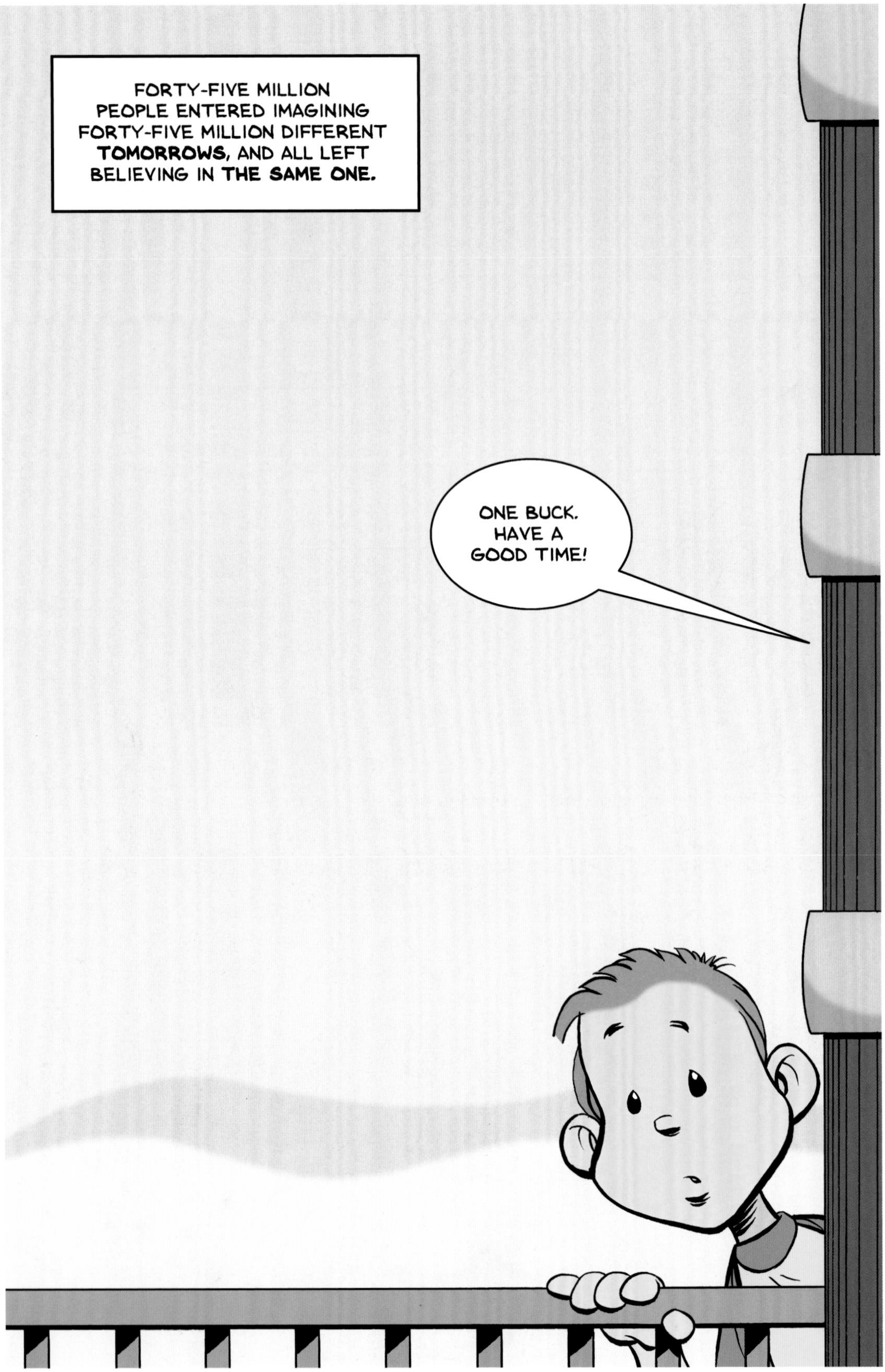
FORTY-FIVE MILLION PEOPLE ENTERED IMAGINING FORTY-FIVE MILLION DIFFERENT **TOMORROWS,** AND ALL LEFT BELIEVING IN **THE SAME ONE.**
ONE BUCK. HAVE A GOOD TIME!

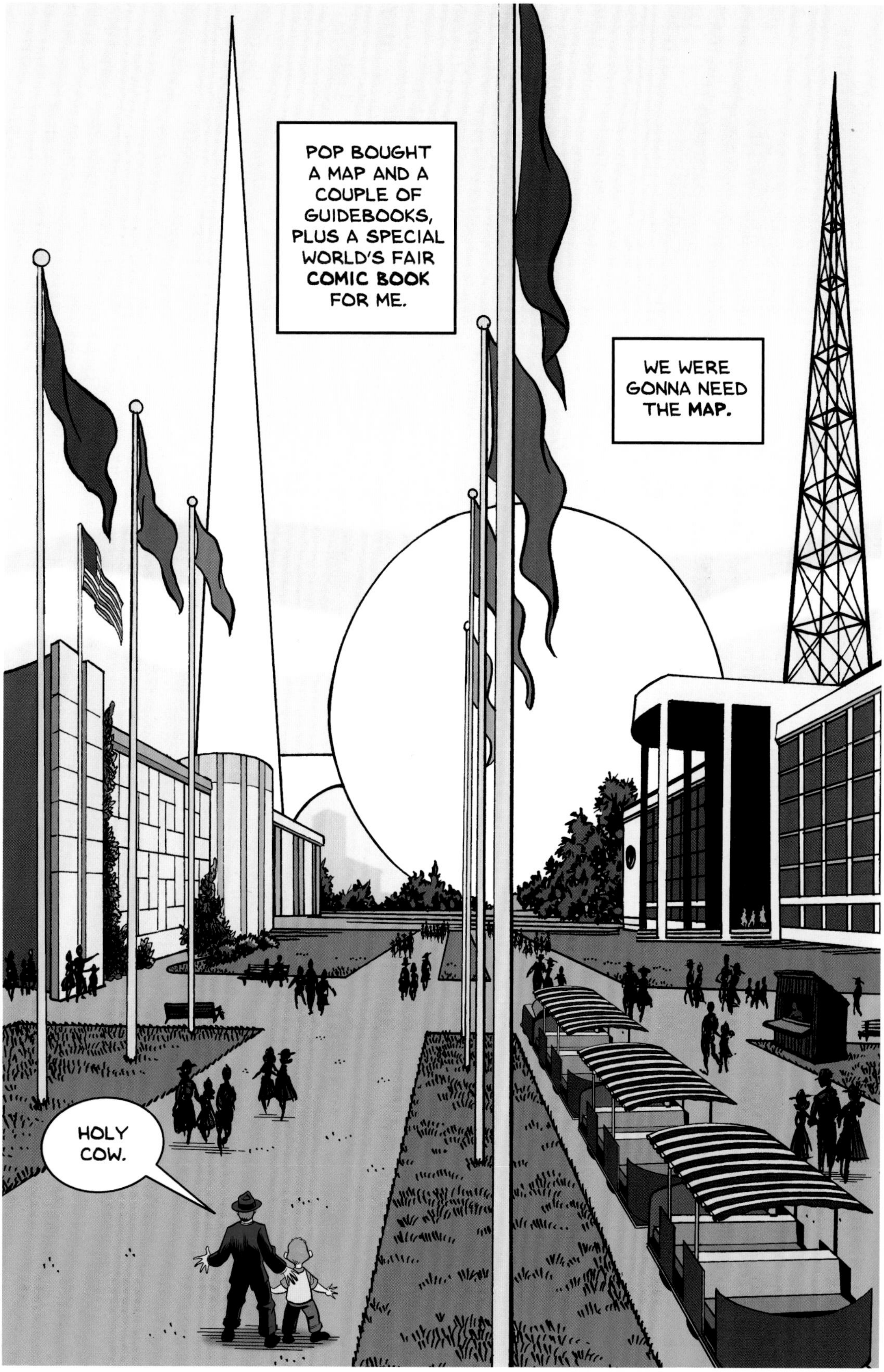
POP BOUGHT A MAP AND A COUPLE OF GUIDEBOOKS, PLUS A SPECIAL WORLD'S FAIR COMIC BOOK FOR ME.
WE WERE GONNA NEED THE MAP.
HOLY COW.

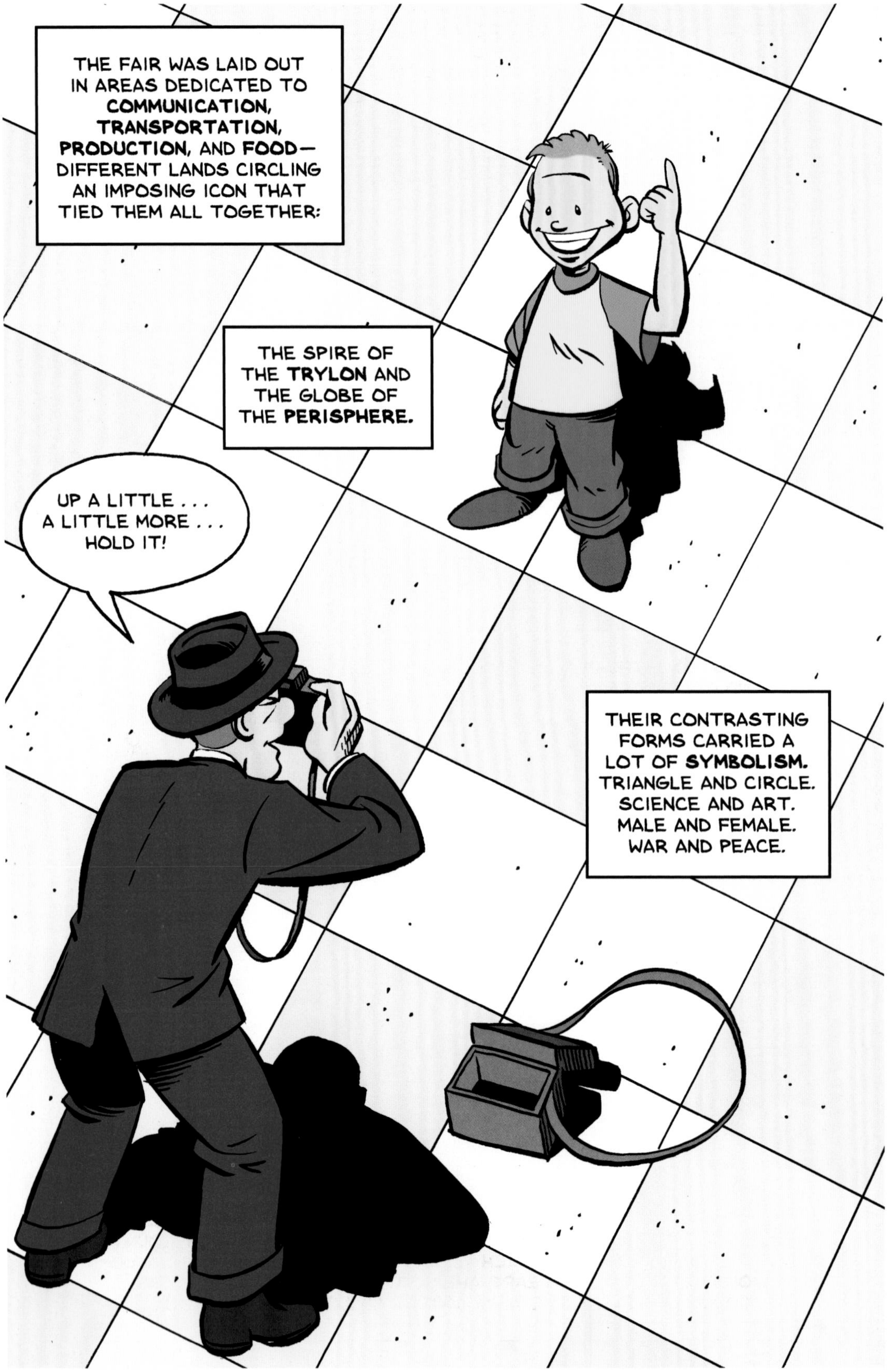
THE FAIR WAS LAID OUT IN AREAS DEDICATED TO **COMMUNICATION, TRANSPORTATION, PRODUCTION,** AND **FOOD**— DIFFERENT LANDS CIRCLING AN IMPOSING ICON THAT TIED THEM ALL TOGETHER:
THE SPIRE OF THE **TRYLON** AND THE GLOBE OF THE **PERISPHERE.**
UP A LITTLE . . . A LITTLE MORE . . . HOLD IT!
THEIR CONTRASTING FORMS CARRIED A LOT OF **SYMBOLISM.** TRIANGLE AND CIRCLE. SCIENCE AND ART. MALE AND FEMALE. WAR AND PEACE.

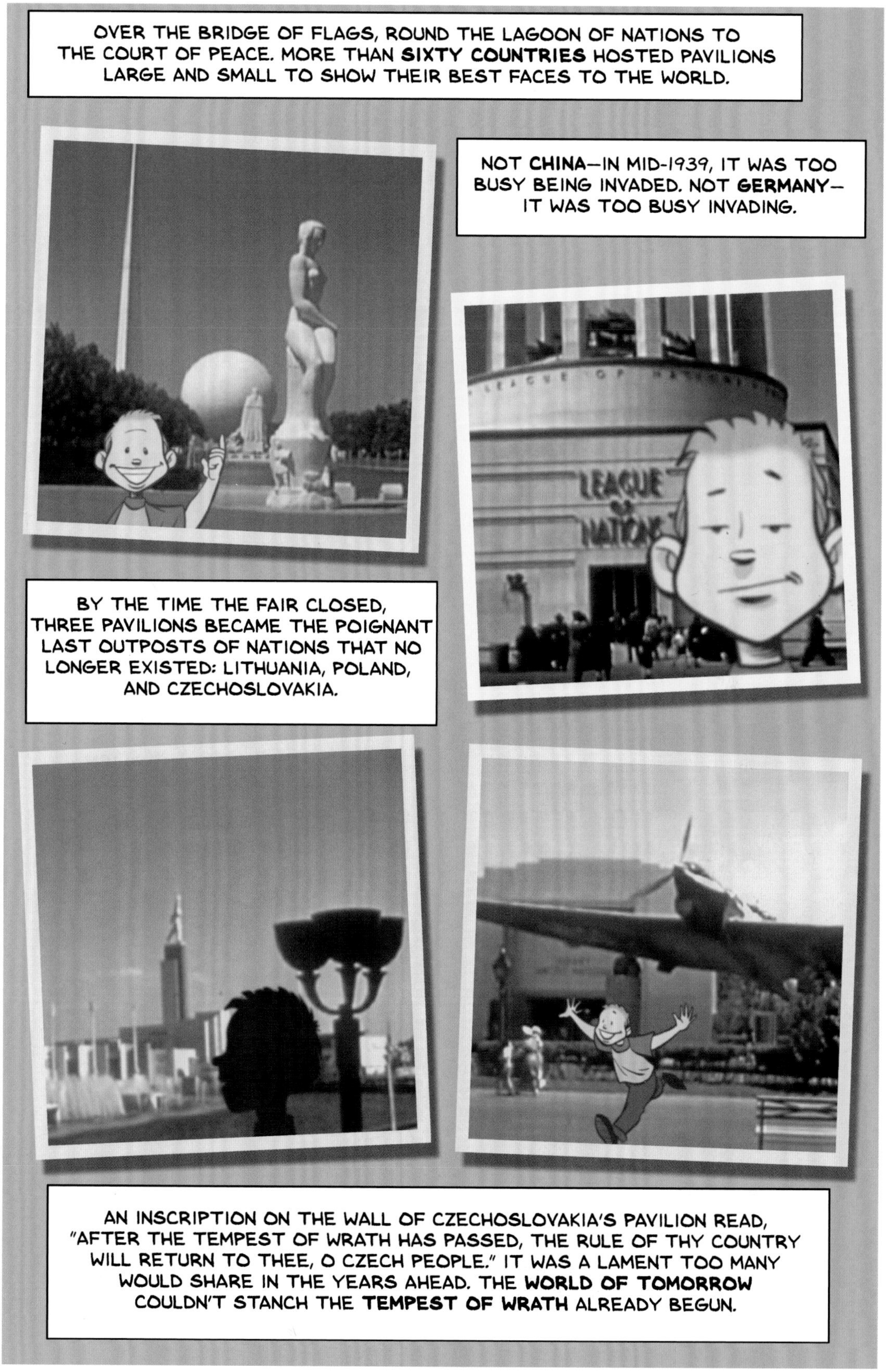
OVER THE BRIDGE OF FLAGS, ROUND THE LAGOON OF NATIONS TO THE COURT OF PEACE. MORE THAN **SIXTY COUNTRIES** HOSTED PAVILIONS LARGE AND SMALL TO SHOW THEIR BEST FACES TO THE WORLD.
NOT **CHINA**—IN MID-1939, IT WAS TOO BUSY BEING INVADED. NOT **GERMANY**—IT WAS TOO BUSY INVADING.
LEAGUE
BY THE TIME THE FAIR CLOSED, THREE PAVILIONS BECAME THE POIGNANT LAST OUTPOSTS OF NATIONS THAT NO LONGER EXISTED: LITHUANIA, POLAND, AND CZECHOSLOVAKIA.
AN INSCRIPTION ON THE WALL OF CZECHOSLOVAKIA'S PAVILION READ, "AFTER THE TEMPEST OF WRATH HAS PASSED, THE RULE OF THY COUNTRY WILL RETURN TO THEE, O CZECH PEOPLE." IT WAS A LAMENT TOO MANY WOULD SHARE IN THE YEARS AHEAD. THE **WORLD OF TOMORROW** COULDN'T STANCH THE **TEMPEST OF WRATH** ALREADY BEGUN.

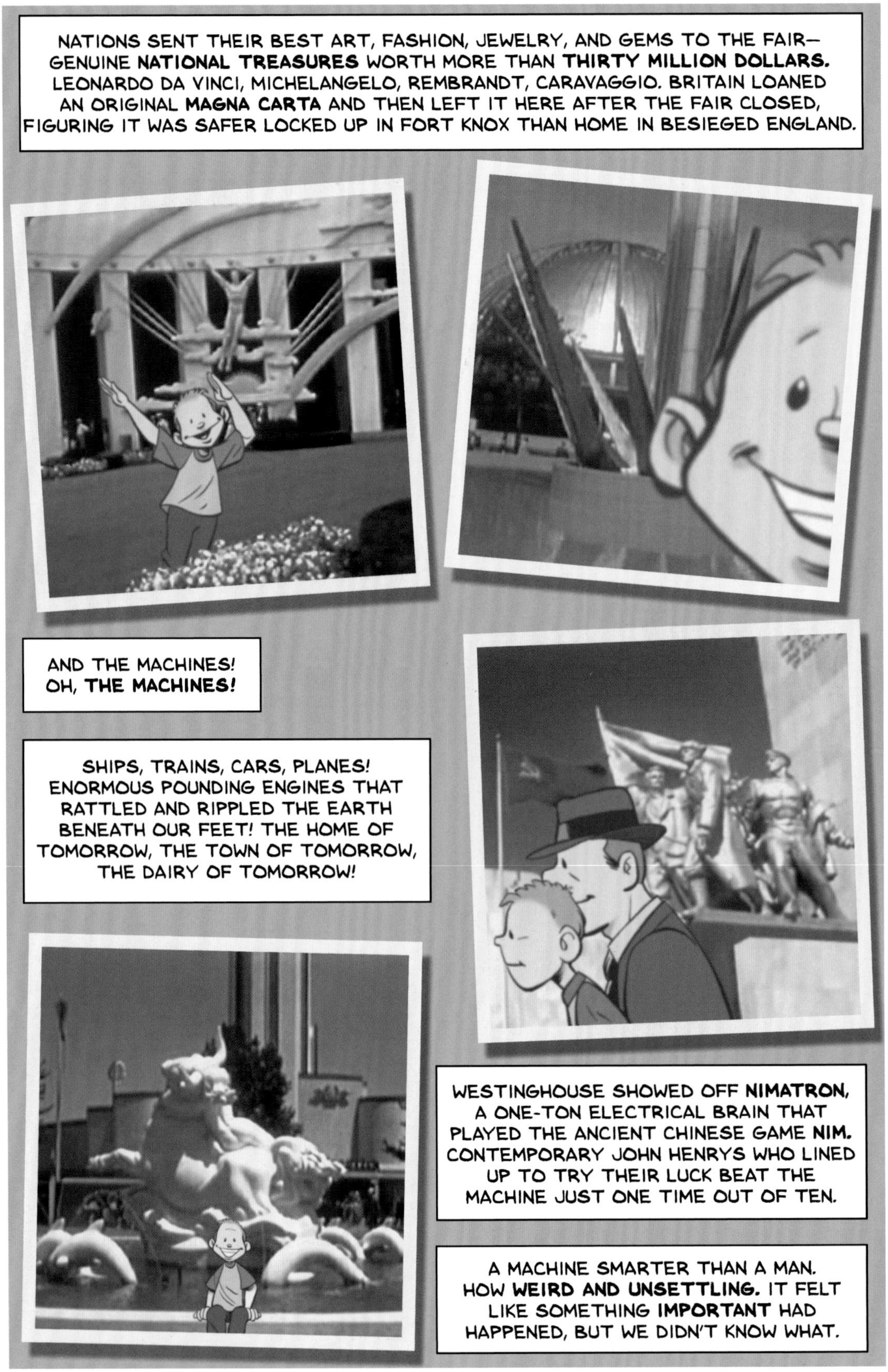
NATIONS SENT THEIR BEST ART, FASHION, JEWELRY, AND GEMS TO THE FAIR—GENUINE NATIONAL TREASURES WORTH MORE THAN THIRTY MILLION DOLLARS. LEONARDO DA VINCI, MICHELANGELO, REMBRANDT, CARAVAGGIO. BRITAIN LOANED AN ORIGINAL MAGNA CARTA AND THEN LEFT IT HERE AFTER THE FAIR CLOSED, FIGURING IT WAS SAFER LOCKED UP IN FORT KNOX THAN HOME IN BESIEGED ENGLAND.
AND THE MACHINES! OH, THE MACHINES!
SHIPS, TRAINS, CARS, PLANES! ENORMOUS POUNDING ENGINES THAT RATTLED AND RIPPLED THE EARTH BENEATH OUR FEET! THE HOME OF TOMORROW, THE TOWN OF TOMORROW, THE DAIRY OF TOMORROW!
WESTINGHOUSE SHOWED OFF NIMATRON, A ONE-TON ELECTRICAL BRAIN THAT PLAYED THE ANCIENT CHINESE GAME NIM. CONTEMPORARY JOHN HENRYS WHO LINED UP TO TRY THEIR LUCK BEAT THE MACHINE JUST ONE TIME OUT OF TEN.
A MACHINE SMARTER THAN A MAN. HOW WEIRD AND UNSETTLING. IT FELT LIKE SOMETHING IMPORTANT HAD HAPPENED, BUT WE DIDN'T KNOW WHAT.

ONCE EVERY HOUR, WESTINGHOUSE PUT AN EIGHT-FOOT-TALL ROBOT NAMED **ELEKTRO** THROUGH HIS PACES, SHOWING THE CROWD HOW HE MOVED, TALKED, ANSWERED QUESTIONS, EVEN SMOKED CIGARETTES.

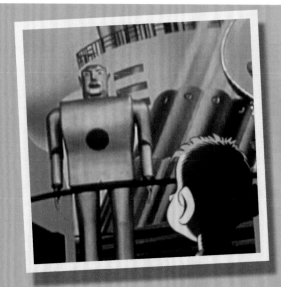

A COPPER-CHROMIUM-SILVER **TIME CAPSULE** IN THE WESTINGHOUSE COURTYARD CONTAINED A CAMERA, ALARM CLOCK, EYEGLASSES, SAFETY PIN, FOUNTAIN PEN, BASEBALL, DECK OF CARDS, POKER CHIPS, CHANGE FOR A DOLLAR, AND MORE, MEANT TO REPRESENT EVERYDAY MODERN LIFE TO THE PEOPLE OF **6939.**

BOOKS DESCRIBING HOW TO FIND THE CAPSULE WERE SENT TO LIBRARIES THROUGHOUT THE WORLD IN THE HOPE THAT **SOME** OF THEM MIGHT SURVIVE **FIVE THOUSAND YEARS.**

WHAT WILL THE **SEVENTIETH CENTURY** MAKE OF A LIPSTICK, A GOLF TEE, HAND-SET PRINTER'S TYPE, "WEIRD TALES" MAGAZINE, OR FILM FOOTAGE OF A MIAMI BEACH FASHION SHOW?

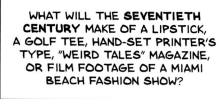

I LIKE TO IMAGINE THEY'LL FIND US AND OUR STUFF BOTH **REASSURINGLY FAMILIAR** AND **UTTERLY BAFFLING.**

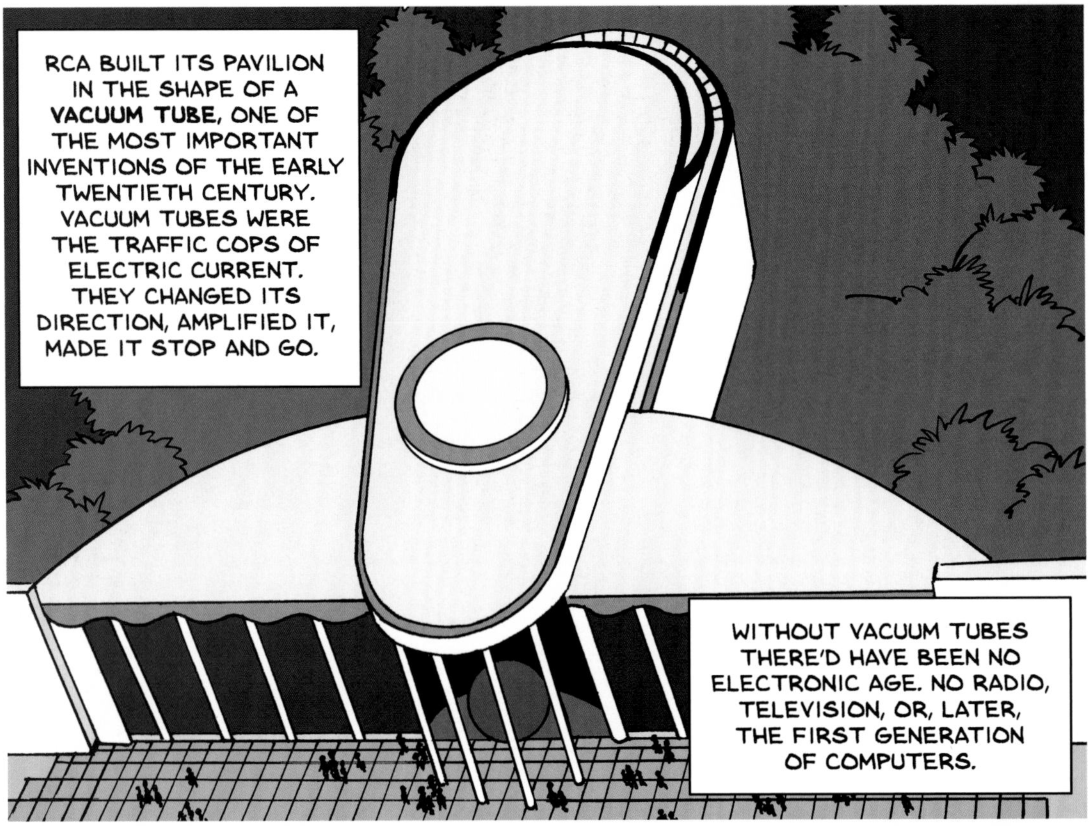
RCA BUILT ITS PAVILION IN THE SHAPE OF A **VACUUM TUBE**, ONE OF THE MOST IMPORTANT INVENTIONS OF THE EARLY TWENTIETH CENTURY. VACUUM TUBES WERE THE TRAFFIC COPS OF ELECTRIC CURRENT. THEY CHANGED ITS DIRECTION, AMPLIFIED IT, MADE IT STOP AND GO.
WITHOUT VACUUM TUBES THERE'D HAVE BEEN NO ELECTRONIC AGE. NO RADIO, TELEVISION, OR, LATER, THE FIRST GENERATION OF COMPUTERS.

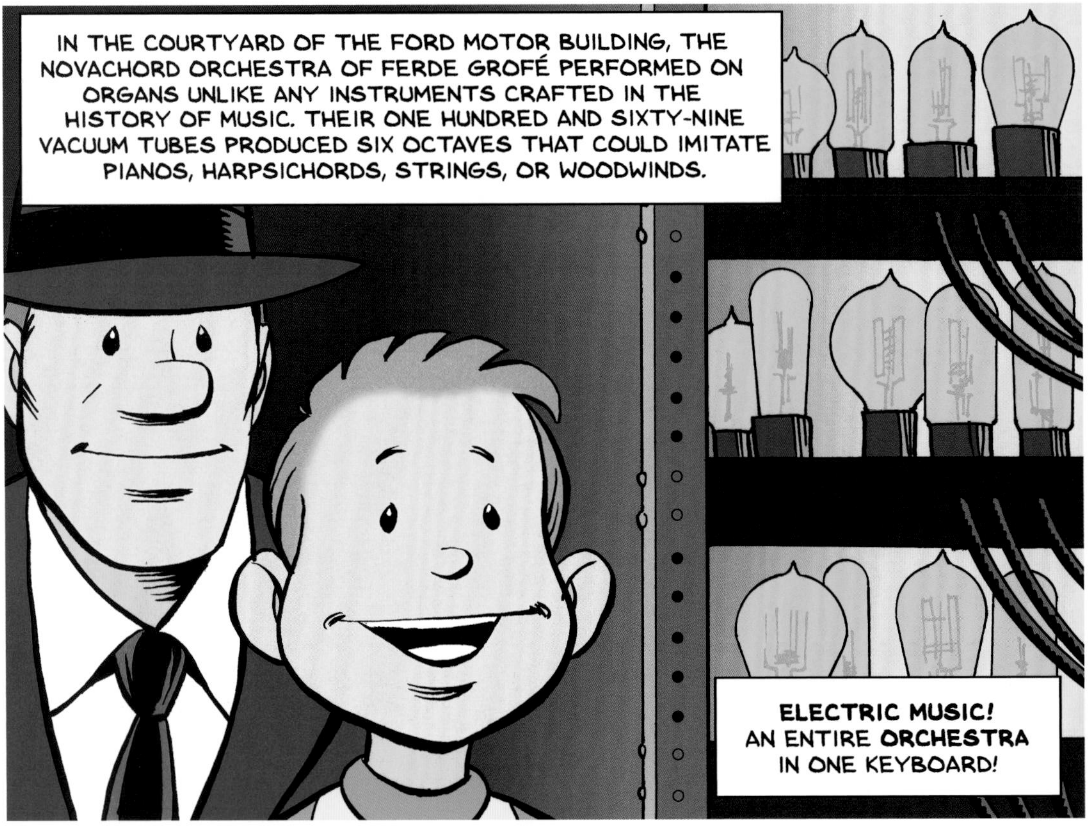
IN THE COURTYARD OF THE FORD MOTOR BUILDING, THE NOVACHORD ORCHESTRA OF FERDE GROFÉ PERFORMED ON ORGANS UNLIKE ANY INSTRUMENTS CRAFTED IN THE HISTORY OF MUSIC. THEIR ONE HUNDRED AND SIXTY-NINE VACUUM TUBES PRODUCED SIX OCTAVES THAT COULD IMITATE PIANOS, HARPSICHORDS, STRINGS, OR WOODWINDS.
**ELECTRIC MUSIC!** AN ENTIRE **ORCHESTRA** IN ONE KEYBOARD!

IN ITS "RADIO LIVING ROOM OF THE FUTURE," RCA DEMONSTRATED A NEW WAY OF BROADCASTING RADIO PROGRAMS USING **FREQUENCY MODULATION.** THE EXHIBIT ALSO HAD A **FACSIMILE MACHINE,** WHICH COULD SEND WORDS AND PICTURES OVER PHONE LINES TO A RECEIVER THAT PRINTED EIGHTEEN PAGES PER MINUTE.

AND THERE WAS TELEVISION.

**TELEVISION!** PICTURE RADIO! MOVIES, CONCERTS, AND PLAYS IN YOUR OWN LIVING ROOM!

**AT HOME!**

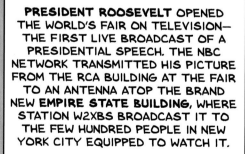

PRESIDENT ROOSEVELT OPENED THE WORLD'S FAIR ON TELEVISION— THE FIRST LIVE BROADCAST OF A PRESIDENTIAL SPEECH. THE NBC NETWORK TRANSMITTED HIS PICTURE FROM THE RCA BUILDING AT THE FAIR TO AN ANTENNA ATOP THE BRAND NEW **EMPIRE STATE BUILDING,** WHERE STATION W2XBS BROADCAST IT TO THE FEW HUNDRED PEOPLE IN NEW YORK CITY EQUIPPED TO WATCH IT.

THROUGHOUT THE FAIR'S RUN, RCA INVITED GUESTS TO BEAM THEIR IMAGES AND VOICES TO THE TELEVISIONS ON DISPLAY NEARBY. OF ALL THE FUTURISTIC MARVELS WE WITNESSED THAT DAY, SEEING **OUR FIRST TV** WAS THE MOMENT POP AND I KNEW NOTHING WOULD EVER BE THE SAME.

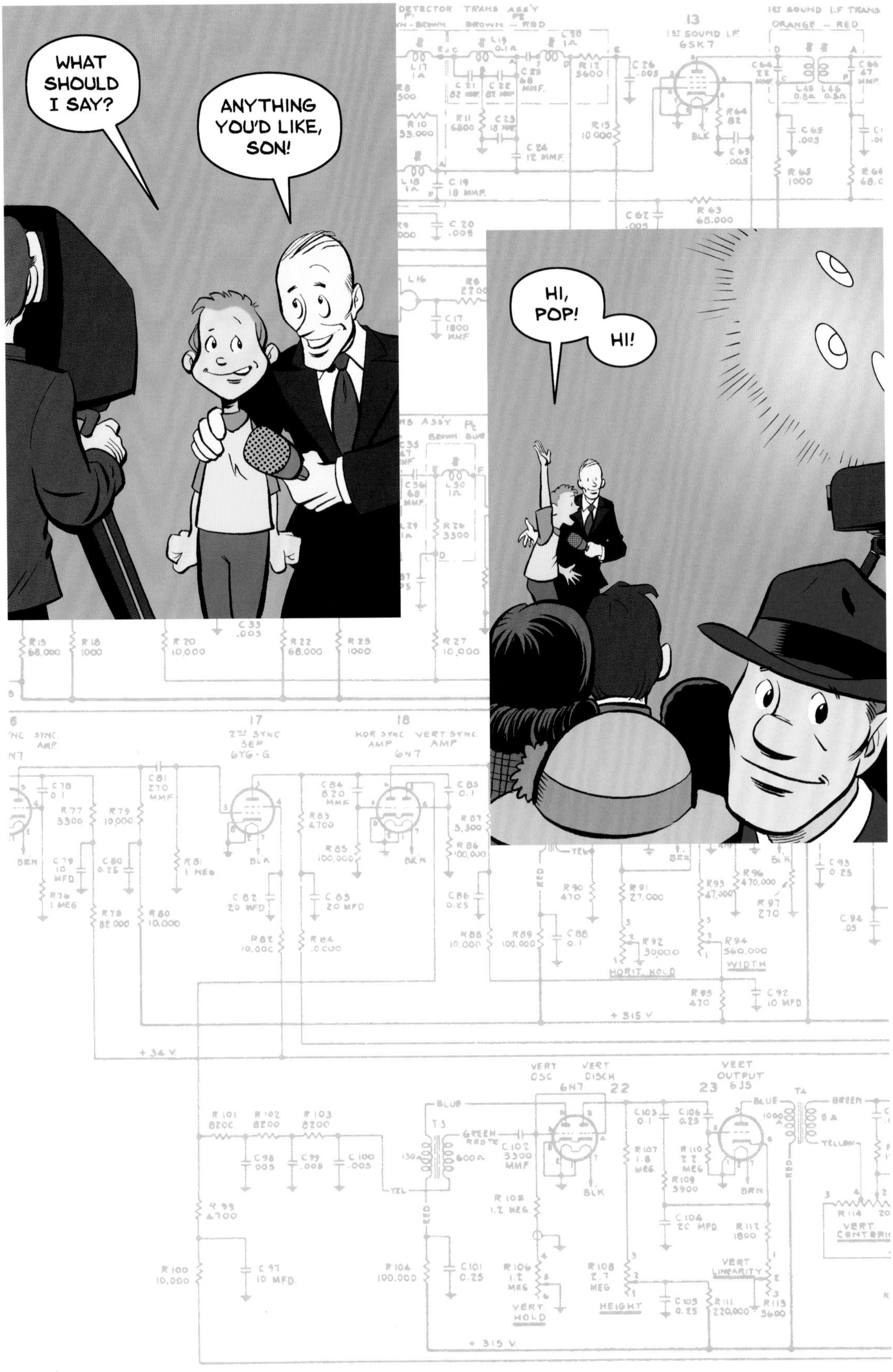
WHAT SHOULD I SAY?
ANYTHING YOU'D LIKE, SON!
HI, POP!
HI!

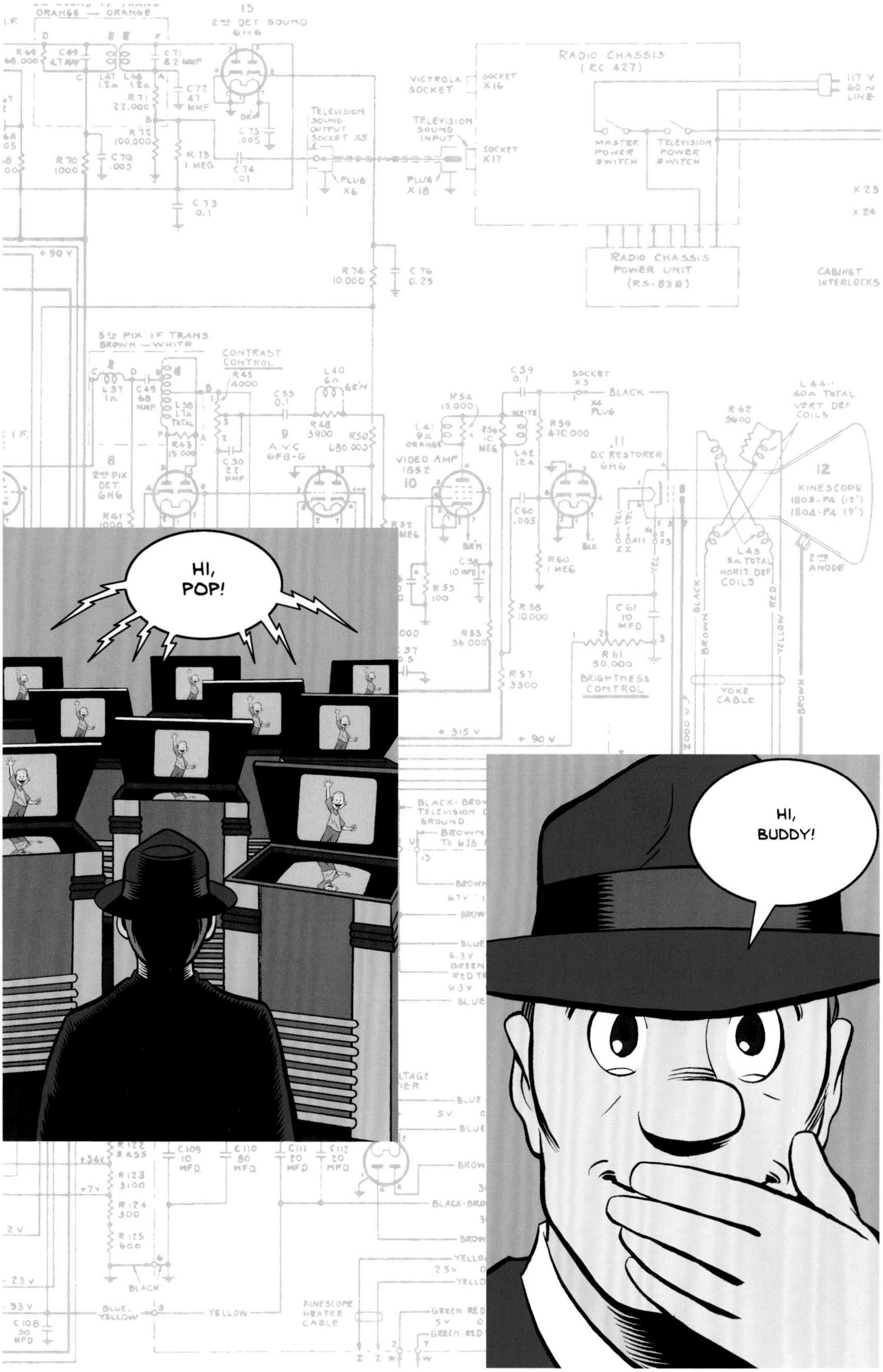
HI, POP!
HI, BUDDY!

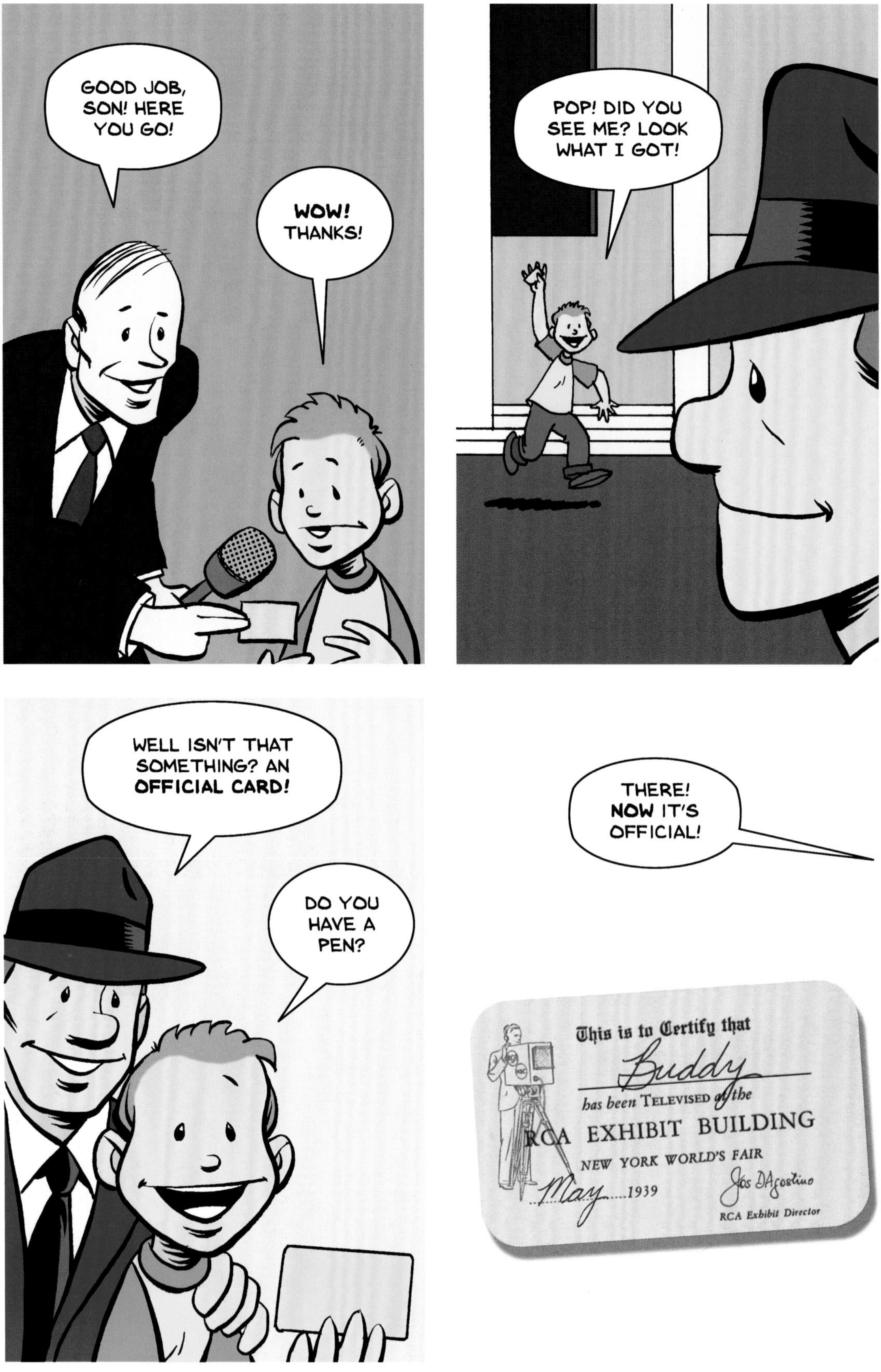
GOOD JOB, SON! HERE YOU GO!
WOW! THANKS!
POP! DID YOU SEE ME? LOOK WHAT I GOT!
WELL ISN'T THAT SOMETHING? AN OFFICIAL CARD!
DO YOU HAVE A PEN?
THERE! NOW IT'S OFFICIAL!
This is to Certify that
Buddy
has been TELEVISED at the
RCA EXHIBIT BUILDING
NEW YORK WORLD'S FAIR
May 1939
Jos DAgostino
RCA Exhibit Director

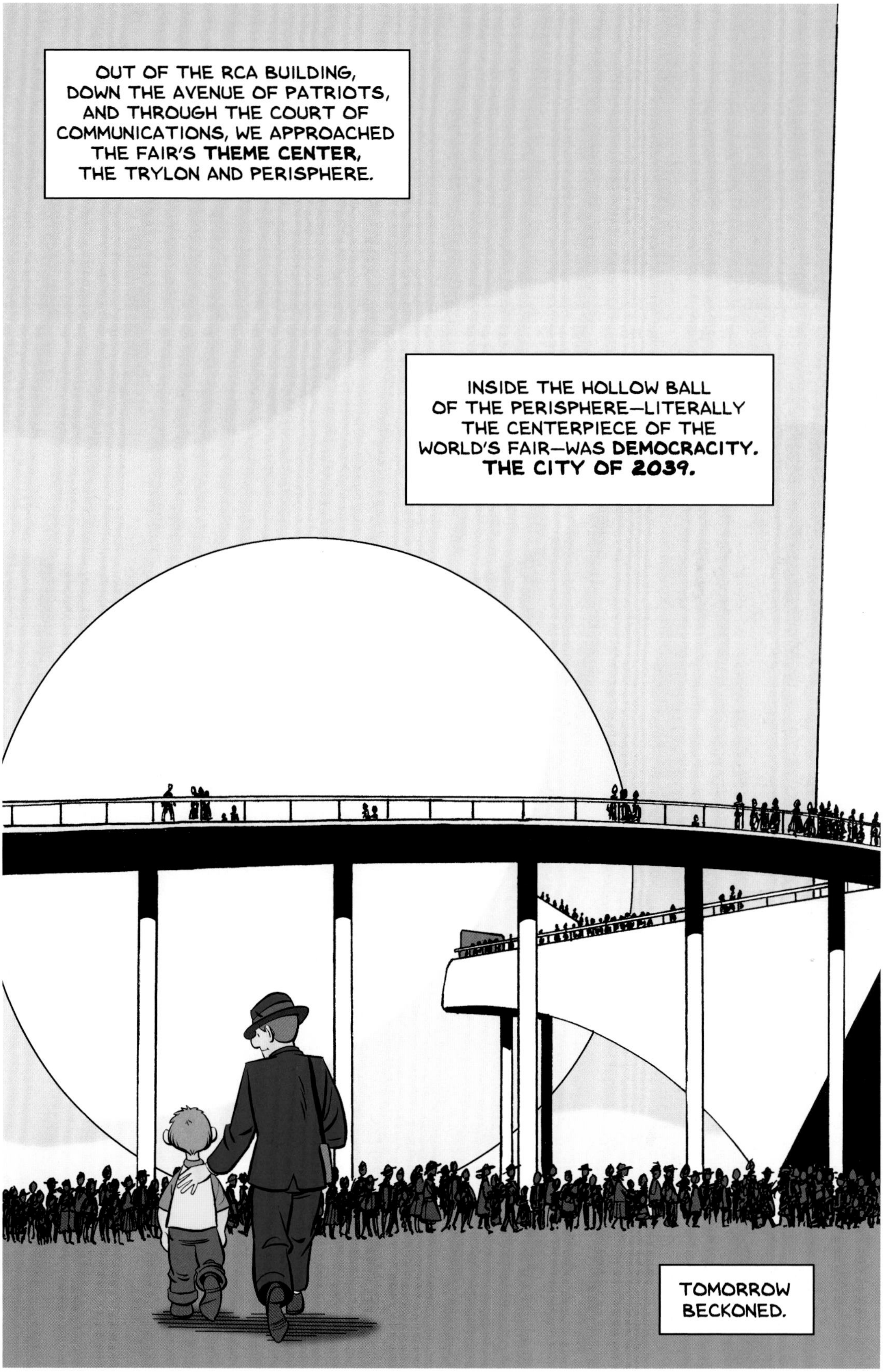
OUT OF THE RCA BUILDING, DOWN THE AVENUE OF PATRIOTS, AND THROUGH THE COURT OF COMMUNICATIONS, WE APPROACHED THE FAIR'S **THEME CENTER**, THE TRYLON AND PERISPHERE.
INSIDE THE HOLLOW BALL OF THE PERISPHERE—LITERALLY THE CENTERPIECE OF THE WORLD'S FAIR—WAS **DEMOCRACITY. THE CITY OF 2039.**
TOMORROW BECKONED.

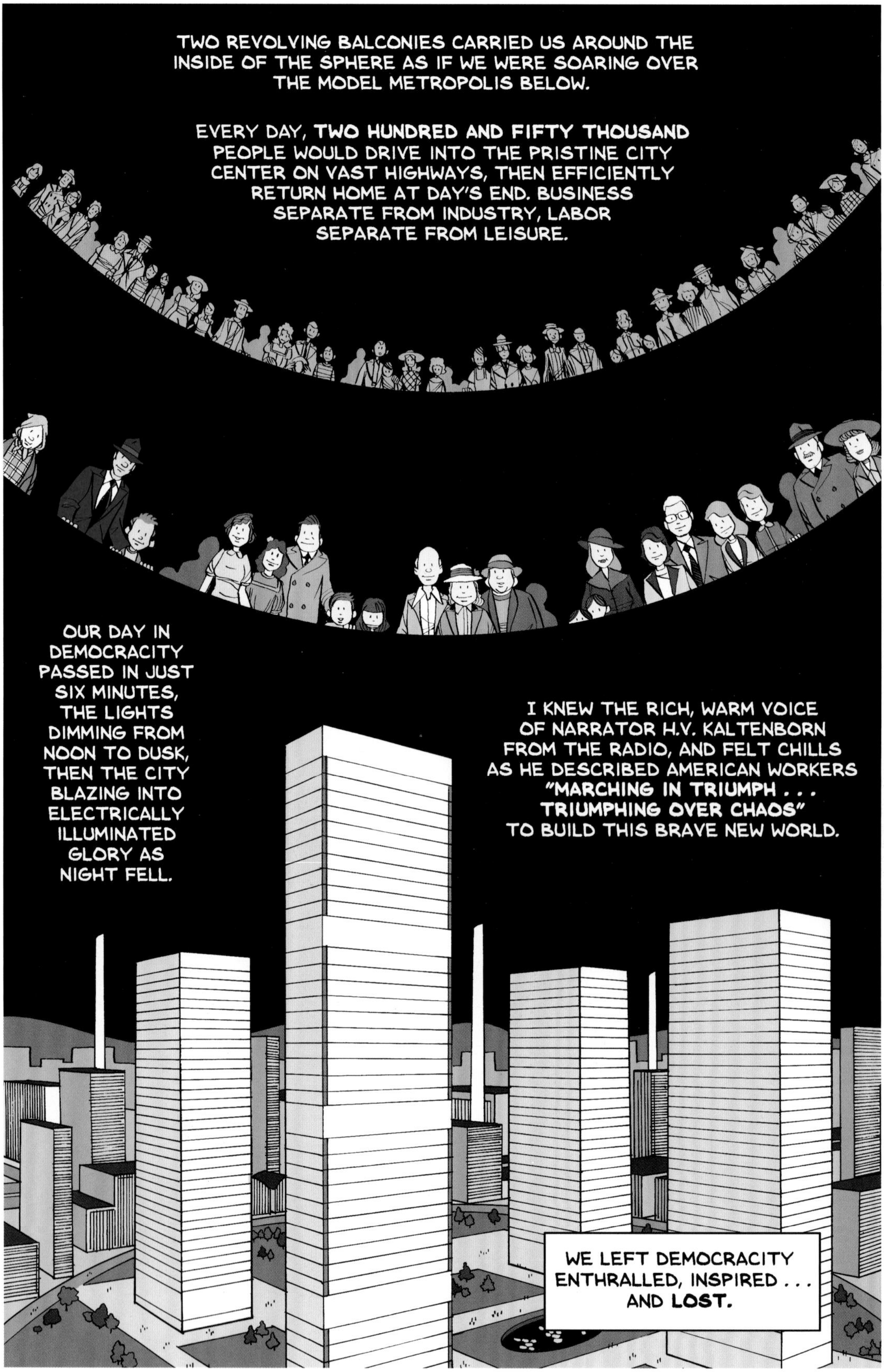
TWO REVOLVING BALCONIES CARRIED US AROUND THE INSIDE OF THE SPHERE AS IF WE WERE SOARING OVER THE MODEL METROPOLIS BELOW.
EVERY DAY, **TWO HUNDRED AND FIFTY THOUSAND** PEOPLE WOULD DRIVE INTO THE PRISTINE CITY CENTER ON VAST HIGHWAYS, THEN EFFICIENTLY RETURN HOME AT DAY'S END. BUSINESS SEPARATE FROM INDUSTRY, LABOR SEPARATE FROM LEISURE.
OUR DAY IN DEMOCRACITY PASSED IN JUST SIX MINUTES, THE LIGHTS DIMMING FROM NOON TO DUSK, THEN THE CITY BLAZING INTO ELECTRICALLY ILLUMINATED GLORY AS NIGHT FELL.
I KNEW THE RICH, WARM VOICE OF NARRATOR H.V. KALTENBORN FROM THE RADIO, AND FELT CHILLS AS HE DESCRIBED AMERICAN WORKERS **"MARCHING IN TRIUMPH . . . TRIUMPHING OVER CHAOS"** TO BUILD THIS BRAVE NEW WORLD.
WE LEFT DEMOCRACITY ENTHRALLED, INSPIRED . . . AND **LOST.**

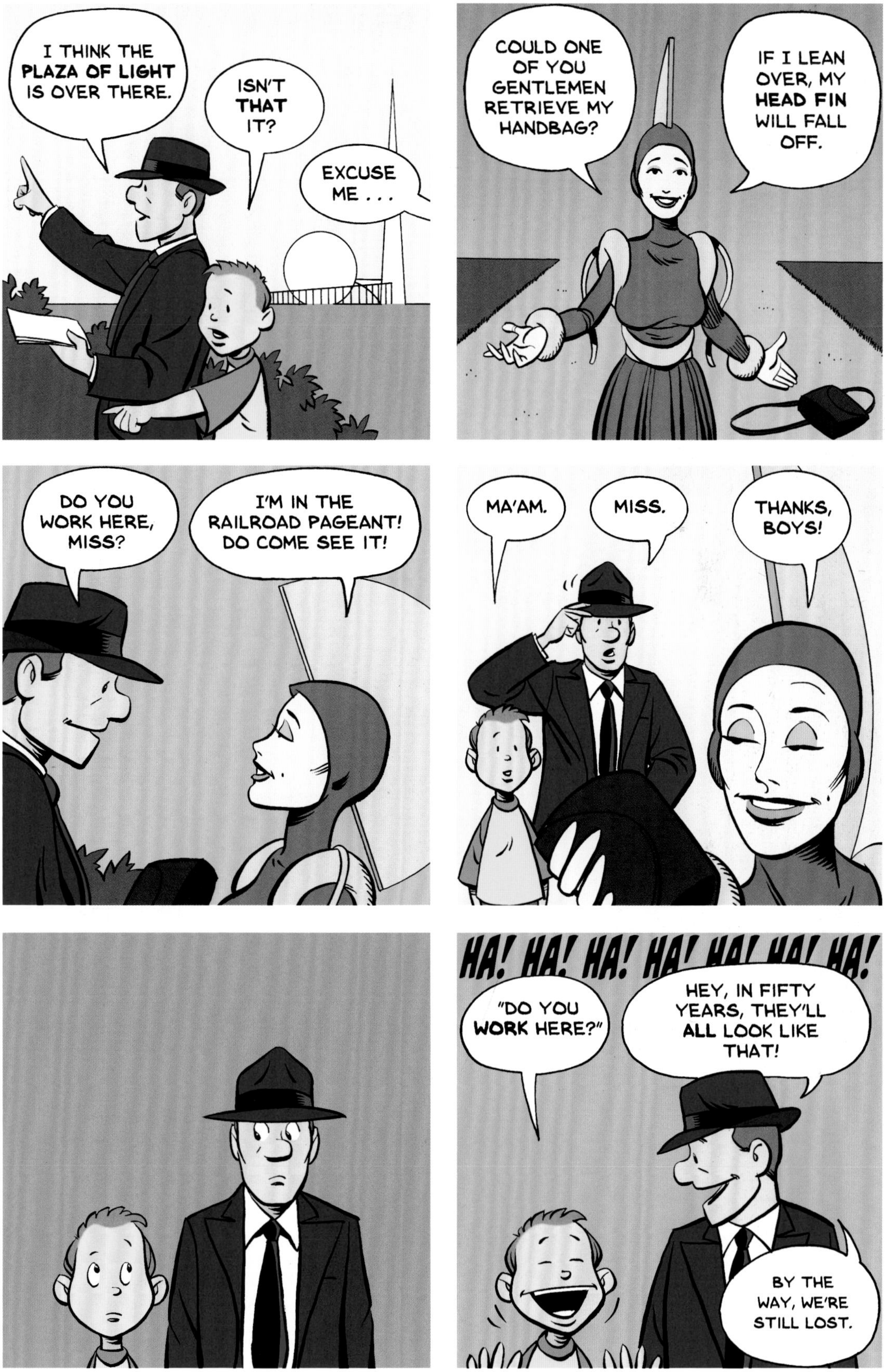
I THINK THE PLAZA OF LIGHT IS OVER THERE.
ISN'T THAT IT?
EXCUSE ME . . .
COULD ONE OF YOU GENTLEMEN RETRIEVE MY HANDBAG?
IF I LEAN OVER, MY HEAD FIN WILL FALL OFF.
DO YOU WORK HERE, MISS?
I'M IN THE RAILROAD PAGEANT! DO COME SEE IT!
MA'AM.
MISS.
THANKS, BOYS!
HA! HA! HA! HA! HA! HA! HA!
"DO YOU WORK HERE?"
HEY, IN FIFTY YEARS, THEY'LL ALL LOOK LIKE THAT!
BY THE WAY, WE'RE STILL LOST.

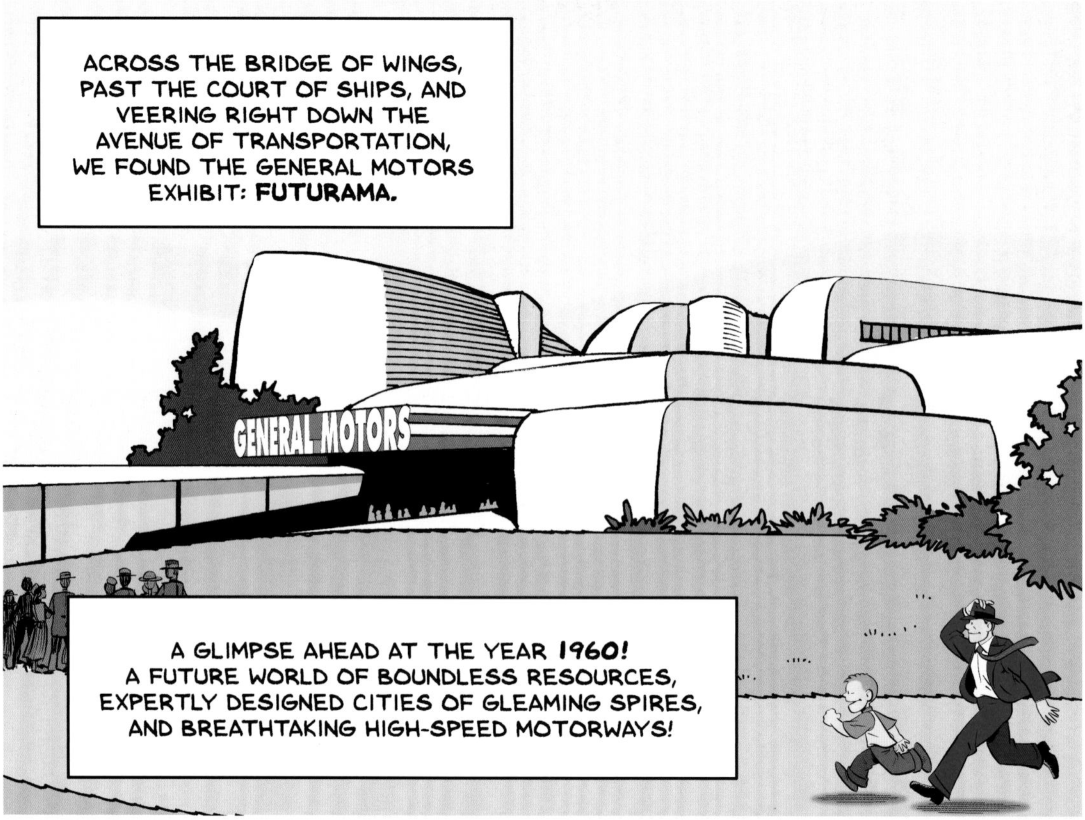
ACROSS THE BRIDGE OF WINGS, PAST THE COURT OF SHIPS, AND VEERING RIGHT DOWN THE AVENUE OF TRANSPORTATION, WE FOUND THE GENERAL MOTORS EXHIBIT: **FUTURAMA.**
GENERAL MOTORS
A GLIMPSE AHEAD AT THE YEAR **1960!** A FUTURE WORLD OF BOUNDLESS RESOURCES, EXPERTLY DESIGNED CITIES OF GLEAMING SPIRES, AND BREATHTAKING HIGH-SPEED MOTORWAYS!

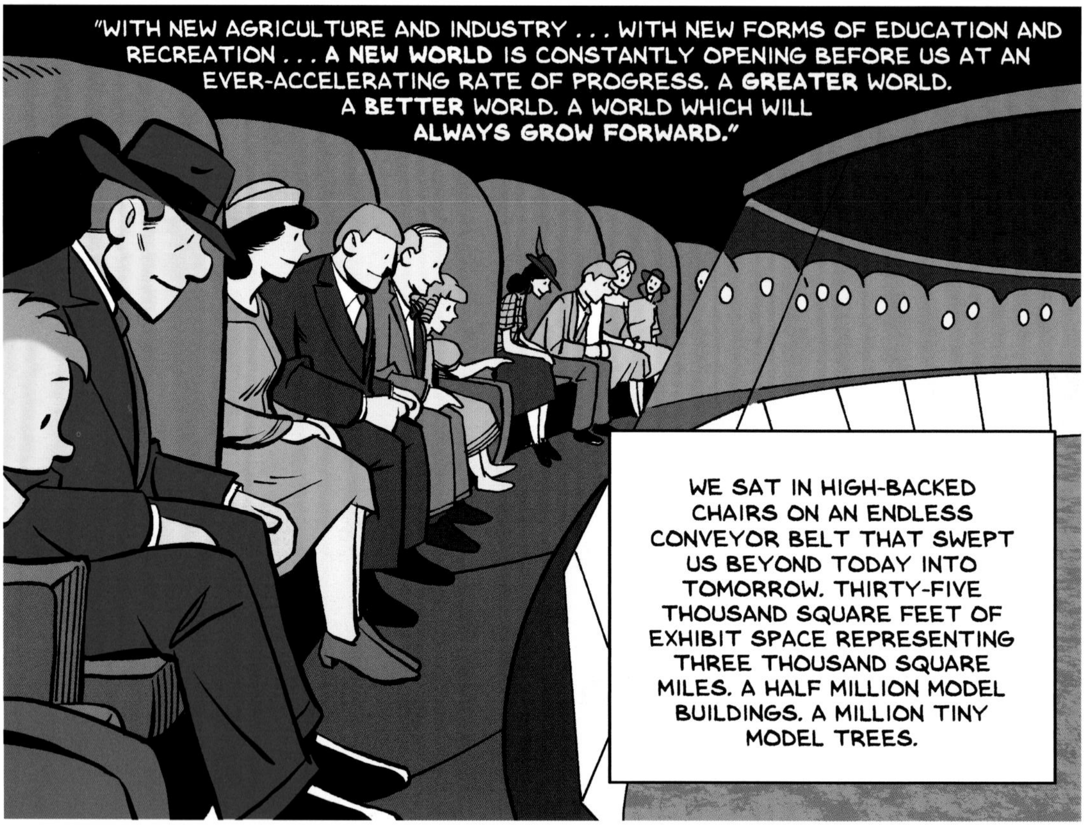
"WITH NEW AGRICULTURE AND INDUSTRY . . . WITH NEW FORMS OF EDUCATION AND RECREATION . . . A **NEW WORLD** IS CONSTANTLY OPENING BEFORE US AT AN EVER-ACCELERATING RATE OF PROGRESS. A **GREATER** WORLD. A **BETTER** WORLD. A WORLD WHICH WILL **ALWAYS GROW FORWARD.**"
WE SAT IN HIGH-BACKED CHAIRS ON AN ENDLESS CONVEYOR BELT THAT SWEPT US BEYOND TODAY INTO TOMORROW. THIRTY-FIVE THOUSAND SQUARE FEET OF EXHIBIT SPACE REPRESENTING THREE THOUSAND SQUARE MILES. A HALF MILLION MODEL BUILDINGS. A MILLION TINY MODEL TREES.

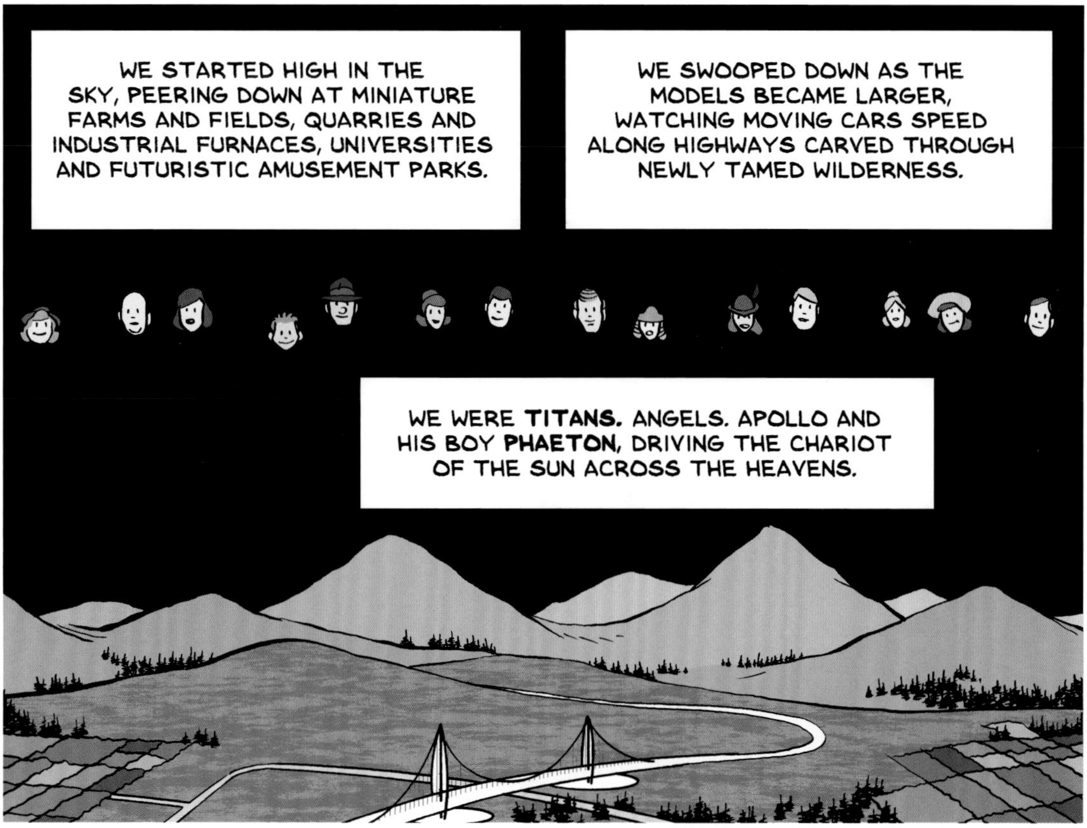
WE STARTED HIGH IN THE SKY, PEERING DOWN AT MINIATURE FARMS AND FIELDS, QUARRIES AND INDUSTRIAL FURNACES, UNIVERSITIES AND FUTURISTIC AMUSEMENT PARKS.
WE SWOOPED DOWN AS THE MODELS BECAME LARGER, WATCHING MOVING CARS SPEED ALONG HIGHWAYS CARVED THROUGH NEWLY TAMED WILDERNESS.
WE WERE **TITANS.** ANGELS. APOLLO AND HIS BOY **PHAETON**, DRIVING THE CHARIOT OF THE SUN ACROSS THE HEAVENS.

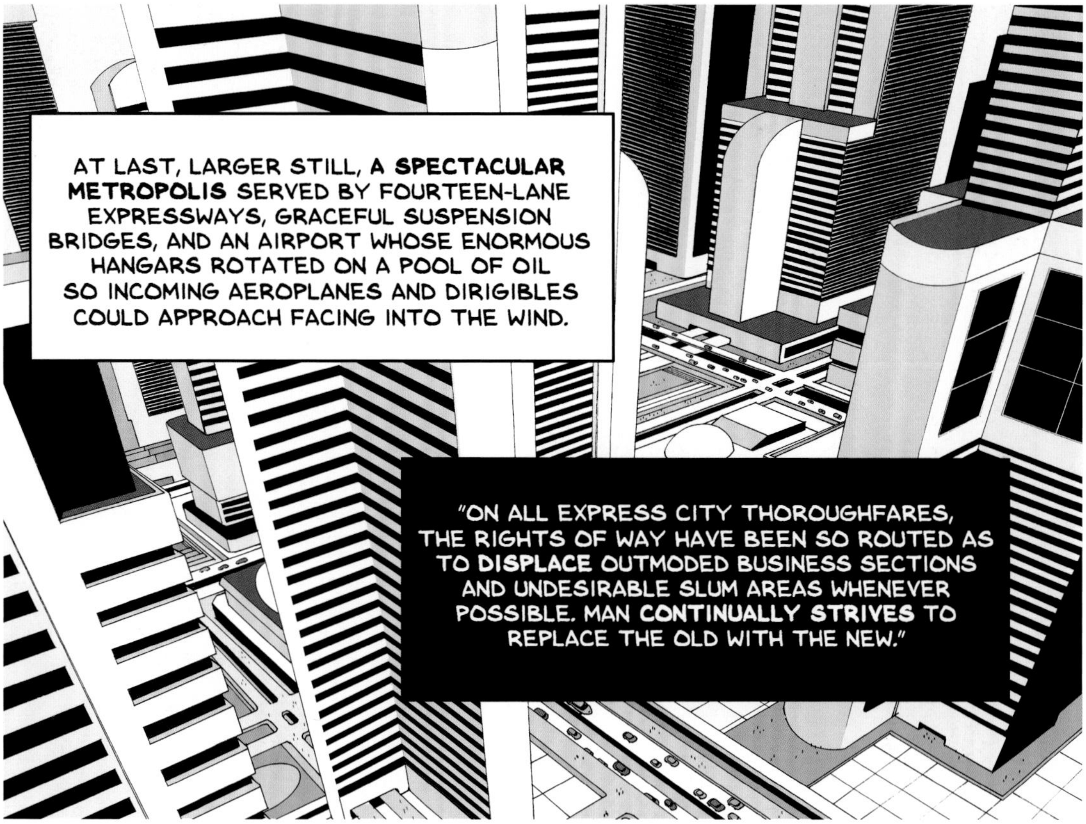
AT LAST, LARGER STILL, A **SPECTACULAR METROPOLIS** SERVED BY FOURTEEN-LANE EXPRESSWAYS, GRACEFUL SUSPENSION BRIDGES, AND AN AIRPORT WHOSE ENORMOUS HANGARS ROTATED ON A POOL OF OIL SO INCOMING AEROPLANES AND DIRIGIBLES COULD APPROACH FACING INTO THE WIND.
"ON ALL EXPRESS CITY THOROUGHFARES, THE RIGHTS OF WAY HAVE BEEN SO ROUTED AS TO **DISPLACE** OUTMODED BUSINESS SECTIONS AND UNDESIRABLE SLUM AREAS WHENEVER POSSIBLE. MAN **CONTINUALLY STRIVES** TO REPLACE THE OLD WITH THE NEW."

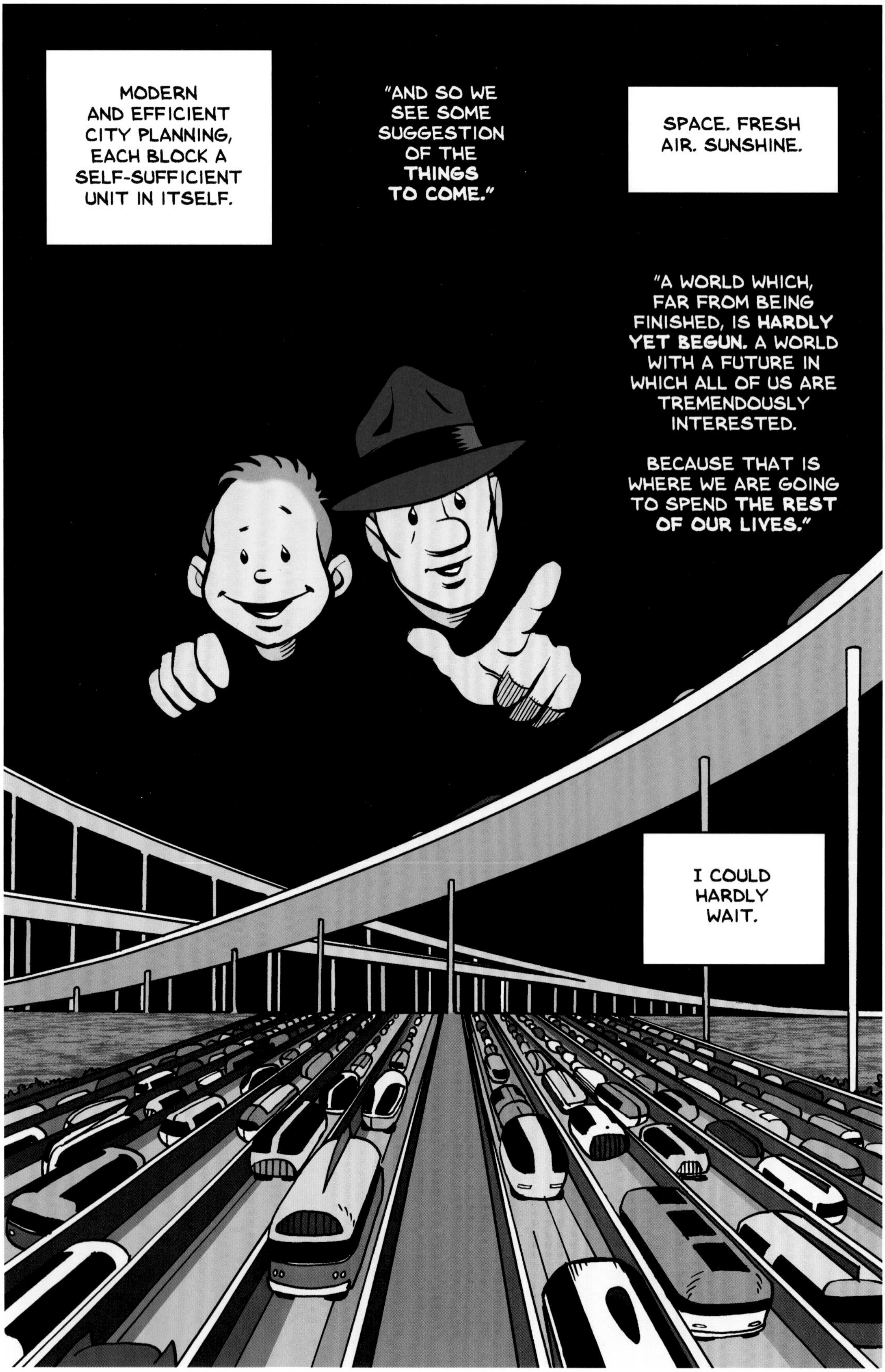
MODERN AND EFFICIENT CITY PLANNING, EACH BLOCK A SELF-SUFFICIENT UNIT IN ITSELF.
"AND SO WE SEE SOME SUGGESTION OF THE THINGS TO COME."
SPACE. FRESH AIR. SUNSHINE.
"A WORLD WHICH, FAR FROM BEING FINISHED, IS HARDLY YET BEGUN. A WORLD WITH A FUTURE IN WHICH ALL OF US ARE TREMENDOUSLY INTERESTED.
BECAUSE THAT IS WHERE WE ARE GOING TO SPEND THE REST OF OUR LIVES."
I COULD HARDLY WAIT.

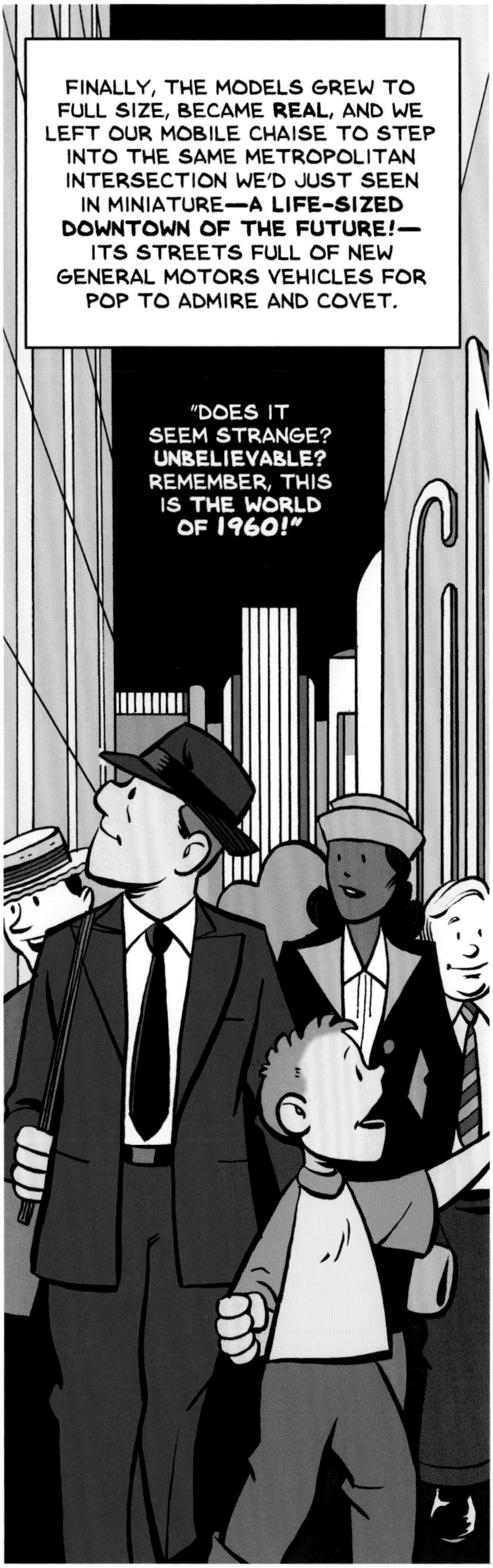
FINALLY, THE MODELS GREW TO FULL SIZE, BECAME **REAL**, AND WE LEFT OUR MOBILE CHAISE TO STEP INTO THE SAME METROPOLITAN INTERSECTION WE'D JUST SEEN IN MINIATURE—**A LIFE-SIZED DOWNTOWN OF THE FUTURE!**— ITS STREETS FULL OF NEW GENERAL MOTORS VEHICLES FOR POP TO ADMIRE AND COVET.
"DOES IT SEEM STRANGE? UNBELIEVABLE? REMEMBER, THIS IS THE WORLD OF 1960!"

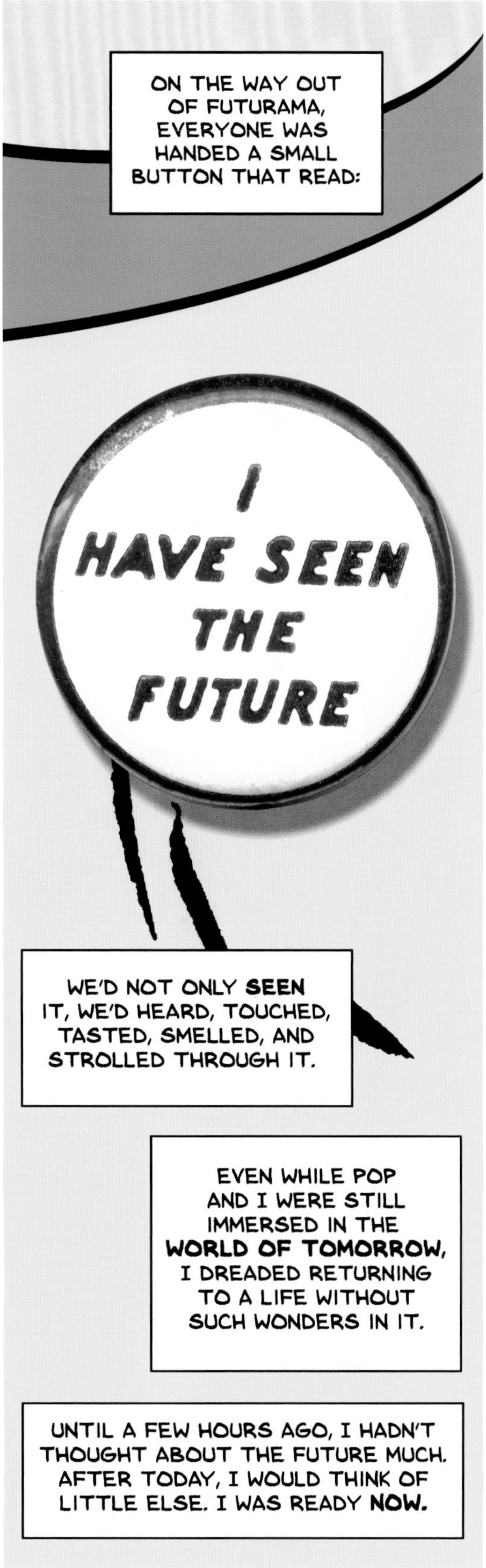
ON THE WAY OUT OF FUTURAMA, EVERYONE WAS HANDED A SMALL BUTTON THAT READ:
I HAVE SEEN THE FUTURE
WE'D NOT ONLY **SEEN** IT, WE'D HEARD, TOUCHED, TASTED, SMELLED, AND STROLLED THROUGH IT.
EVEN WHILE POP AND I WERE STILL IMMERSED IN THE **WORLD OF TOMORROW**, I DREADED RETURNING TO A LIFE WITHOUT SUCH WONDERS IN IT.
UNTIL A FEW HOURS AGO, I HADN'T THOUGHT ABOUT THE FUTURE MUCH. AFTER TODAY, I WOULD THINK OF LITTLE ELSE. I WAS READY **NOW.**

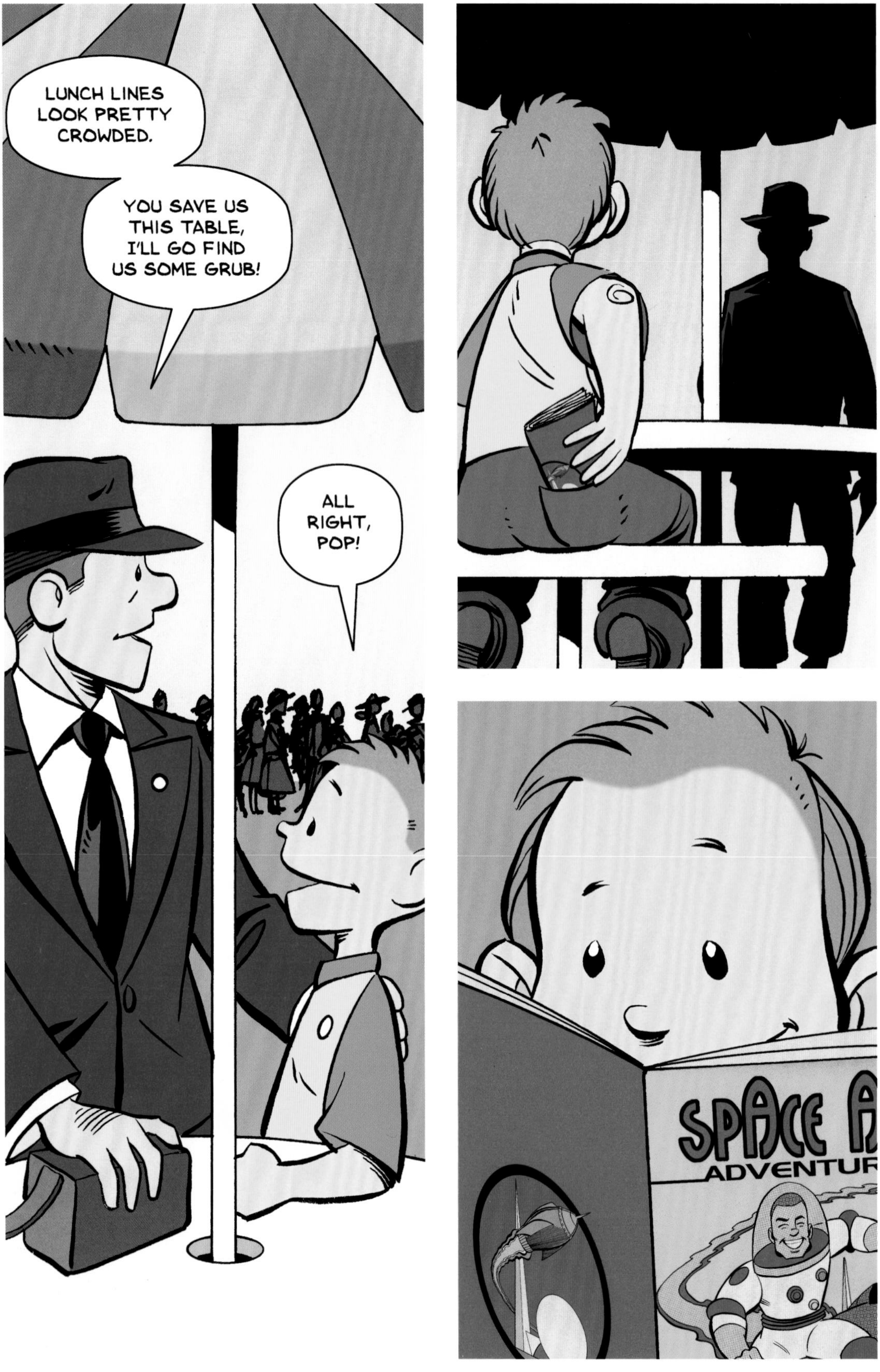
LUNCH LINES LOOK PRETTY CROWDED.
YOU SAVE US THIS TABLE, I'LL GO FIND US SOME GRUB!
ALL RIGHT, POP!

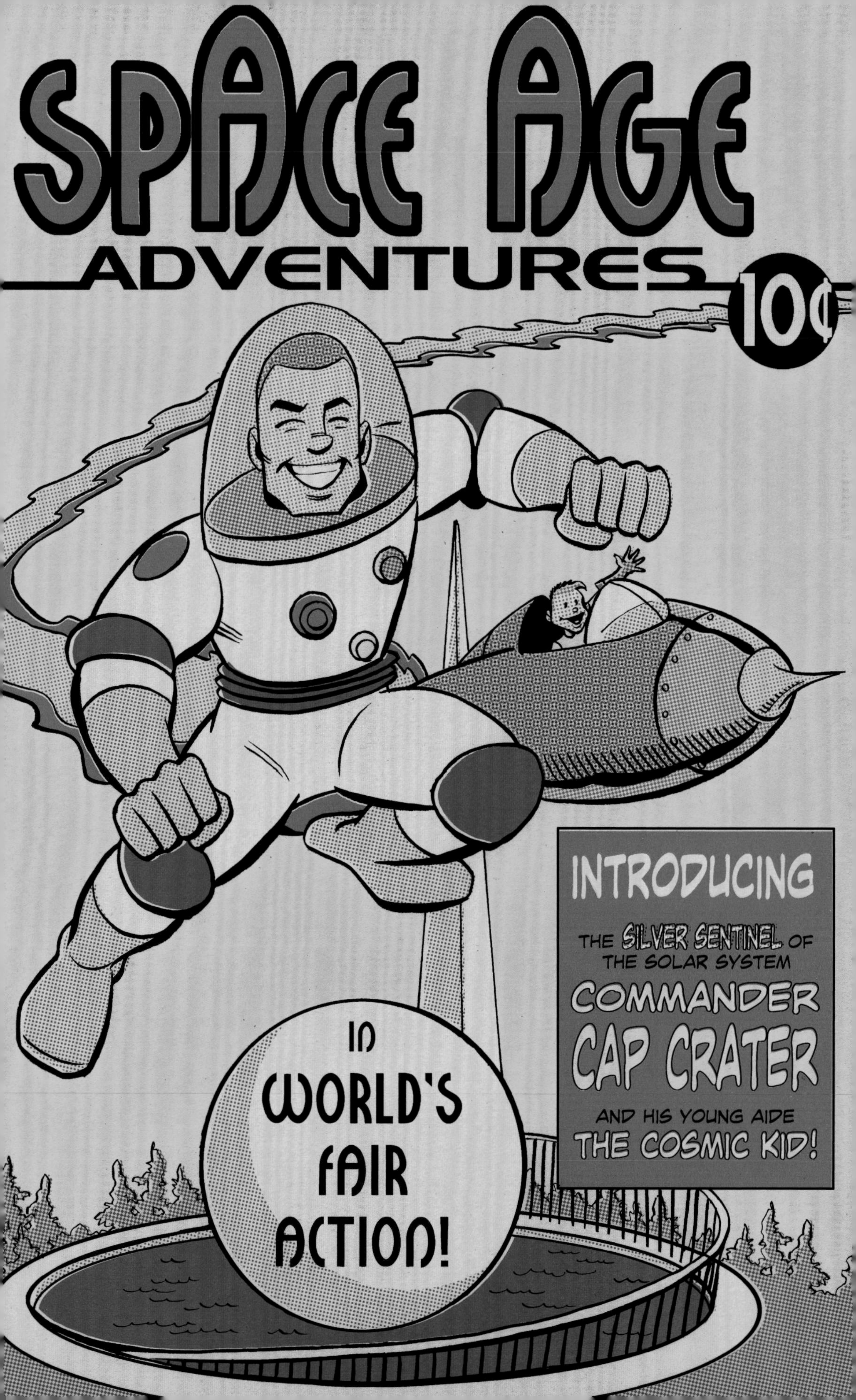
SPACE AGE
ADVENTURES
10¢
INTRODUCING
THE SILVER SENTINEL OF
THE SOLAR SYSTEM
COMMANDER
CAP CRATER
AND HIS YOUNG AIDE
THE COSMIC KID!
IN
WORLD'S
FAIR
ACTION!

# Your Guide to the New York World's Fair!

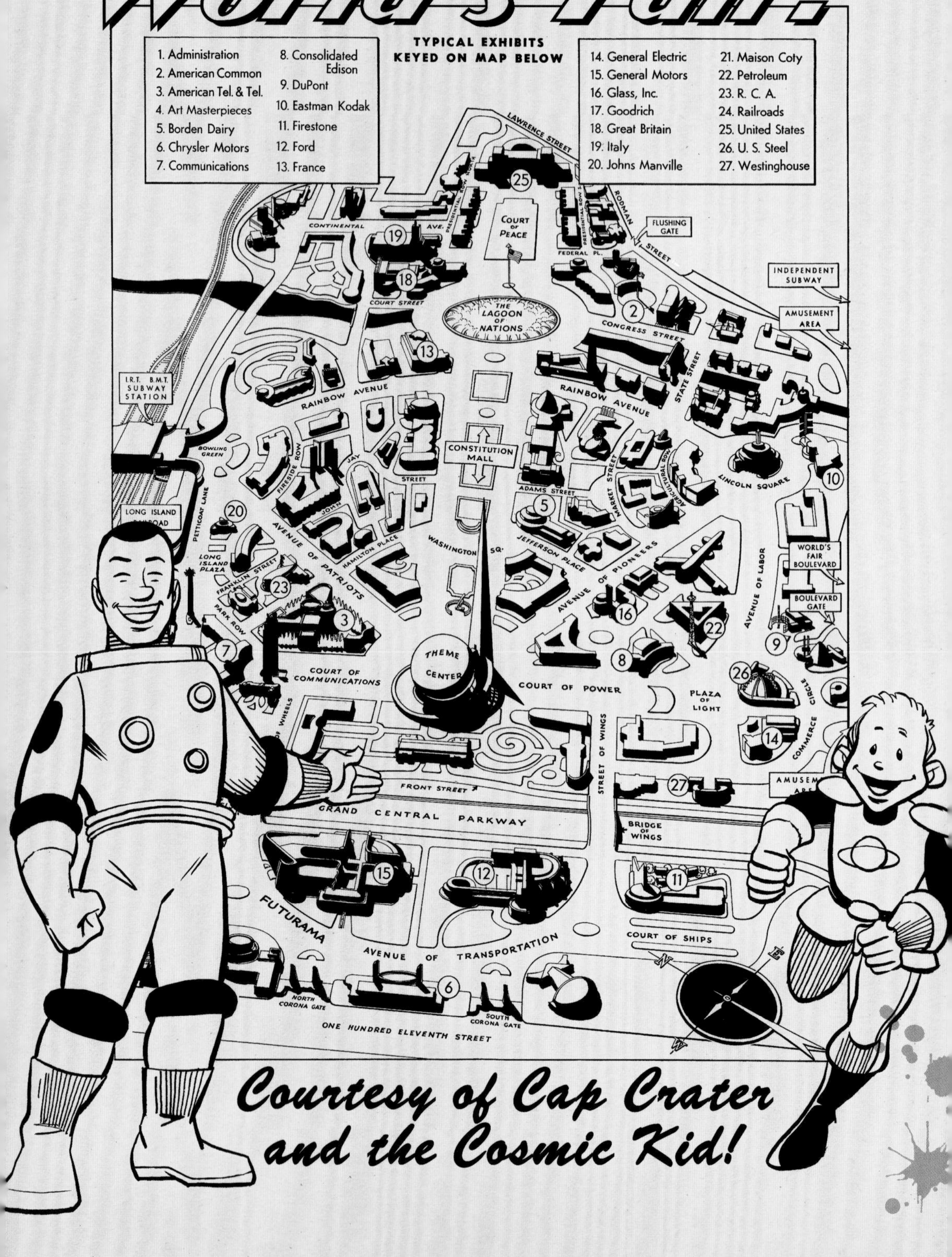
TYPICAL EXHIBITS KEYED ON MAP BELOW
1. Administration
2. American Common
3. American Tel. & Tel.
4. Art Masterpieces
5. Borden Dairy
6. Chrysler Motors
7. Communications
8. Consolidated Edison
9. DuPont
10. Eastman Kodak
11. Firestone
12. Ford
13. France
14. General Electric
15. General Motors
16. Glass, Inc.
17. Goodrich
18. Great Britain
19. Italy
20. Johns Manville
21. Maison Coty
22. Petroleum
23. R. C. A.
24. Railroads
25. United States
26. U. S. Steel
27. Westinghouse
LAWRENCE STREET
RODMAN
FLUSHING GATE
STREET
INDEPENDENT SUBWAY
AMUSEMENT AREA
COURT OF PEACE
CONTINENTAL AVE.
FEDERAL PL.
COURT STREET
THE LAGOON OF NATIONS
CONGRESS STREET
STATE STREET
RAINBOW AVENUE
RAINBOW AVENUE
I.R.T. B.M.T. SUBWAY STATION
BOWLING GREEN
CONSTITUTION MALL
JAY STREET
ADAMS STREET
MARKET STREET
AGRICULTURAL ROW
LINCOLN SQUARE
FIRESIDE ROW
JOHN
LONG ISLAND RAILROAD
PETTICOAT LANE
WASHINGTON SQ.
JEFFERSON PLACE
HAMILTON PLACE
AVENUE OF PATRIOTS
AVENUE OF PIONEERS
AVENUE OF LABOR
WORLD'S FAIR BOULEVARD
BOULEVARD GATE
LONG ISLAND PLAZA
FRANKLIN STREET
PARK ROW
THEME CENTER
COURT OF COMMUNICATIONS
COURT OF POWER
PLAZA OF LIGHT
CIRCLE
COMMERCE
STREET OF WHEELS
STREET OF WINGS
FRONT STREET
GRAND CENTRAL PARKWAY
BRIDGE OF WINGS
FUTURAMA
AVENUE OF TRANSPORTATION
COURT OF SHIPS
NORTH CORONA GATE
SOUTH CORONA GATE
ONE HUNDRED ELEVENTH STREET
N
E
W
Courtesy of Cap Crater and the Cosmic Kid!

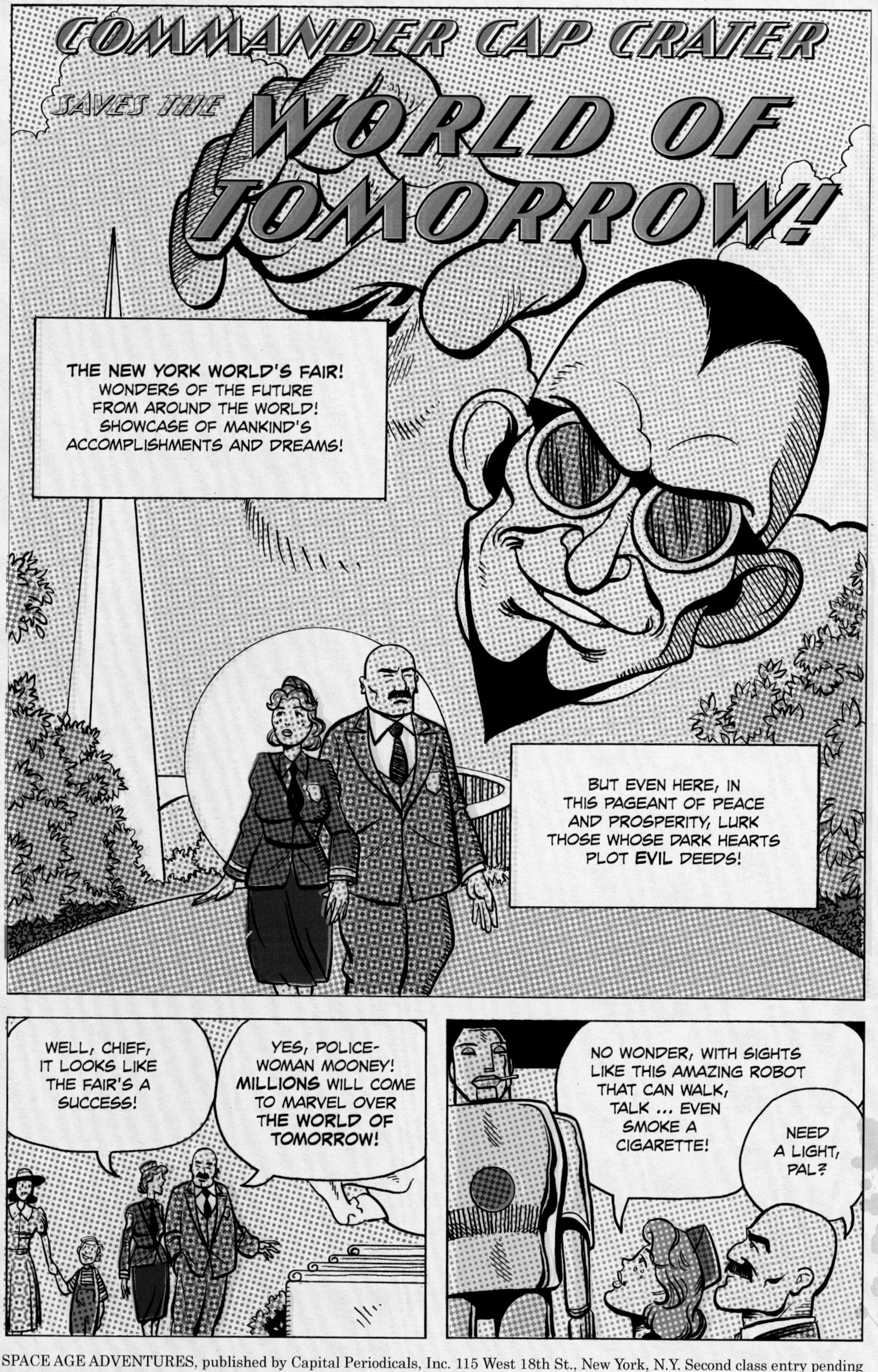
COMMANDER CAP CRATER
SAVES THE
WORLD OF TOMORROW!
THE NEW YORK WORLD'S FAIR! WONDERS OF THE FUTURE FROM AROUND THE WORLD! SHOWCASE OF MANKIND'S ACCOMPLISHMENTS AND DREAMS!
BUT EVEN HERE, IN THIS PAGEANT OF PEACE AND PROSPERITY, LURK THOSE WHOSE DARK HEARTS PLOT EVIL DEEDS!
WELL, CHIEF, IT LOOKS LIKE THE FAIR'S A SUCCESS!
YES, POLICE-WOMAN MOONEY! MILLIONS WILL COME TO MARVEL OVER THE WORLD OF TOMORROW!
NO WONDER, WITH SIGHTS LIKE THIS AMAZING ROBOT THAT CAN WALK, TALK ... EVEN SMOKE A CIGARETTE!
NEED A LIGHT, PAL?

SPACE AGE ADVENTURES, published by Capital Periodicals, Inc. 115 West 18th St., New York, N.Y. Second class entry pending at Post Office, New York, N.Y., under the Act of March 3, 1879.

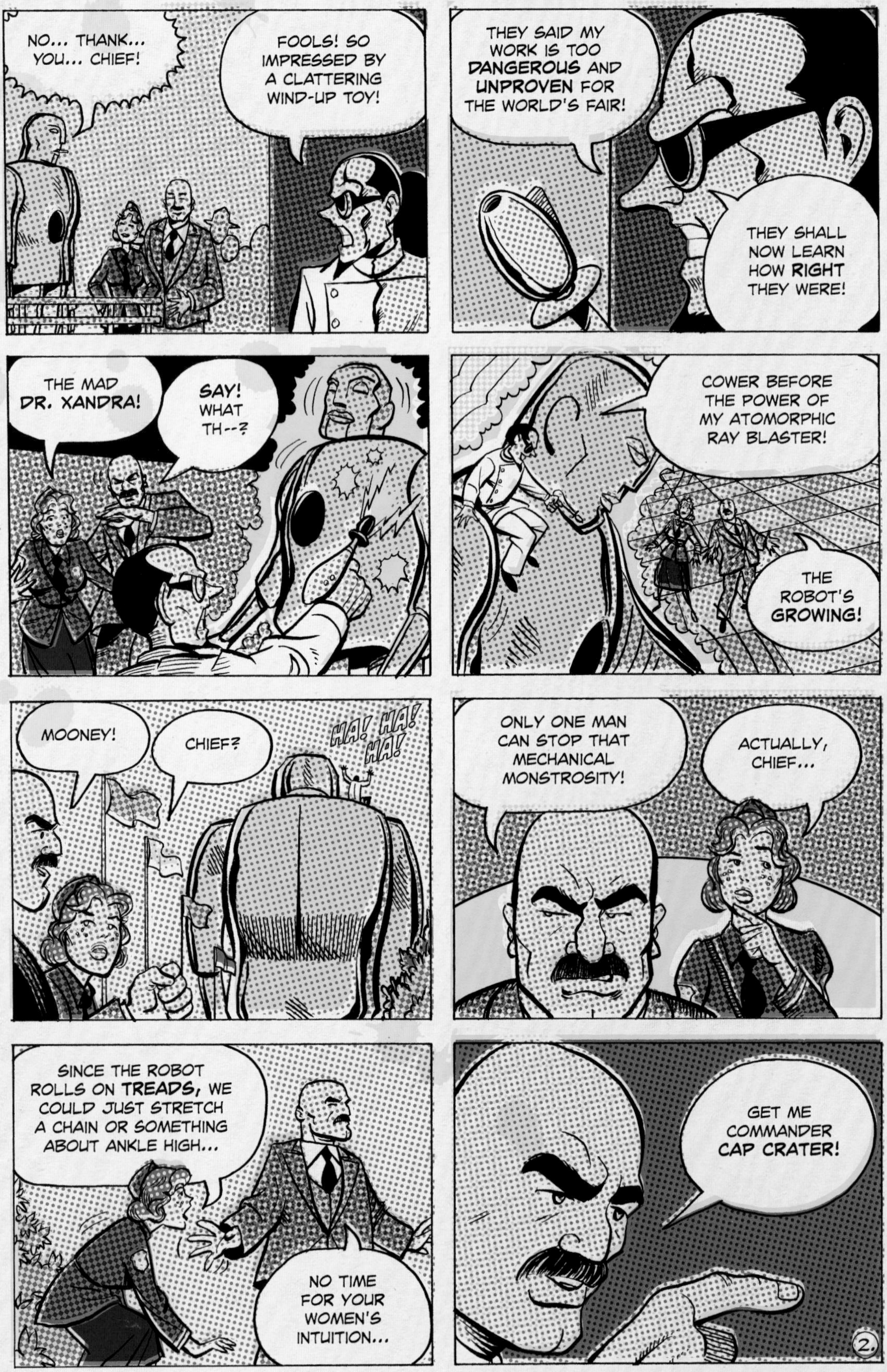
NO... THANK... YOU... CHIEF!
FOOLS! SO IMPRESSED BY A CLATTERING WIND-UP TOY!
THEY SAID MY WORK IS TOO **DANGEROUS** AND **UNPROVEN** FOR THE WORLD'S FAIR!
THEY SHALL NOW LEARN HOW **RIGHT** THEY WERE!
THE MAD **DR. XANDRA!**
**SAY!** WHAT TH--?
COWER BEFORE THE POWER OF MY ATOMORPHIC RAY BLASTER!
THE ROBOT'S **GROWING!**
MOONEY!
CHIEF?
HA! HA! HA!
ONLY ONE MAN CAN STOP THAT MECHANICAL MONSTROSITY!
ACTUALLY, CHIEF...
SINCE THE ROBOT ROLLS ON **TREADS,** WE COULD JUST STRETCH A CHAIN OR SOMETHING ABOUT ANKLE HIGH...
NO TIME FOR YOUR WOMEN'S INTUITION...
GET ME COMMANDER **CAP CRATER!**

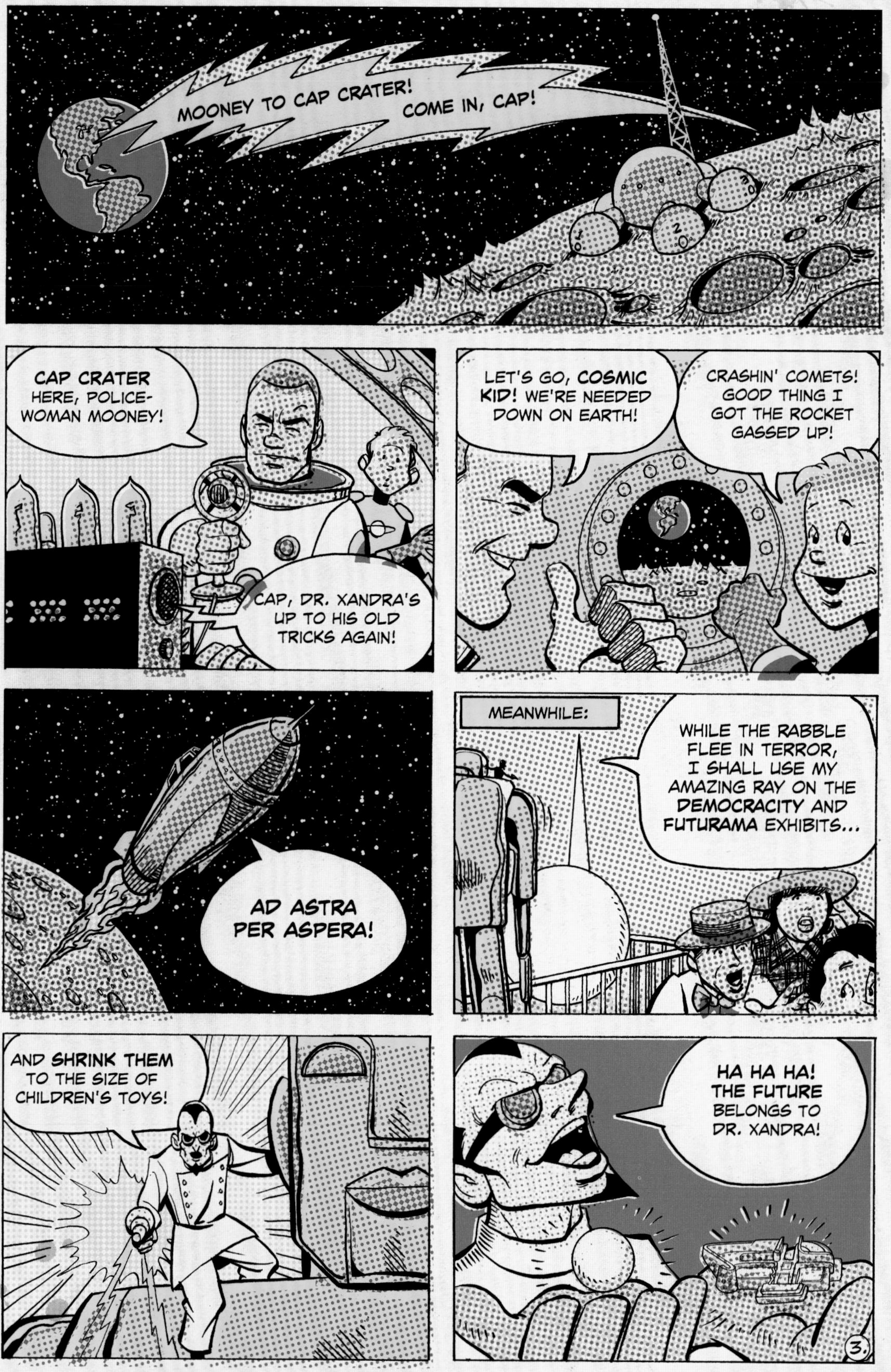
MOONEY TO CAP CRATER! COME IN, CAP!
CAP CRATER HERE, POLICE-WOMAN MOONEY!
CAP, DR. XANDRA'S UP TO HIS OLD TRICKS AGAIN!
LET'S GO, COSMIC KID! WE'RE NEEDED DOWN ON EARTH!
CRASHIN' COMETS! GOOD THING I GOT THE ROCKET GASSED UP!
AD ASTRA PER ASPERA!
MEANWHILE:
WHILE THE RABBLE FLEE IN TERROR, I SHALL USE MY AMAZING RAY ON THE DEMOCRACITY AND FUTURAMA EXHIBITS...
AND SHRINK THEM TO THE SIZE OF CHILDREN'S TOYS!
HA HA HA! THE FUTURE BELONGS TO DR. XANDRA!

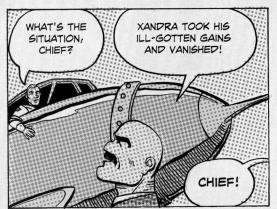

WHAT'S THE SITUATION, CHIEF?

XANDRA TOOK HIS ILL-GOTTEN GAINS AND VANISHED!

CHIEF!

IT'S INCREDIBLE! SOMEHOW AN ENTIRE FUTURISTIC CITY HAS SPRUNG UP IN THE REMOTE FARMLANDS OF NEW JERSEY!

IT CAN ONLY BE XANDRA'S DOING!

PREPARE THE AUTOGYRO, YOUNG CHUM!

GOLLY, CAP! WHAT'S XANDRA'S EVIL SCHEME?

IT'S HARD TO FATHOM A MIND SO TWISTED...

SOME PEOPLE FEAR THE FUTURE, COSMIC KID! THEY DON'T UNDERSTAND THAT MEN OF SCIENCE, INDUSTRY, AND GOVERNMENT ARE WORKING TOGETHER TO BUILD A BETTER TOMORROW FOR EVERYONE!

I GUESS I NEVER LOOKED AT IT LIKE THAT BEFORE!

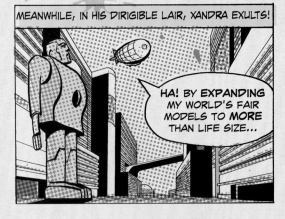

MEANWHILE, IN HIS DIRIGIBLE LAIR, XANDRA EXULTS!

HA! BY EXPANDING MY WORLD'S FAIR MODELS TO MORE THAN LIFE SIZE...

...I'VE BUILT MY OWN FUTURISTIC KINGDOM, GUARDED BY AN INVINCIBLE ROBOT, IN MERE MINUTES!

EH?

4.

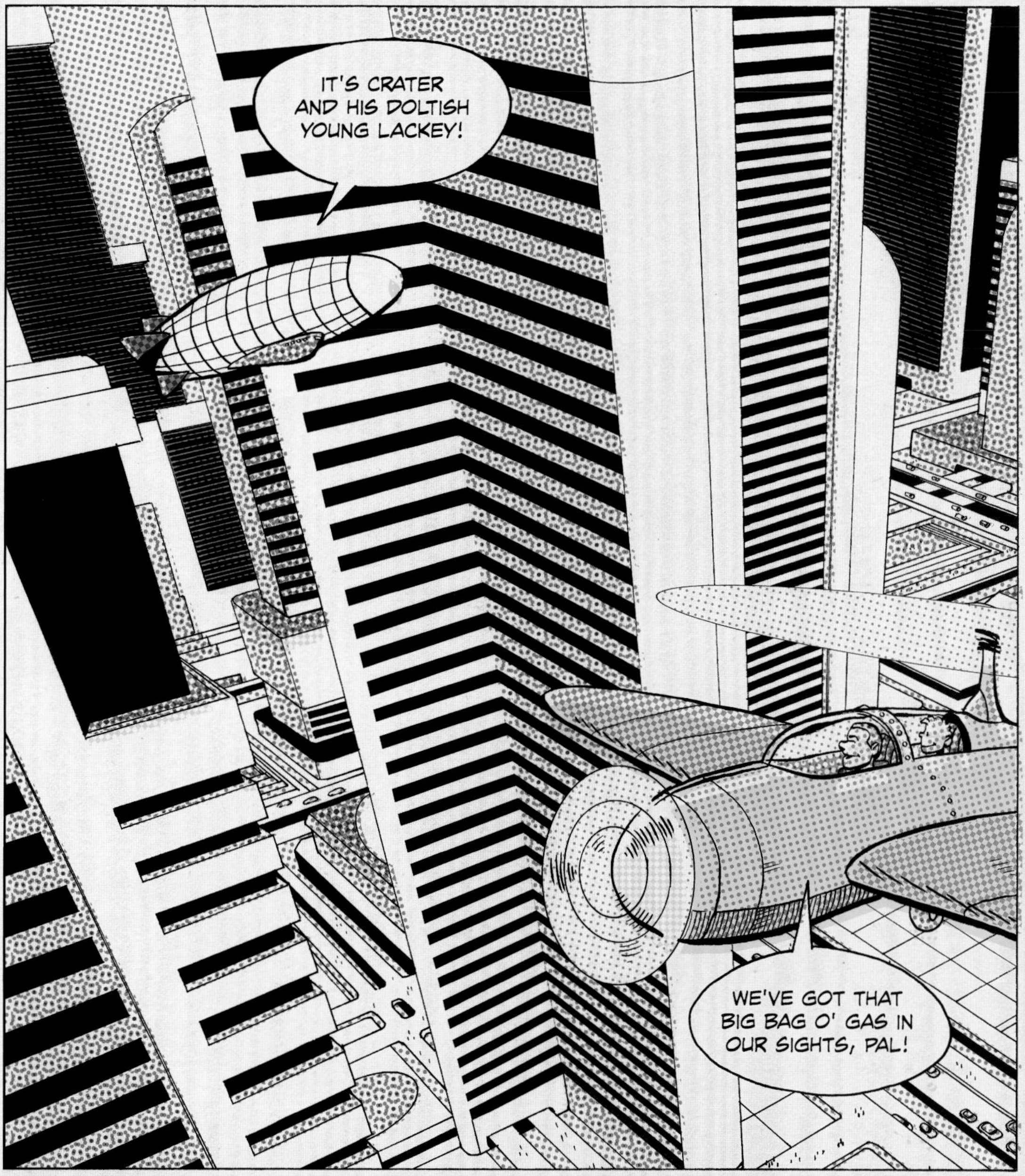
IT'S CRATER AND HIS DOLTISH YOUNG LACKEY!
WE'VE GOT THAT BIG BAG O' GAS IN OUR SIGHTS, PAL!

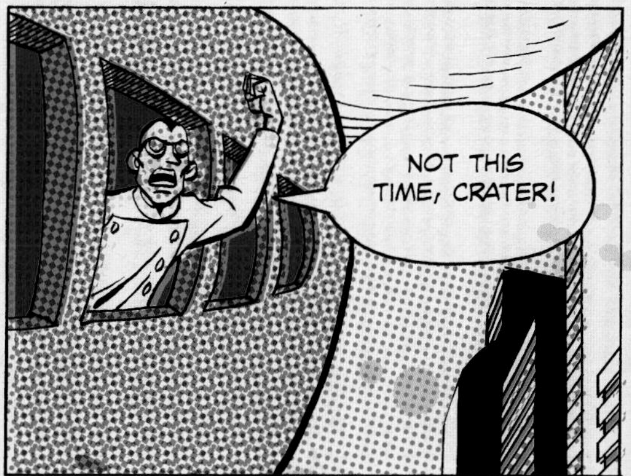
NOT THIS TIME, CRATER!

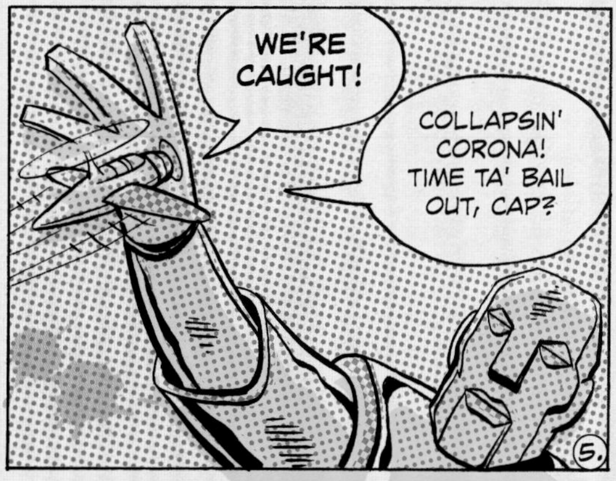
WE'RE CAUGHT!
COLLAPSIN' CORONA! TIME TA' BAIL OUT, CAP?

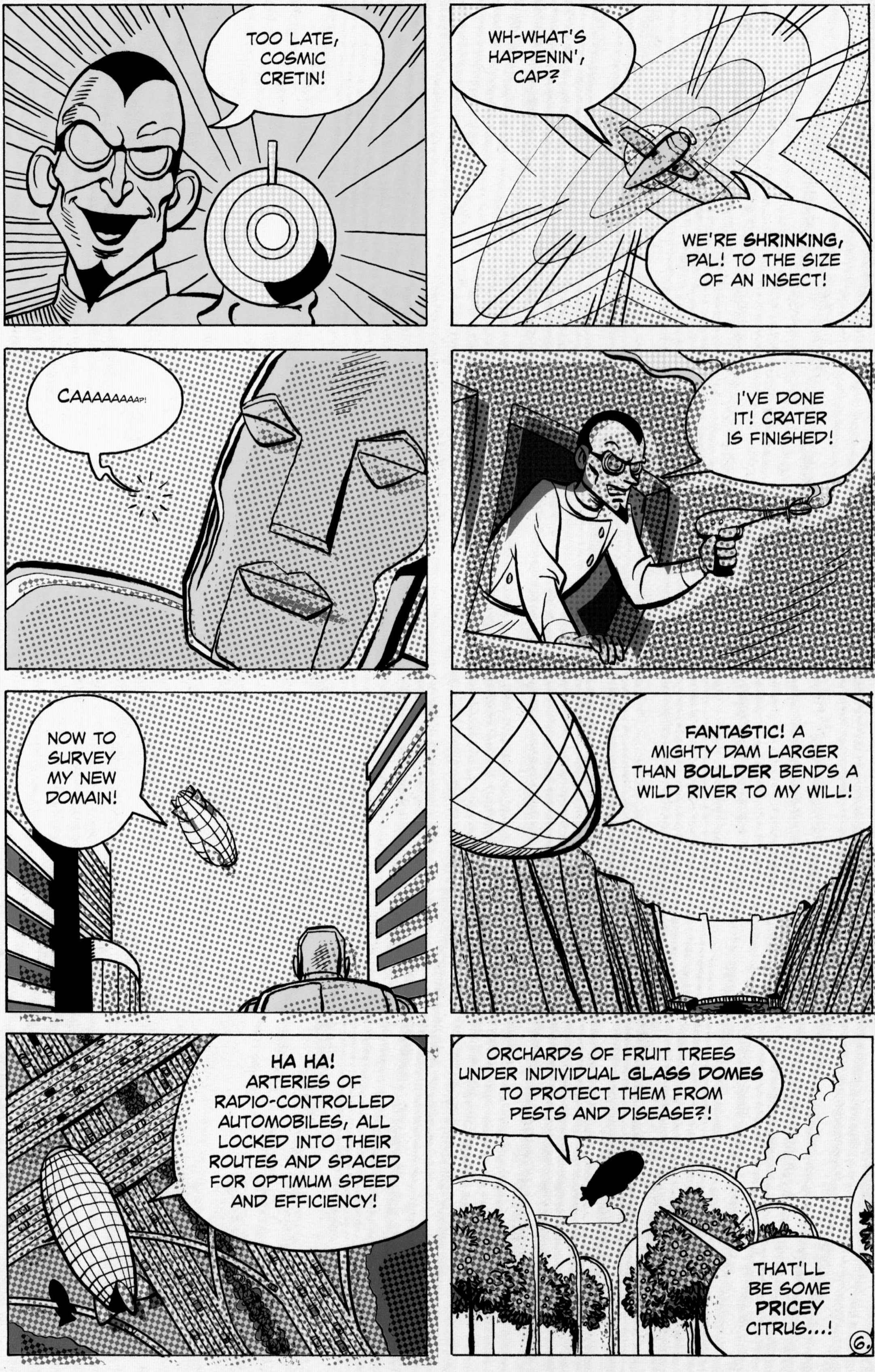
TOO LATE, COSMIC CRETIN!
WH-WHAT'S HAPPENIN', CAP?
WE'RE SHRINKING, PAL! TO THE SIZE OF AN INSECT!
CAAAAAAAAP!
I'VE DONE IT! CRATER IS FINISHED!
NOW TO SURVEY MY NEW DOMAIN!
FANTASTIC! A MIGHTY DAM LARGER THAN BOULDER BENDS A WILD RIVER TO MY WILL!
HA HA! ARTERIES OF RADIO-CONTROLLED AUTOMOBILES, ALL LOCKED INTO THEIR ROUTES AND SPACED FOR OPTIMUM SPEED AND EFFICIENCY!
ORCHARDS OF FRUIT TREES UNDER INDIVIDUAL GLASS DOMES TO PROTECT THEM FROM PESTS AND DISEASE?!
THAT'LL BE SOME PRICEY CITRUS...!
6.

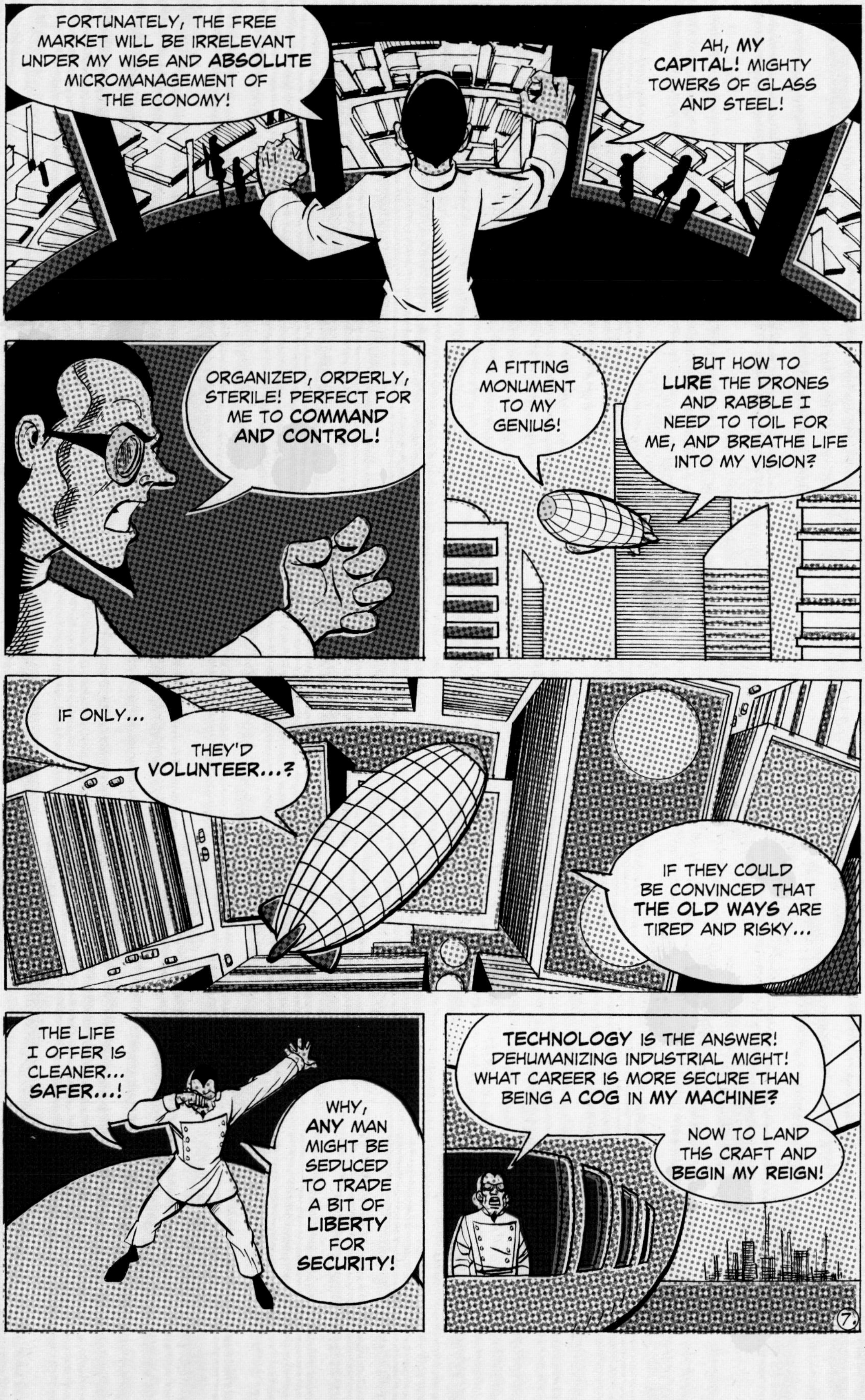
FORTUNATELY, THE FREE MARKET WILL BE IRRELEVANT UNDER MY WISE AND ABSOLUTE MICROMANAGEMENT OF THE ECONOMY!
AH, MY CAPITAL! MIGHTY TOWERS OF GLASS AND STEEL!
ORGANIZED, ORDERLY, STERILE! PERFECT FOR ME TO COMMAND AND CONTROL!
A FITTING MONUMENT TO MY GENIUS!
BUT HOW TO LURE THE DRONES AND RABBLE I NEED TO TOIL FOR ME, AND BREATHE LIFE INTO MY VISION?
IF ONLY...
THEY'D VOLUNTEER...?
IF THEY COULD BE CONVINCED THAT THE OLD WAYS ARE TIRED AND RISKY...
THE LIFE I OFFER IS CLEANER... SAFER...!
WHY, ANY MAN MIGHT BE SEDUCED TO TRADE A BIT OF LIBERTY FOR SECURITY!
TECHNOLOGY IS THE ANSWER! DEHUMANIZING INDUSTRIAL MIGHT! WHAT CAREER IS MORE SECURE THAN BEING A COG IN MY MACHINE?
NOW TO LAND THS CRAFT AND BEGIN MY REIGN!

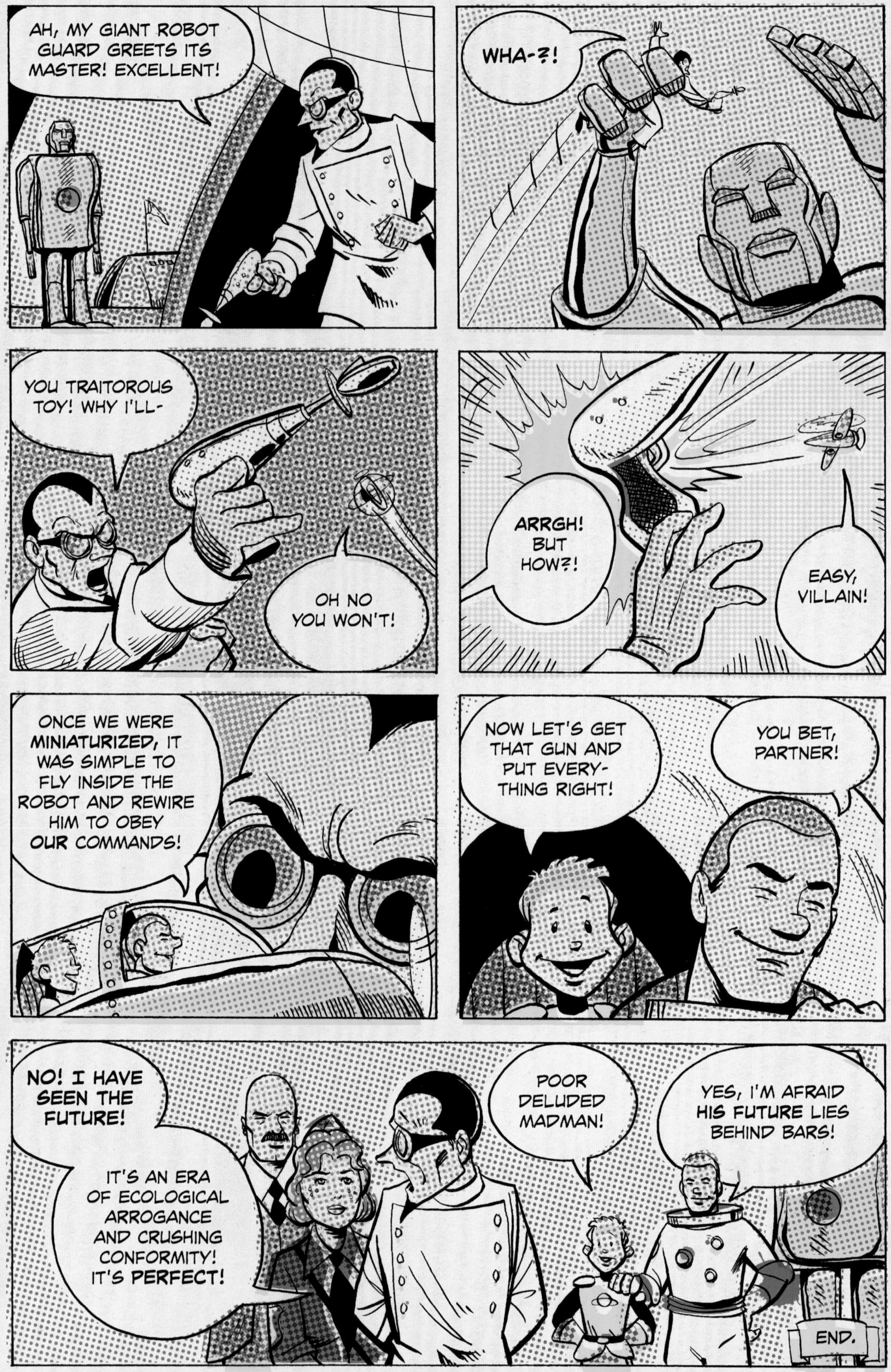
AH, MY GIANT ROBOT GUARD GREETS ITS MASTER! EXCELLENT!
WHA-?!
YOU TRAITOROUS TOY! WHY I'LL-
OH NO YOU WON'T!
ARRGH! BUT HOW?!
EASY, VILLAIN!
ONCE WE WERE MINIATURIZED, IT WAS SIMPLE TO FLY INSIDE THE ROBOT AND REWIRE HIM TO OBEY OUR COMMANDS!
NOW LET'S GET THAT GUN AND PUT EVERY-THING RIGHT!
YOU BET, PARTNER!
NO! I HAVE SEEN THE FUTURE!
IT'S AN ERA OF ECOLOGICAL ARROGANCE AND CRUSHING CONFORMITY! IT'S PERFECT!
POOR DELUDED MADMAN!
YES, I'M AFRAID HIS FUTURE LIES BEHIND BARS!
END.

# President Roosevelt Opens the New York World's Fair

April 30, 1939

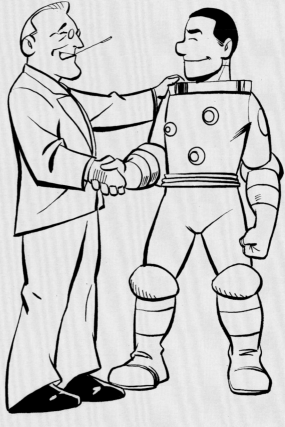

Here at the New York World's Fair of 1939, many nations are represented--indeed, most of the nations of the world--and the theme is "The World of Tomorrow."

This general, and I might almost say spontaneous, participation by other countries is a gesture of friendship and good will toward the United States for which I render most grateful thanks. It is not through the physical exhibits alone that this gesture has manifested itself. The magic of modern communications makes possible a continuing participation by word of mouth itself. Already, on Sunday afternoon radio programs, no fewer than seventeen foreign nations have shown their good will to this country since the first of January this year.

All who come to this World's Fair in New York will, I need not tell them, receive the heartiest of welcomes. They will find that the eyes of the United States are fixed on the future.

Yes, our wagon is still hitched to a star.

But it is a star of friendship, a star of progress for mankind, a star of greater happiness and less hardship, a star of international good will. And, above all, a star of peace.

May the months to come carry us forward in the rays of that eternal hope.

And so, my friends, the time has come for me to announce with solemnity, perhaps, but with great happiness, a fact: I hereby dedicate the New York World's Fair of 1939, and I declare it open to all mankind.

Franklin D. Roosevelt

KIDS!
DON'T MISS THE GREAT RIDES, FUN, AND FIREWORKS IN THE AMUSEMENT ZONE!
THERE'S PLENTY TO ENTERTAIN YOUR PARENTS AS WELL!

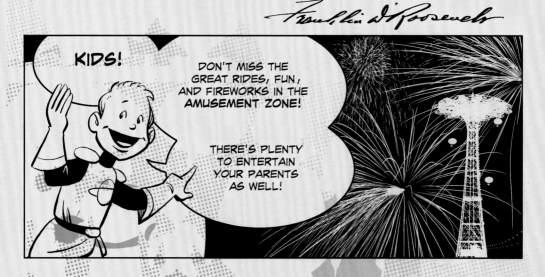

OFFICIAL SOUVENIR OF THE NEW YORK WORLD'S FAIR

TEN CENTS

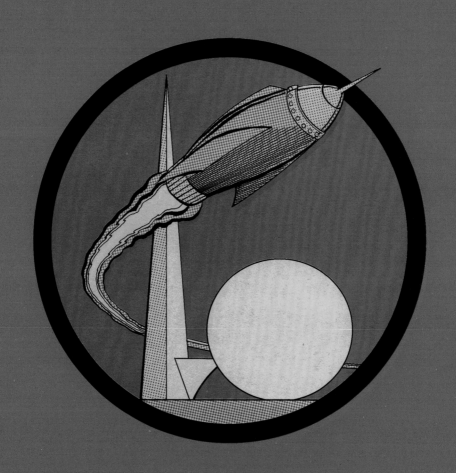

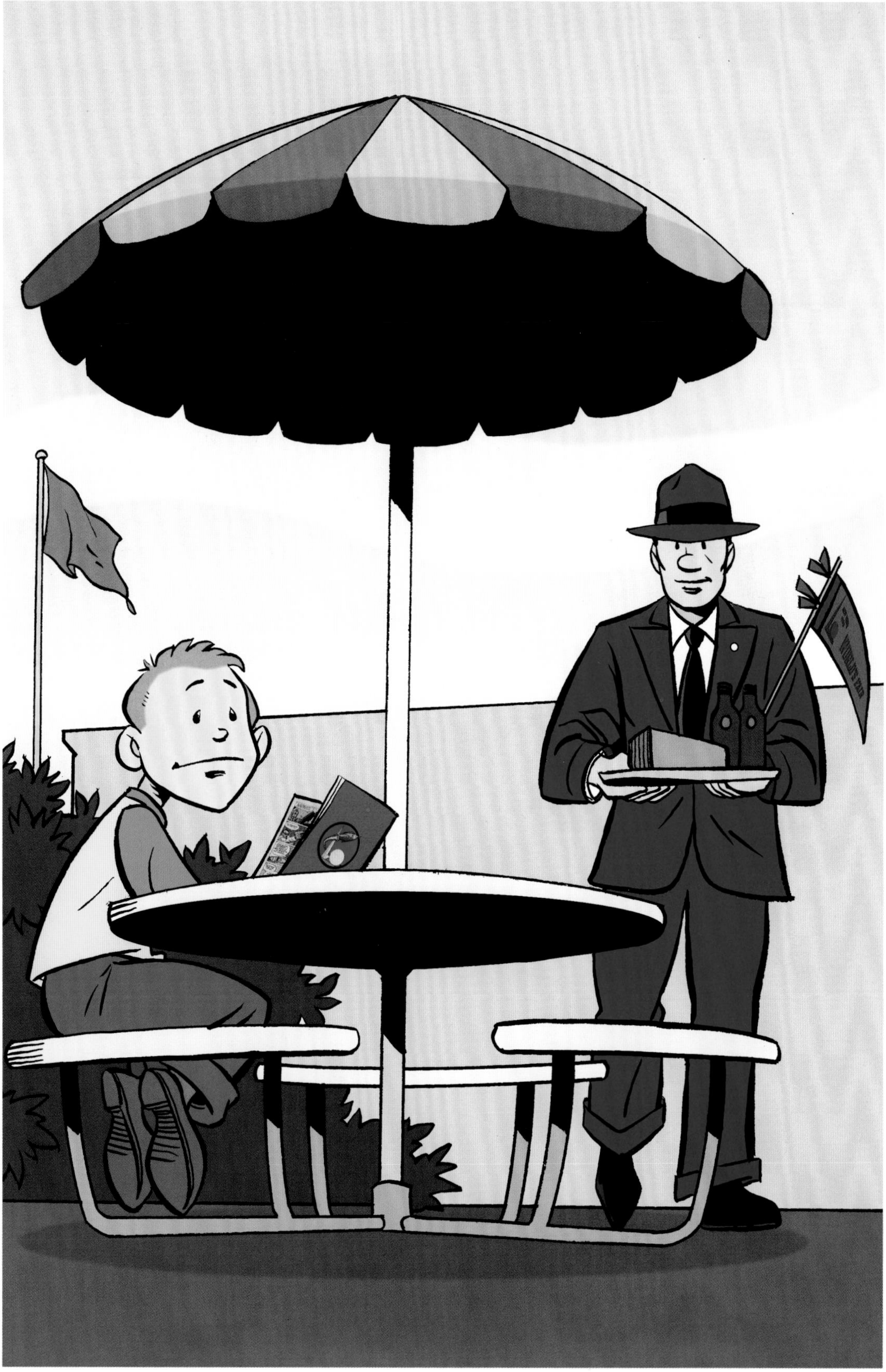
WORLD'S FAIR

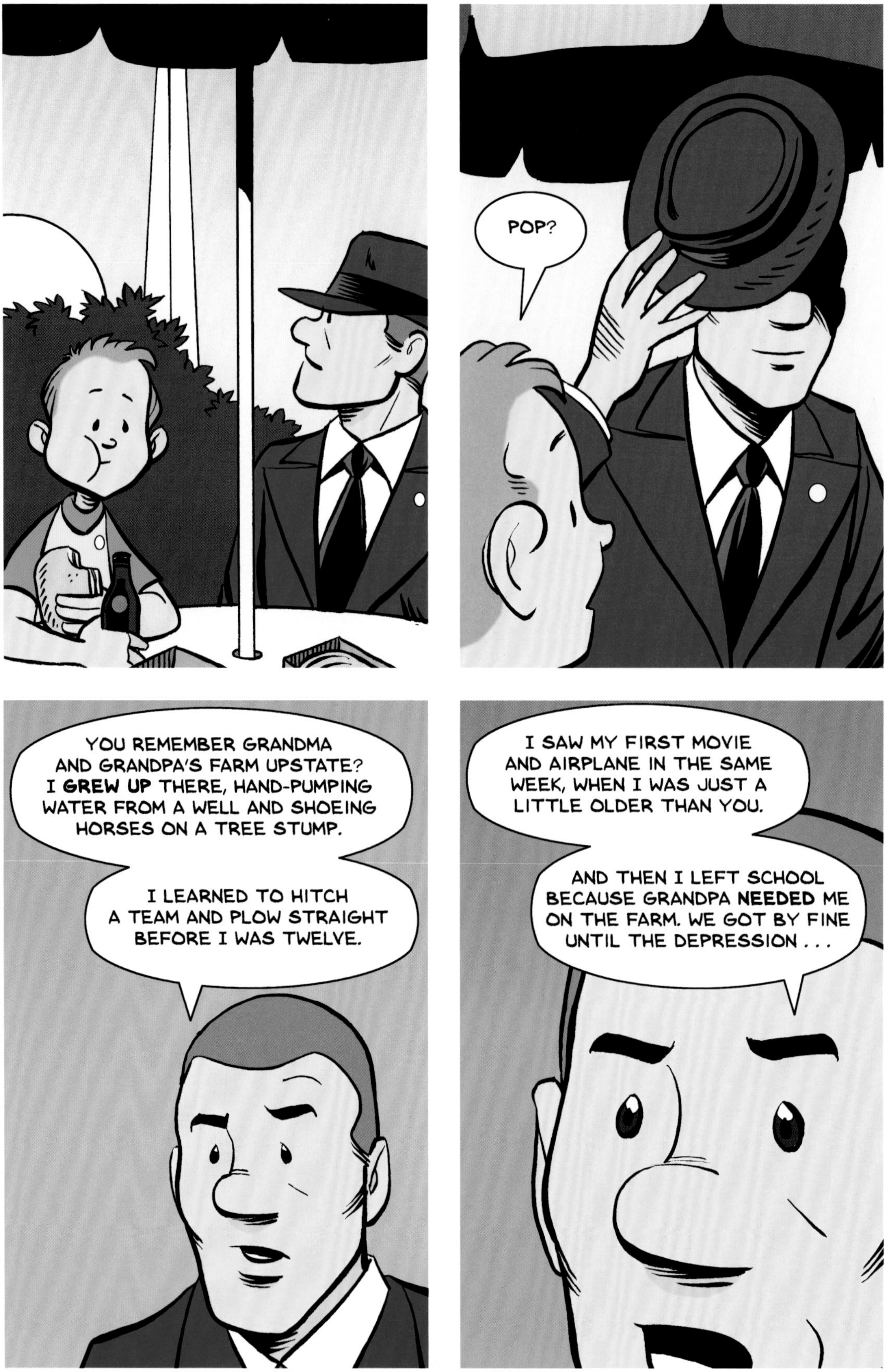
POP?
YOU REMEMBER GRANDMA AND GRANDPA'S FARM UPSTATE? I **GREW UP** THERE, HAND-PUMPING WATER FROM A WELL AND SHOEING HORSES ON A TREE STUMP.
I LEARNED TO HITCH A TEAM AND PLOW STRAIGHT BEFORE I WAS TWELVE.
I SAW MY FIRST MOVIE AND AIRPLANE IN THE SAME WEEK, WHEN I WAS JUST A LITTLE OLDER THAN YOU.
AND THEN I LEFT SCHOOL BECAUSE GRANDPA **NEEDED** ME ON THE FARM. WE GOT BY FINE UNTIL THE DEPRESSION . . .

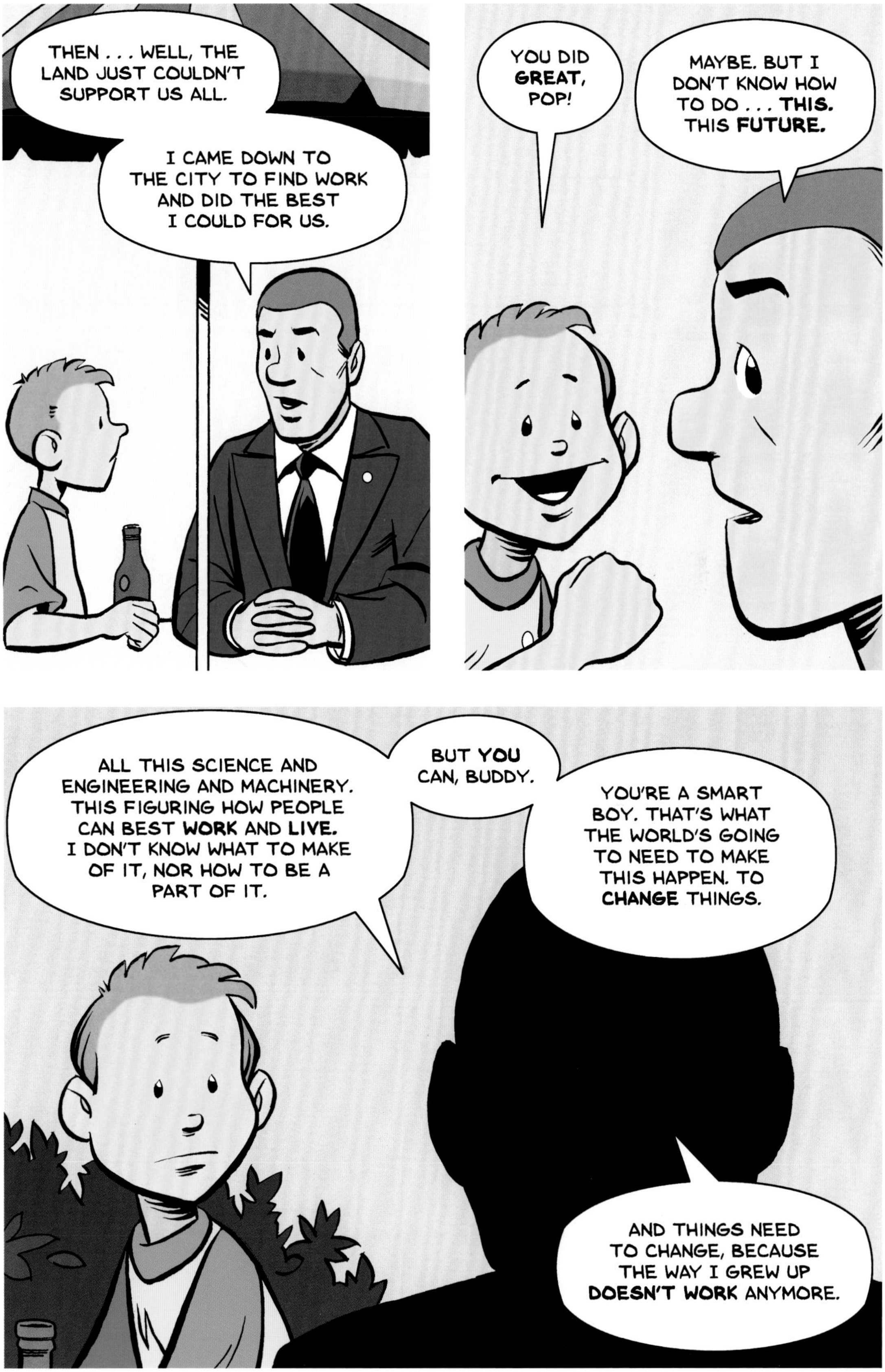
THEN . . . WELL, THE LAND JUST COULDN'T SUPPORT US ALL.
I CAME DOWN TO THE CITY TO FIND WORK AND DID THE BEST I COULD FOR US.
YOU DID **GREAT,** POP!
MAYBE. BUT I DON'T KNOW HOW TO DO . . . **THIS.** THIS **FUTURE.**
ALL THIS SCIENCE AND ENGINEERING AND MACHINERY. THIS FIGURING HOW PEOPLE CAN BEST **WORK** AND **LIVE.** I DON'T KNOW WHAT TO MAKE OF IT, NOR HOW TO BE A PART OF IT.
BUT **YOU** CAN, BUDDY.
YOU'RE A SMART BOY. THAT'S WHAT THE WORLD'S GOING TO NEED TO MAKE THIS HAPPEN. TO **CHANGE** THINGS.
AND THINGS NEED TO CHANGE, BECAUSE THE WAY I GREW UP **DOESN'T WORK** ANYMORE.

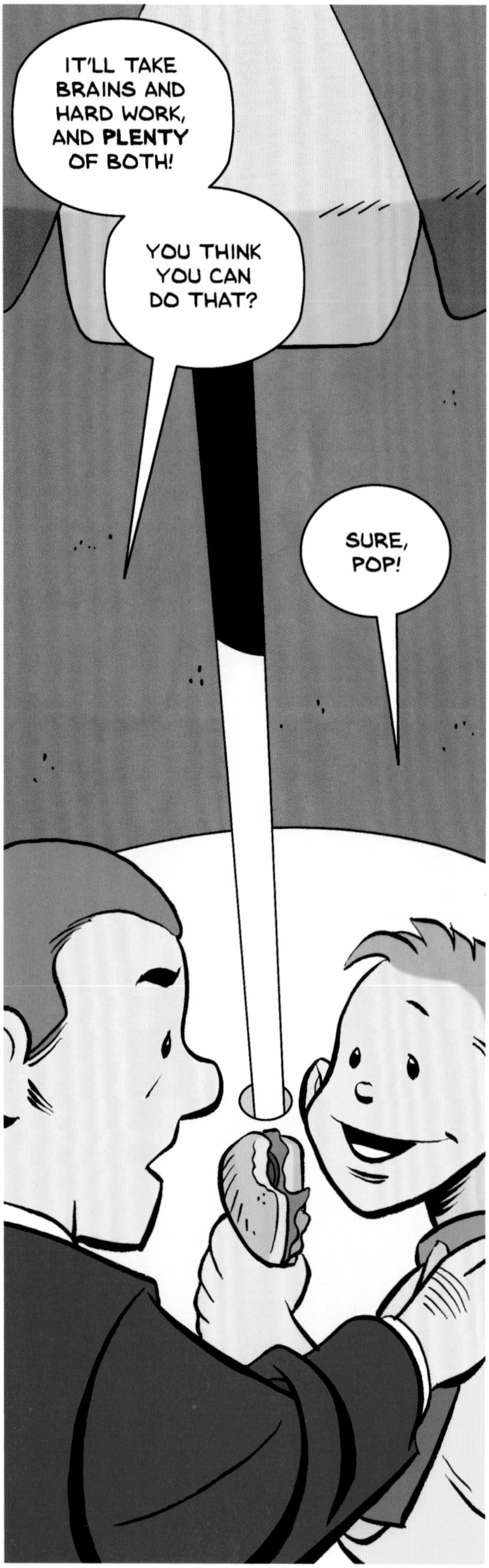
IT'LL TAKE BRAINS AND HARD WORK, AND **PLENTY** OF BOTH!
YOU THINK YOU CAN DO THAT?
SURE, POP!

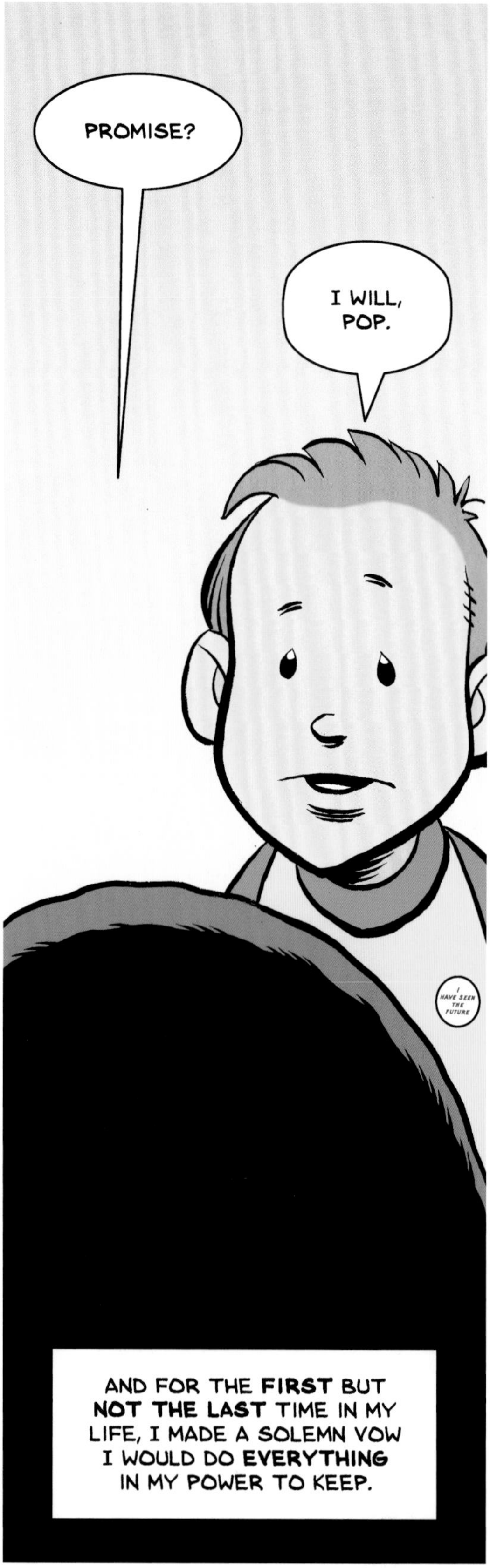
PROMISE?
I WILL, POP.
I HAVE SEEN THE FUTURE
AND FOR THE **FIRST** BUT **NOT THE LAST** TIME IN MY LIFE, I MADE A SOLEMN VOW I WOULD DO **EVERYTHING** IN MY POWER TO KEEP.

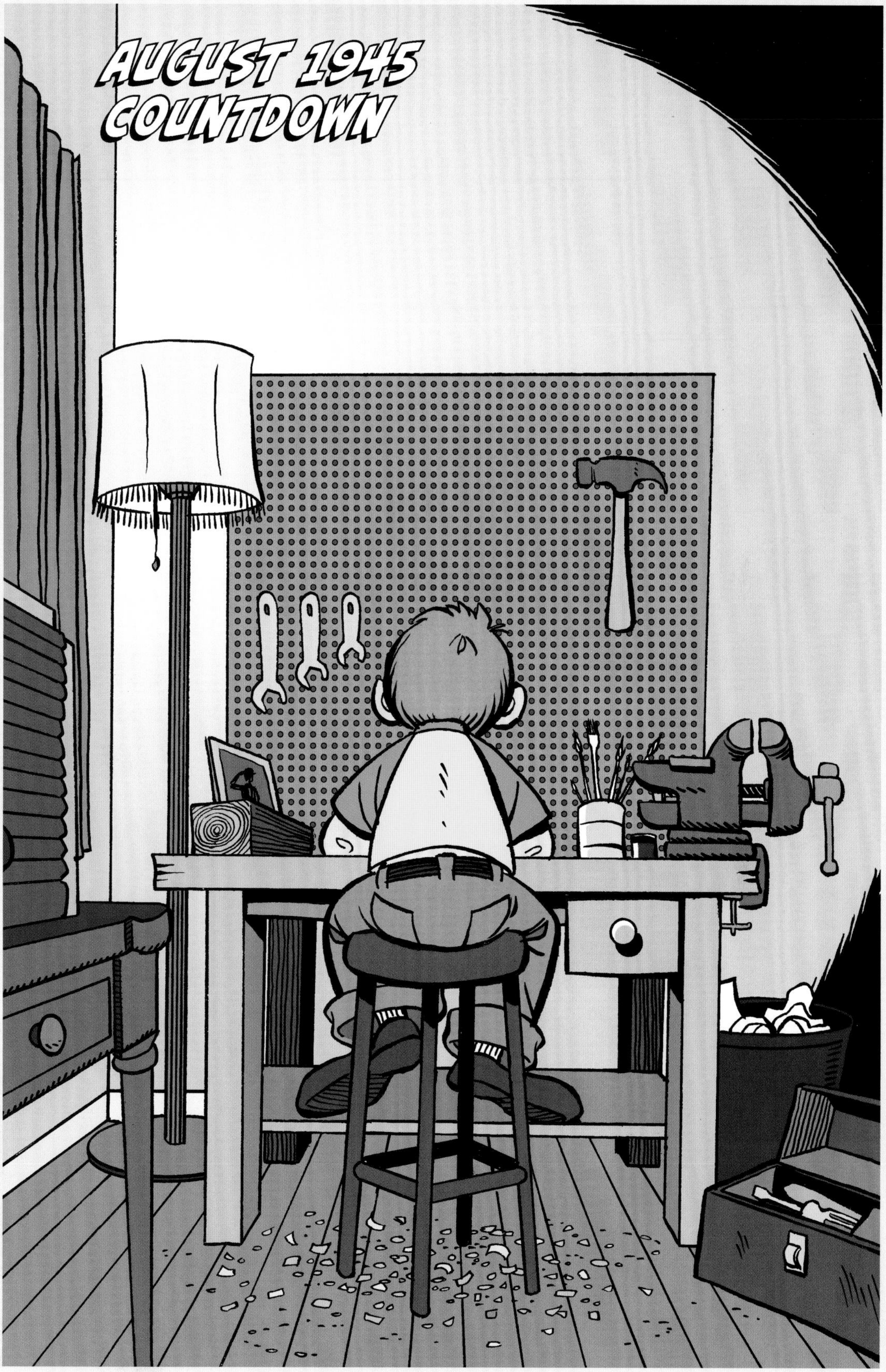
AUGUST 1945
COUNTDOWN

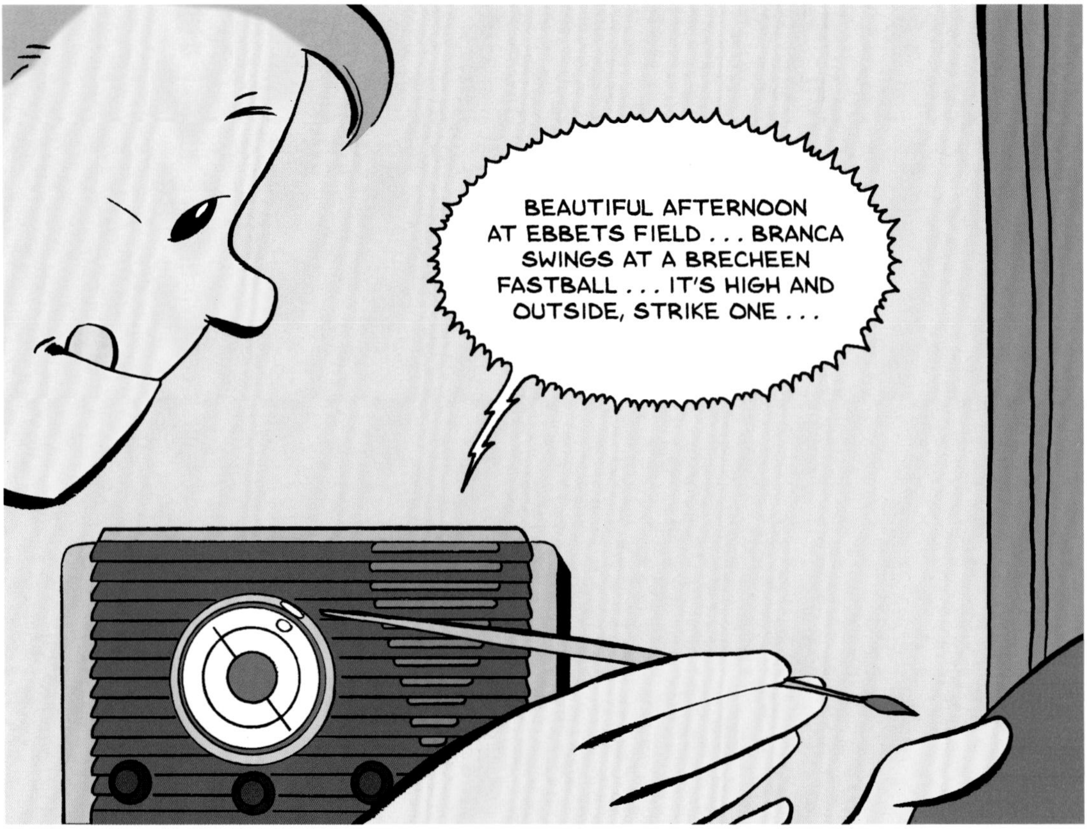
BEAUTIFUL AFTERNOON AT EBBETS FIELD . . . BRANCA SWINGS AT A BRECHEEN FASTBALL . . . IT'S HIGH AND OUTSIDE, STRIKE ONE . . .

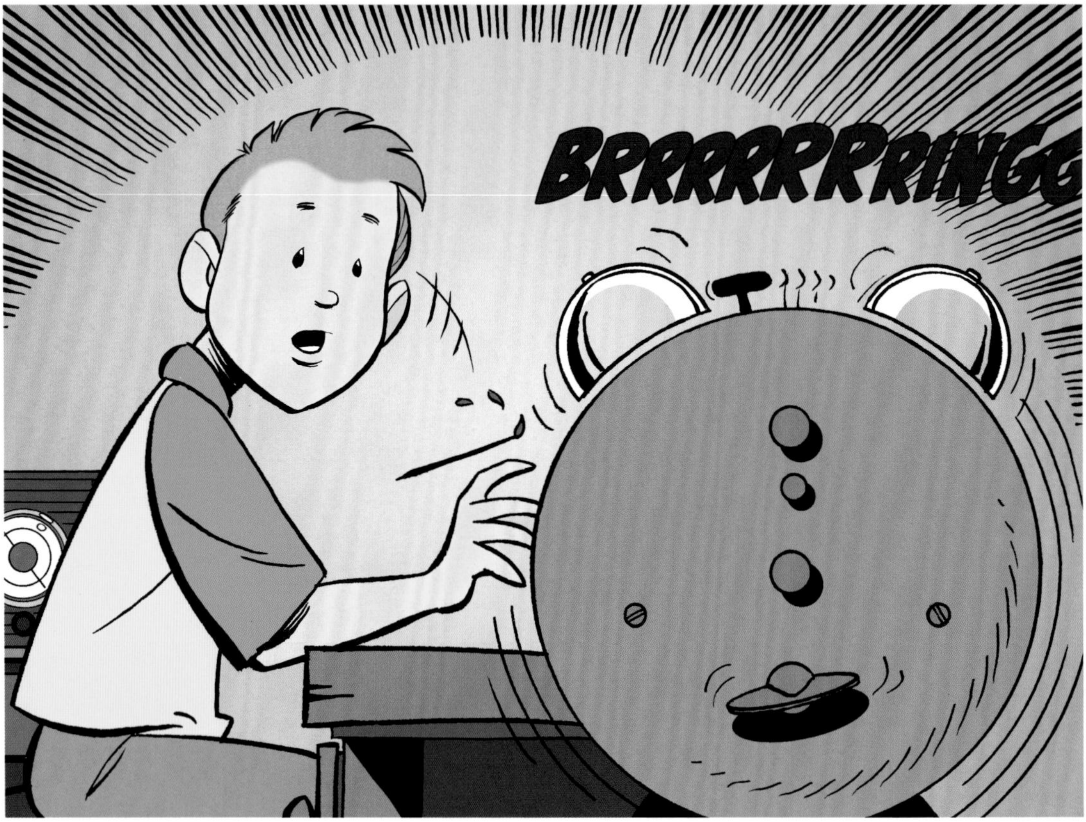
BRRRRRRRINGG

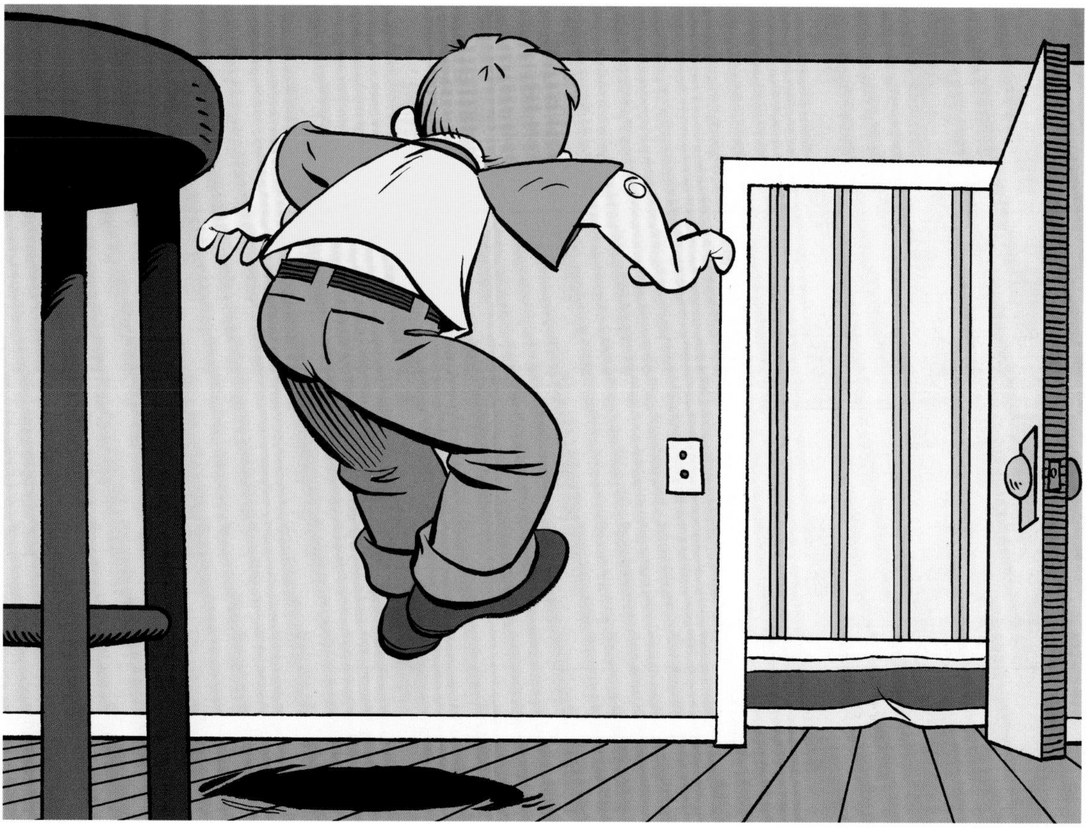

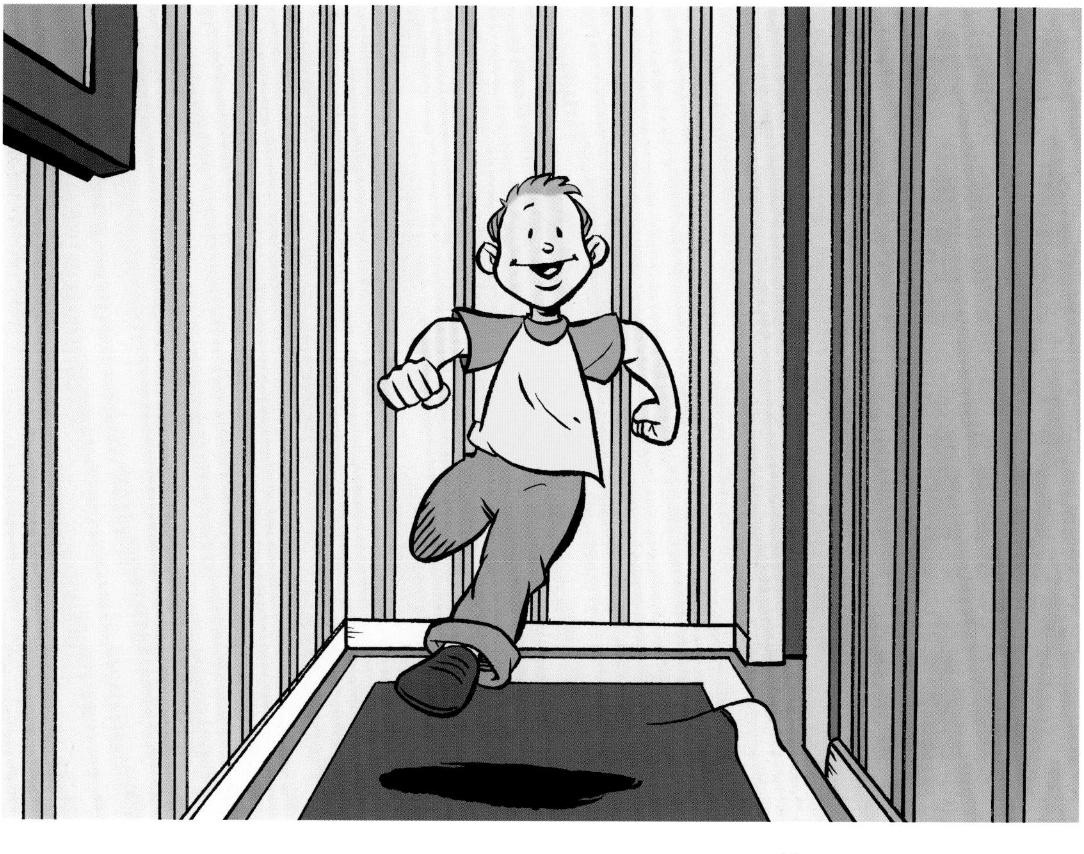

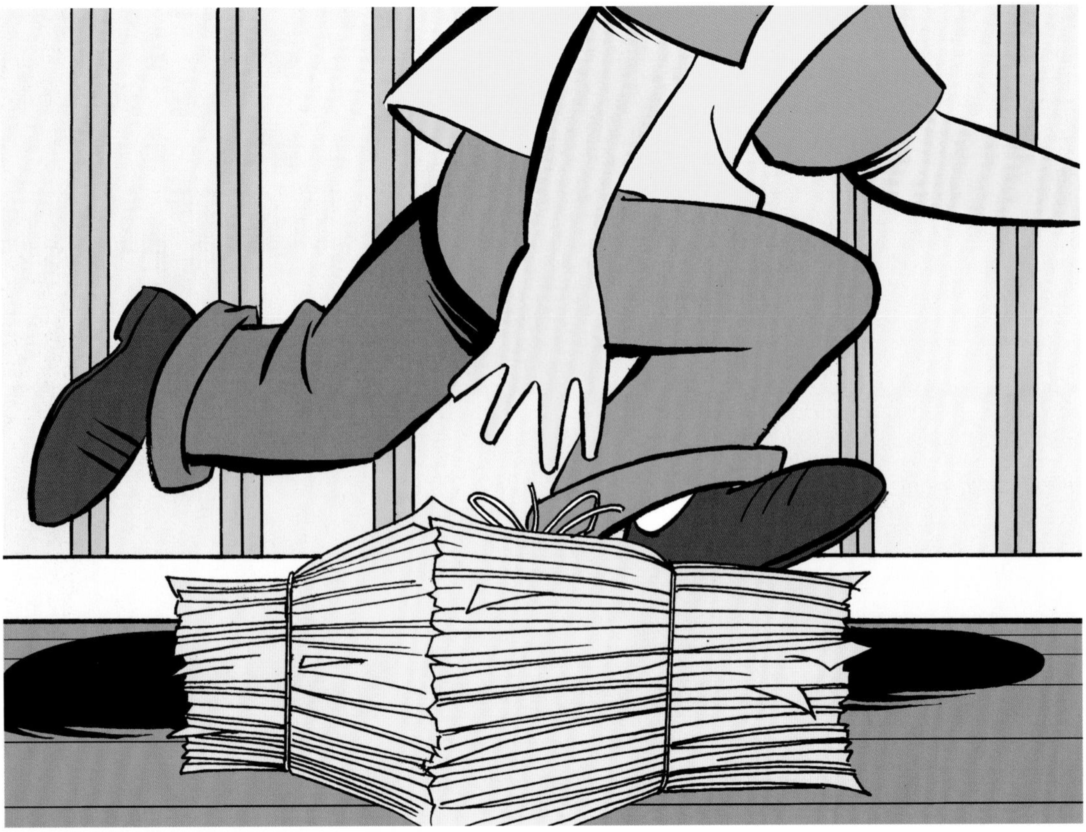

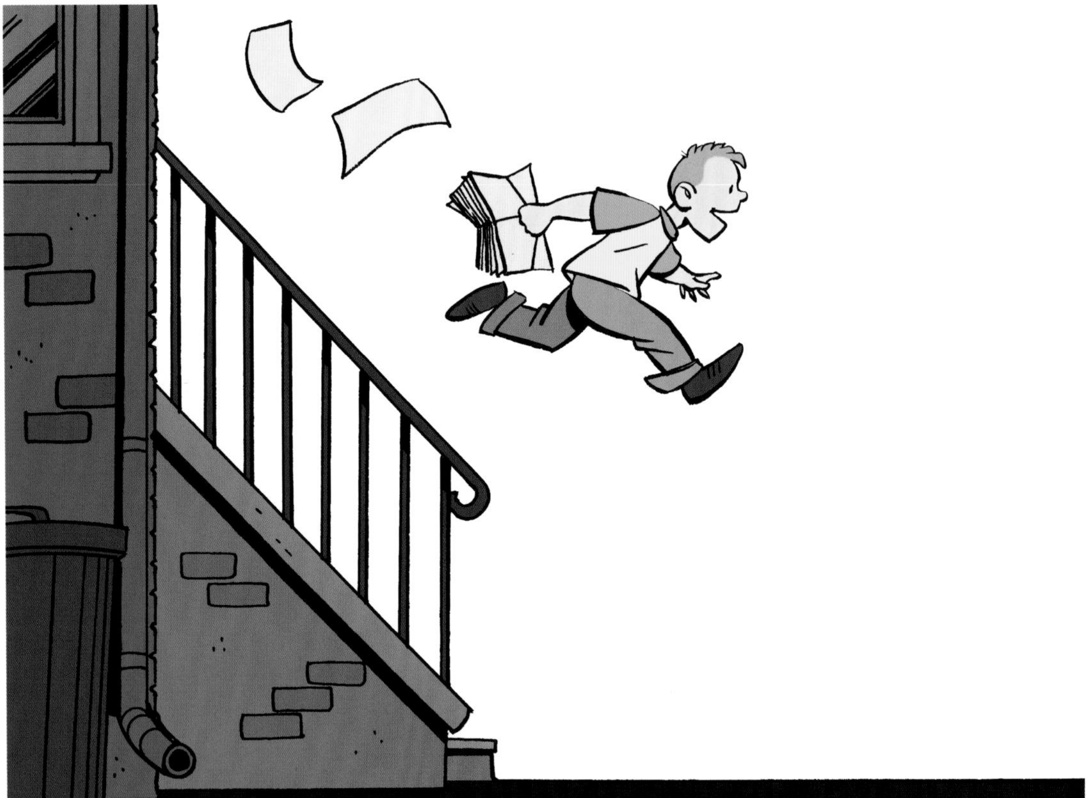

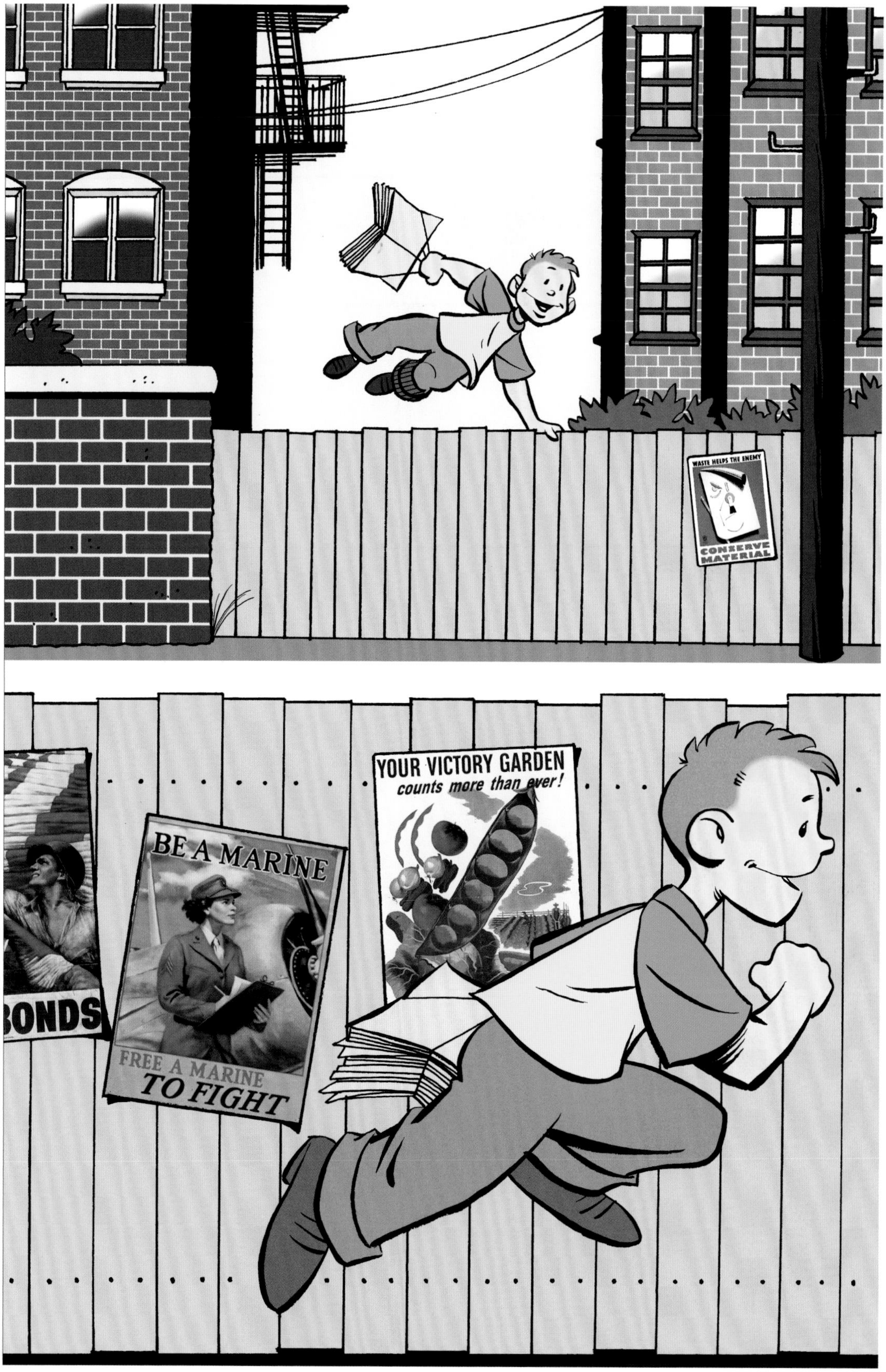
WASTE HELPS THE ENEMY
CONSERVE MATERIAL
BONDS
BE A MARINE
FREE A MARINE
TO FIGHT
YOUR VICTORY GARDEN
counts more than ever!

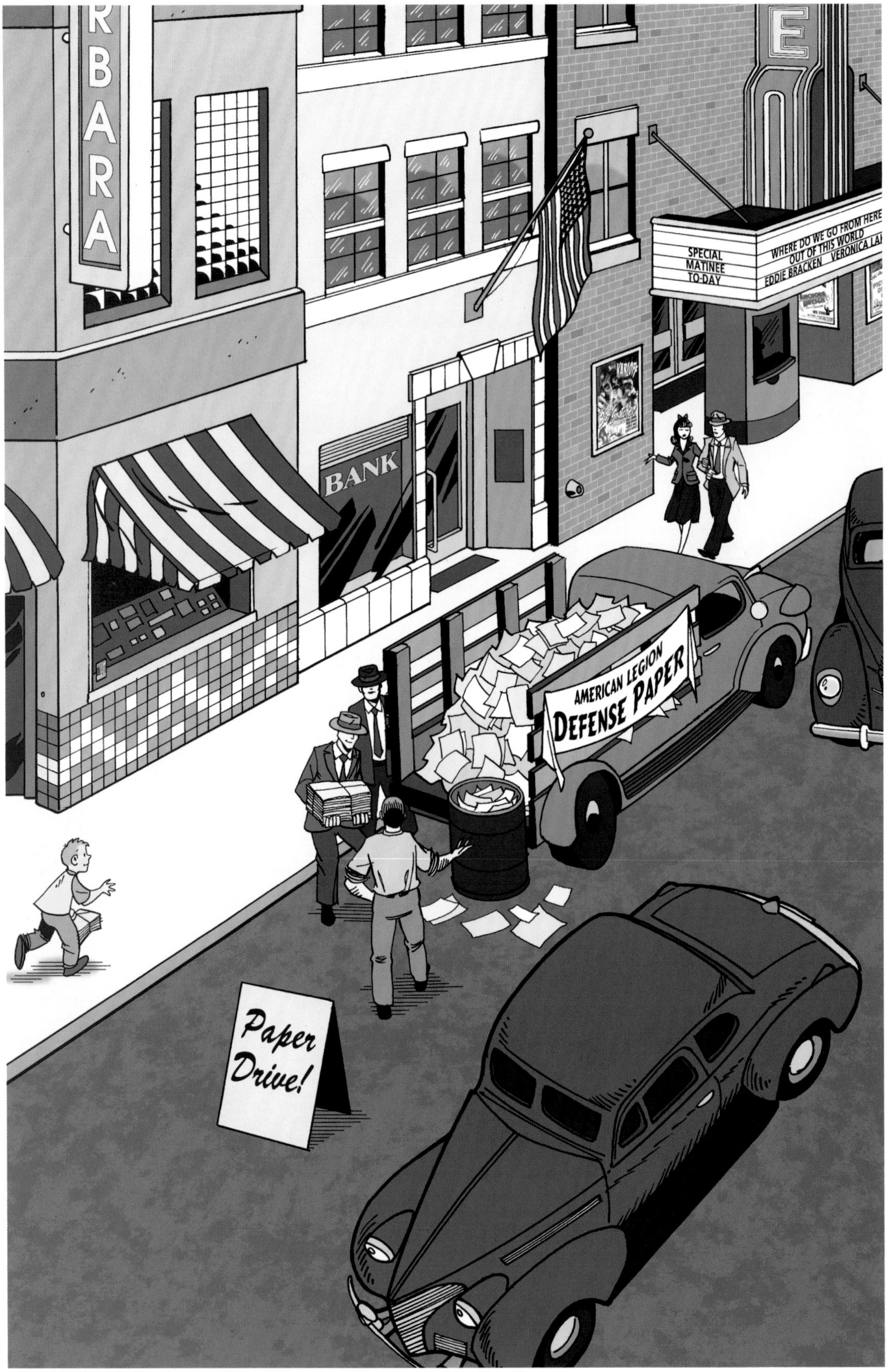
RBARA
BANK
SPECIAL
MATINEE
TO-DAY
WHERE DO WE GO FROM HERE
OUT OF THIS WORLD
EDDIE BRACKEN VERONICA LA
AMERICAN LEGION
DEFENSE PAPER
Paper
Drive!

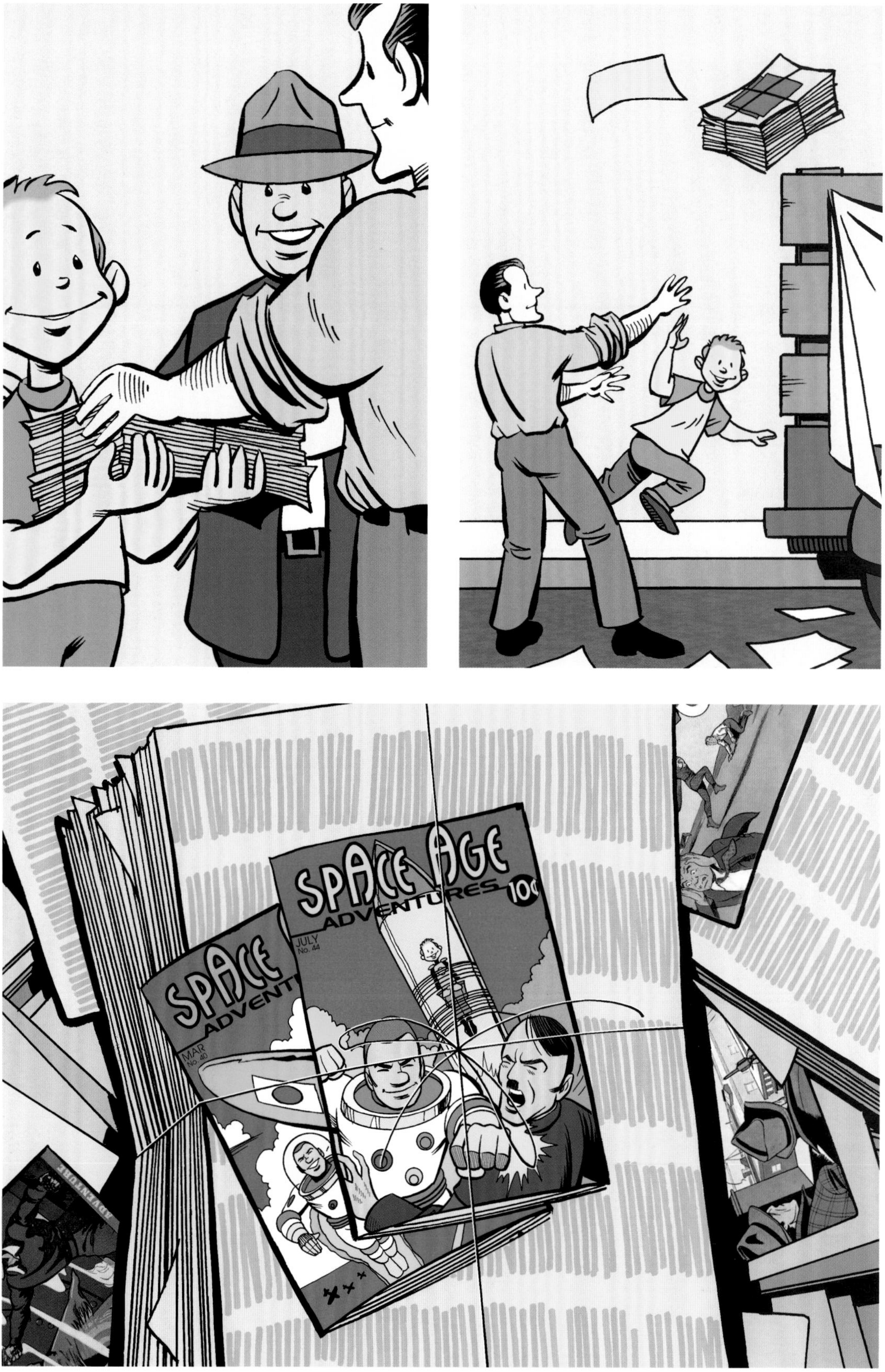
SPACE AGE
ADVENTURES
10¢
JULY
No. 44
MAR
No. 40

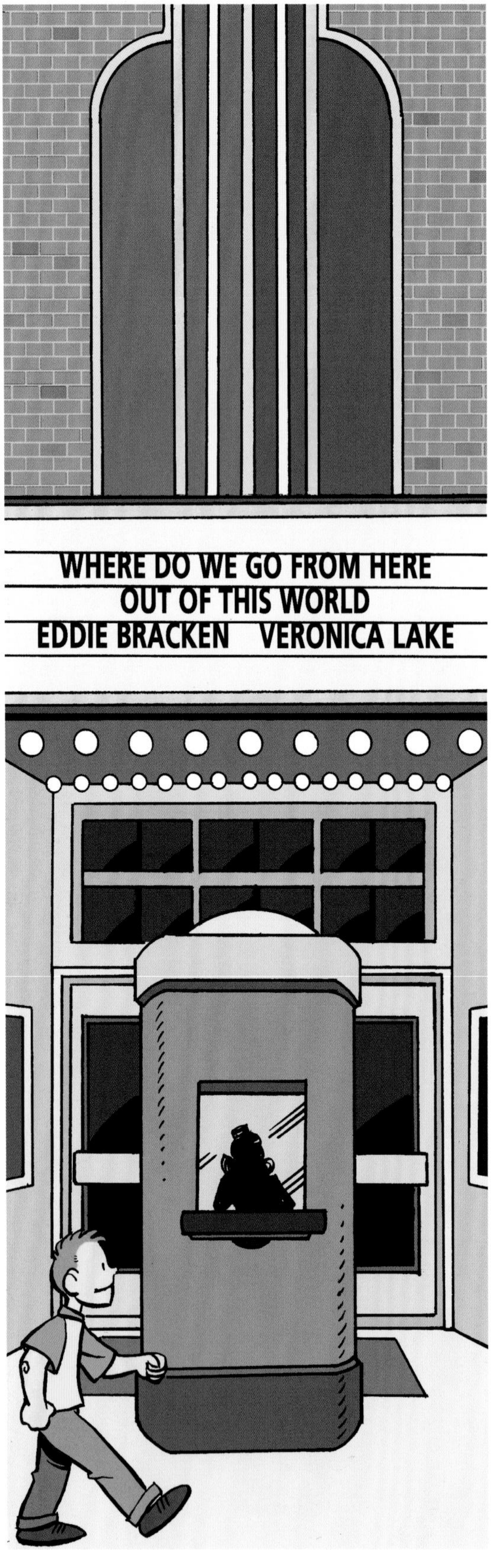
WHERE DO WE GO FROM HERE
OUT OF THIS WORLD
EDDIE BRACKEN VERONICA LAKE

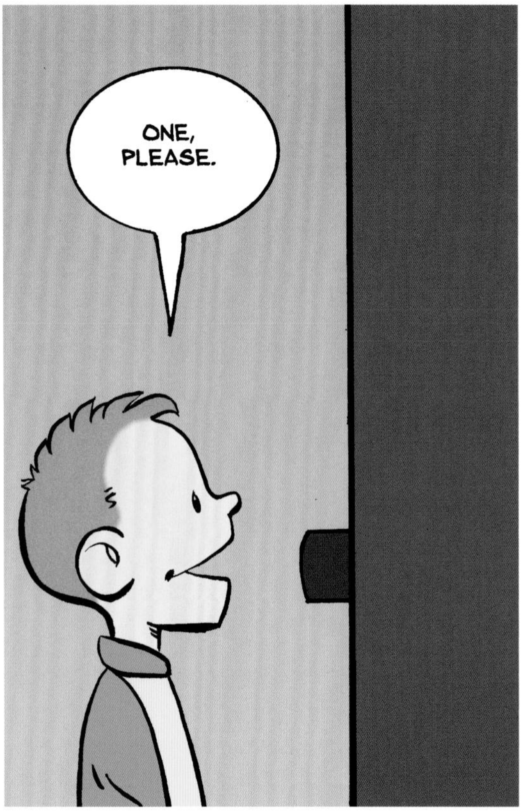
ONE, PLEASE.

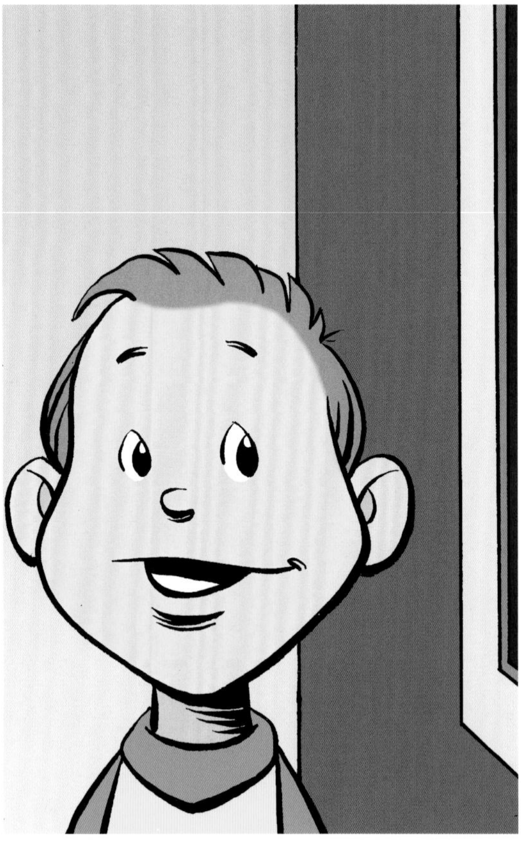

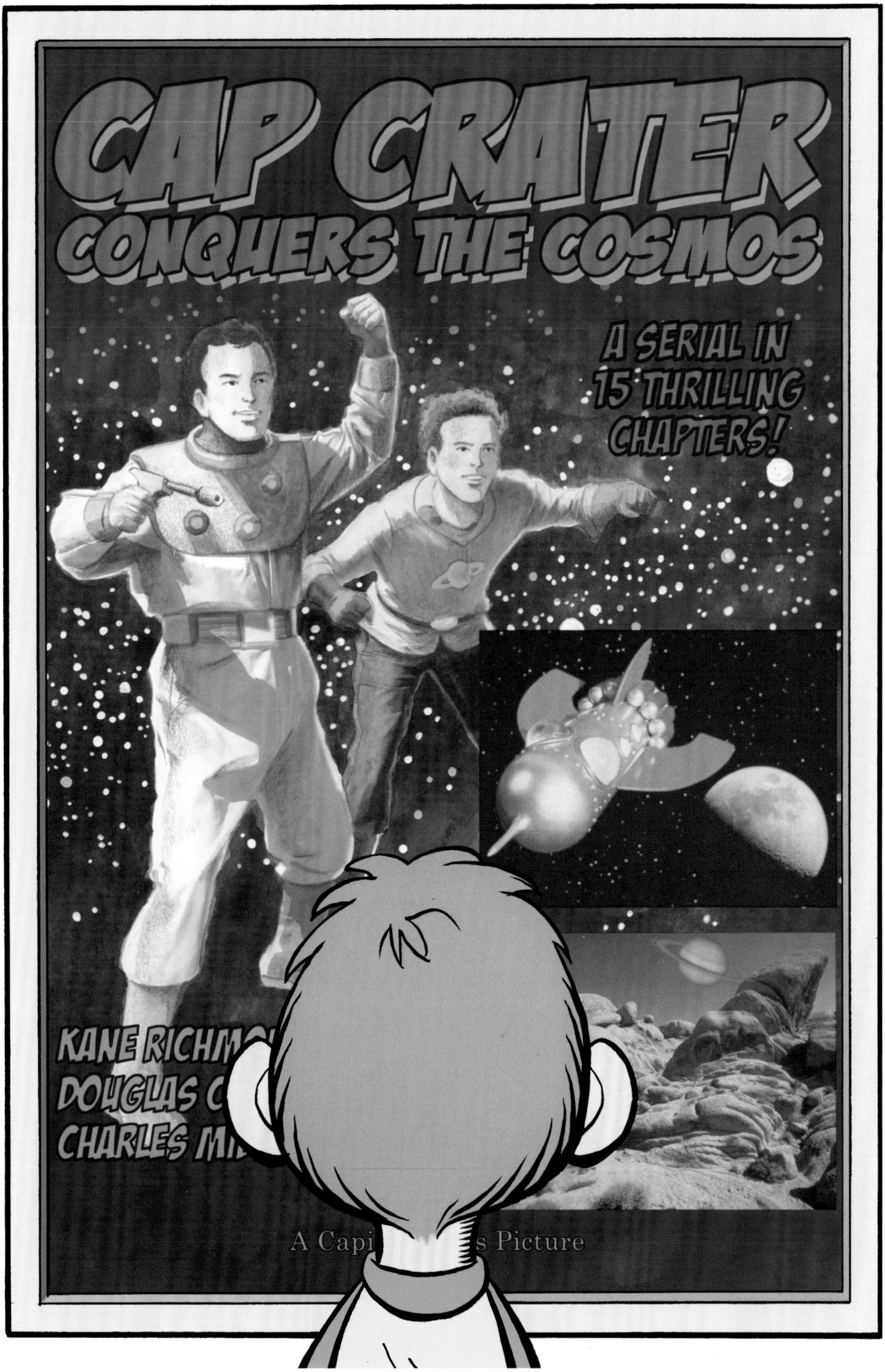
CAP CRATER
CONQUERS THE COSMOS
A SERIAL IN
15 THRILLING
CHAPTERS!

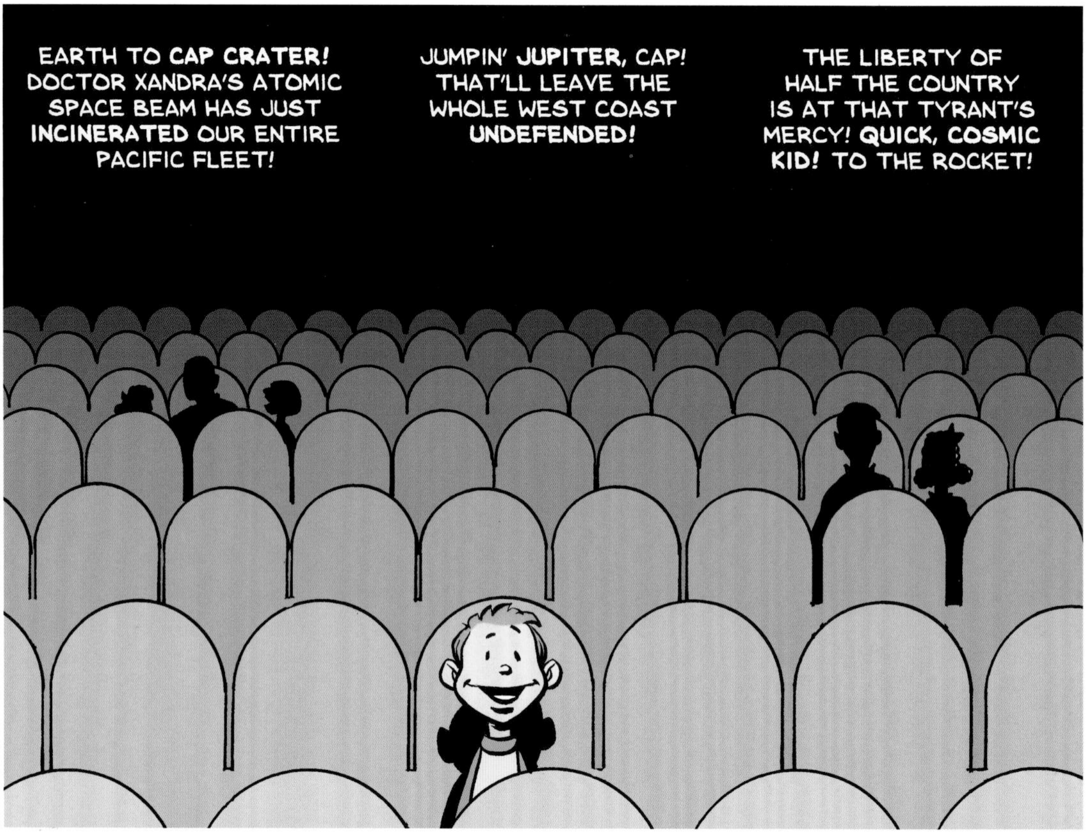
EARTH TO CAP CRATER! DOCTOR XANDRA'S ATOMIC SPACE BEAM HAS JUST INCINERATED OUR ENTIRE PACIFIC FLEET!
JUMPIN' JUPITER, CAP! THAT'LL LEAVE THE WHOLE WEST COAST UNDEFENDED!
THE LIBERTY OF HALF THE COUNTRY IS AT THAT TYRANT'S MERCY! QUICK, COSMIC KID! TO THE ROCKET!

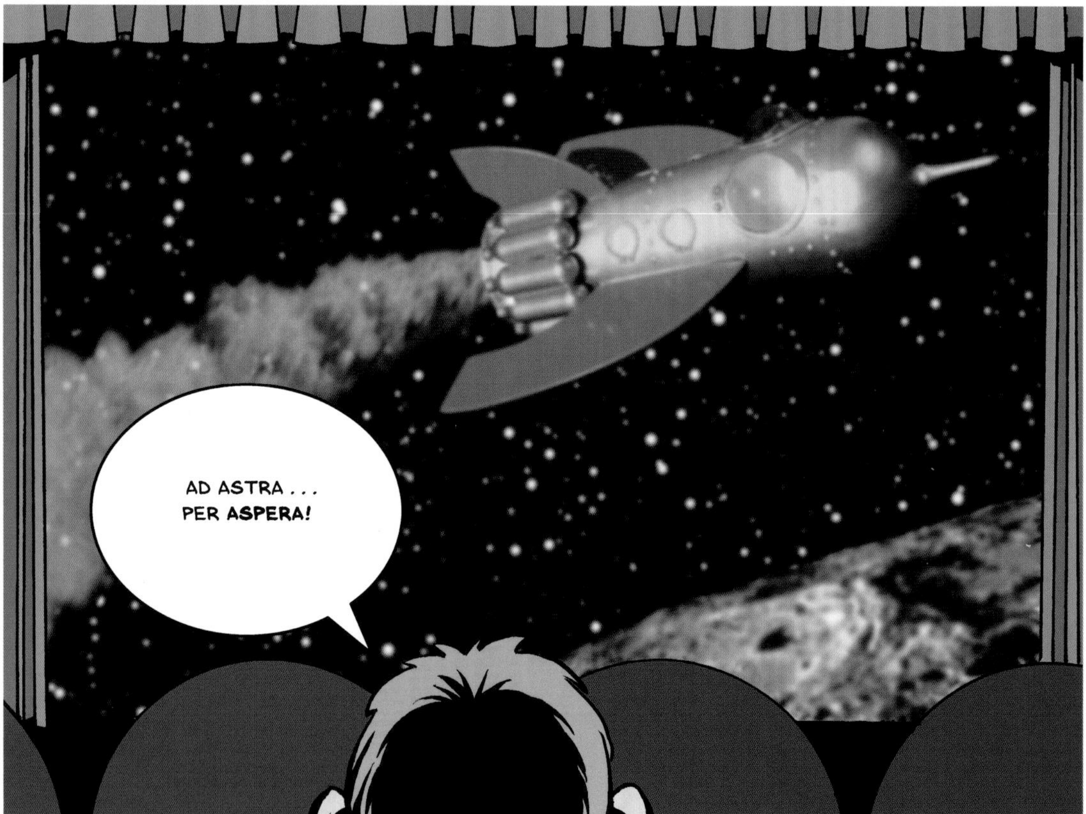
AD ASTRA . . . PER ASPERA!

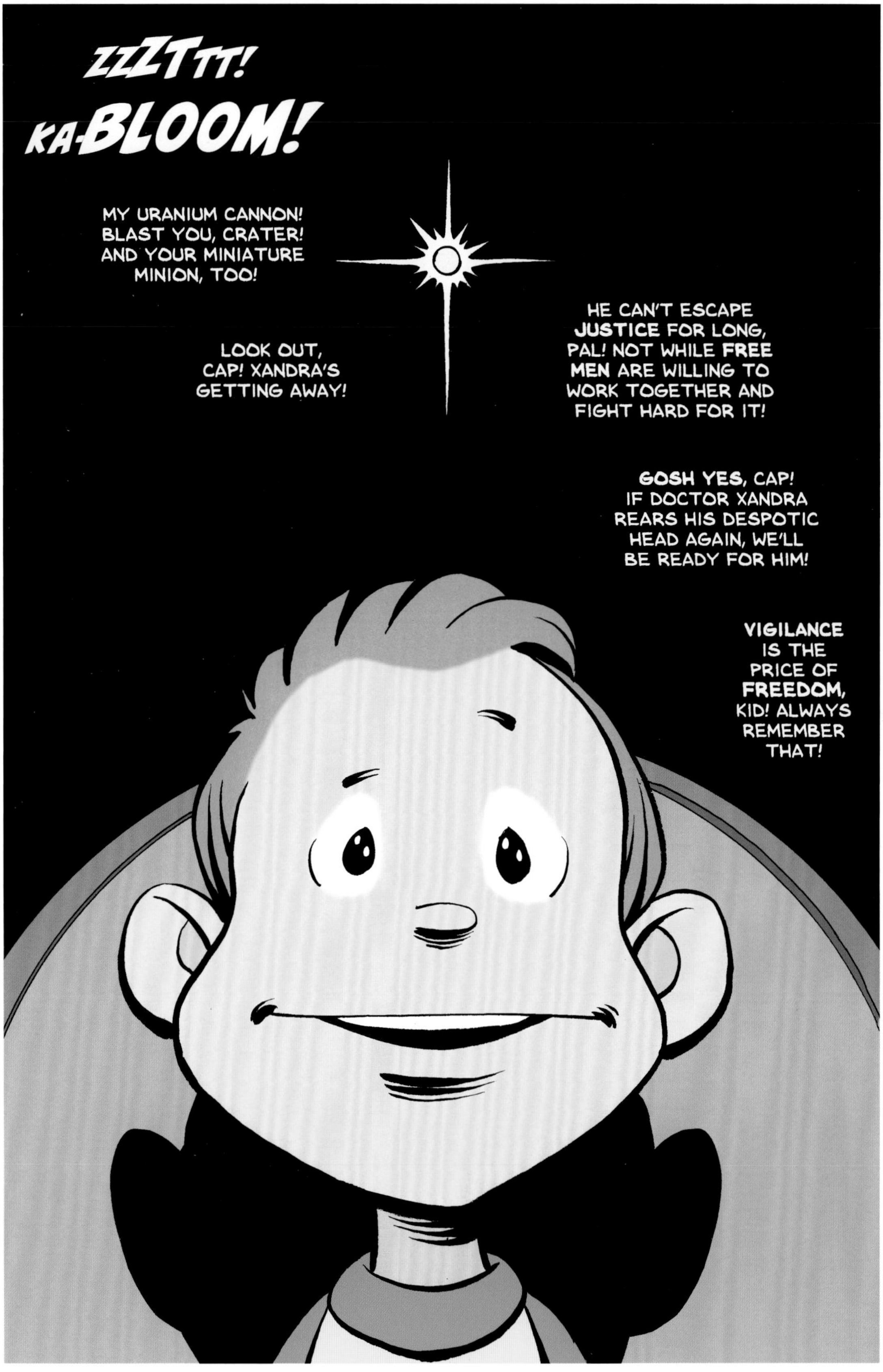
ZZZTTT!
KA-BLOOM!
MY URANIUM CANNON! BLAST YOU, CRATER! AND YOUR MINIATURE MINION, TOO!
LOOK OUT, CAP! XANDRA'S GETTING AWAY!
HE CAN'T ESCAPE JUSTICE FOR LONG, PAL! NOT WHILE FREE MEN ARE WILLING TO WORK TOGETHER AND FIGHT HARD FOR IT!
GOSH YES, CAP! IF DOCTOR XANDRA REARS HIS DESPOTIC HEAD AGAIN, WE'LL BE READY FOR HIM!
VIGILANCE IS THE PRICE OF FREEDOM, KID! ALWAYS REMEMBER THAT!

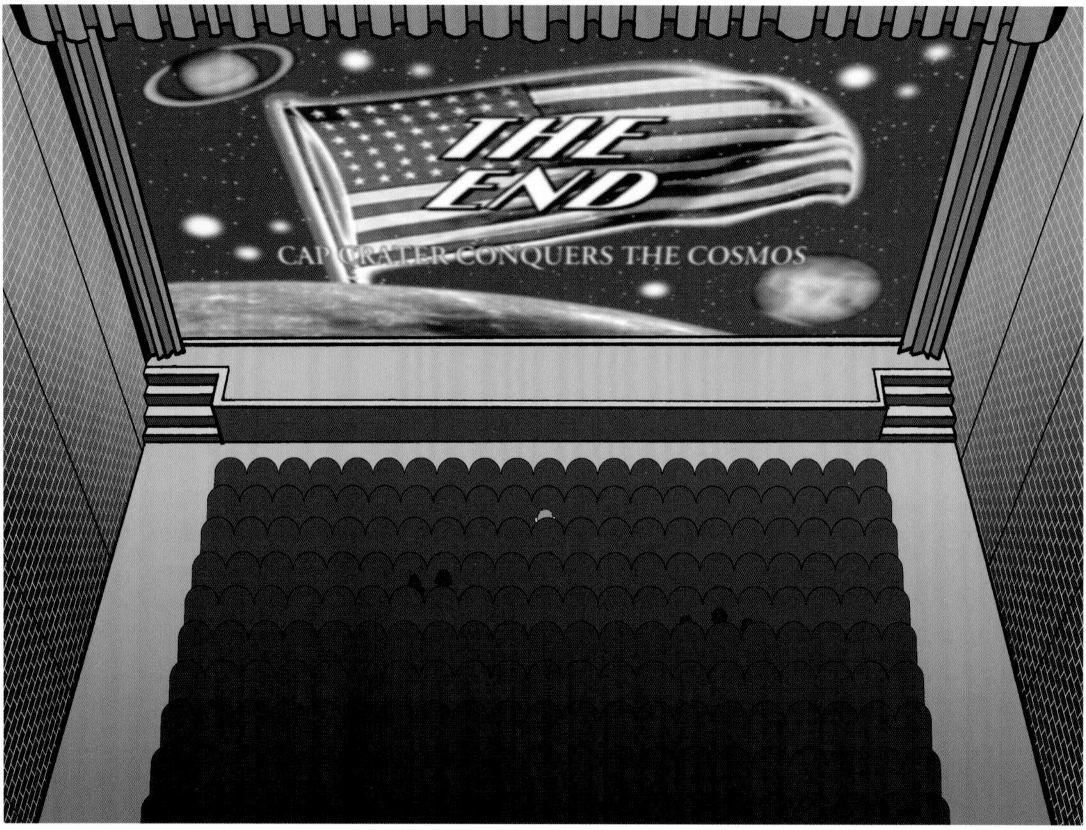
THE END
CONQUERS THE COSMOS

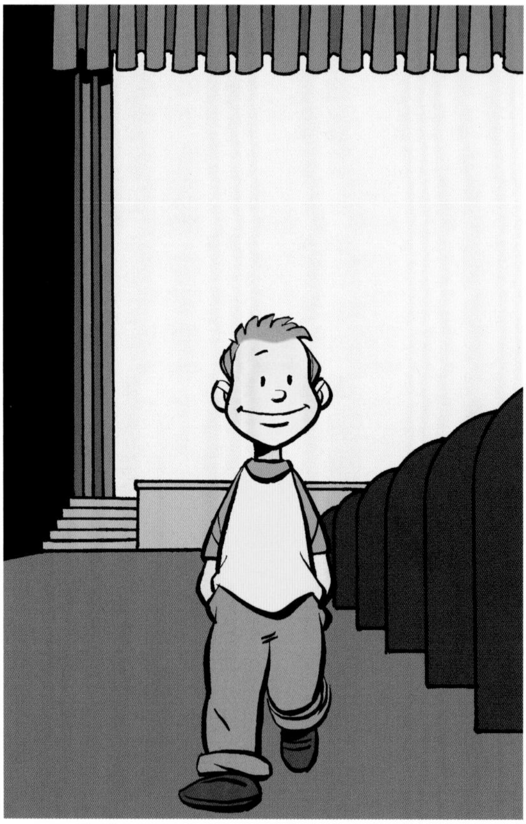

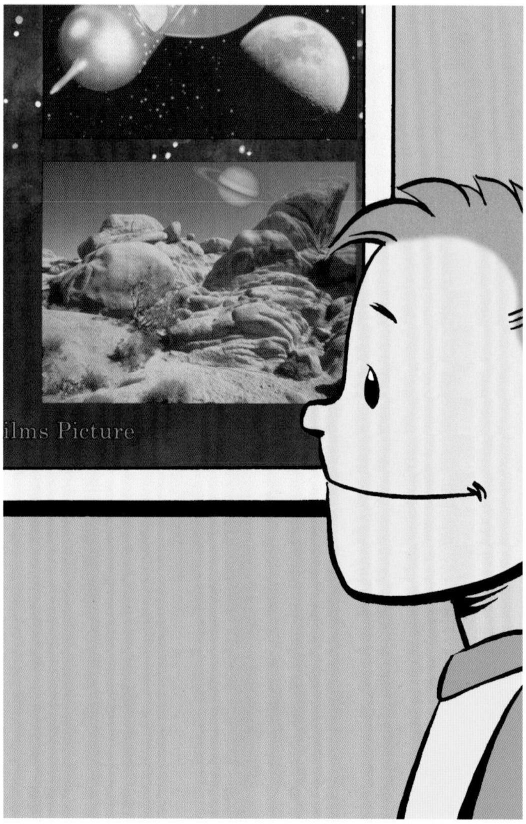
ilms Picture

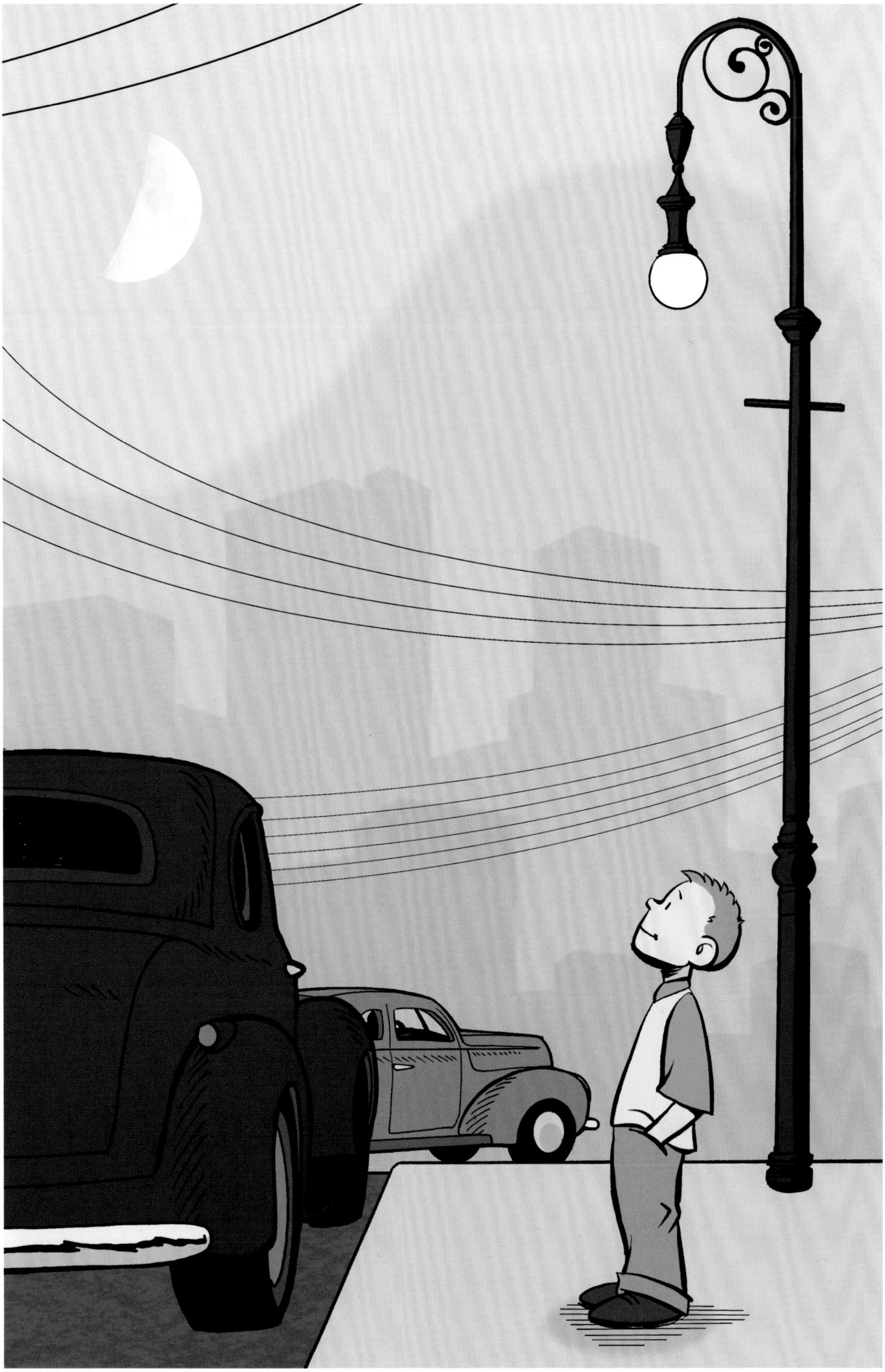

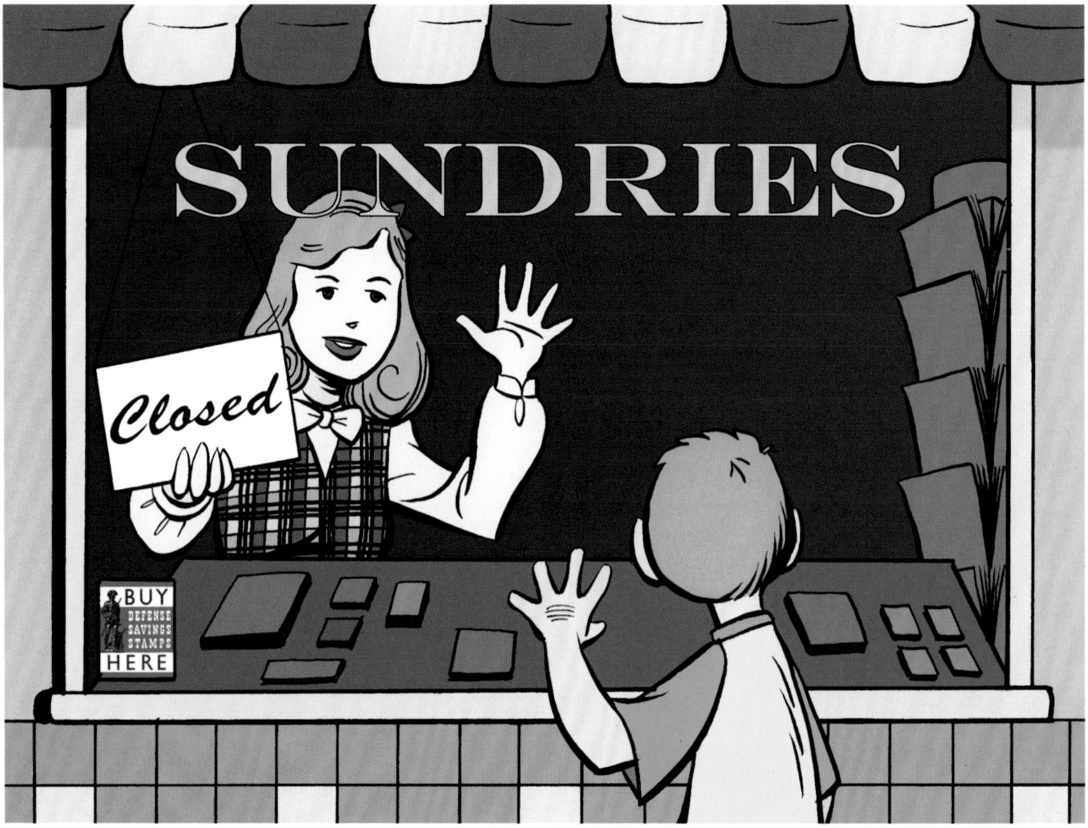
SUNDRIES
Closed
BUY DEFENSE SAVINGS STAMPS HERE

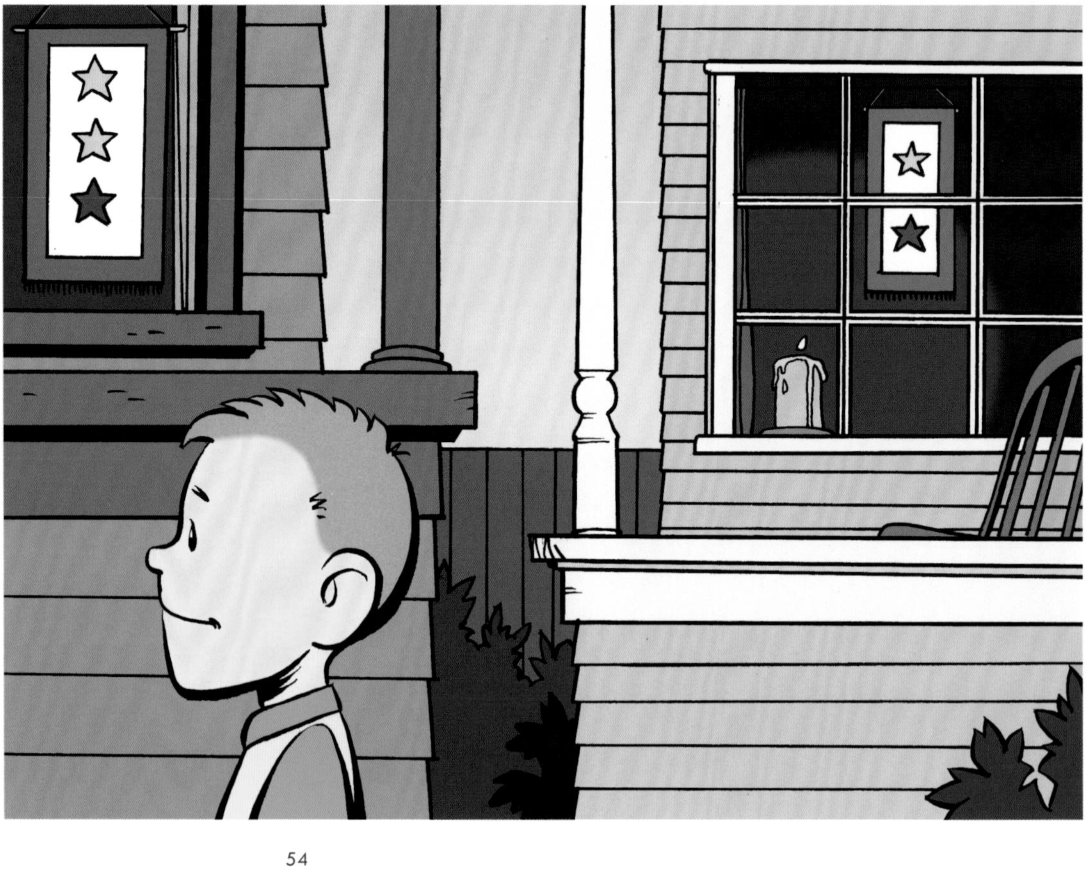

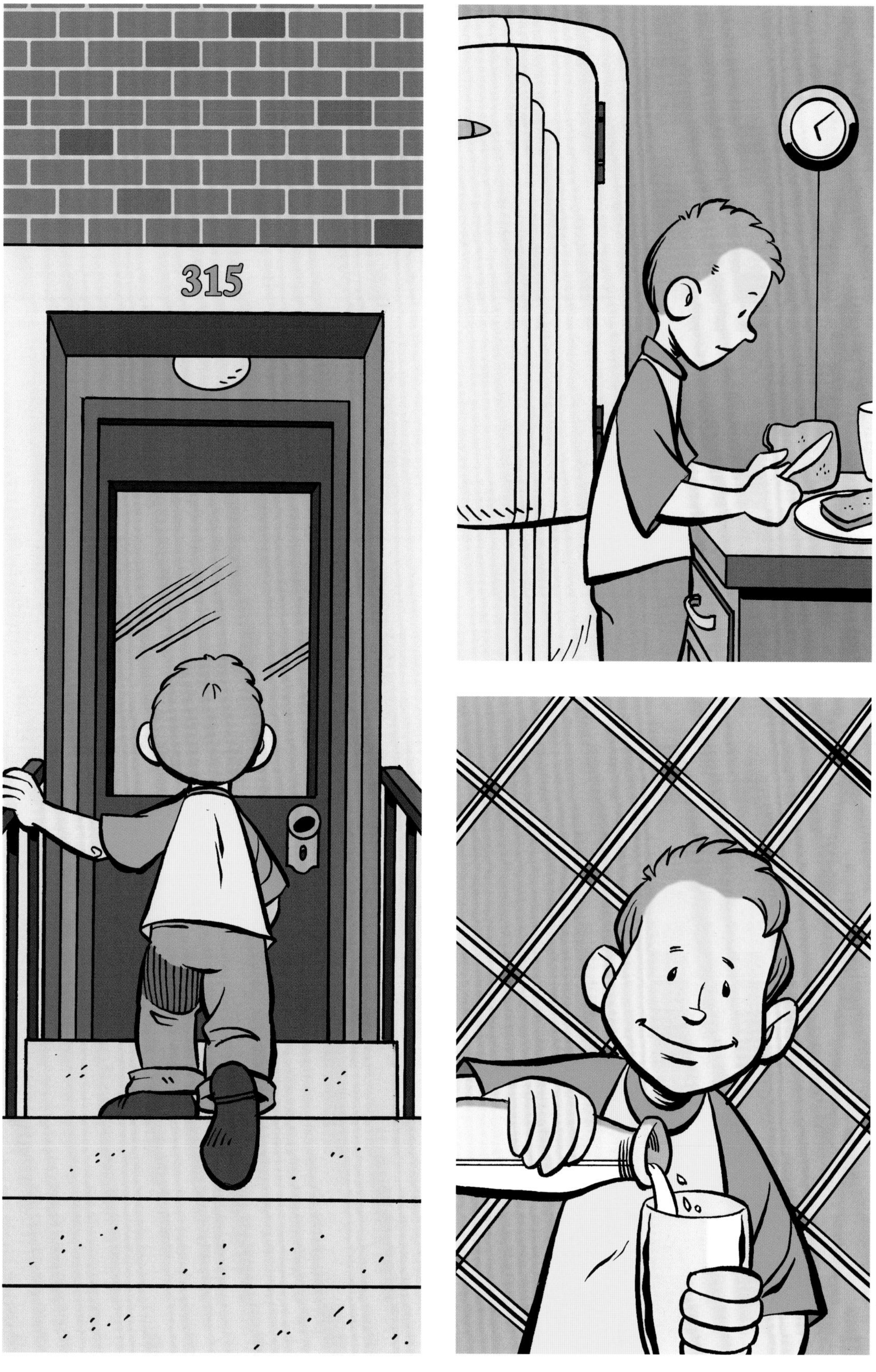
315

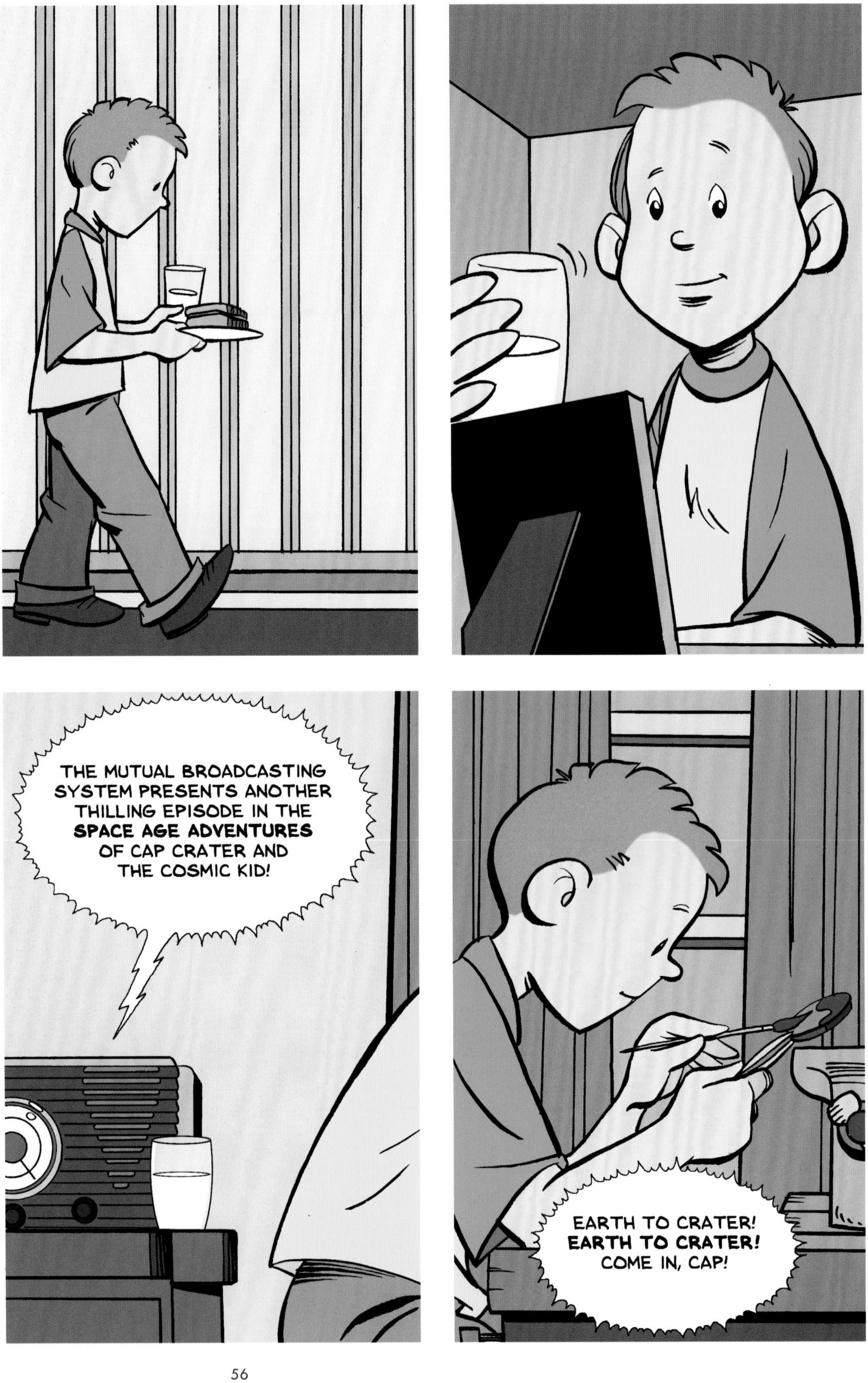
THE MUTUAL BROADCASTING SYSTEM PRESENTS ANOTHER THILLING EPISODE IN THE **SPACE AGE ADVENTURES** OF CAP CRATER AND THE COSMIC KID!
EARTH TO CRATER! **EARTH TO CRATER!** COME IN, CAP!

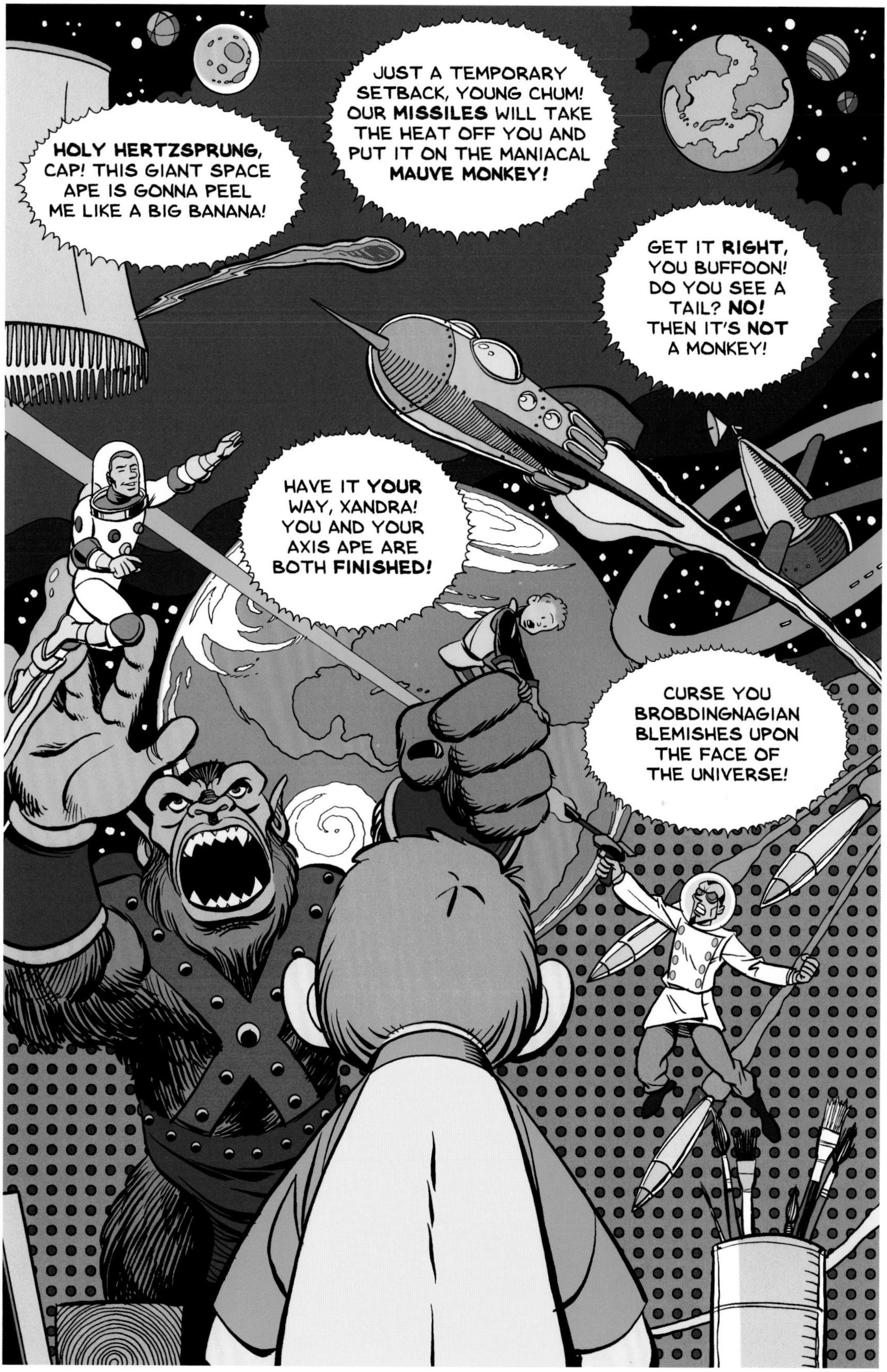
HOLY HERTZSPRUNG, CAP! THIS GIANT SPACE APE IS GONNA PEEL ME LIKE A BIG BANANA!
JUST A TEMPORARY SETBACK, YOUNG CHUM! OUR MISSILES WILL TAKE THE HEAT OFF YOU AND PUT IT ON THE MANIACAL MAUVE MONKEY!
GET IT RIGHT, YOU BUFFOON! DO YOU SEE A TAIL? NO! THEN IT'S NOT A MONKEY!
HAVE IT YOUR WAY, XANDRA! YOU AND YOUR AXIS APE ARE BOTH FINISHED!
CURSE YOU BROBDINGNAGIAN BLEMISHES UPON THE FACE OF THE UNIVERSE!

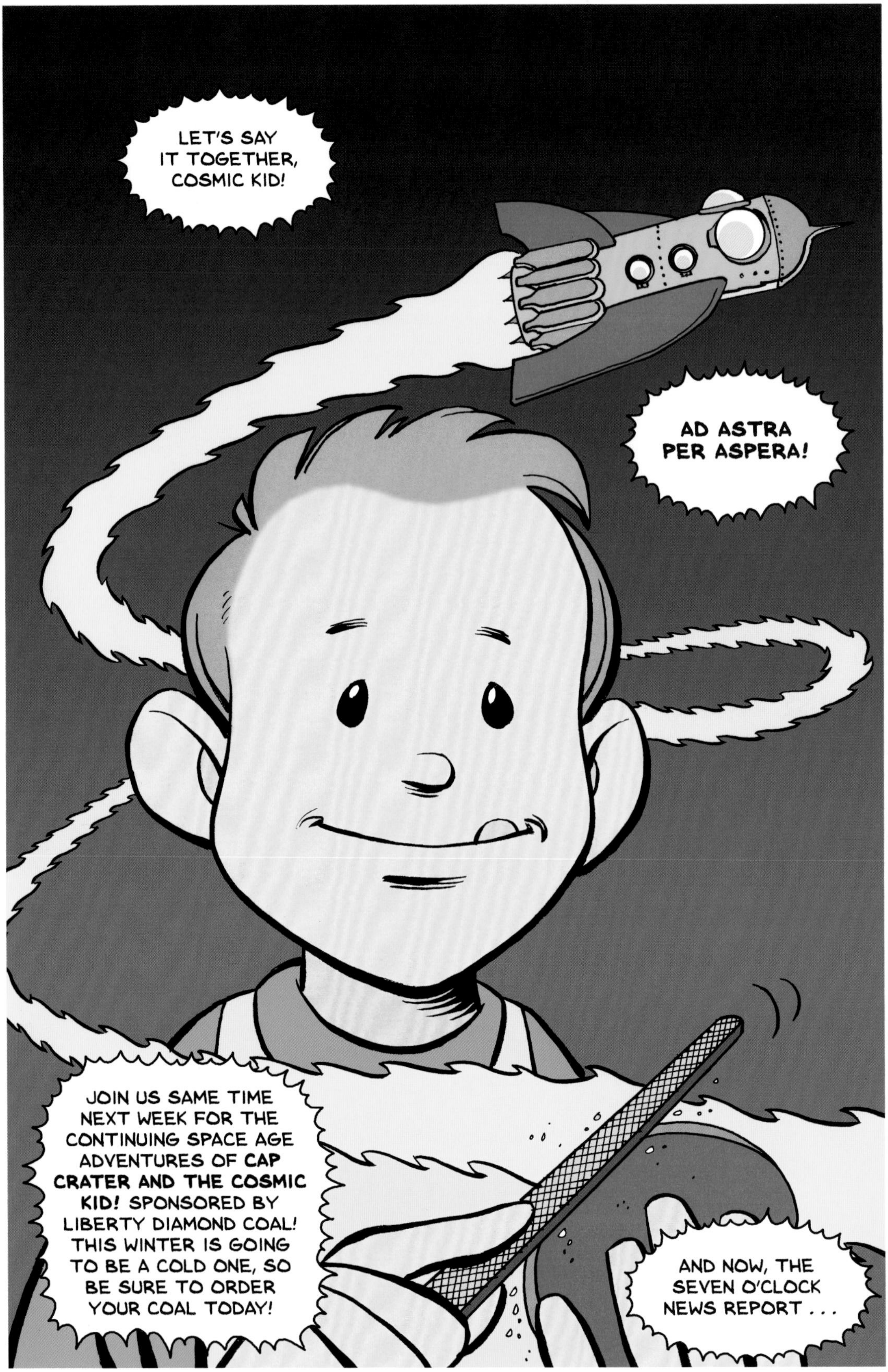
LET'S SAY IT TOGETHER, COSMIC KID!
AD ASTRA PER ASPERA!
JOIN US SAME TIME NEXT WEEK FOR THE CONTINUING SPACE AGE ADVENTURES OF CAP CRATER AND THE COSMIC KID! SPONSORED BY LIBERTY DIAMOND COAL! THIS WINTER IS GOING TO BE A COLD ONE, SO BE SURE TO ORDER YOUR COAL TODAY!
AND NOW, THE SEVEN O'CLOCK NEWS REPORT . . .

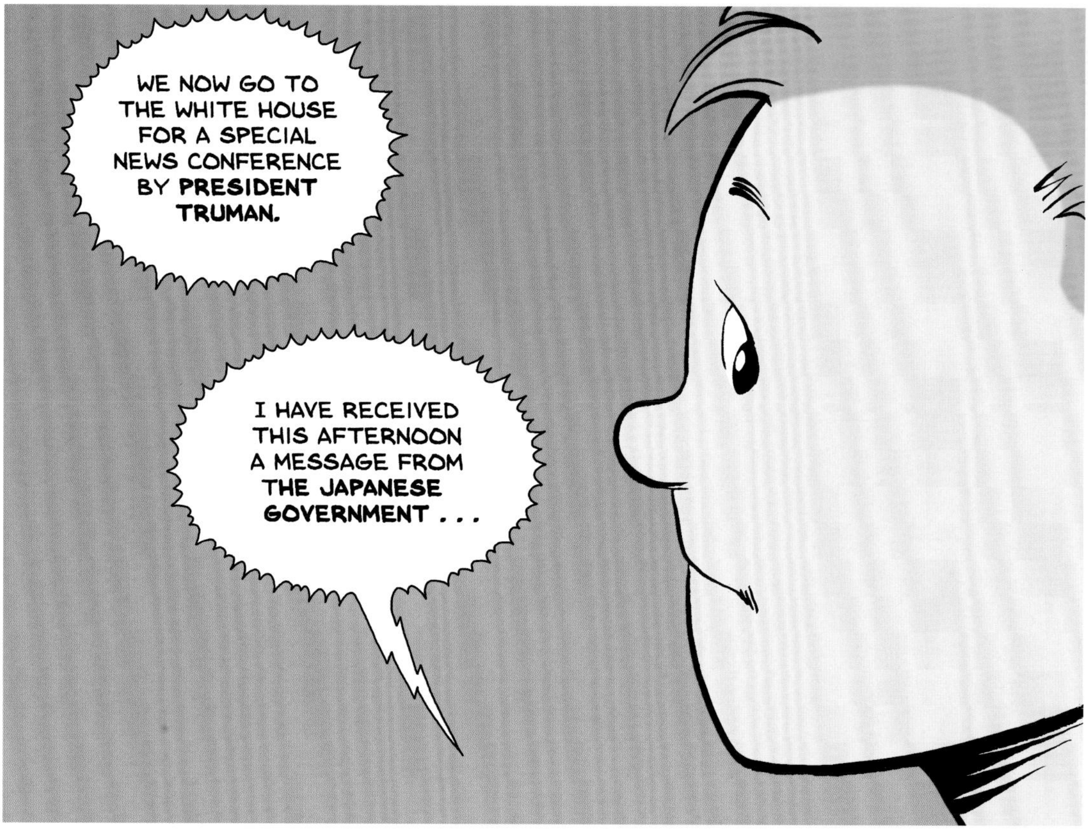
WE NOW GO TO THE WHITE HOUSE FOR A SPECIAL NEWS CONFERENCE BY **PRESIDENT TRUMAN.**
I HAVE RECEIVED THIS AFTERNOON A MESSAGE FROM **THE JAPANESE GOVERNMENT . . .**

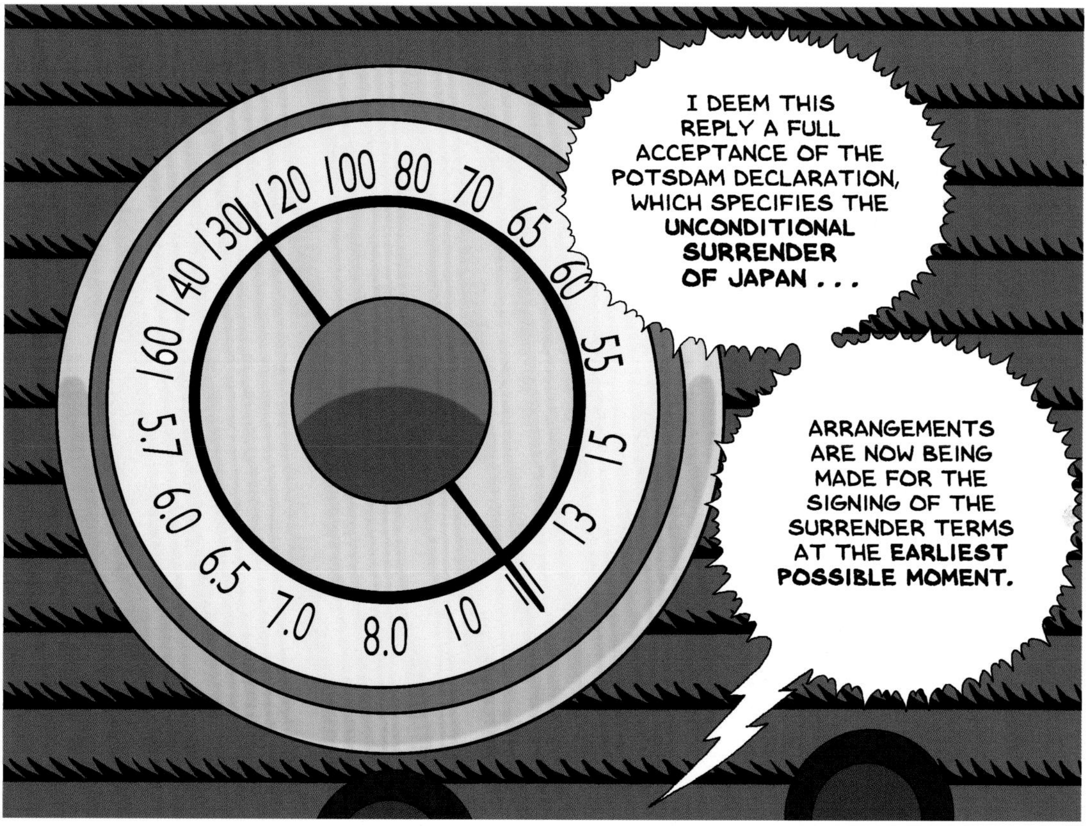
160 140 130 120 100 80 70 65 60 55
5.7 6.0 6.5 7.0 8.0 10 11 13 15
I DEEM THIS REPLY A FULL ACCEPTANCE OF THE POTSDAM DECLARATION, WHICH SPECIFIES THE **UNCONDITIONAL SURRENDER OF JAPAN . . .**
ARRANGEMENTS ARE NOW BEING MADE FOR THE SIGNING OF THE SURRENDER TERMS AT THE **EARLIEST POSSIBLE MOMENT.**

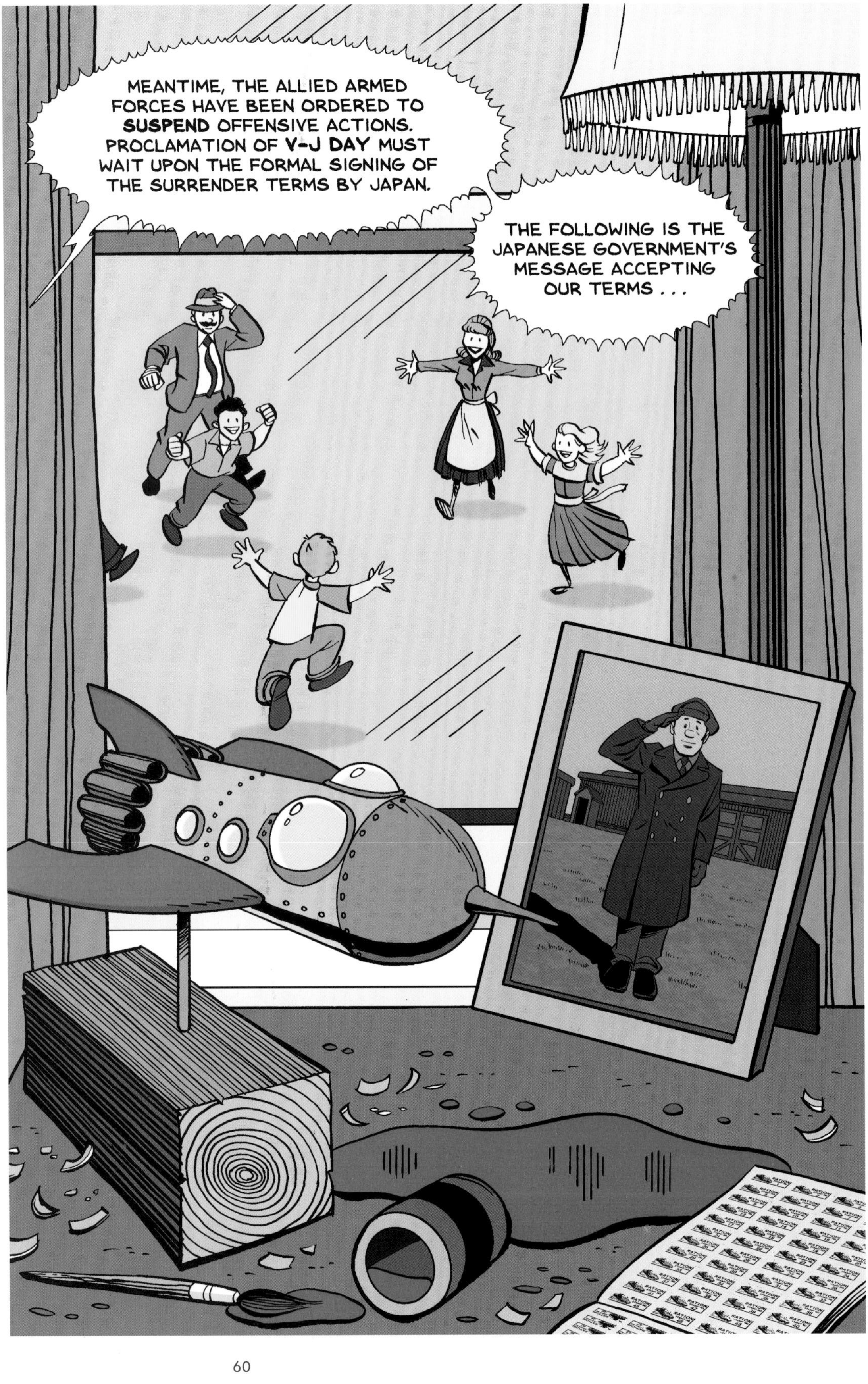
MEANTIME, THE ALLIED ARMED FORCES HAVE BEEN ORDERED TO **SUSPEND** OFFENSIVE ACTIONS. PROCLAMATION OF **V-J DAY** MUST WAIT UPON THE FORMAL SIGNING OF THE SURRENDER TERMS BY JAPAN.
THE FOLLOWING IS THE JAPANESE GOVERNMENT'S MESSAGE ACCEPTING OUR TERMS . . .

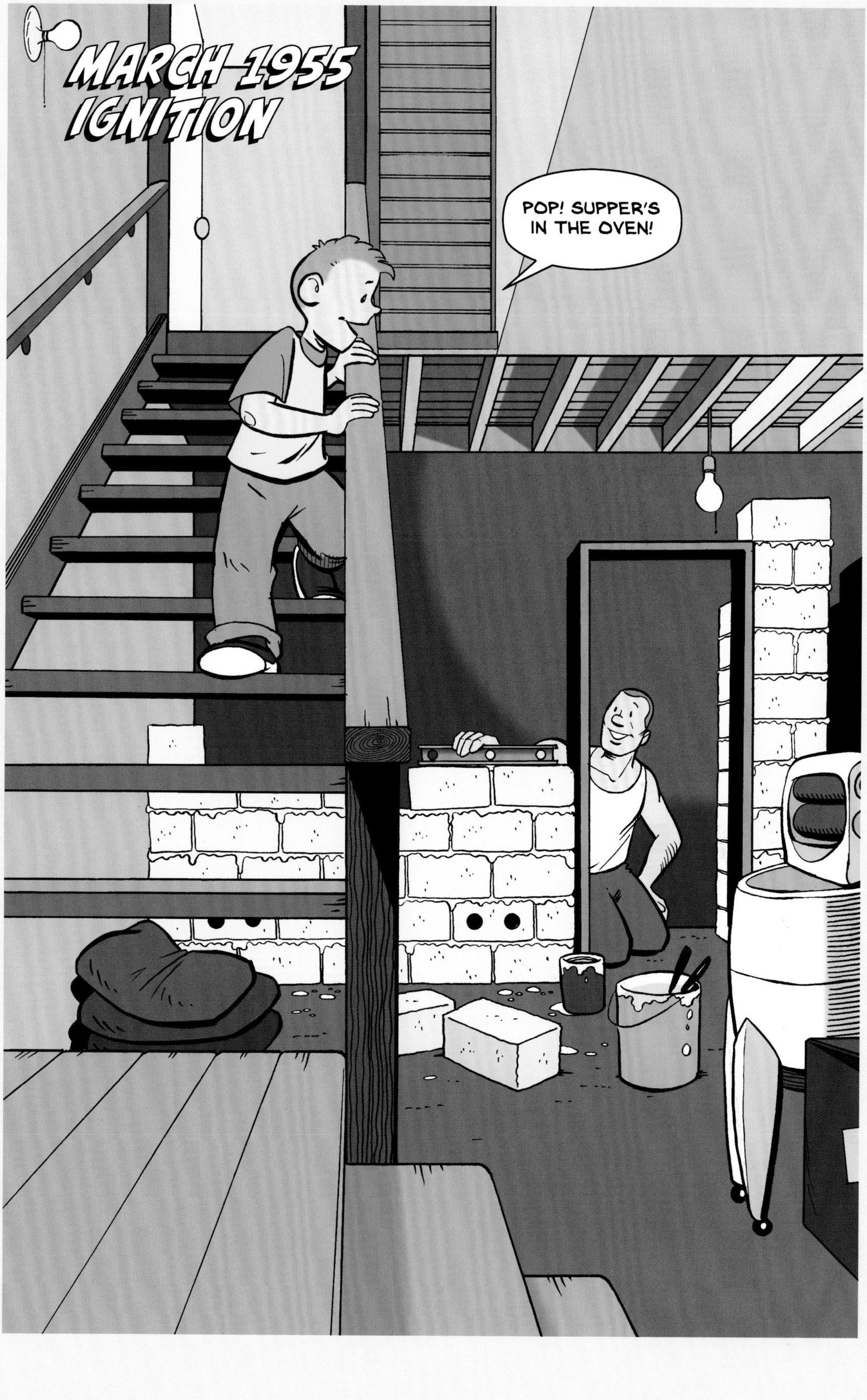
MARCH 1955
IGNITION
POP! SUPPER'S IN THE OVEN!

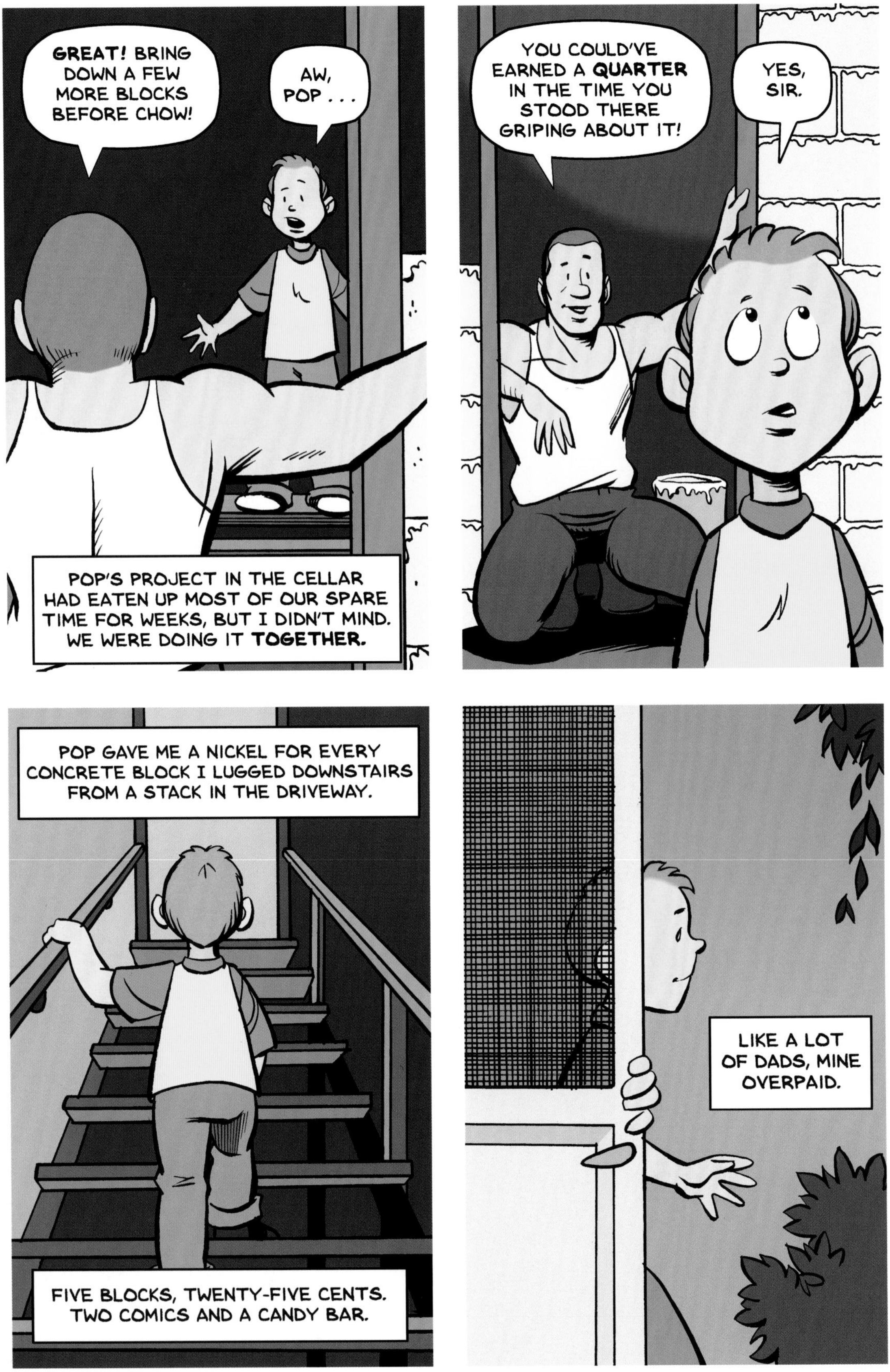
GREAT! BRING DOWN A FEW MORE BLOCKS BEFORE CHOW!
AW, POP . . .
POP'S PROJECT IN THE CELLAR HAD EATEN UP MOST OF OUR SPARE TIME FOR WEEKS, BUT I DIDN'T MIND. WE WERE DOING IT TOGETHER.
YOU COULD'VE EARNED A QUARTER IN THE TIME YOU STOOD THERE GRIPING ABOUT IT!
YES, SIR.
POP GAVE ME A NICKEL FOR EVERY CONCRETE BLOCK I LUGGED DOWNSTAIRS FROM A STACK IN THE DRIVEWAY.
FIVE BLOCKS, TWENTY-FIVE CENTS. TWO COMICS AND A CANDY BAR.
LIKE A LOT OF DADS, MINE OVERPAID.

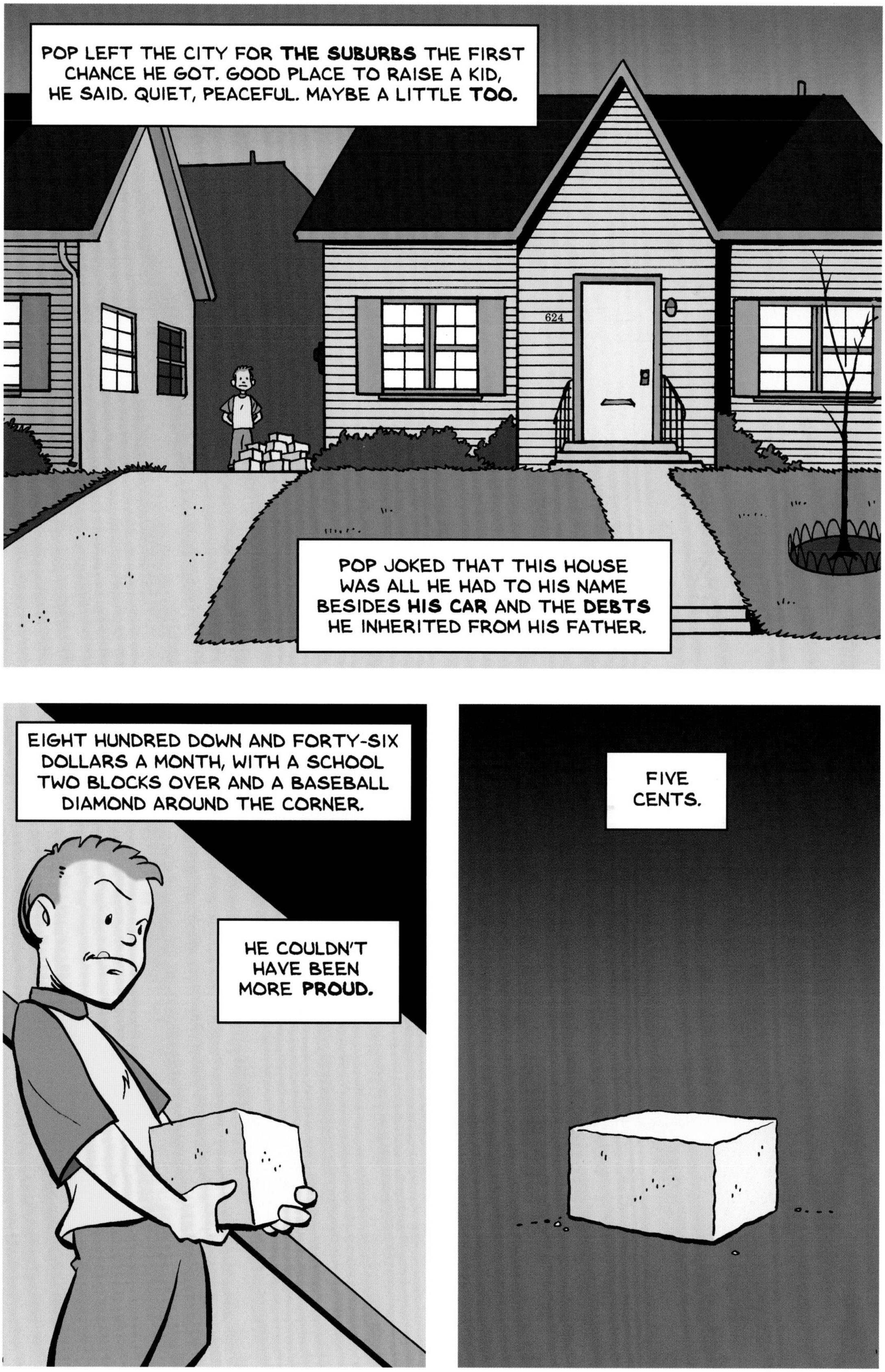
POP LEFT THE CITY FOR THE SUBURBS THE FIRST CHANCE HE GOT. GOOD PLACE TO RAISE A KID, HE SAID. QUIET, PEACEFUL. MAYBE A LITTLE TOO.
624
POP JOKED THAT THIS HOUSE WAS ALL HE HAD TO HIS NAME BESIDES HIS CAR AND THE DEBTS HE INHERITED FROM HIS FATHER.
EIGHT HUNDRED DOWN AND FORTY-SIX DOLLARS A MONTH, WITH A SCHOOL TWO BLOCKS OVER AND A BASEBALL DIAMOND AROUND THE CORNER.
HE COULDN'T HAVE BEEN MORE PROUD.
FIVE CENTS.

A GENERATION AGO, HALF OF NORTH AMERICA STILL LACKED ELECTRICITY, TELEPHONES, AND INDOOR PLUMBING. WITH THE POST-DEPRESSION PUBLIC WILLING TO INVEST IN INFRASTRUCTURE, THAT ALL CHANGED.

THE WIRING OF THE NATION THAT BEGAN WITH THE RURAL ELECTRIFICATION ACT OF 1936 WAS MOSTLY DONE NOW. TEAMS OF HARDWORKING LINEMEN SWEPT THROUGH THE COUNTRYSIDE LIKE AN ADVANCING ARMY.

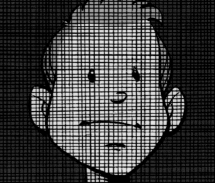

EXCEPT FOR THOSE IN A FEW DOGGED BACKWATERS, EVERY HOME IN AMERICA HAD AT LEAST A SIXTY-AMP CIRCUIT FOR A RANGE, A TWENTY-AMP CIRCUIT IN THE KITCHEN, AND TWO FIFTEEN-AMP CIRCUITS POWERING OUTLETS IN EVERY ROOM.

THE FLOOD CONTROL ACT OF 1944 FUNDED THOUSANDS OF DAMS AND LEVEES THAT DOMESTICATED RIVERS AND GENERATED POWER **THROUGHOUT THE COUNTRY.**

THE ATOMIC ENERGY ACT OF 1954 OPENED THE GOVERNMENT'S MONOPOLY ON NUCLEAR POWER TO **COMMERCIAL** DEVELOPMENT.

TEN.

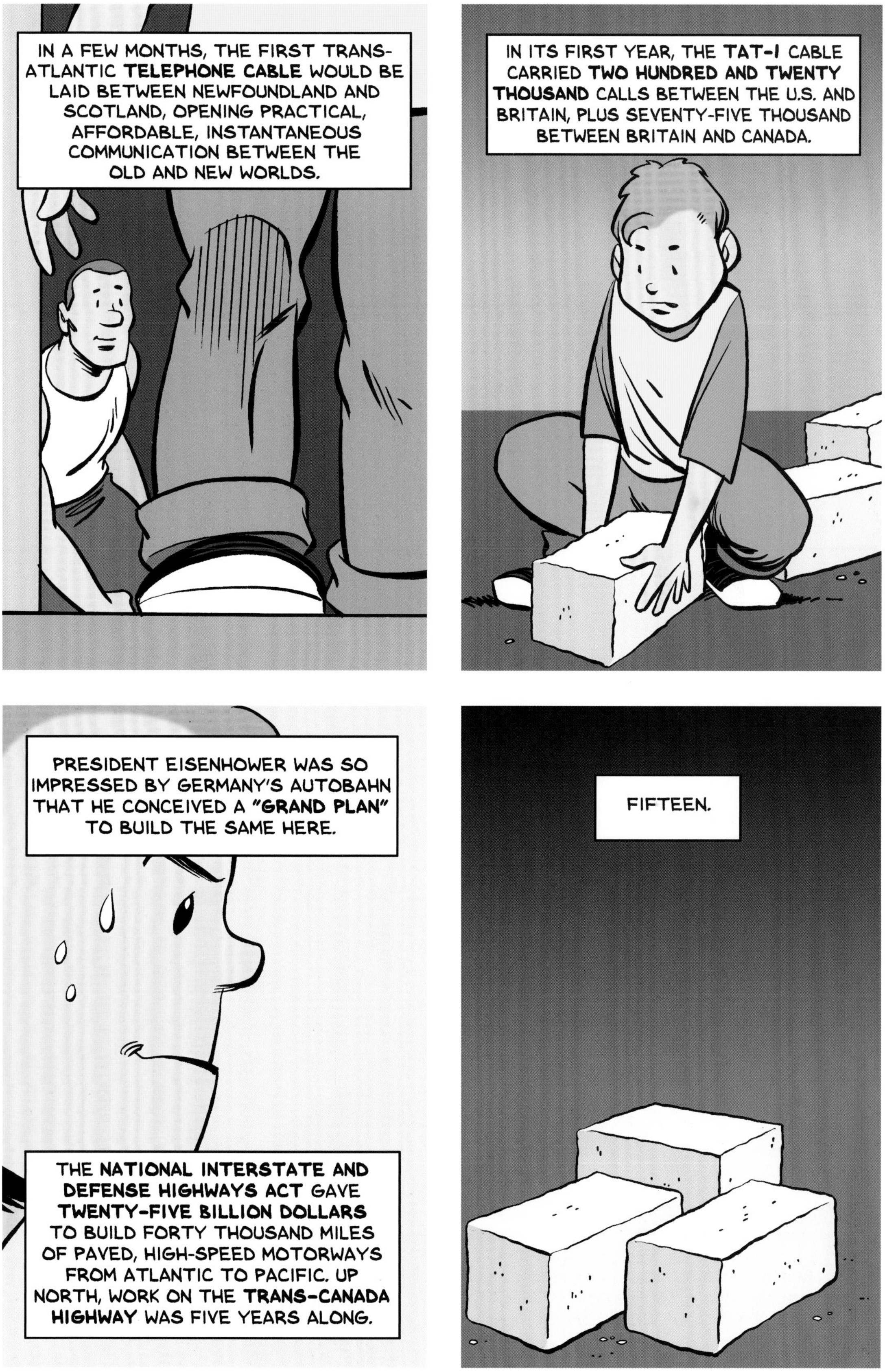
IN A FEW MONTHS, THE FIRST TRANS-ATLANTIC TELEPHONE CABLE WOULD BE LAID BETWEEN NEWFOUNDLAND AND SCOTLAND, OPENING PRACTICAL, AFFORDABLE, INSTANTANEOUS COMMUNICATION BETWEEN THE OLD AND NEW WORLDS.
IN ITS FIRST YEAR, THE TAT-1 CABLE CARRIED TWO HUNDRED AND TWENTY THOUSAND CALLS BETWEEN THE U.S. AND BRITAIN, PLUS SEVENTY-FIVE THOUSAND BETWEEN BRITAIN AND CANADA.
PRESIDENT EISENHOWER WAS SO IMPRESSED BY GERMANY'S AUTOBAHN THAT HE CONCEIVED A "GRAND PLAN" TO BUILD THE SAME HERE.
THE NATIONAL INTERSTATE AND DEFENSE HIGHWAYS ACT GAVE TWENTY-FIVE BILLION DOLLARS TO BUILD FORTY THOUSAND MILES OF PAVED, HIGH-SPEED MOTORWAYS FROM ATLANTIC TO PACIFIC. UP NORTH, WORK ON THE TRANS-CANADA HIGHWAY WAS FIVE YEARS ALONG.
FIFTEEN.

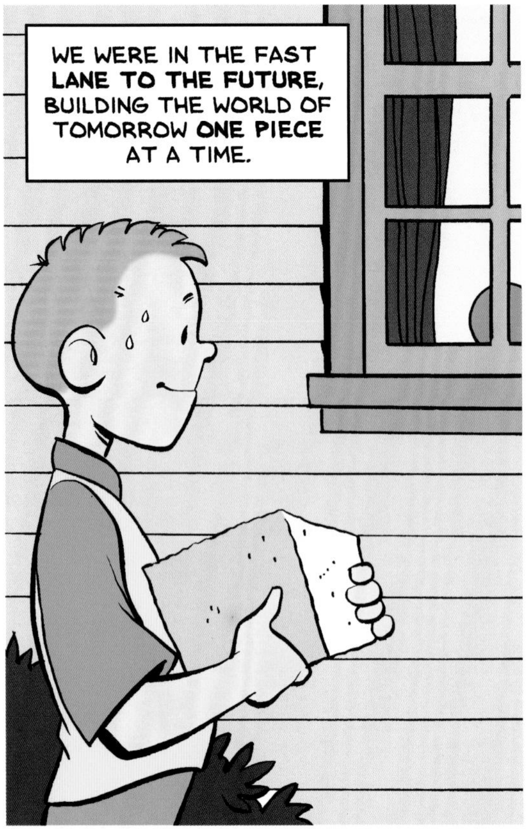

WE WERE IN THE FAST LANE TO THE FUTURE, BUILDING THE WORLD OF TOMORROW ONE PIECE AT A TIME.


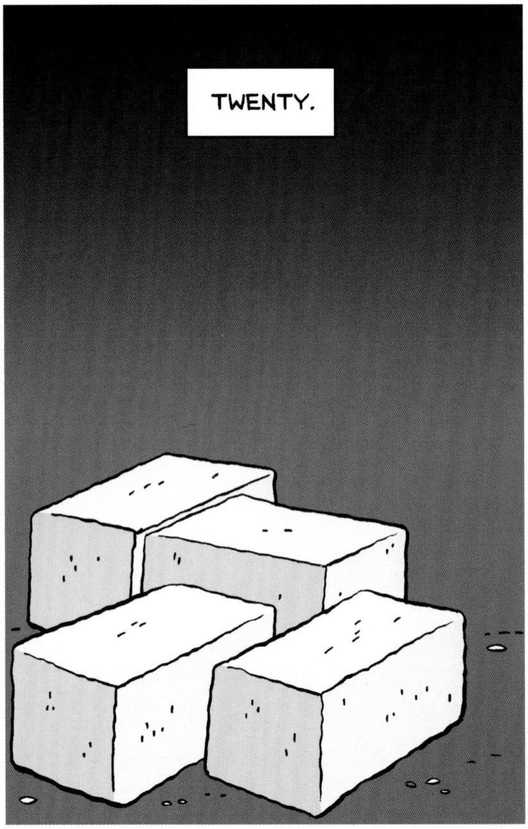

TWENTY.


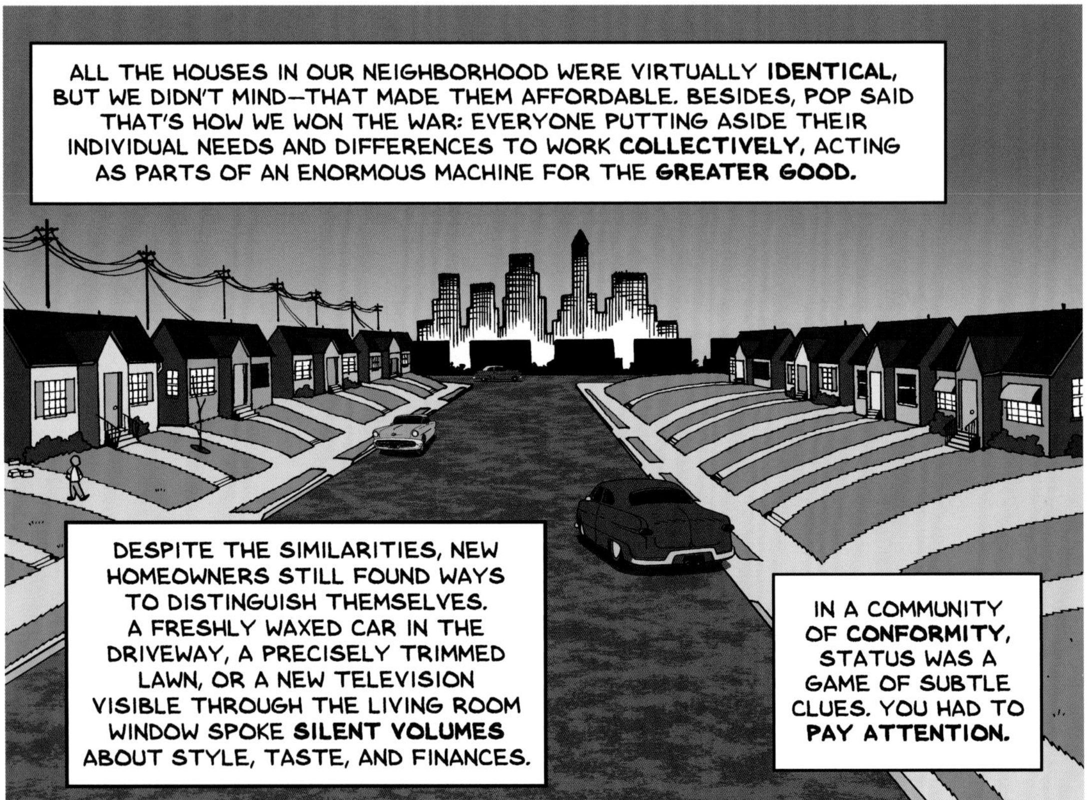

ALL THE HOUSES IN OUR NEIGHBORHOOD WERE VIRTUALLY IDENTICAL, BUT WE DIDN'T MIND—THAT MADE THEM AFFORDABLE. BESIDES, POP SAID THAT'S HOW WE WON THE WAR: EVERYONE PUTTING ASIDE THEIR INDIVIDUAL NEEDS AND DIFFERENCES TO WORK COLLECTIVELY, ACTING AS PARTS OF AN ENORMOUS MACHINE FOR THE GREATER GOOD.
DESPITE THE SIMILARITIES, NEW HOMEOWNERS STILL FOUND WAYS TO DISTINGUISH THEMSELVES. A FRESHLY WAXED CAR IN THE DRIVEWAY, A PRECISELY TRIMMED LAWN, OR A NEW TELEVISION VISIBLE THROUGH THE LIVING ROOM WINDOW SPOKE SILENT VOLUMES ABOUT STYLE, TASTE, AND FINANCES.
IN A COMMUNITY OF CONFORMITY, STATUS WAS A GAME OF SUBTLE CLUES. YOU HAD TO PAY ATTENTION.

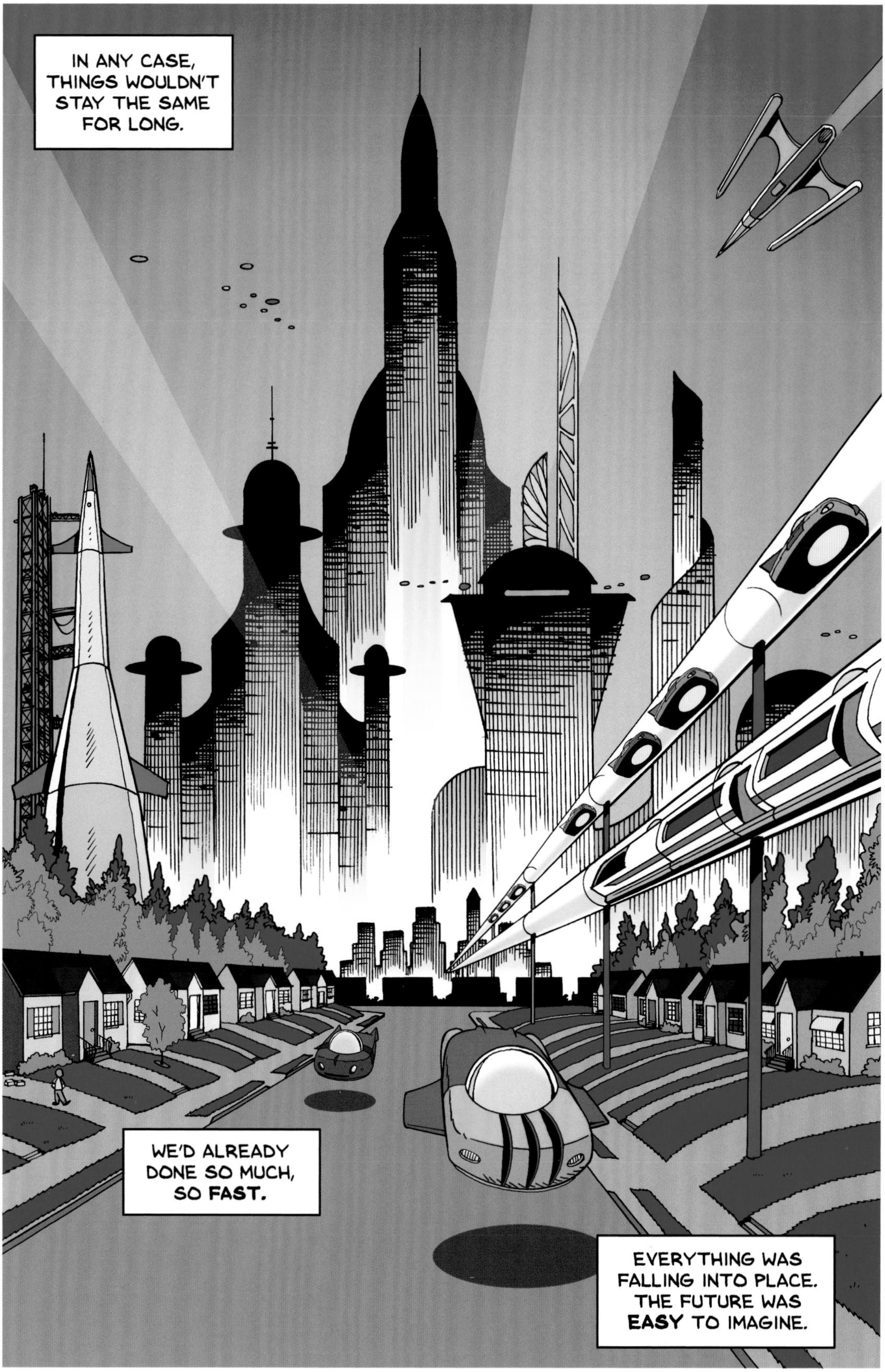
IN ANY CASE, THINGS WOULDN'T STAY THE SAME FOR LONG.
WE'D ALREADY DONE SO MUCH, SO **FAST.**
EVERYTHING WAS FALLING INTO PLACE. THE FUTURE WAS **EASY** TO IMAGINE.

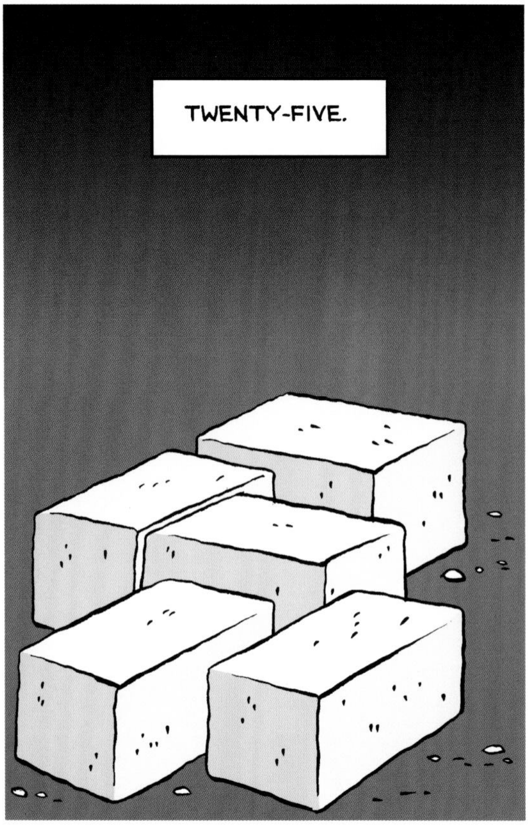
TWENTY-FIVE.

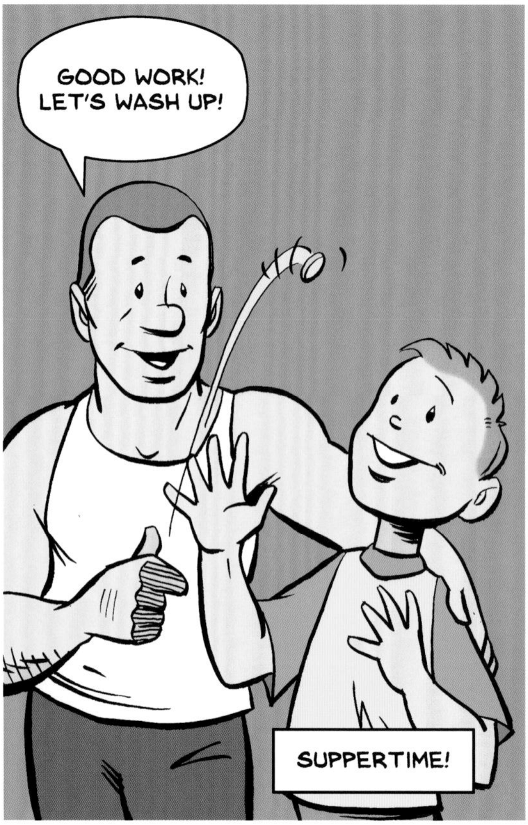
GOOD WORK! LET'S WASH UP!
SUPPERTIME!

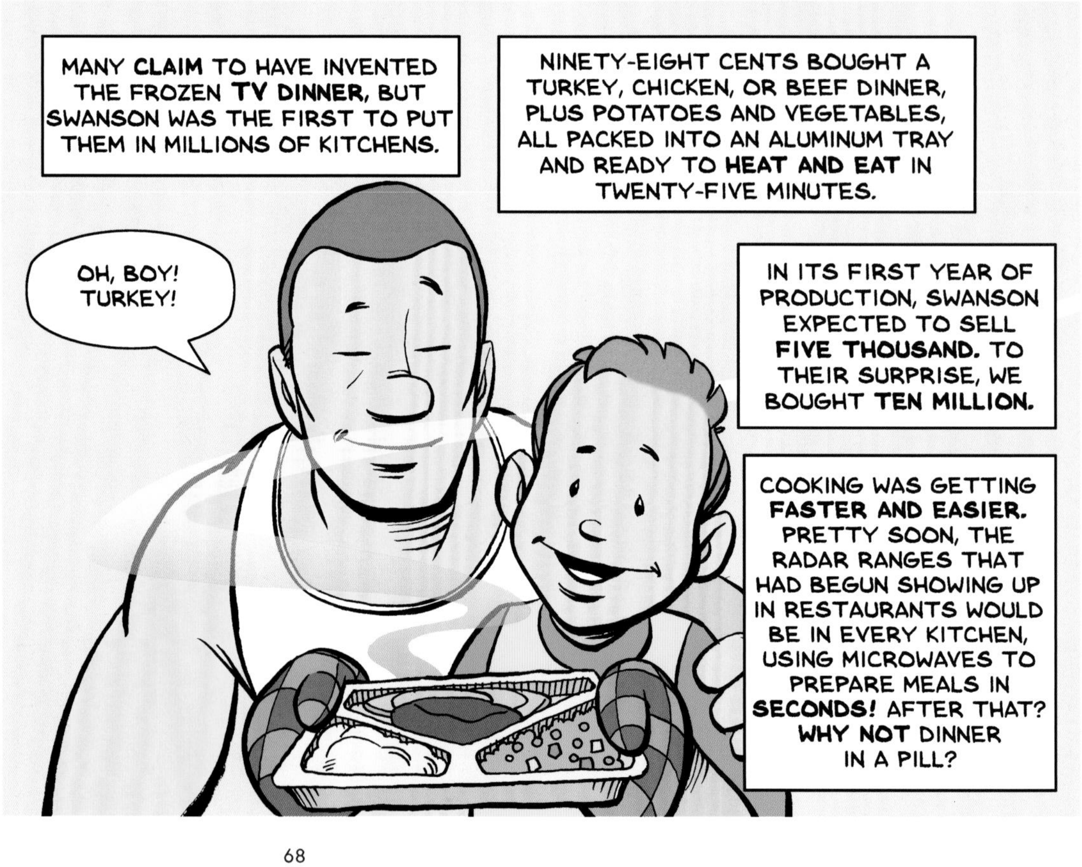
MANY **CLAIM** TO HAVE INVENTED THE FROZEN **TV DINNER**, BUT SWANSON WAS THE FIRST TO PUT THEM IN MILLIONS OF KITCHENS.
NINETY-EIGHT CENTS BOUGHT A TURKEY, CHICKEN, OR BEEF DINNER, PLUS POTATOES AND VEGETABLES, ALL PACKED INTO AN ALUMINUM TRAY AND READY TO **HEAT AND EAT** IN TWENTY-FIVE MINUTES.
OH, BOY! TURKEY!
IN ITS FIRST YEAR OF PRODUCTION, SWANSON EXPECTED TO SELL **FIVE THOUSAND.** TO THEIR SURPRISE, WE BOUGHT **TEN MILLION.**
COOKING WAS GETTING **FASTER AND EASIER.** PRETTY SOON, THE RADAR RANGES THAT HAD BEGUN SHOWING UP IN RESTAURANTS WOULD BE IN EVERY KITCHEN, USING MICROWAVES TO PREPARE MEALS IN **SECONDS!** AFTER THAT? **WHY NOT** DINNER IN A PILL?

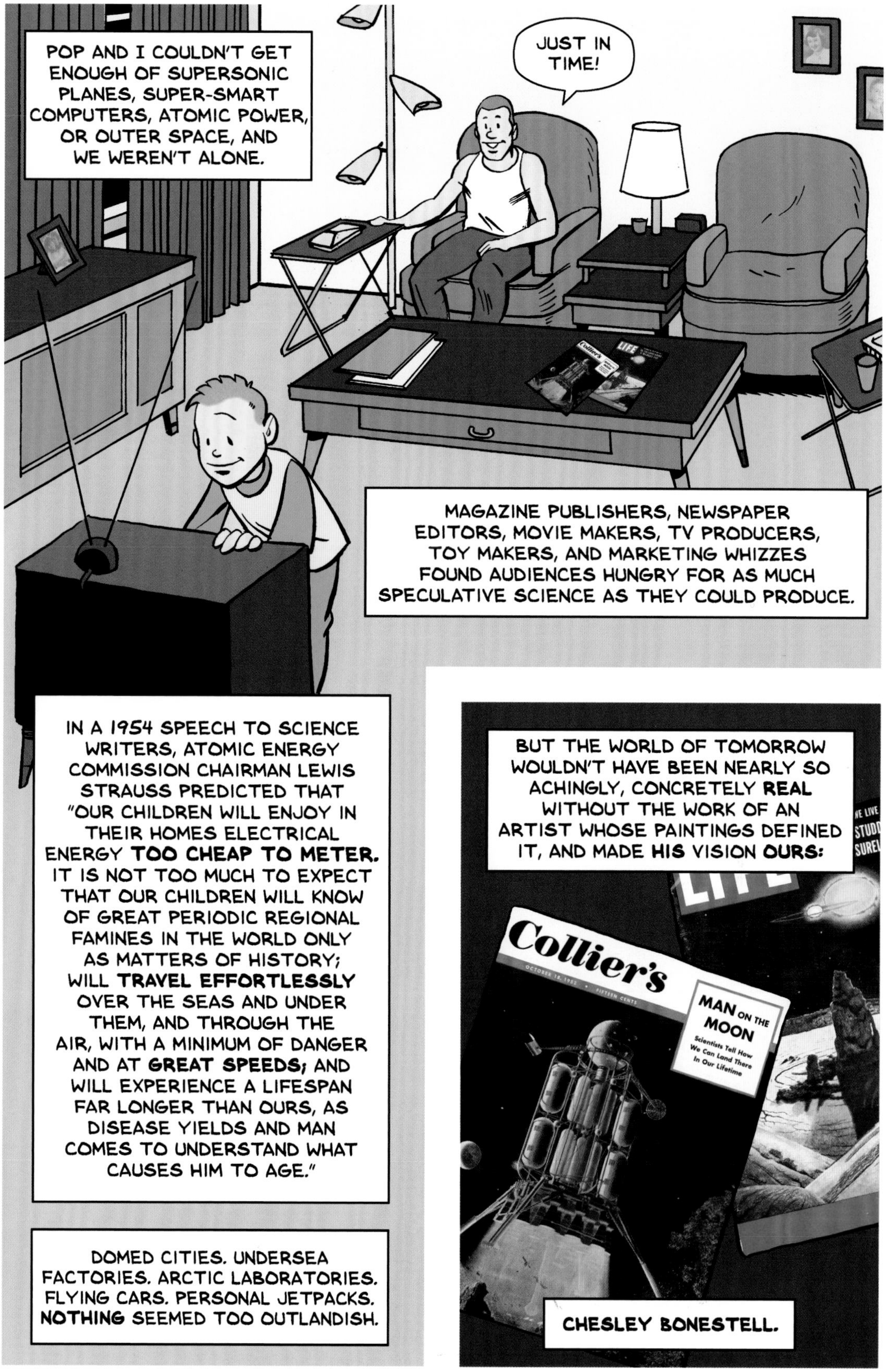
POP AND I COULDN'T GET ENOUGH OF SUPERSONIC PLANES, SUPER-SMART COMPUTERS, ATOMIC POWER, OR OUTER SPACE, AND WE WEREN'T ALONE.
JUST IN TIME!
LIFE
MAGAZINE PUBLISHERS, NEWSPAPER EDITORS, MOVIE MAKERS, TV PRODUCERS, TOY MAKERS, AND MARKETING WHIZZES FOUND AUDIENCES HUNGRY FOR AS MUCH SPECULATIVE SCIENCE AS THEY COULD PRODUCE.
IN A 1954 SPEECH TO SCIENCE WRITERS, ATOMIC ENERGY COMMISSION CHAIRMAN LEWIS STRAUSS PREDICTED THAT "OUR CHILDREN WILL ENJOY IN THEIR HOMES ELECTRICAL ENERGY **TOO CHEAP TO METER.** IT IS NOT TOO MUCH TO EXPECT THAT OUR CHILDREN WILL KNOW OF GREAT PERIODIC REGIONAL FAMINES IN THE WORLD ONLY AS MATTERS OF HISTORY; WILL **TRAVEL EFFORTLESSLY** OVER THE SEAS AND UNDER THEM, AND THROUGH THE AIR, WITH A MINIMUM OF DANGER AND AT **GREAT SPEEDS;** AND WILL EXPERIENCE A LIFESPAN FAR LONGER THAN OURS, AS DISEASE YIELDS AND MAN COMES TO UNDERSTAND WHAT CAUSES HIM TO AGE."
DOMED CITIES. UNDERSEA FACTORIES. ARCTIC LABORATORIES. FLYING CARS. PERSONAL JETPACKS. **NOTHING** SEEMED TOO OUTLANDISH.
BUT THE WORLD OF TOMORROW WOULDN'T HAVE BEEN NEARLY SO ACHINGLY, CONCRETELY **REAL** WITHOUT THE WORK OF AN ARTIST WHOSE PAINTINGS DEFINED IT, AND MADE **HIS** VISION **OURS:**
Collier's
MAN ON THE MOON
Scientists Tell How We Can Land There In Our Lifetime
**CHESLEY BONESTELL.**

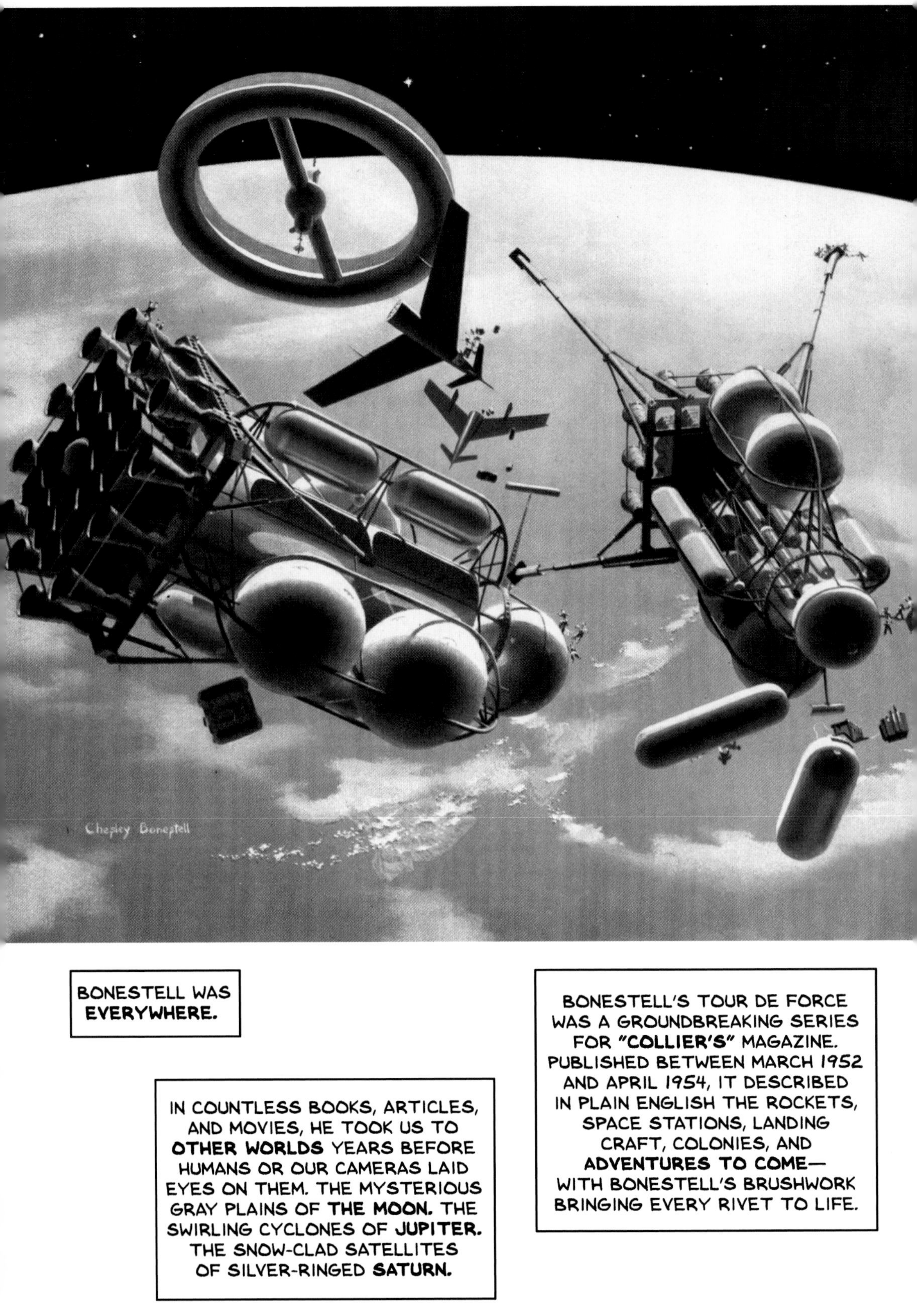
Chesley Bonestell

BONESTELL WAS **EVERYWHERE.**

IN COUNTLESS BOOKS, ARTICLES, AND MOVIES, HE TOOK US TO **OTHER WORLDS** YEARS BEFORE HUMANS OR OUR CAMERAS LAID EYES ON THEM. THE MYSTERIOUS GRAY PLAINS OF **THE MOON.** THE SWIRLING CYCLONES OF **JUPITER.** THE SNOW-CLAD SATELLITES OF SILVER-RINGED **SATURN.**

BONESTELL'S TOUR DE FORCE WAS A GROUNDBREAKING SERIES FOR **"COLLIER'S"** MAGAZINE. PUBLISHED BETWEEN MARCH 1952 AND APRIL 1954, IT DESCRIBED IN PLAIN ENGLISH THE ROCKETS, SPACE STATIONS, LANDING CRAFT, COLONIES, AND **ADVENTURES TO COME—** WITH BONESTELL'S BRUSHWORK BRINGING EVERY RIVET TO LIFE.

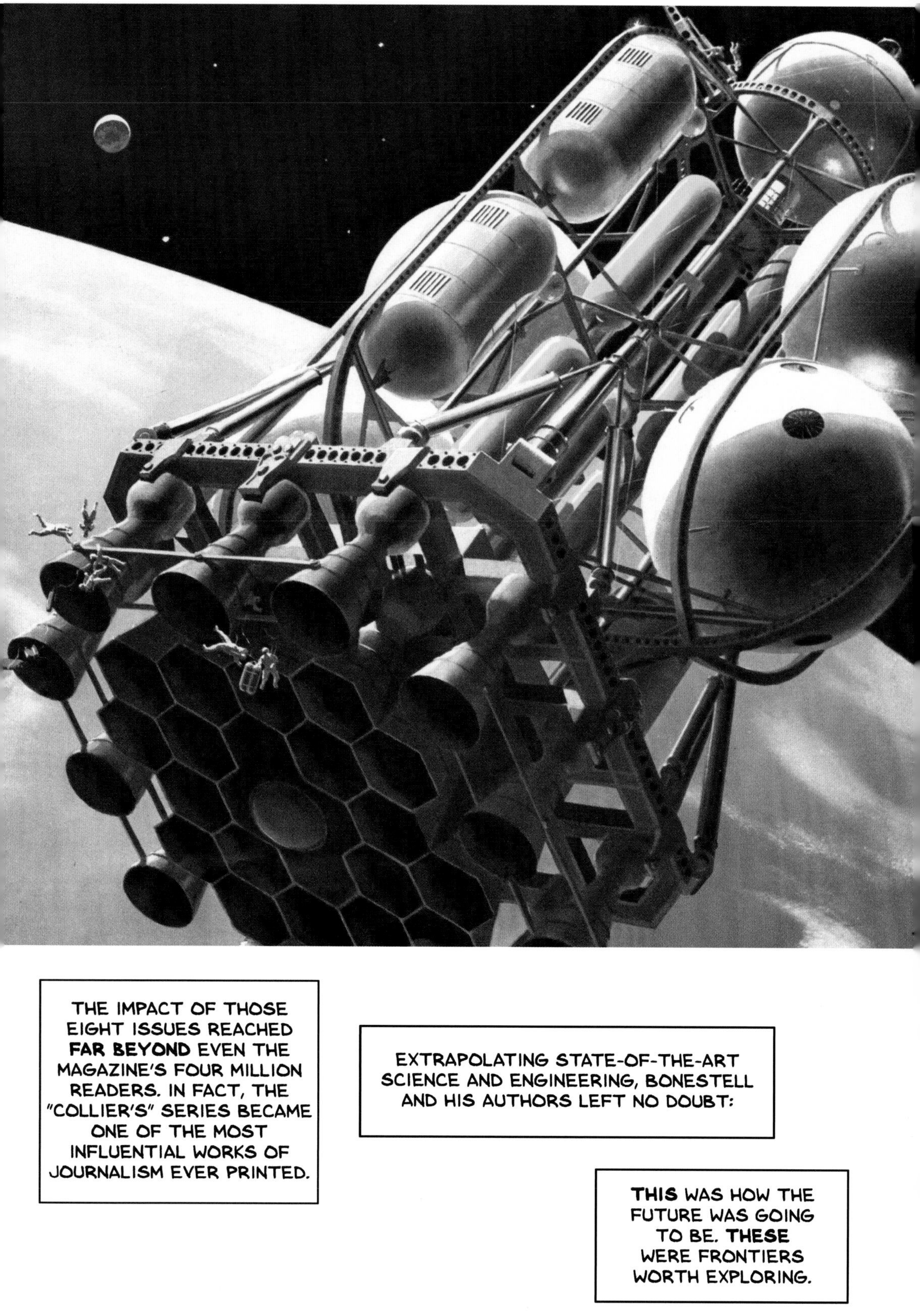

THE IMPACT OF THOSE EIGHT ISSUES REACHED **FAR BEYOND** EVEN THE MAGAZINE'S FOUR MILLION READERS. IN FACT, THE "COLLIER'S" SERIES BECAME ONE OF THE MOST INFLUENTIAL WORKS OF JOURNALISM EVER PRINTED.

EXTRAPOLATING STATE-OF-THE-ART SCIENCE AND ENGINEERING, BONESTELL AND HIS AUTHORS LEFT NO DOUBT:

**THIS** WAS HOW THE FUTURE WAS GOING TO BE. **THESE** WERE FRONTIERS WORTH EXPLORING.

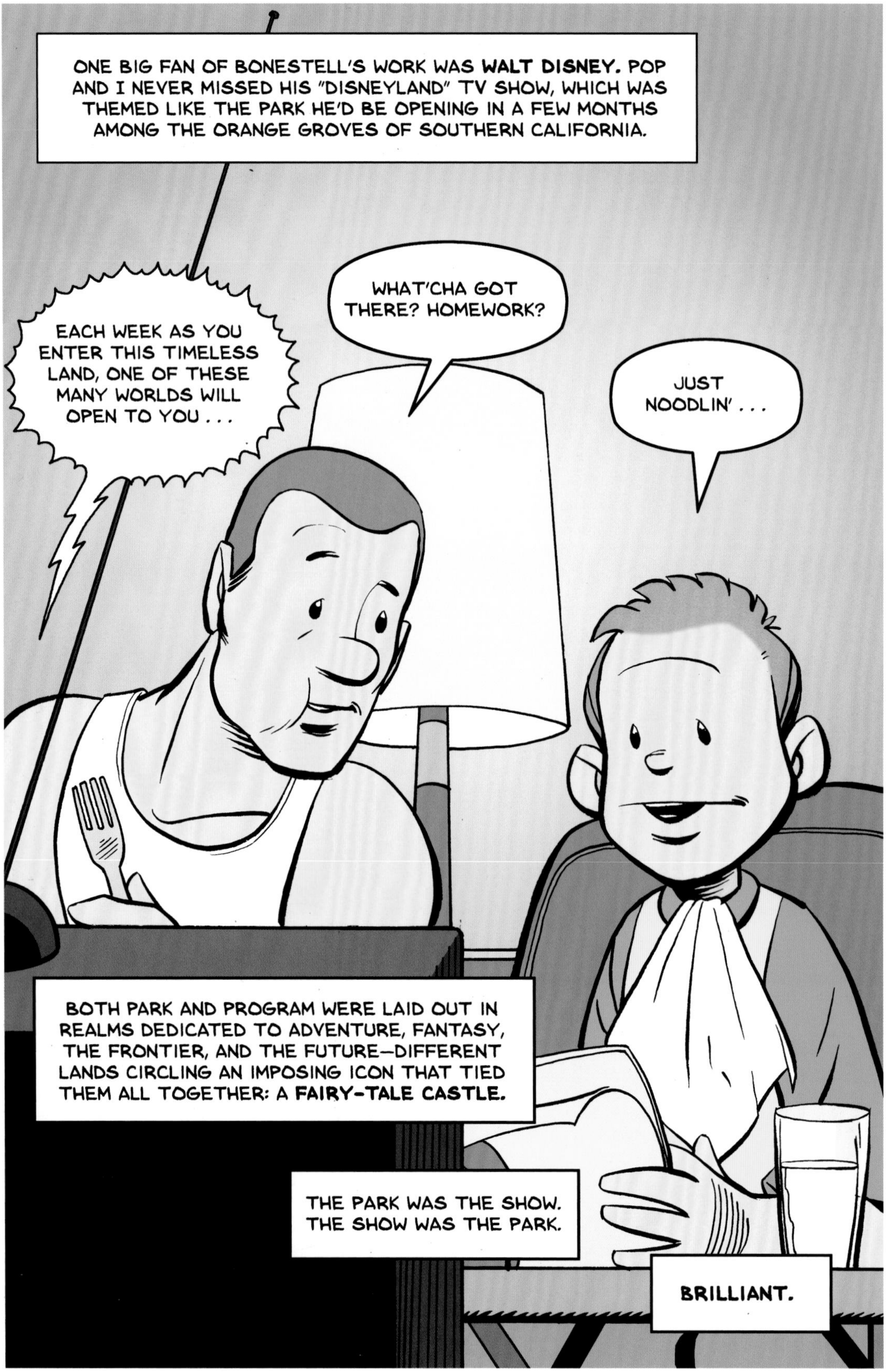
ONE BIG FAN OF BONESTELL'S WORK WAS **WALT DISNEY.** POP AND I NEVER MISSED HIS "DISNEYLAND" TV SHOW, WHICH WAS THEMED LIKE THE PARK HE'D BE OPENING IN A FEW MONTHS AMONG THE ORANGE GROVES OF SOUTHERN CALIFORNIA.
EACH WEEK AS YOU ENTER THIS TIMELESS LAND, ONE OF THESE MANY WORLDS WILL OPEN TO YOU . . .
WHAT'CHA GOT THERE? HOMEWORK?
JUST NOODLIN' . . .
BOTH PARK AND PROGRAM WERE LAID OUT IN REALMS DEDICATED TO ADVENTURE, FANTASY, THE FRONTIER, AND THE FUTURE—DIFFERENT LANDS CIRCLING AN IMPOSING ICON THAT TIED THEM ALL TOGETHER: A **FAIRY-TALE CASTLE.**
THE PARK WAS THE SHOW. THE SHOW WAS THE PARK.
**BRILLIANT.**

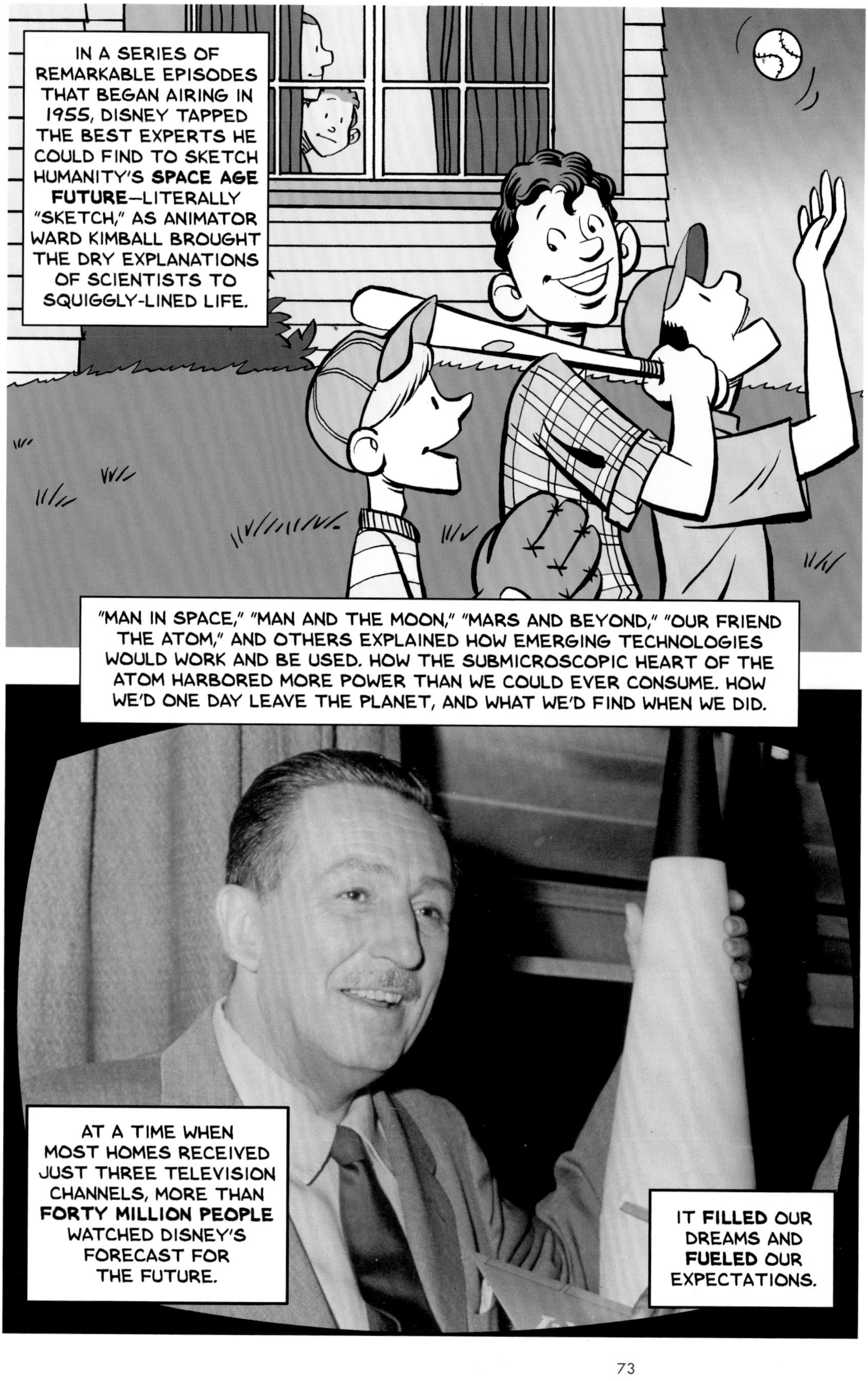
IN A SERIES OF REMARKABLE EPISODES THAT BEGAN AIRING IN 1955, DISNEY TAPPED THE BEST EXPERTS HE COULD FIND TO SKETCH HUMANITY'S **SPACE AGE FUTURE**—LITERALLY "SKETCH," AS ANIMATOR WARD KIMBALL BROUGHT THE DRY EXPLANATIONS OF SCIENTISTS TO SQUIGGLY-LINED LIFE.
"MAN IN SPACE," "MAN AND THE MOON," "MARS AND BEYOND," "OUR FRIEND THE ATOM," AND OTHERS EXPLAINED HOW EMERGING TECHNOLOGIES WOULD WORK AND BE USED. HOW THE SUBMICROSCOPIC HEART OF THE ATOM HARBORED MORE POWER THAN WE COULD EVER CONSUME. HOW WE'D ONE DAY LEAVE THE PLANET, AND WHAT WE'D FIND WHEN WE DID.
AT A TIME WHEN MOST HOMES RECEIVED JUST THREE TELEVISION CHANNELS, MORE THAN **FORTY MILLION PEOPLE** WATCHED DISNEY'S FORECAST FOR THE FUTURE.
IT **FILLED** OUR DREAMS AND **FUELED** OUR EXPECTATIONS.

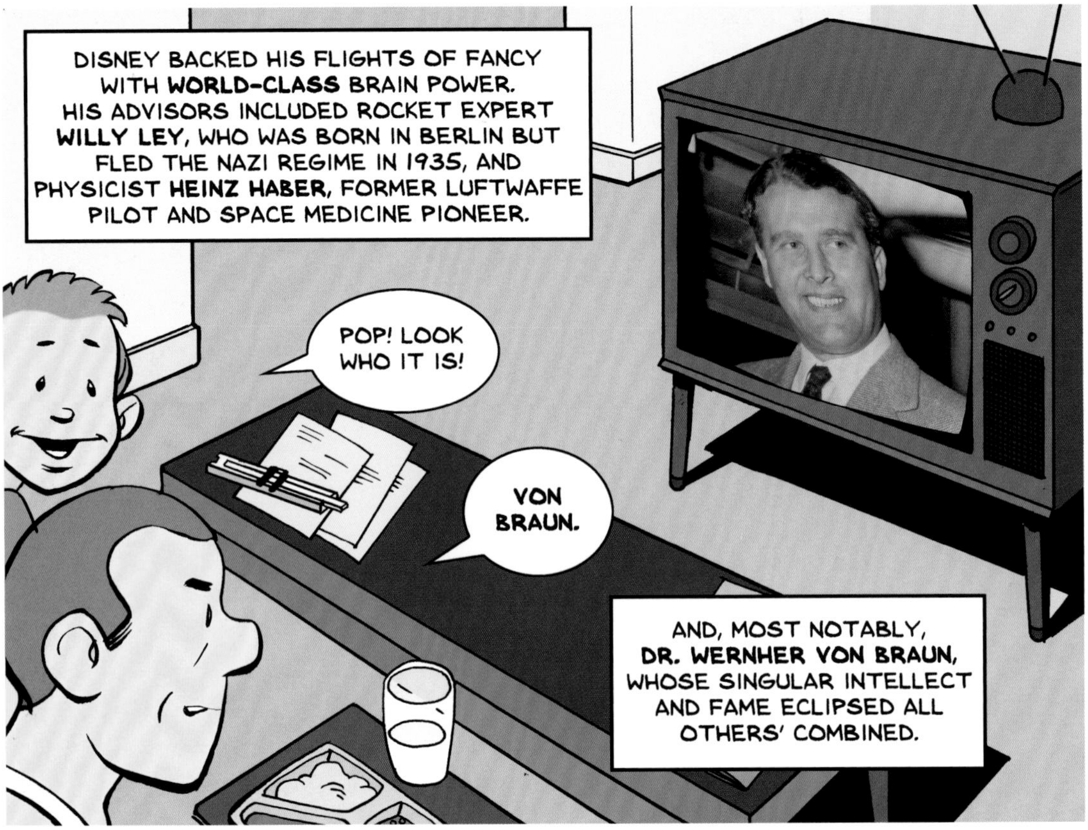
DISNEY BACKED HIS FLIGHTS OF FANCY WITH **WORLD-CLASS** BRAIN POWER. HIS ADVISORS INCLUDED ROCKET EXPERT **WILLY LEY**, WHO WAS BORN IN BERLIN BUT FLED THE NAZI REGIME IN 1935, AND PHYSICIST **HEINZ HABER**, FORMER LUFTWAFFE PILOT AND SPACE MEDICINE PIONEER.
POP! LOOK WHO IT IS!
**VON BRAUN.**
AND, MOST NOTABLY, **DR. WERNHER VON BRAUN**, WHOSE SINGULAR INTELLECT AND FAME ECLIPSED ALL OTHERS' COMBINED.

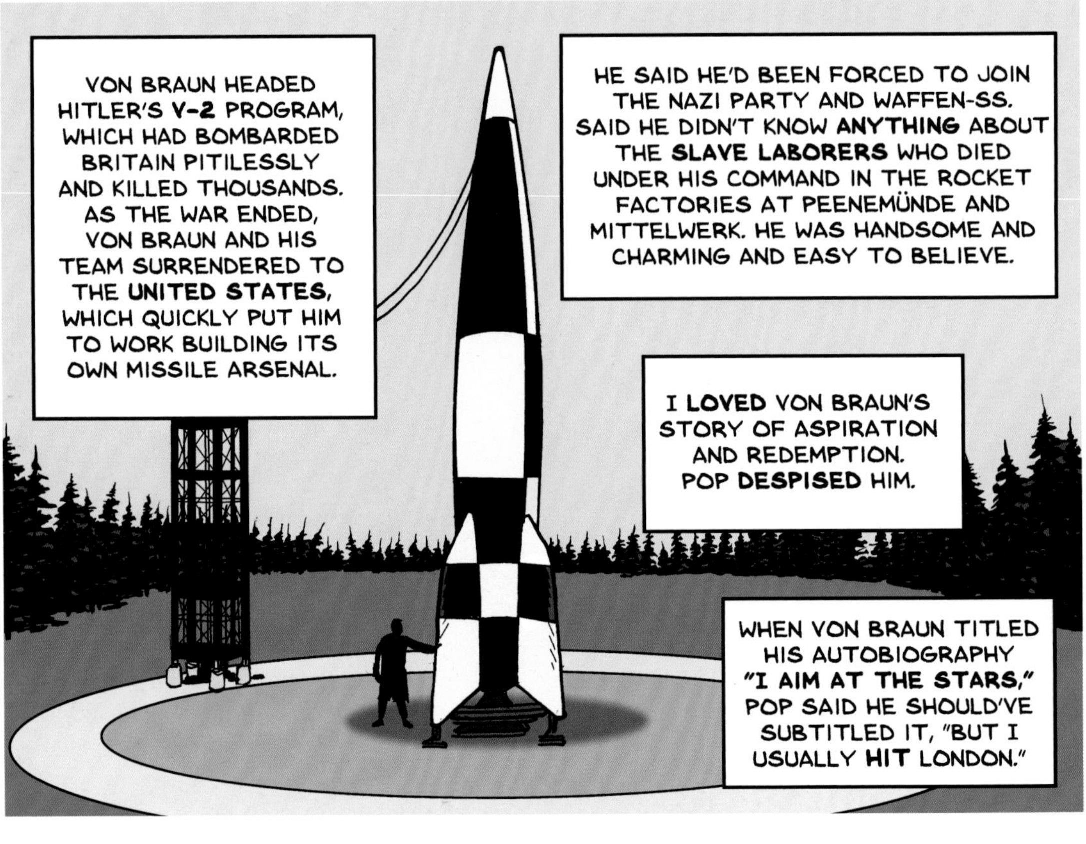
VON BRAUN HEADED HITLER'S **V-2** PROGRAM, WHICH HAD BOMBARDED BRITAIN PITILESSLY AND KILLED THOUSANDS. AS THE WAR ENDED, VON BRAUN AND HIS TEAM SURRENDERED TO THE **UNITED STATES**, WHICH QUICKLY PUT HIM TO WORK BUILDING ITS OWN MISSILE ARSENAL.
HE SAID HE'D BEEN FORCED TO JOIN THE NAZI PARTY AND WAFFEN-SS. SAID HE DIDN'T KNOW **ANYTHING** ABOUT THE **SLAVE LABORERS** WHO DIED UNDER HIS COMMAND IN THE ROCKET FACTORIES AT PEENEMÜNDE AND MITTELWERK. HE WAS HANDSOME AND CHARMING AND EASY TO BELIEVE.
I **LOVED** VON BRAUN'S STORY OF ASPIRATION AND REDEMPTION. POP **DESPISED** HIM.
WHEN VON BRAUN TITLED HIS AUTOBIOGRAPHY **"I AIM AT THE STARS,"** POP SAID HE SHOULD'VE SUBTITLED IT, "BUT I USUALLY **HIT** LONDON."

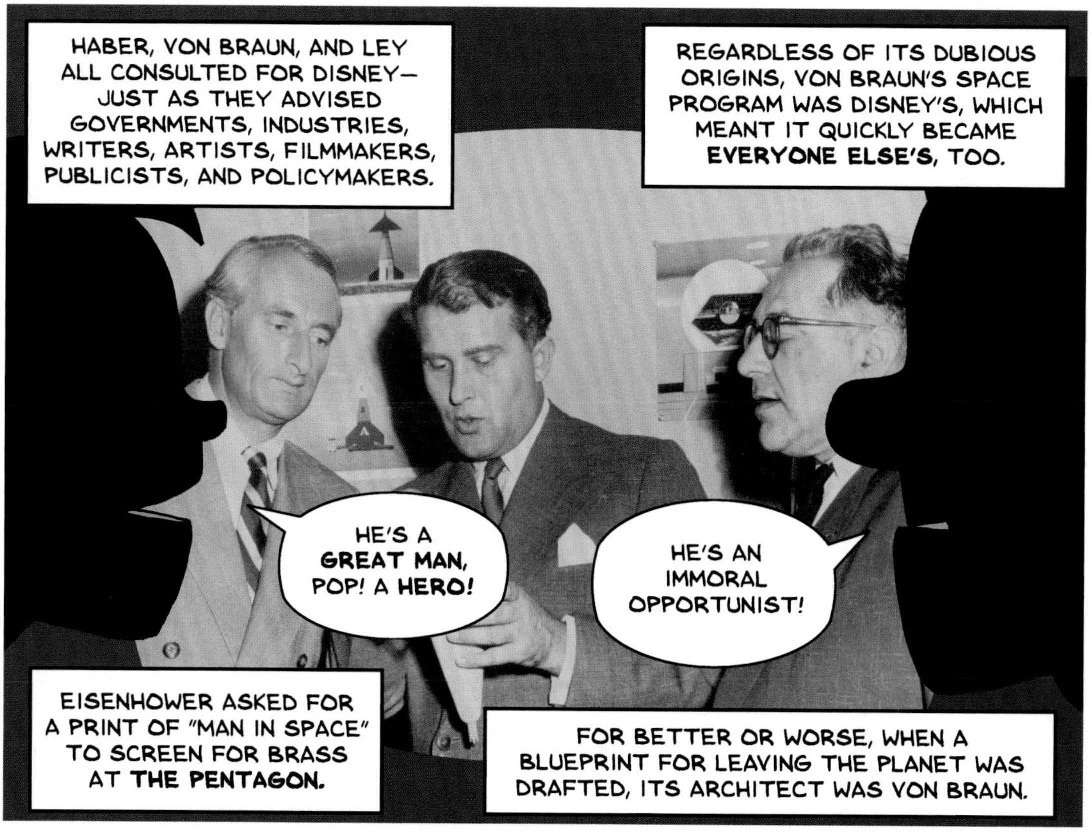
HABER, VON BRAUN, AND LEY ALL CONSULTED FOR DISNEY—JUST AS THEY ADVISED GOVERNMENTS, INDUSTRIES, WRITERS, ARTISTS, FILMMAKERS, PUBLICISTS, AND POLICYMAKERS.
REGARDLESS OF ITS DUBIOUS ORIGINS, VON BRAUN'S SPACE PROGRAM WAS DISNEY'S, WHICH MEANT IT QUICKLY BECAME **EVERYONE ELSE'S**, TOO.
HE'S A **GREAT MAN**, POP! A **HERO!**
HE'S AN IMMORAL OPPORTUNIST!
EISENHOWER ASKED FOR A PRINT OF "MAN IN SPACE" TO SCREEN FOR BRASS AT **THE PENTAGON.**
FOR BETTER OR WORSE, WHEN A BLUEPRINT FOR LEAVING THE PLANET WAS DRAFTED, ITS ARCHITECT WAS VON BRAUN.

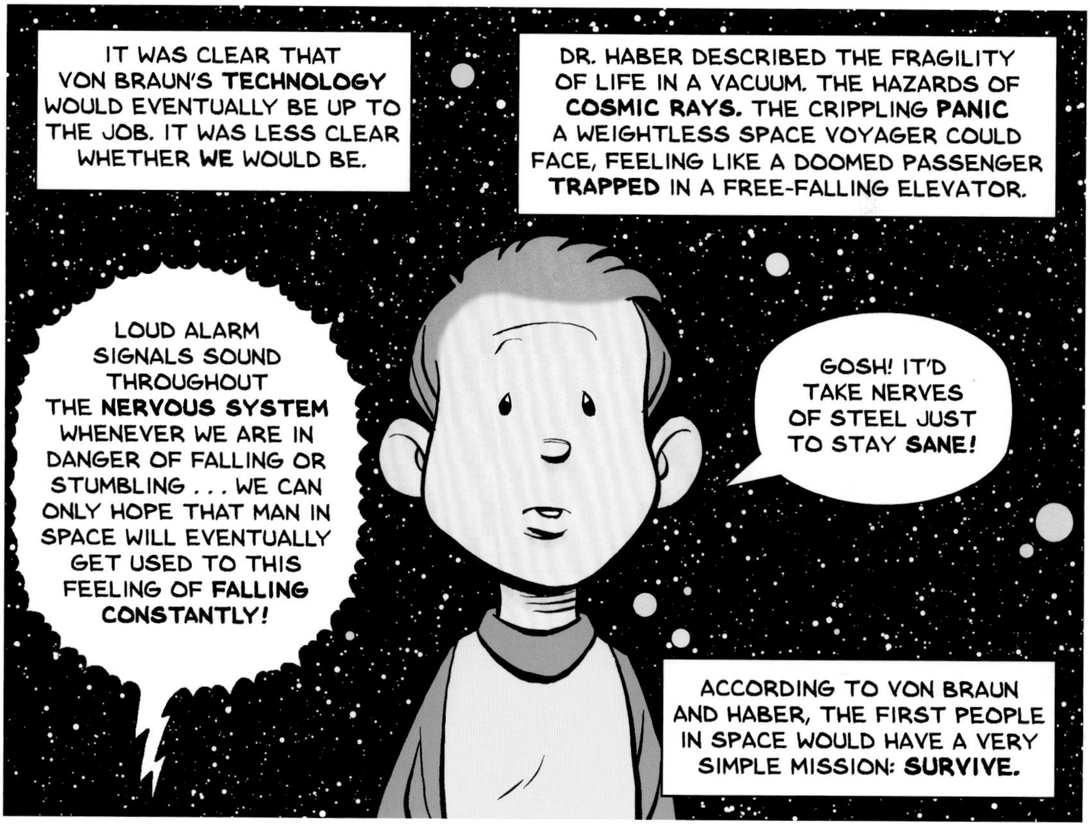
IT WAS CLEAR THAT VON BRAUN'S **TECHNOLOGY** WOULD EVENTUALLY BE UP TO THE JOB. IT WAS LESS CLEAR WHETHER **WE** WOULD BE.
DR. HABER DESCRIBED THE FRAGILITY OF LIFE IN A VACUUM. THE HAZARDS OF **COSMIC RAYS.** THE CRIPPLING **PANIC** A WEIGHTLESS SPACE VOYAGER COULD FACE, FEELING LIKE A DOOMED PASSENGER **TRAPPED** IN A FREE-FALLING ELEVATOR.
LOUD ALARM SIGNALS SOUND THROUGHOUT THE **NERVOUS SYSTEM** WHENEVER WE ARE IN DANGER OF FALLING OR STUMBLING . . . WE CAN ONLY HOPE THAT MAN IN SPACE WILL EVENTUALLY GET USED TO THIS FEELING OF **FALLING CONSTANTLY!**
GOSH! IT'D TAKE NERVES OF STEEL JUST TO STAY **SANE!**
ACCORDING TO VON BRAUN AND HABER, THE FIRST PEOPLE IN SPACE WOULD HAVE A VERY SIMPLE MISSION: **SURVIVE.**

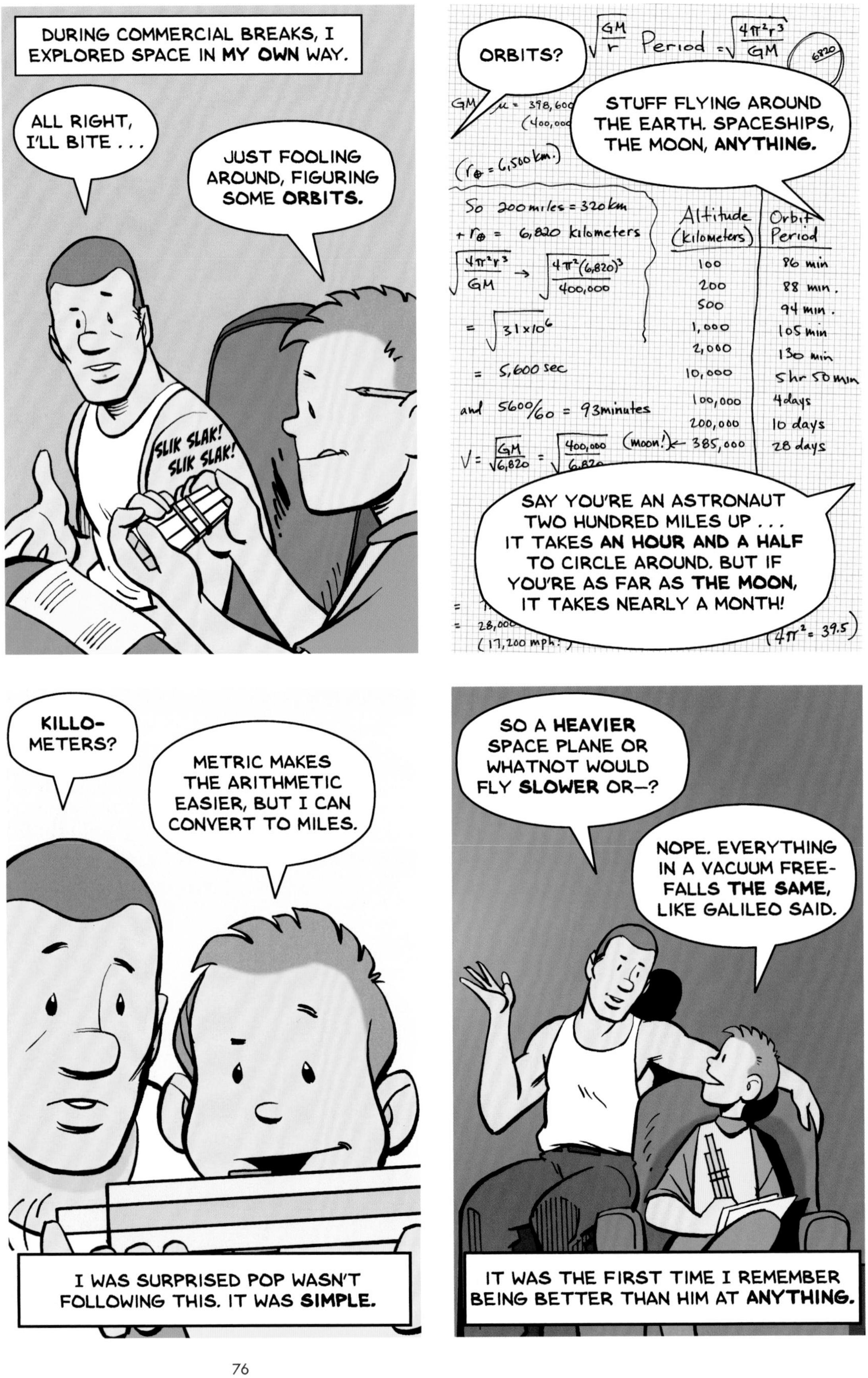
DURING COMMERCIAL BREAKS, I EXPLORED SPACE IN MY OWN WAY.
ALL RIGHT, I'LL BITE . . .
JUST FOOLING AROUND, FIGURING SOME ORBITS.
SLIK SLAK! SLIK SLAK!
ORBITS?
STUFF FLYING AROUND THE EARTH. SPACESHIPS, THE MOON, ANYTHING.
Period
So 200 miles = 320 km
+ r = 6,820 kilometers
= 5,600 sec
and 5600/60 = 93 minutes
Altitude (kilometers)
Orbit Period
100 86 min
200 88 min.
500 94 min.
1,000 105 min
2,000 130 min
10,000 5 hr 50 min
100,000 4 days
200,000 10 days
(moon!) 385,000 28 days
SAY YOU'RE AN ASTRONAUT TWO HUNDRED MILES UP . . . IT TAKES AN HOUR AND A HALF TO CIRCLE AROUND. BUT IF YOU'RE AS FAR AS THE MOON, IT TAKES NEARLY A MONTH!
KILLO-METERS?
METRIC MAKES THE ARITHMETIC EASIER, BUT I CAN CONVERT TO MILES.
I WAS SURPRISED POP WASN'T FOLLOWING THIS. IT WAS SIMPLE.
SO A HEAVIER SPACE PLANE OR WHATNOT WOULD FLY SLOWER OR—?
NOPE. EVERYTHING IN A VACUUM FREE-FALLS THE SAME, LIKE GALILEO SAID.
IT WAS THE FIRST TIME I REMEMBER BEING BETTER THAN HIM AT ANYTHING.

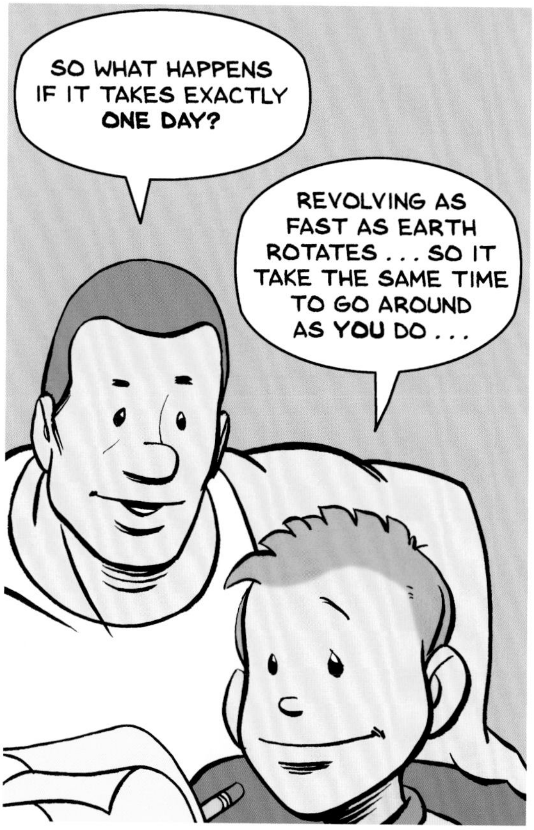
SO WHAT HAPPENS IF IT TAKES EXACTLY ONE DAY?
REVOLVING AS FAST AS EARTH ROTATES . . . SO IT TAKE THE SAME TIME TO GO AROUND AS YOU DO . . .

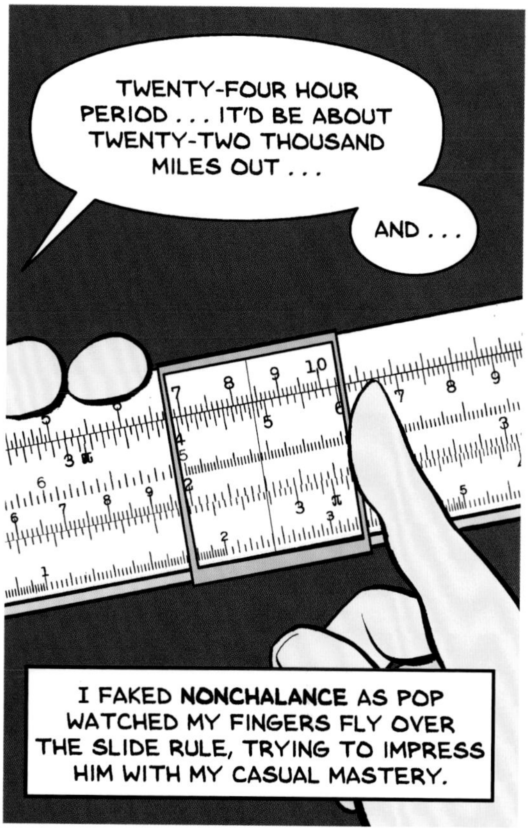
TWENTY-FOUR HOUR PERIOD . . . IT'D BE ABOUT TWENTY-TWO THOUSAND MILES OUT . . .
AND . . .
I FAKED NONCHALANCE AS POP WATCHED MY FINGERS FLY OVER THE SLIDE RULE, TRYING TO IMPRESS HIM WITH MY CASUAL MASTERY.

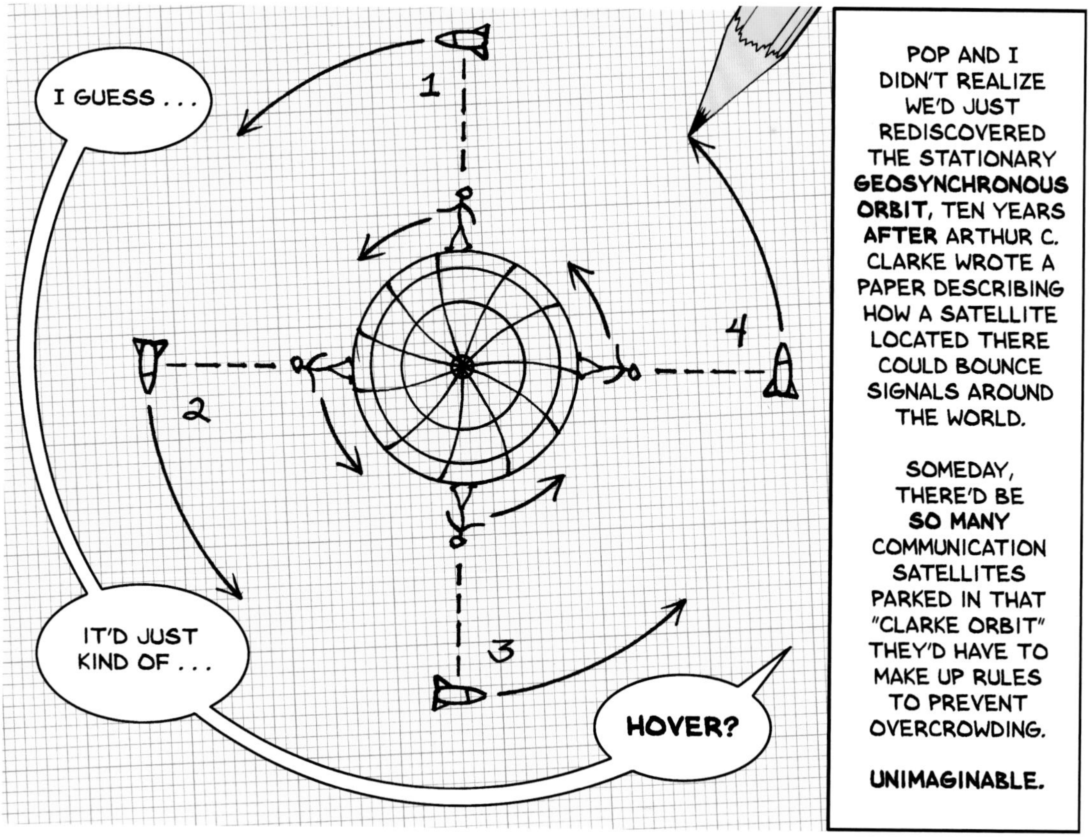
I GUESS . . .
IT'D JUST KIND OF . . .
HOVER?
POP AND I DIDN'T REALIZE WE'D JUST REDISCOVERED THE STATIONARY GEOSYNCHRONOUS ORBIT, TEN YEARS AFTER ARTHUR C. CLARKE WROTE A PAPER DESCRIBING HOW A SATELLITE LOCATED THERE COULD BOUNCE SIGNALS AROUND THE WORLD.
SOMEDAY, THERE'D BE SO MANY COMMUNICATION SATELLITES PARKED IN THAT "CLARKE ORBIT" THEY'D HAVE TO MAKE UP RULES TO PREVENT OVERCROWDING.
UNIMAGINABLE.

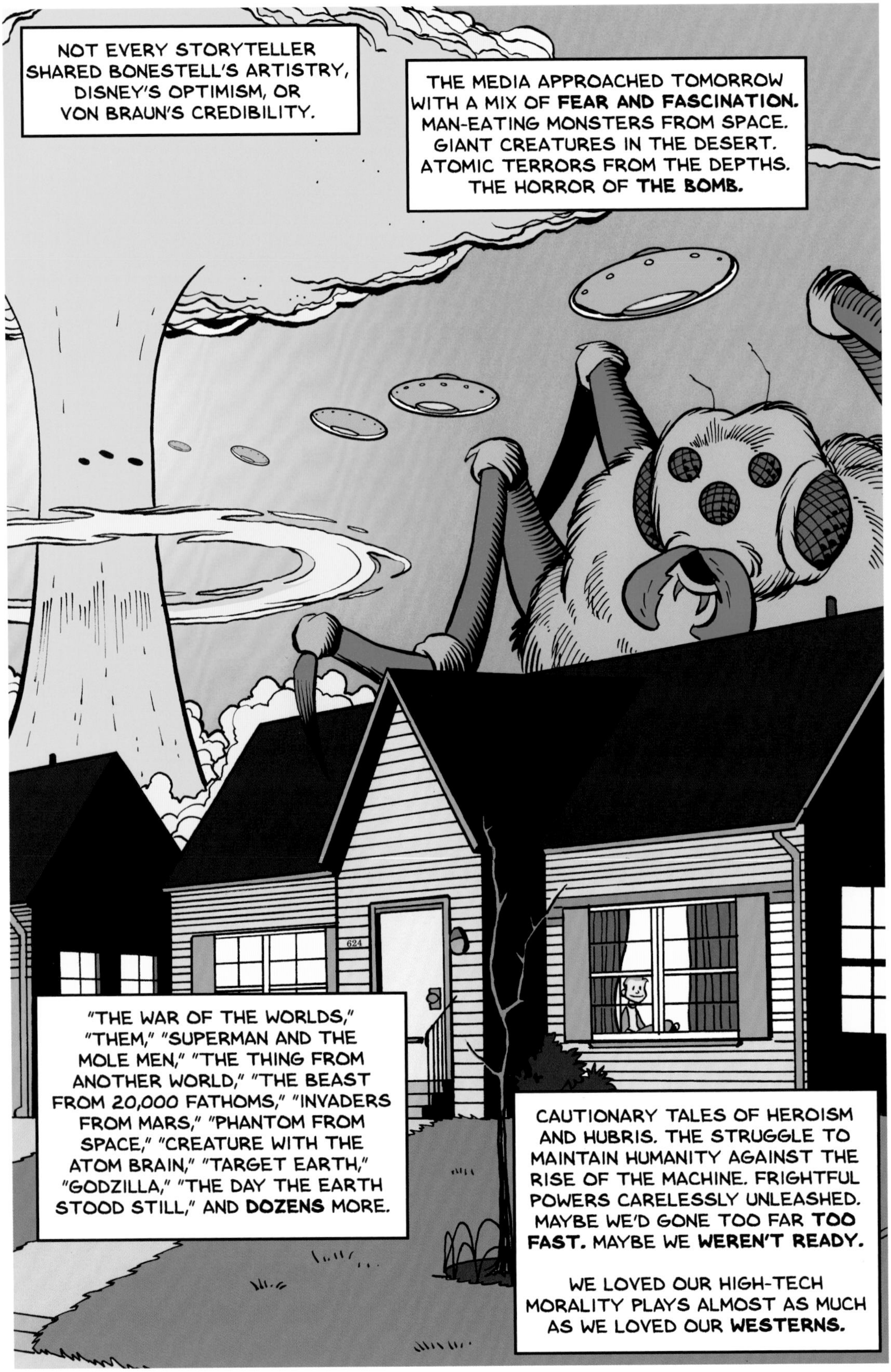
NOT EVERY STORYTELLER SHARED BONESTELL'S ARTISTRY, DISNEY'S OPTIMISM, OR VON BRAUN'S CREDIBILITY.
THE MEDIA APPROACHED TOMORROW WITH A MIX OF **FEAR AND FASCINATION.** MAN-EATING MONSTERS FROM SPACE. GIANT CREATURES IN THE DESERT. ATOMIC TERRORS FROM THE DEPTHS. THE HORROR OF **THE BOMB.**
624
"THE WAR OF THE WORLDS," "THEM," "SUPERMAN AND THE MOLE MEN," "THE THING FROM ANOTHER WORLD," "THE BEAST FROM 20,000 FATHOMS," "INVADERS FROM MARS," "PHANTOM FROM SPACE," "CREATURE WITH THE ATOM BRAIN," "TARGET EARTH," "GODZILLA," "THE DAY THE EARTH STOOD STILL," AND **DOZENS** MORE.
CAUTIONARY TALES OF HEROISM AND HUBRIS. THE STRUGGLE TO MAINTAIN HUMANITY AGAINST THE RISE OF THE MACHINE. FRIGHTFUL POWERS CARELESSLY UNLEASHED. MAYBE WE'D GONE TOO FAR **TOO FAST.** MAYBE WE **WEREN'T READY.**
WE LOVED OUR HIGH-TECH MORALITY PLAYS ALMOST AS MUCH AS WE LOVED OUR **WESTERNS.**

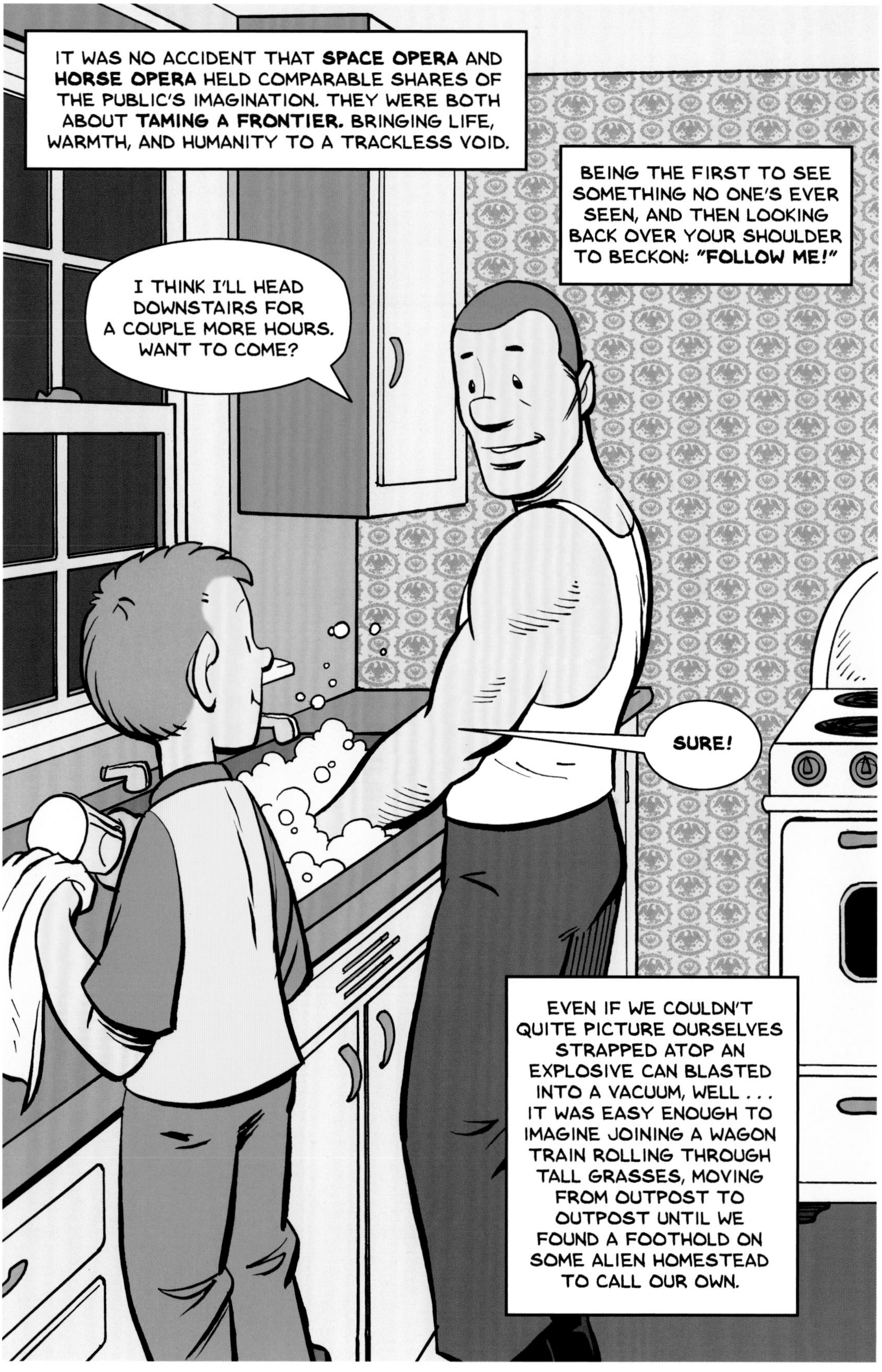
IT WAS NO ACCIDENT THAT SPACE OPERA AND HORSE OPERA HELD COMPARABLE SHARES OF THE PUBLIC'S IMAGINATION. THEY WERE BOTH ABOUT TAMING A FRONTIER. BRINGING LIFE, WARMTH, AND HUMANITY TO A TRACKLESS VOID.
BEING THE FIRST TO SEE SOMETHING NO ONE'S EVER SEEN, AND THEN LOOKING BACK OVER YOUR SHOULDER TO BECKON: "FOLLOW ME!"
I THINK I'LL HEAD DOWNSTAIRS FOR A COUPLE MORE HOURS. WANT TO COME?
SURE!
EVEN IF WE COULDN'T QUITE PICTURE OURSELVES STRAPPED ATOP AN EXPLOSIVE CAN BLASTED INTO A VACUUM, WELL . . . IT WAS EASY ENOUGH TO IMAGINE JOINING A WAGON TRAIN ROLLING THROUGH TALL GRASSES, MOVING FROM OUTPOST TO OUTPOST UNTIL WE FOUND A FOOTHOLD ON SOME ALIEN HOMESTEAD TO CALL OUR OWN.

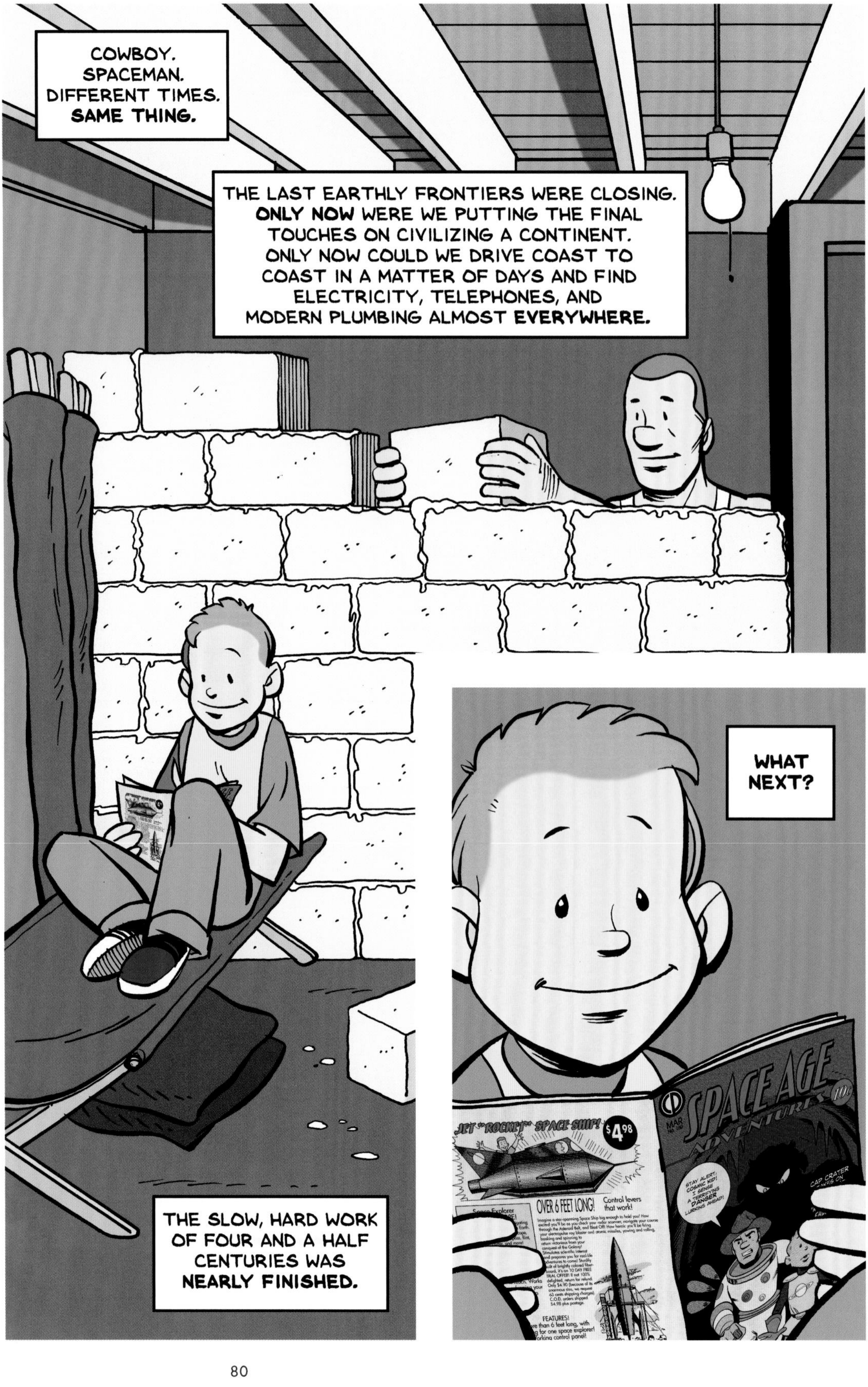
COWBOY. SPACEMAN. DIFFERENT TIMES. SAME THING.
THE LAST EARTHLY FRONTIERS WERE CLOSING. ONLY NOW WERE WE PUTTING THE FINAL TOUCHES ON CIVILIZING A CONTINENT. ONLY NOW COULD WE DRIVE COAST TO COAST IN A MATTER OF DAYS AND FIND ELECTRICITY, TELEPHONES, AND MODERN PLUMBING ALMOST EVERYWHERE.
THE SLOW, HARD WORK OF FOUR AND A HALF CENTURIES WAS NEARLY FINISHED.
WHAT NEXT?
JET "ROCKET" SPACE SHIP!
$4.98
OVER 6 FEET LONG!
Control levers that work!
SPACE AGE ADVENTURES
10¢
STAY ALERT, COSMIC KID! I SENSE A TERRIFYING DANGER LURKING AHEAD!
CAP CRATER

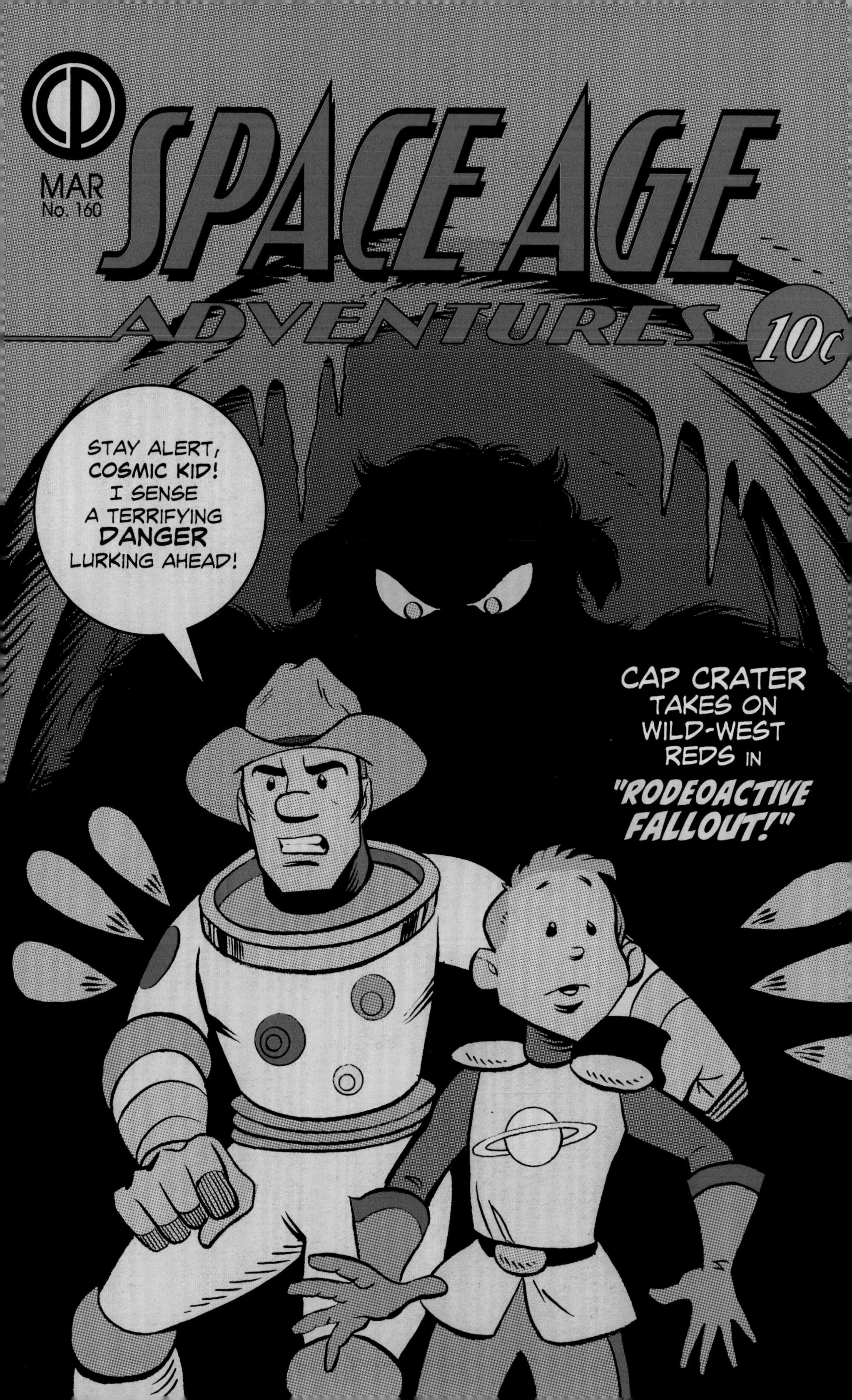
SPACE AGE ADVENTURES
MAR
No. 160
10¢
STAY ALERT, COSMIC KID! I SENSE A TERRIFYING DANGER LURKING AHEAD!
CAP CRATER TAKES ON WILD-WEST REDS IN "RODEOACTIVE FALLOUT!"

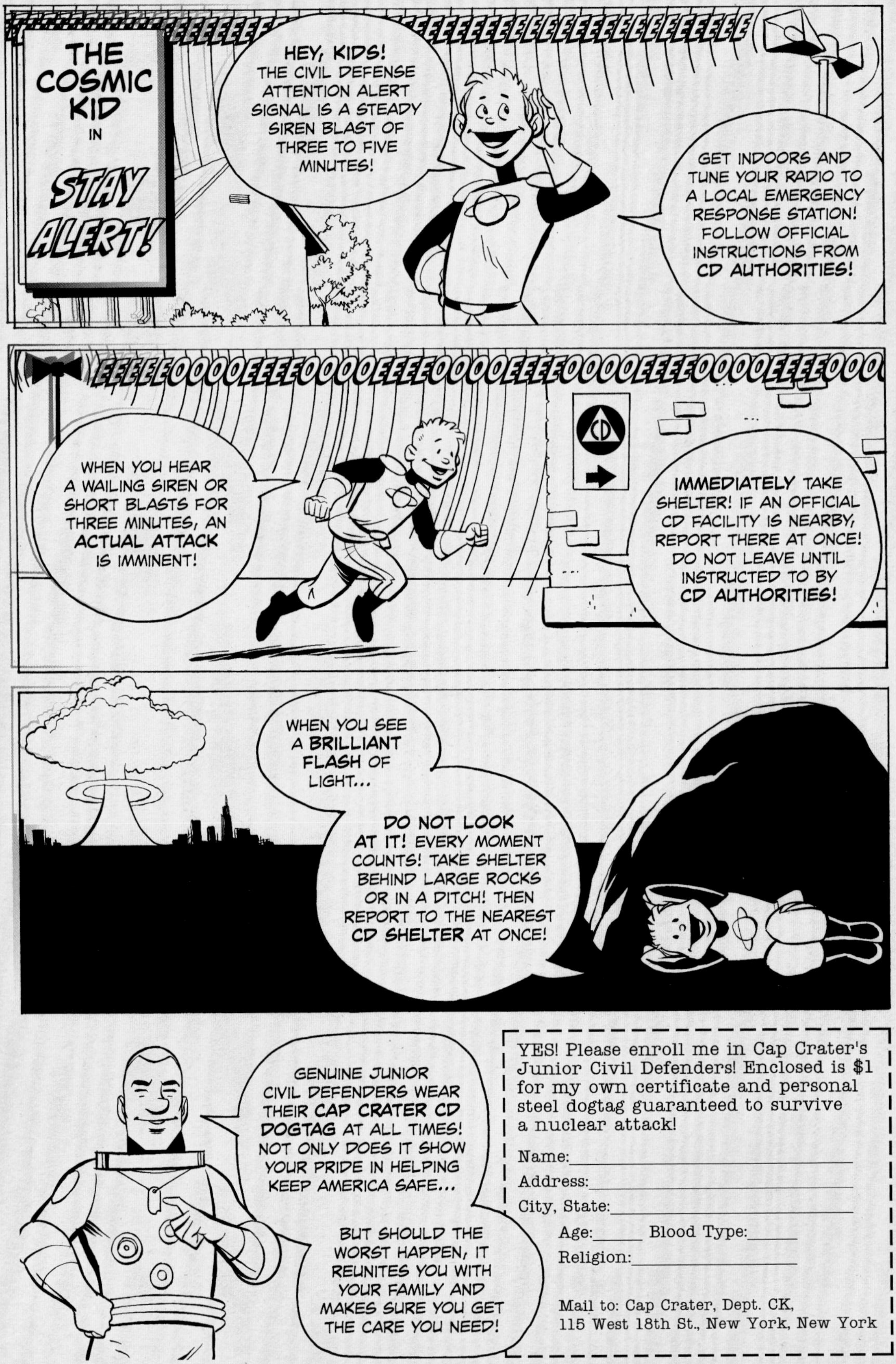

THE COSMIC KID IN STAY ALERT!
EEEEEEEEEEEEEEEEEEEEEEEEEEEEEEEEEEE
HEY, KIDS! THE CIVIL DEFENSE ATTENTION ALERT SIGNAL IS A STEADY SIREN BLAST OF THREE TO FIVE MINUTES!
GET INDOORS AND TUNE YOUR RADIO TO A LOCAL EMERGENCY RESPONSE STATION! FOLLOW OFFICIAL INSTRUCTIONS FROM CD AUTHORITIES!
EEEEOOOOEEEEOOOOEEEEOOOOEEEEOOOOEEEEOOOOEEEEOOOOEEEEOOO
WHEN YOU HEAR A WAILING SIREN OR SHORT BLASTS FOR THREE MINUTES, AN ACTUAL ATTACK IS IMMINENT!
CD
IMMEDIATELY TAKE SHELTER! IF AN OFFICIAL CD FACILITY IS NEARBY, REPORT THERE AT ONCE! DO NOT LEAVE UNTIL INSTRUCTED TO BY CD AUTHORITIES!
WHEN YOU SEE A BRILLIANT FLASH OF LIGHT...
DO NOT LOOK AT IT! EVERY MOMENT COUNTS! TAKE SHELTER BEHIND LARGE ROCKS OR IN A DITCH! THEN REPORT TO THE NEAREST CD SHELTER AT ONCE!
GENUINE JUNIOR CIVIL DEFENDERS WEAR THEIR CAP CRATER CD DOGTAG AT ALL TIMES! NOT ONLY DOES IT SHOW YOUR PRIDE IN HELPING KEEP AMERICA SAFE...
BUT SHOULD THE WORST HAPPEN, IT REUNITES YOU WITH YOUR FAMILY AND MAKES SURE YOU GET THE CARE YOU NEED!
YES! Please enroll me in Cap Crater's Junior Civil Defenders! Enclosed is $1 for my own certificate and personal steel dogtag guaranteed to survive a nuclear attack!
Name:
Address:
City, State:
Age: Blood Type:
Religion:
Mail to: Cap Crater, Dept. CK,
115 West 18th St., New York, New York

**SPACE AGE ADVENTURES,** No. 160, March, 1955. Published monthly by CAPITAL PERIODICALS, INC., 115 W. 18th St., New York 11, N.Y. ENTERED AS SECOND-CLASS MATTER at the post office at New York, N.Y., under the act of March 3, 1879. Yearly subscription in the U.S. $1.50 including postage. Foreign, $3.00 in American funds. Copyright 1955 by Capital Periodicals, Inc., All rights reserved under International and Pan-American Copyright Conventions. Except for those who have authorized use of their names, the stories, characters, and incidents mentioned in this periodical are entirely imaginary and fictitious, and no identification with actual persons, living or dead, is intended or should be inferred.
Printed in U.S.A.

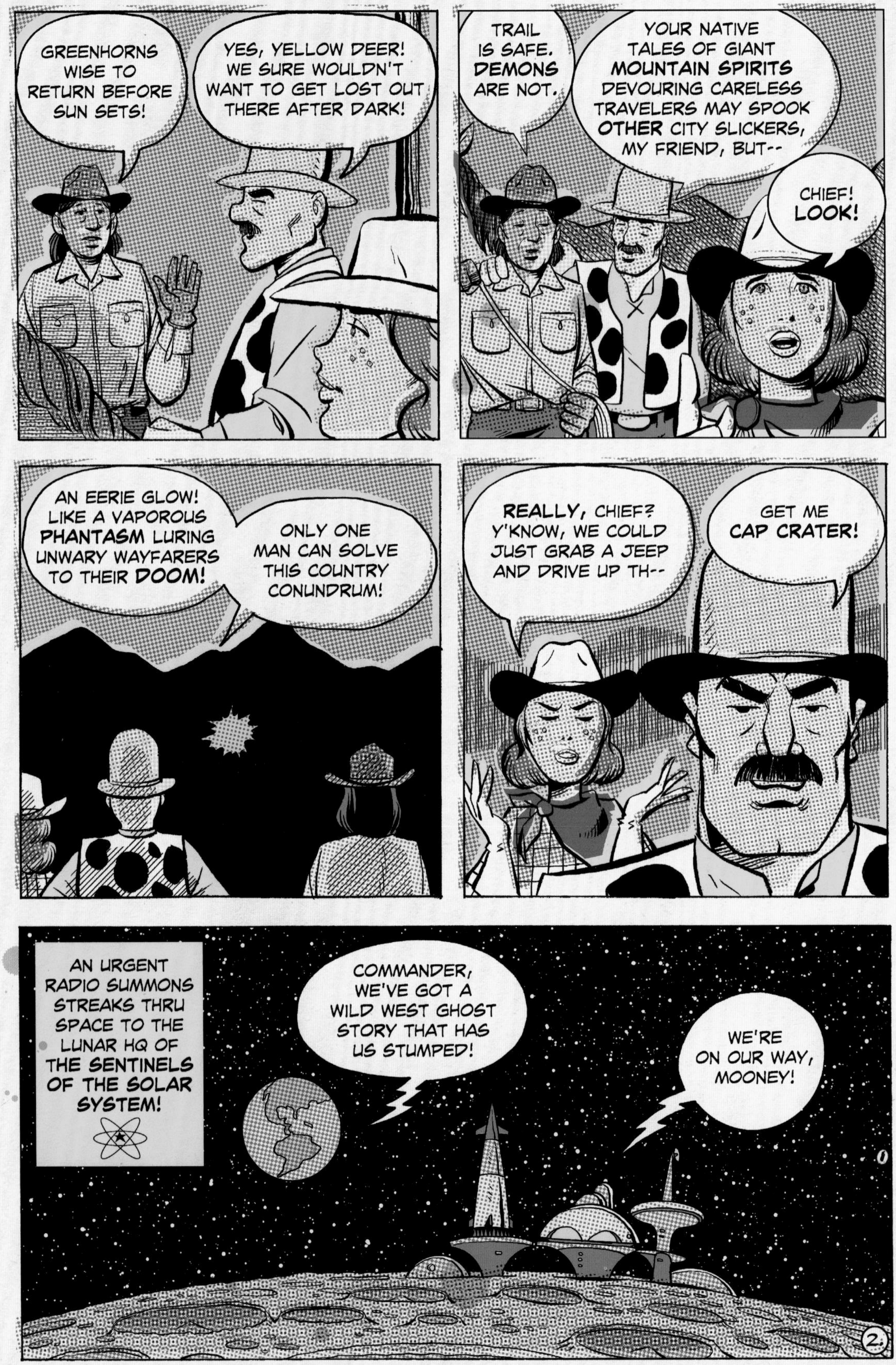
GREENHORNS WISE TO RETURN BEFORE SUN SETS!
YES, YELLOW DEER! WE SURE WOULDN'T WANT TO GET LOST OUT THERE AFTER DARK!
TRAIL IS SAFE. DEMONS ARE NOT.
YOUR NATIVE TALES OF GIANT MOUNTAIN SPIRITS DEVOURING CARELESS TRAVELERS MAY SPOOK OTHER CITY SLICKERS, MY FRIEND, BUT--
CHIEF! LOOK!
AN EERIE GLOW! LIKE A VAPOROUS PHANTASM LURING UNWARY WAYFARERS TO THEIR DOOM!
ONLY ONE MAN CAN SOLVE THIS COUNTRY CONUNDRUM!
REALLY, CHIEF? Y'KNOW, WE COULD JUST GRAB A JEEP AND DRIVE UP TH--
GET ME CAP CRATER!
AN URGENT RADIO SUMMONS STREAKS THRU SPACE TO THE LUNAR HQ OF THE SENTINELS OF THE SOLAR SYSTEM!
COMMANDER, WE'VE GOT A WILD WEST GHOST STORY THAT HAS US STUMPED!
WE'RE ON OUR WAY, MOONEY!

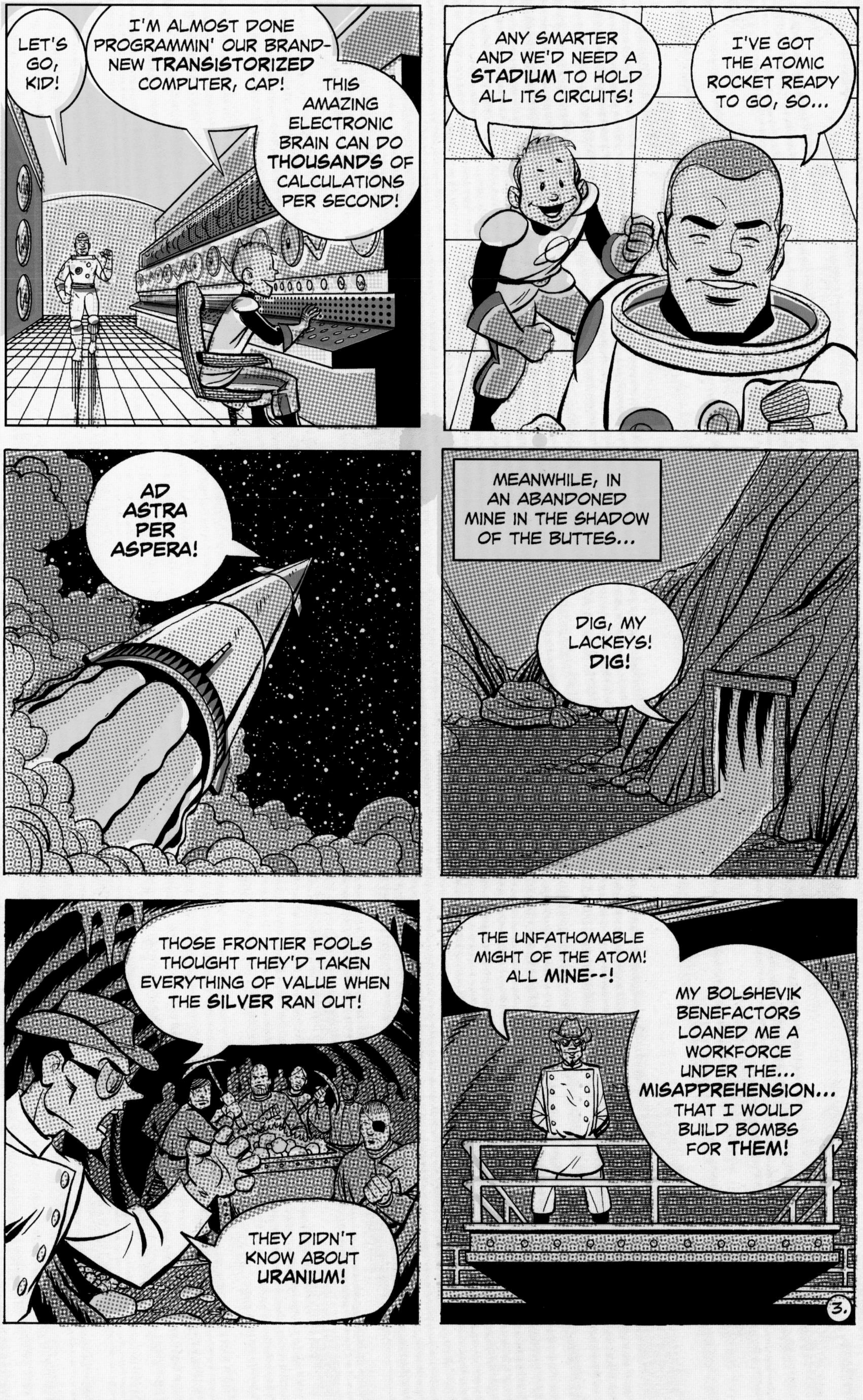
LET'S GO, KID!
I'M ALMOST DONE PROGRAMMIN' OUR BRAND-NEW TRANSISTORIZED COMPUTER, CAP!
THIS AMAZING ELECTRONIC BRAIN CAN DO THOUSANDS OF CALCULATIONS PER SECOND!
ANY SMARTER AND WE'D NEED A STADIUM TO HOLD ALL ITS CIRCUITS!
I'VE GOT THE ATOMIC ROCKET READY TO GO, SO...
AD ASTRA PER ASPERA!
MEANWHILE, IN AN ABANDONED MINE IN THE SHADOW OF THE BUTTES...
DIG, MY LACKEYS! DIG!
THOSE FRONTIER FOOLS THOUGHT THEY'D TAKEN EVERYTHING OF VALUE WHEN THE SILVER RAN OUT!
THEY DIDN'T KNOW ABOUT URANIUM!
THE UNFATHOMABLE MIGHT OF THE ATOM! ALL MINE--!
MY BOLSHEVIK BENEFACTORS LOANED ME A WORKFORCE UNDER THE... MISAPPREHENSION... THAT I WOULD BUILD BOMBS FOR THEM!

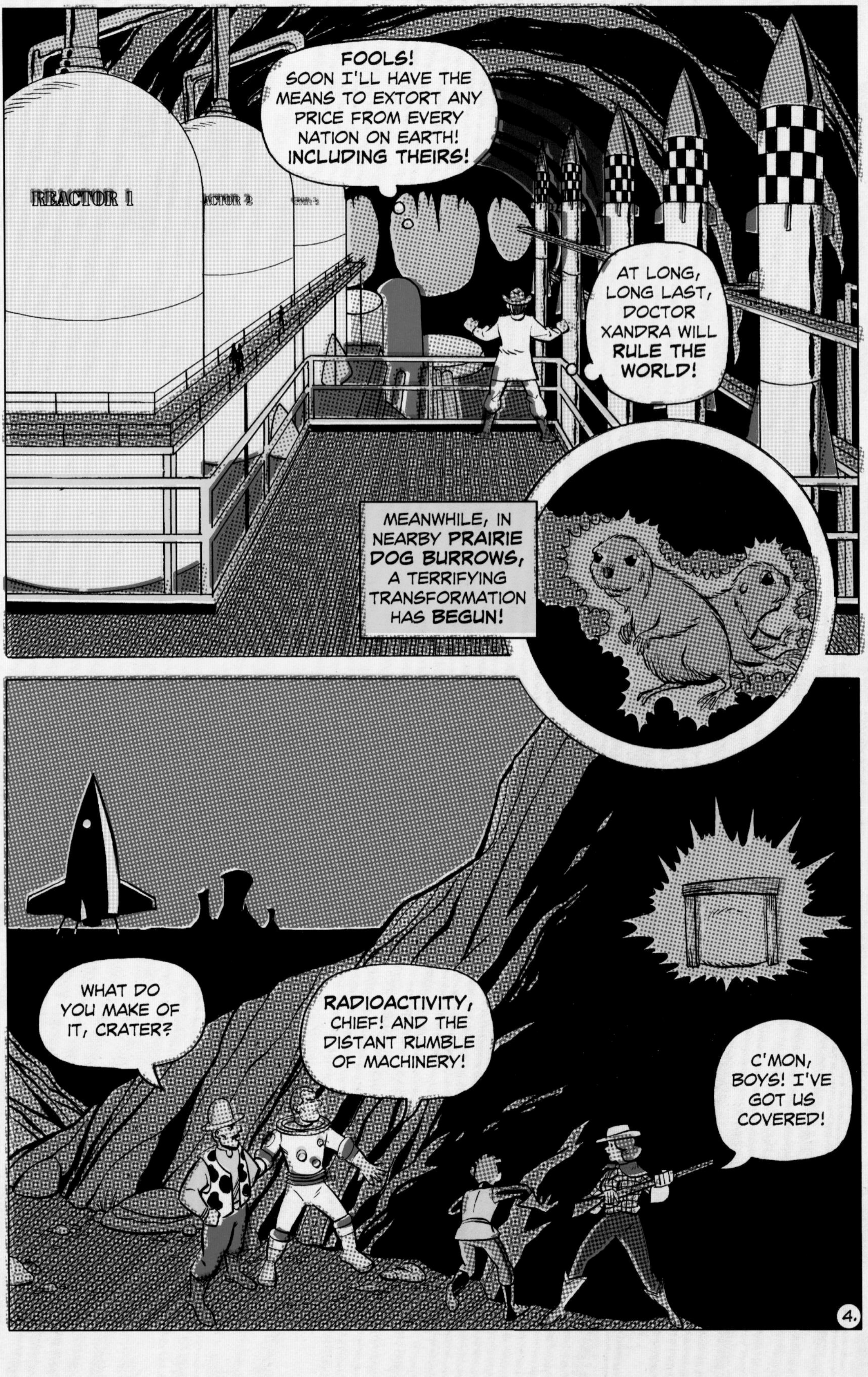
REACTOR 1
FOOLS! SOON I'LL HAVE THE MEANS TO EXTORT ANY PRICE FROM EVERY NATION ON EARTH! INCLUDING THEIRS!
AT LONG, LONG LAST, DOCTOR XANDRA WILL RULE THE WORLD!
MEANWHILE, IN NEARBY PRAIRIE DOG BURROWS, A TERRIFYING TRANSFORMATION HAS BEGUN!
WHAT DO YOU MAKE OF IT, CRATER?
RADIOACTIVITY, CHIEF! AND THE DISTANT RUMBLE OF MACHINERY!
C'MON, BOYS! I'VE GOT US COVERED!

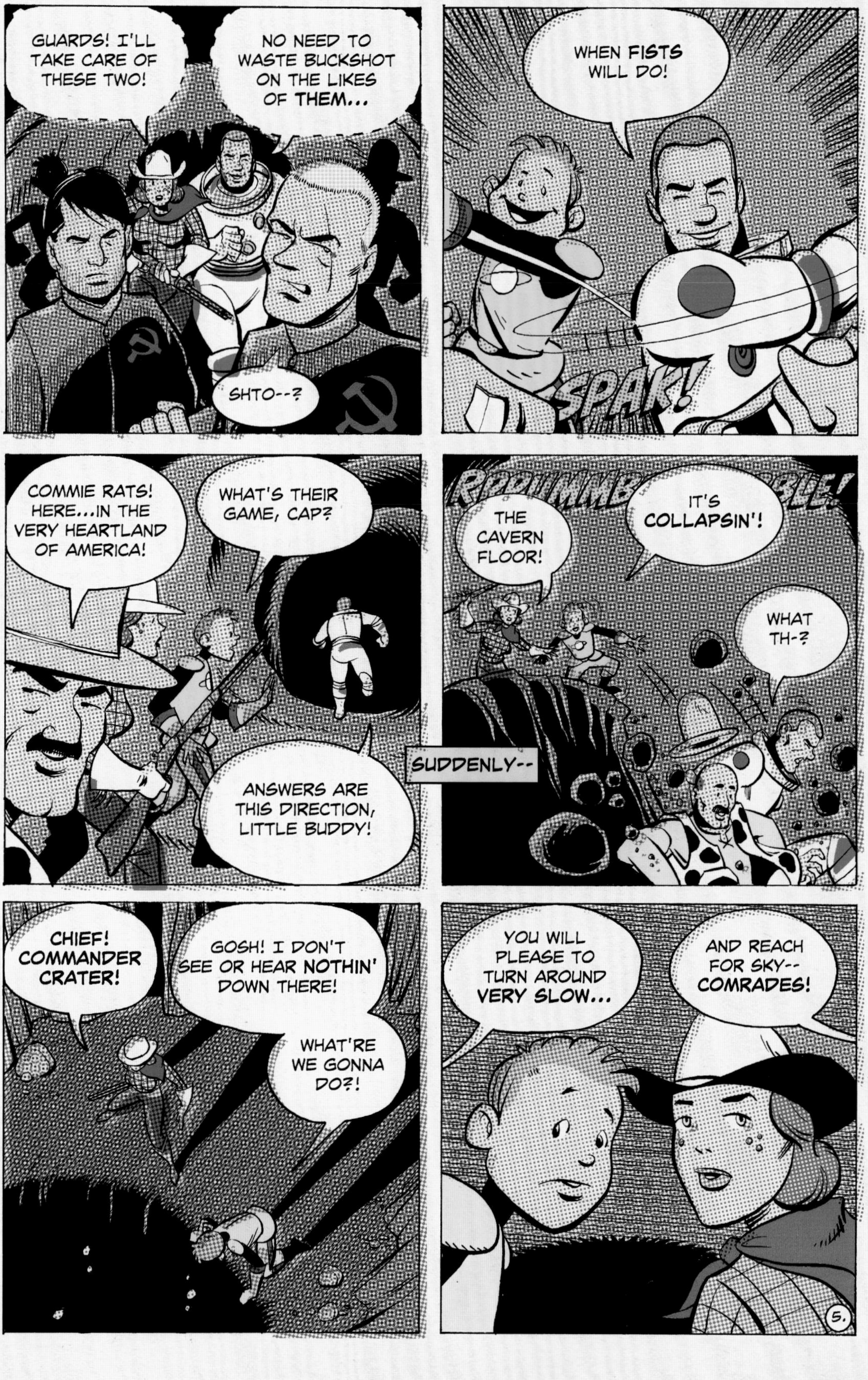
GUARDS! I'LL TAKE CARE OF THESE TWO!
NO NEED TO WASTE BUCKSHOT ON THE LIKES OF THEM...
SHTO--?
WHEN FISTS WILL DO!
SPAK!
COMMIE RATS! HERE...IN THE VERY HEARTLAND OF AMERICA!
WHAT'S THEIR GAME, CAP?
ANSWERS ARE THIS DIRECTION, LITTLE BUDDY!
SUDDENLY--
THE CAVERN FLOOR!
IT'S COLLAPSIN'!
WHAT TH-?
CHIEF! COMMANDER CRATER!
GOSH! I DON'T SEE OR HEAR NOTHIN' DOWN THERE!
WHAT'RE WE GONNA DO?!
YOU WILL PLEASE TO TURN AROUND VERY SLOW...
AND REACH FOR SKY-- COMRADES!

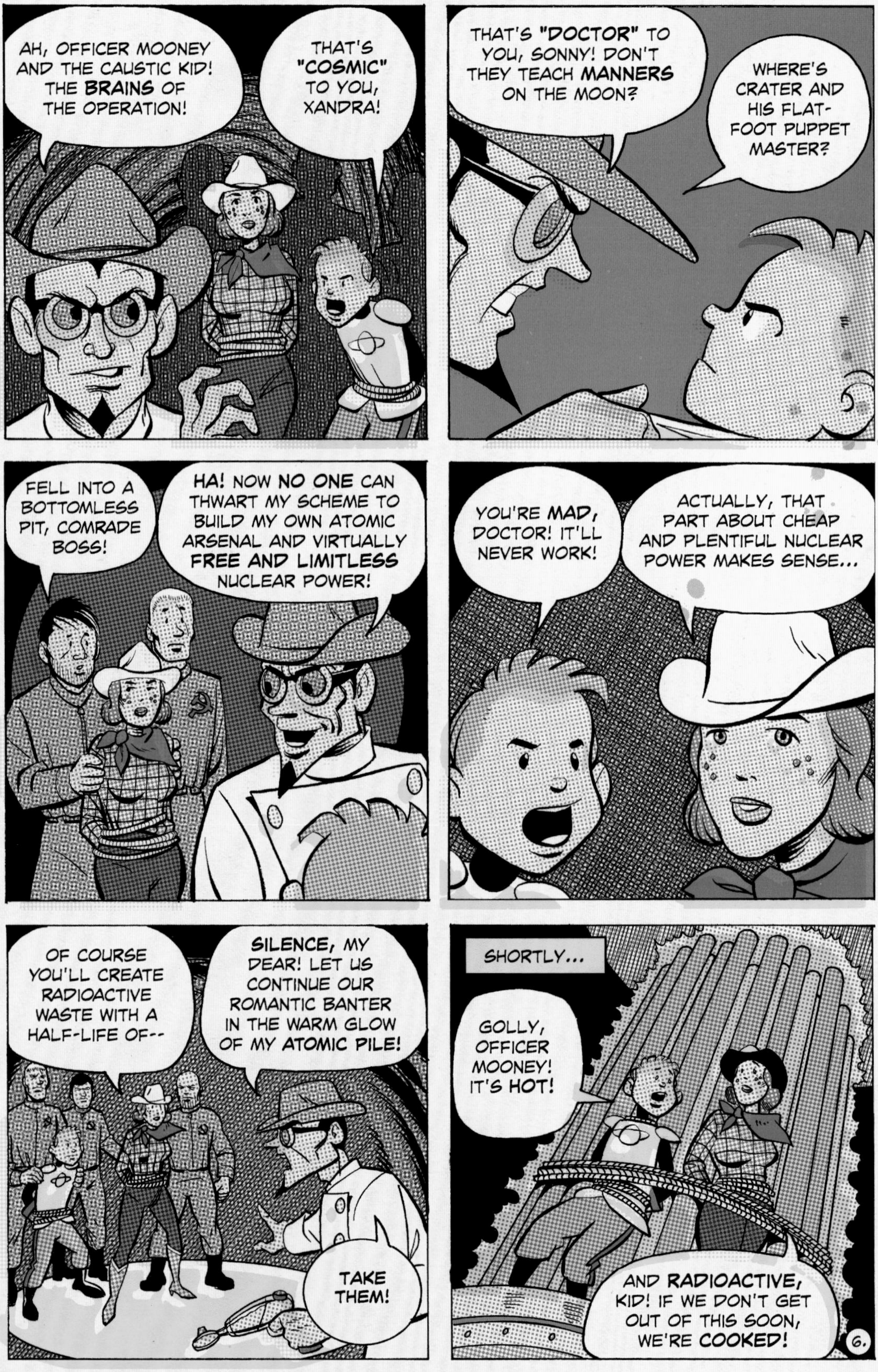
AH, OFFICER MOONEY AND THE CAUSTIC KID! THE **BRAINS** OF THE OPERATION!
THAT'S **"COSMIC"** TO YOU, XANDRA!
THAT'S **"DOCTOR"** TO YOU, SONNY! DON'T THEY TEACH **MANNERS** ON THE MOON?
WHERE'S CRATER AND HIS FLAT-FOOT PUPPET MASTER?
FELL INTO A BOTTOMLESS PIT, COMRADE BOSS!
**HA!** NOW **NO ONE** CAN THWART MY SCHEME TO BUILD MY OWN ATOMIC ARSENAL AND VIRTUALLY **FREE AND LIMITLESS** NUCLEAR POWER!
YOU'RE **MAD**, DOCTOR! IT'LL NEVER WORK!
ACTUALLY, THAT PART ABOUT CHEAP AND PLENTIFUL NUCLEAR POWER MAKES SENSE...
OF COURSE YOU'LL CREATE RADIOACTIVE WASTE WITH A HALF-LIFE OF--
**SILENCE,** MY DEAR! LET US CONTINUE OUR ROMANTIC BANTER IN THE WARM GLOW OF MY **ATOMIC PILE!**
**TAKE THEM!**
SHORTLY...
GOLLY, OFFICER MOONEY! IT'S **HOT!**
AND **RADIOACTIVE,** KID! IF WE DON'T GET OUT OF THIS SOON, WE'RE **COOKED!**
6.

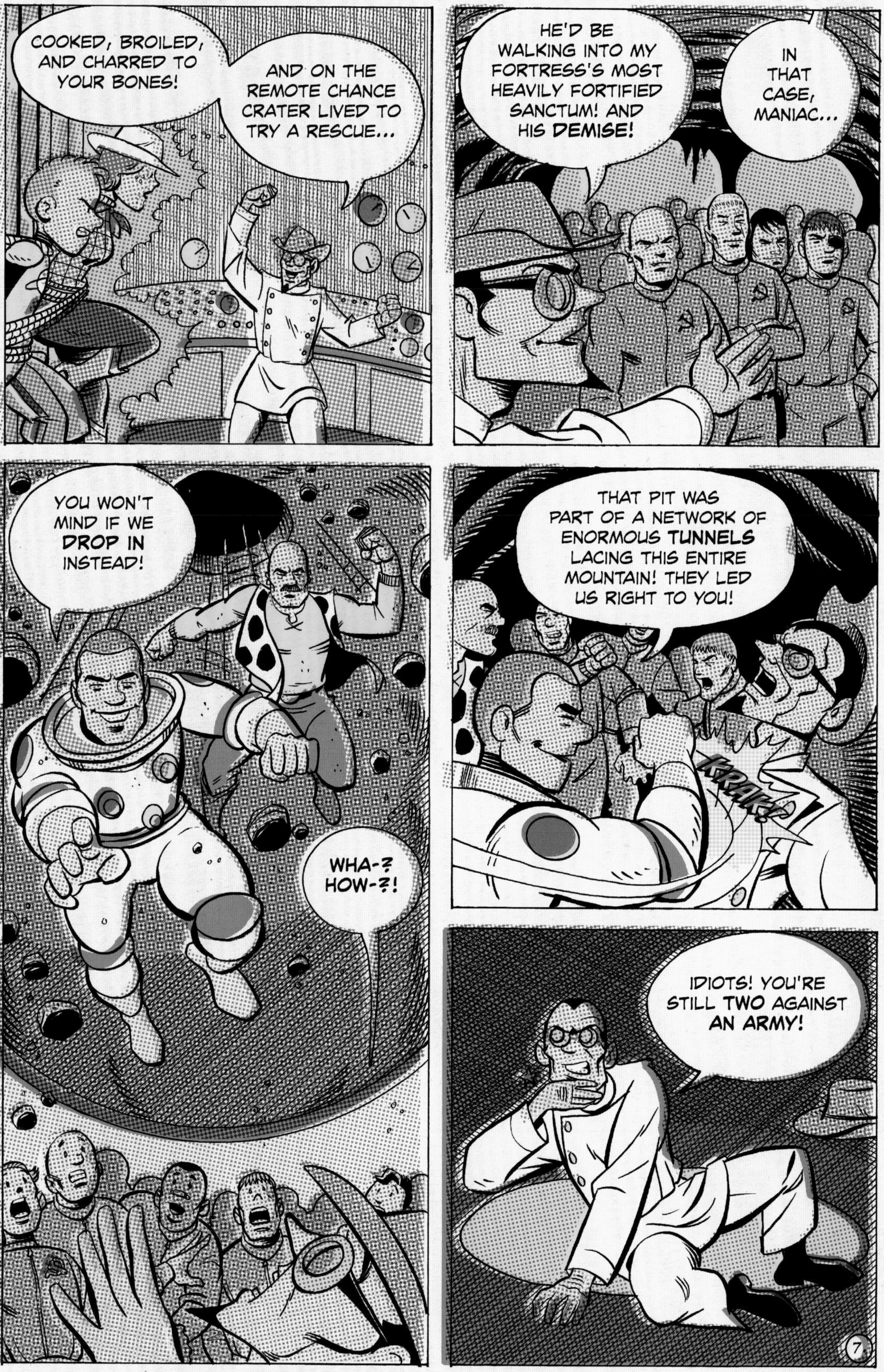
COOKED, BROILED, AND CHARRED TO YOUR BONES!
AND ON THE REMOTE CHANCE CRATER LIVED TO TRY A RESCUE...
HE'D BE WALKING INTO MY FORTRESS'S MOST HEAVILY FORTIFIED SANCTUM! AND HIS DEMISE!
IN THAT CASE, MANIAC...
YOU WON'T MIND IF WE DROP IN INSTEAD!
WHA-? HOW-?!
THAT PIT WAS PART OF A NETWORK OF ENORMOUS TUNNELS LACING THIS ENTIRE MOUNTAIN! THEY LED US RIGHT TO YOU!
KRAK!
IDIOTS! YOU'RE STILL TWO AGAINST AN ARMY!

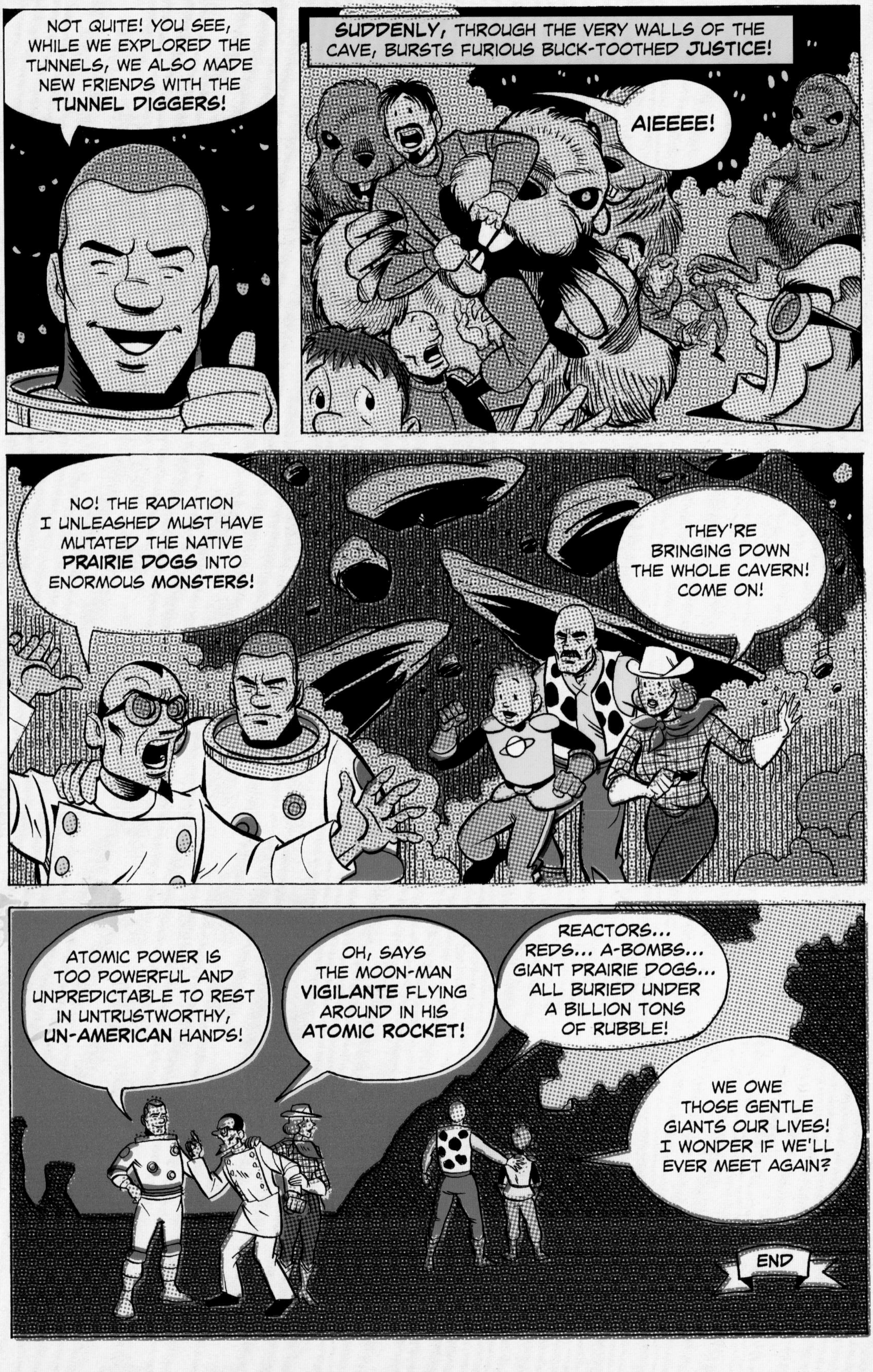
NOT QUITE! YOU SEE, WHILE WE EXPLORED THE TUNNELS, WE ALSO MADE NEW FRIENDS WITH THE TUNNEL DIGGERS!
SUDDENLY, THROUGH THE VERY WALLS OF THE CAVE, BURSTS FURIOUS BUCK-TOOTHED JUSTICE!
AIEEEE!
NO! THE RADIATION I UNLEASHED MUST HAVE MUTATED THE NATIVE PRAIRIE DOGS INTO ENORMOUS MONSTERS!
THEY'RE BRINGING DOWN THE WHOLE CAVERN! COME ON!
ATOMIC POWER IS TOO POWERFUL AND UNPREDICTABLE TO REST IN UNTRUSTWORTHY, UN-AMERICAN HANDS!
OH, SAYS THE MOON-MAN VIGILANTE FLYING AROUND IN HIS ATOMIC ROCKET!
REACTORS... REDS... A-BOMBS... GIANT PRAIRIE DOGS... ALL BURIED UNDER A BILLION TONS OF RUBBLE!
WE OWE THOSE GENTLE GIANTS OUR LIVES! I WONDER IF WE'LL EVER MEET AGAIN?
END

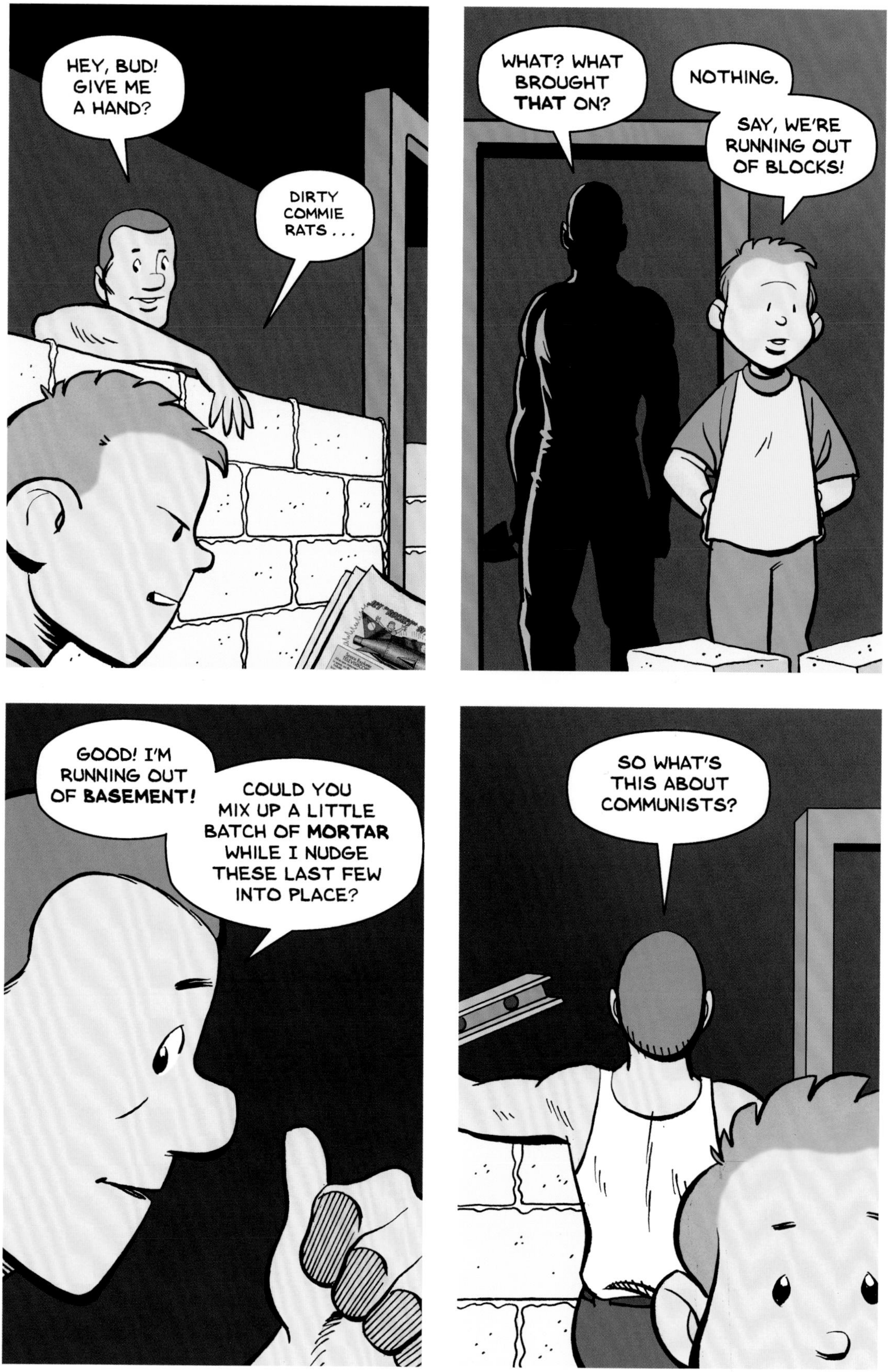
HEY, BUD! GIVE ME A HAND?
DIRTY COMMIE RATS . . .
WHAT? WHAT BROUGHT **THAT** ON?
NOTHING.
SAY, WE'RE RUNNING OUT OF BLOCKS!
GOOD! I'M RUNNING OUT OF **BASEMENT!**
COULD YOU MIX UP A LITTLE BATCH OF **MORTAR** WHILE I NUDGE THESE LAST FEW INTO PLACE?
SO WHAT'S THIS ABOUT COMMUNISTS?

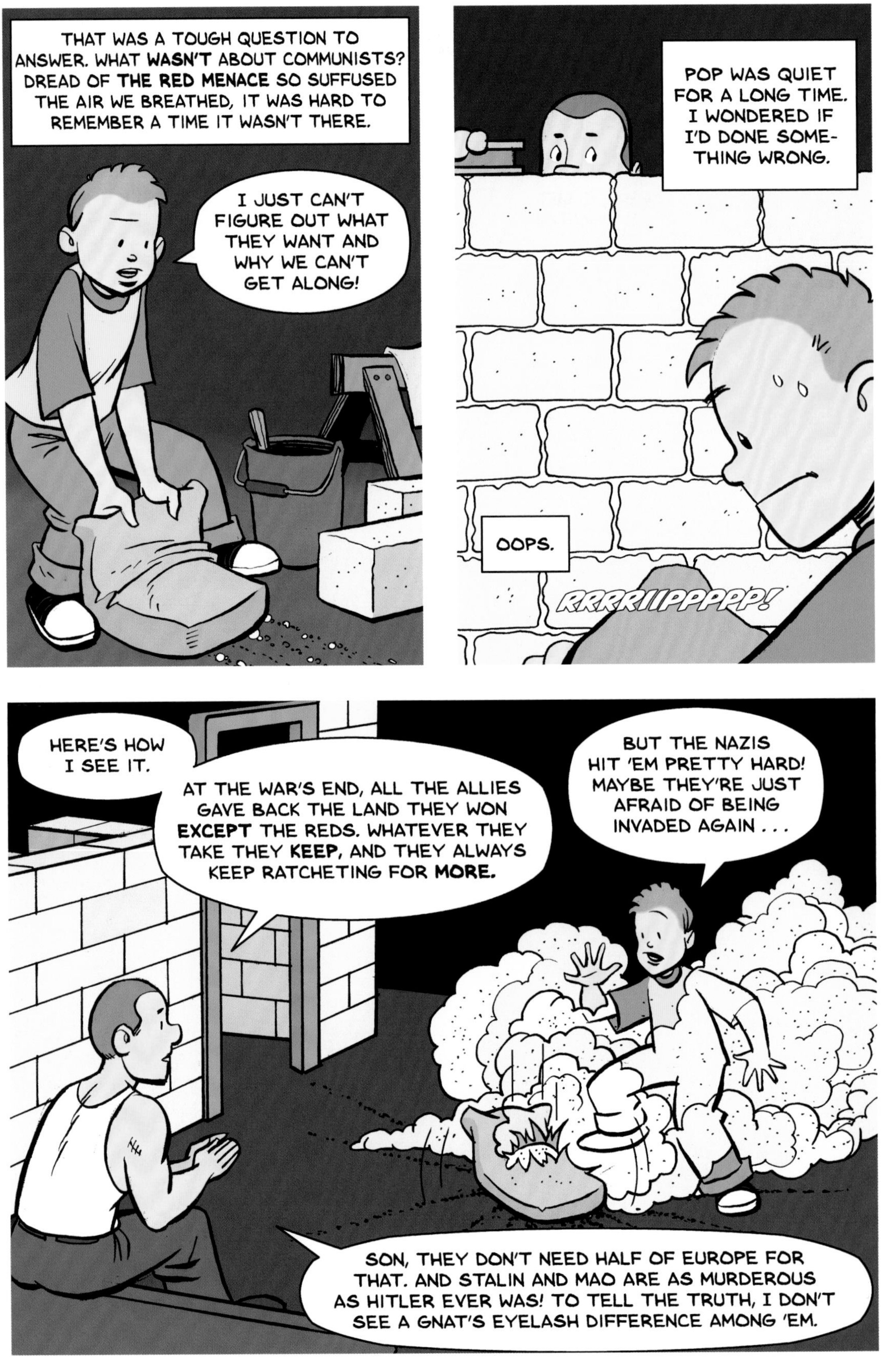
THAT WAS A TOUGH QUESTION TO ANSWER. WHAT WASN'T ABOUT COMMUNISTS? DREAD OF THE RED MENACE SO SUFFUSED THE AIR WE BREATHED, IT WAS HARD TO REMEMBER A TIME IT WASN'T THERE.
I JUST CAN'T FIGURE OUT WHAT THEY WANT AND WHY WE CAN'T GET ALONG!
POP WAS QUIET FOR A LONG TIME. I WONDERED IF I'D DONE SOME-THING WRONG.
OOPS.
RRRRIIPPPPPP!
HERE'S HOW I SEE IT.
AT THE WAR'S END, ALL THE ALLIES GAVE BACK THE LAND THEY WON EXCEPT THE REDS. WHATEVER THEY TAKE THEY KEEP, AND THEY ALWAYS KEEP RATCHETING FOR MORE.
BUT THE NAZIS HIT 'EM PRETTY HARD! MAYBE THEY'RE JUST AFRAID OF BEING INVADED AGAIN . . .
SON, THEY DON'T NEED HALF OF EUROPE FOR THAT. AND STALIN AND MAO ARE AS MURDEROUS AS HITLER EVER WAS! TO TELL THE TRUTH, I DON'T SEE A GNAT'S EYELASH DIFFERENCE AMONG 'EM.

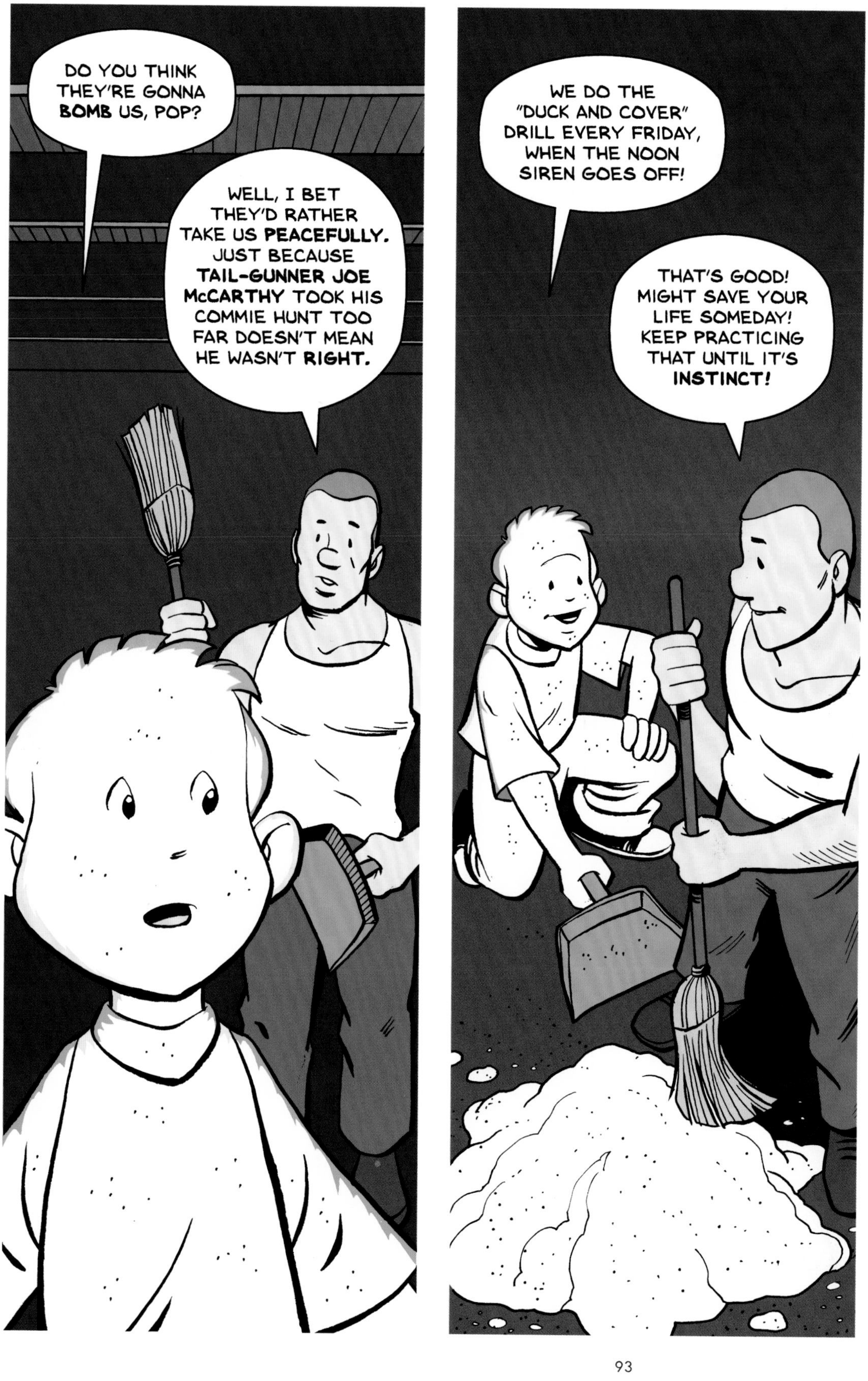
DO YOU THINK THEY'RE GONNA **BOMB** US, POP?
WELL, I BET THEY'D RATHER TAKE US **PEACEFULLY.** JUST BECAUSE **TAIL-GUNNER JOE McCARTHY** TOOK HIS COMMIE HUNT TOO FAR DOESN'T MEAN HE WASN'T **RIGHT.**
WE DO THE "DUCK AND COVER" DRILL EVERY FRIDAY, WHEN THE NOON SIREN GOES OFF!
THAT'S GOOD! MIGHT SAVE YOUR LIFE SOMEDAY! KEEP PRACTICING THAT UNTIL IT'S **INSTINCT!**

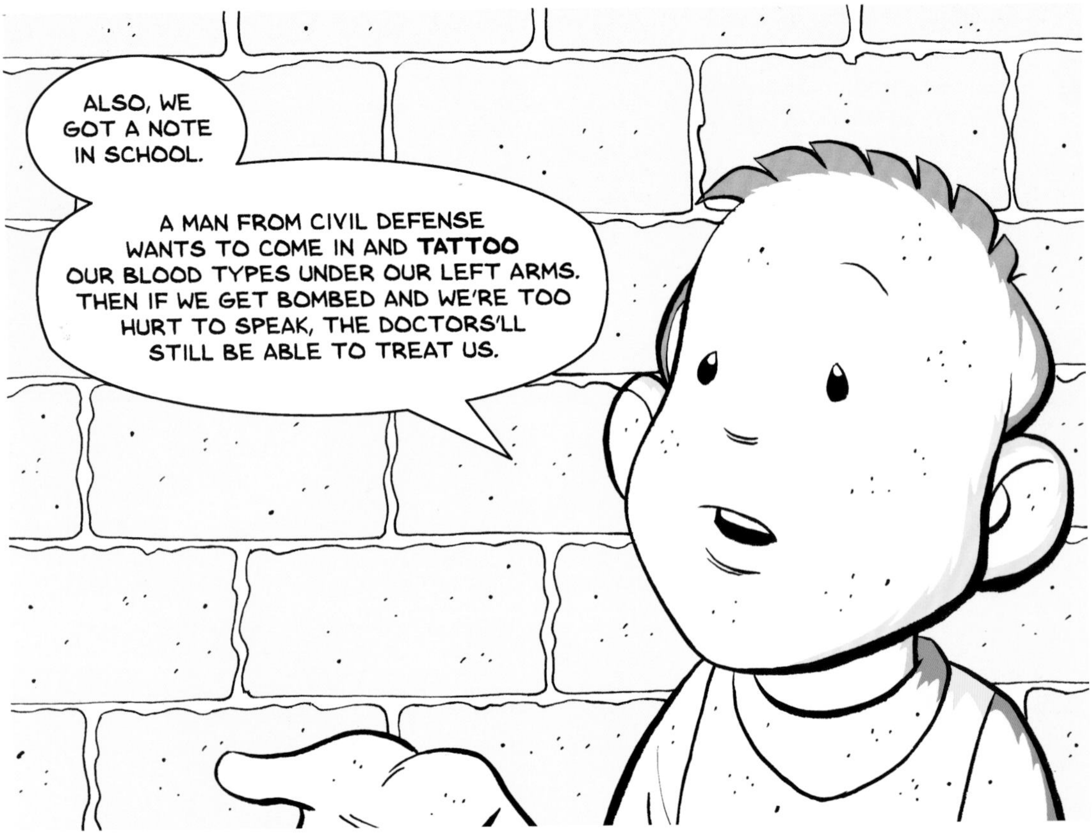
ALSO, WE GOT A NOTE IN SCHOOL.
A MAN FROM CIVIL DEFENSE WANTS TO COME IN AND **TATTOO** OUR BLOOD TYPES UNDER OUR LEFT ARMS. THEN IF WE GET BOMBED AND WE'RE TOO HURT TO SPEAK, THE DOCTORS'LL STILL BE ABLE TO TREAT US.

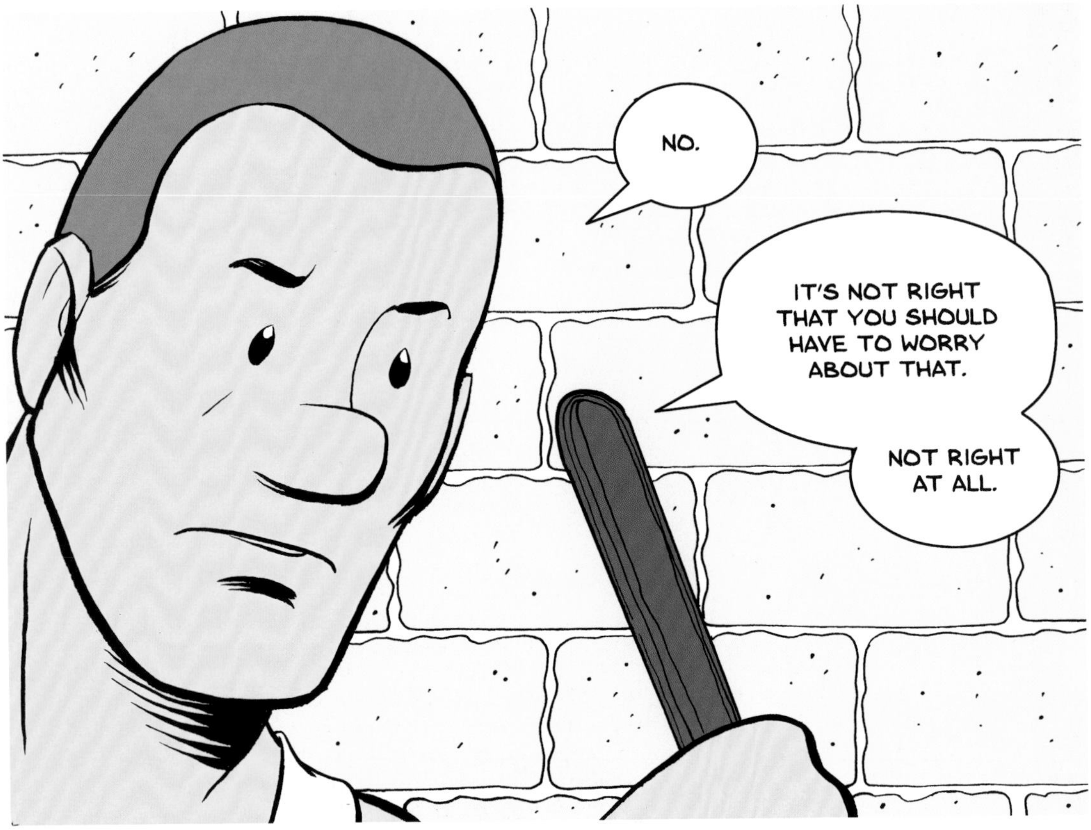
NO.
IT'S NOT RIGHT THAT YOU SHOULD HAVE TO WORRY ABOUT THAT.
NOT RIGHT AT ALL.

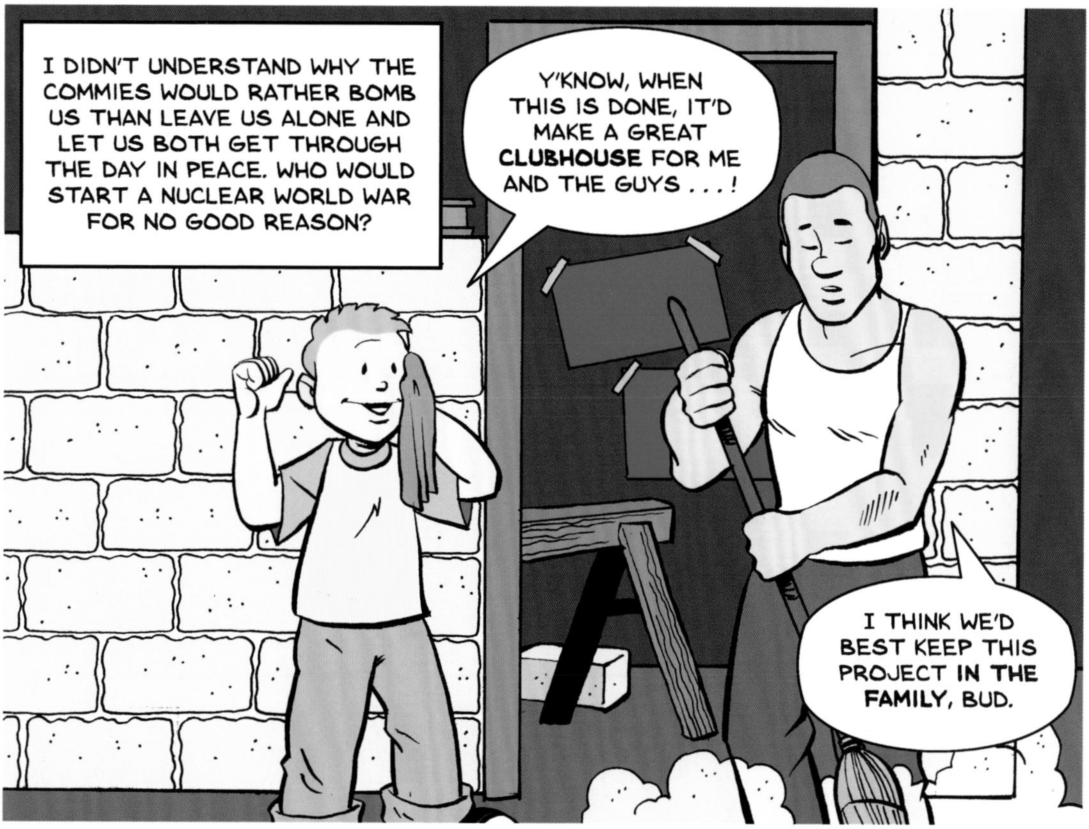
I DIDN'T UNDERSTAND WHY THE COMMIES WOULD RATHER BOMB US THAN LEAVE US ALONE AND LET US BOTH GET THROUGH THE DAY IN PEACE. WHO WOULD START A NUCLEAR WORLD WAR FOR NO GOOD REASON?
Y'KNOW, WHEN THIS IS DONE, IT'D MAKE A GREAT **CLUBHOUSE** FOR ME AND THE GUYS . . . !
I THINK WE'D BEST KEEP THIS PROJECT **IN THE FAMILY**, BUD.

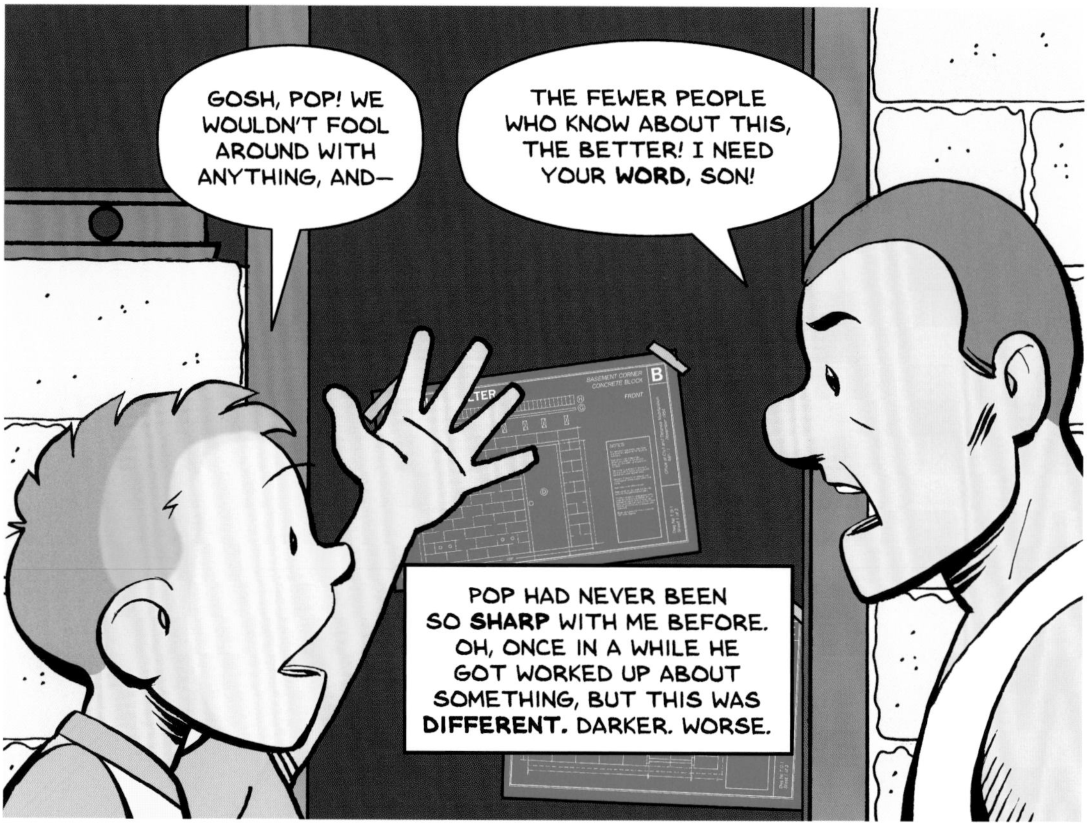
GOSH, POP! WE WOULDN'T FOOL AROUND WITH ANYTHING, AND—
THE FEWER PEOPLE WHO KNOW ABOUT THIS, THE BETTER! I NEED YOUR **WORD**, SON!
POP HAD NEVER BEEN SO **SHARP** WITH ME BEFORE. OH, ONCE IN A WHILE HE GOT WORKED UP ABOUT SOMETHING, BUT THIS WAS **DIFFERENT.** DARKER. WORSE.

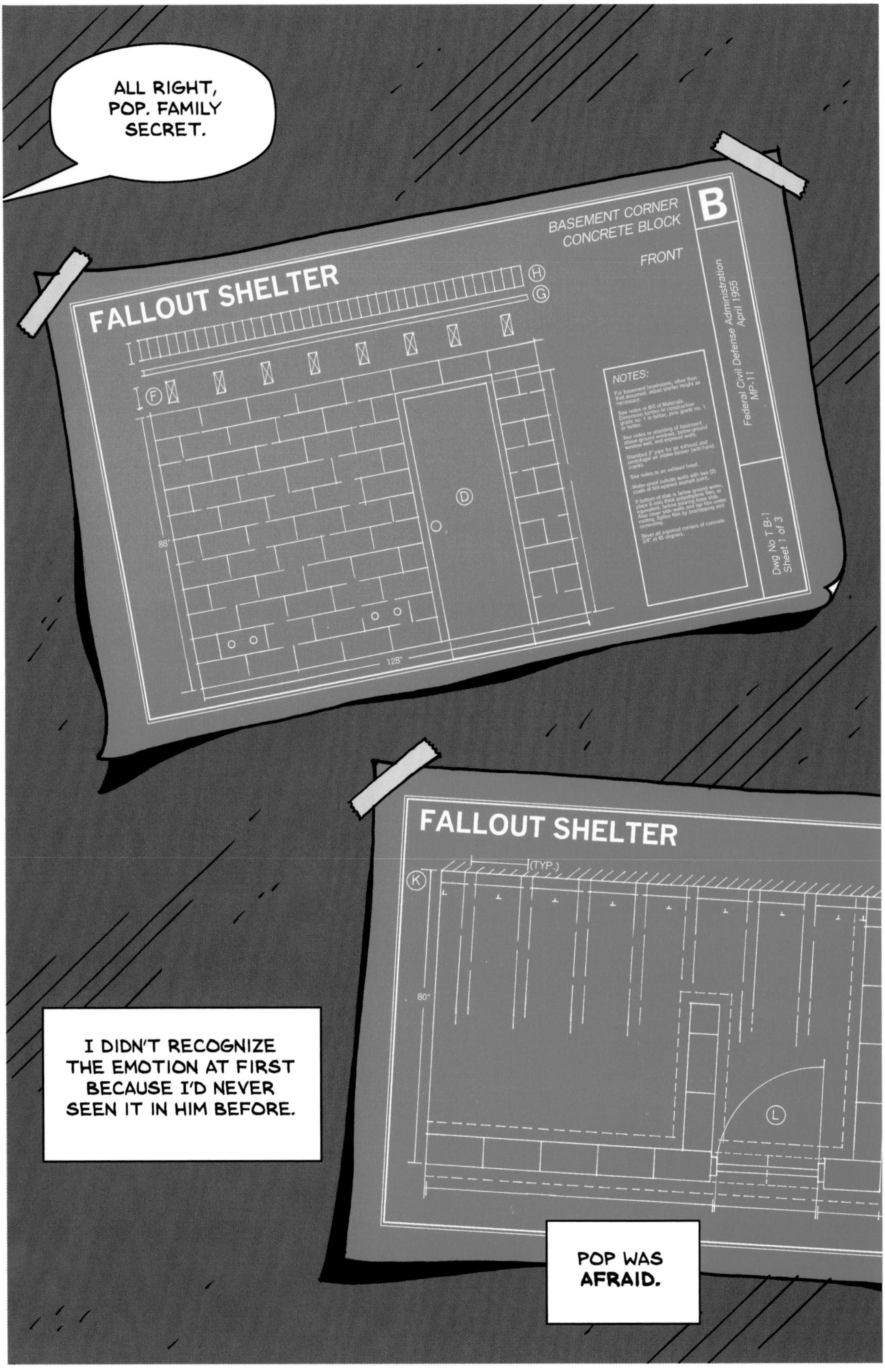
ALL RIGHT, POP. FAMILY SECRET.
FALLOUT SHELTER
BASEMENT CORNER
CONCRETE BLOCK
FRONT
B
Federal Civil Defense Administration
April 1955
MP-11
NOTES:
Dwg No T B-1
Sheet 1 of 3
88"
128"
FALLOUT SHELTER
(TYP.)
80"
I DIDN'T RECOGNIZE THE EMOTION AT FIRST BECAUSE I'D NEVER SEEN IT IN HIM BEFORE.
POP WAS AFRAID.

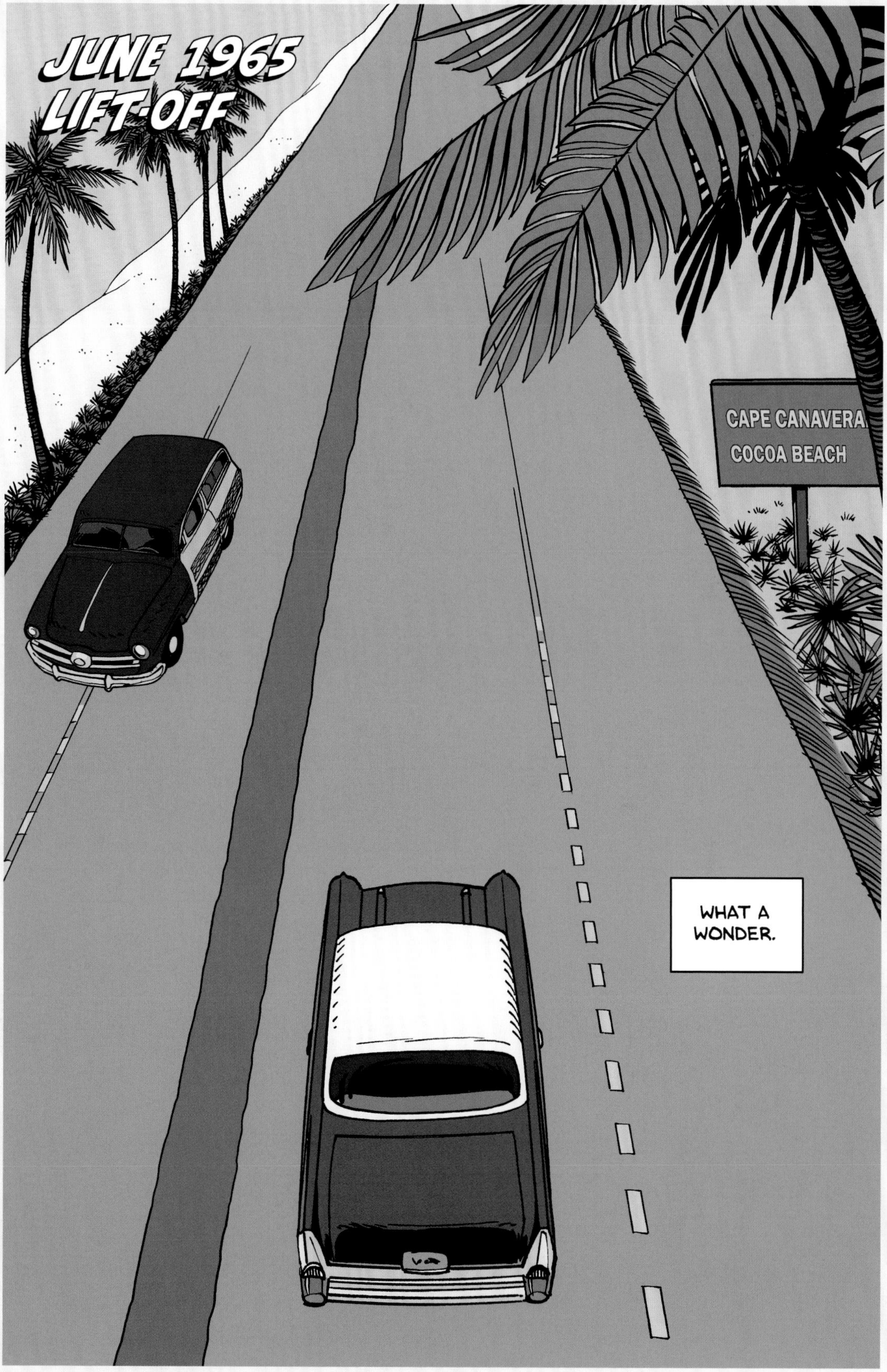
JUNE 1965
LIFT-OFF
CAPE CANAVERAL
COCOA BEACH
WHAT A WONDER.

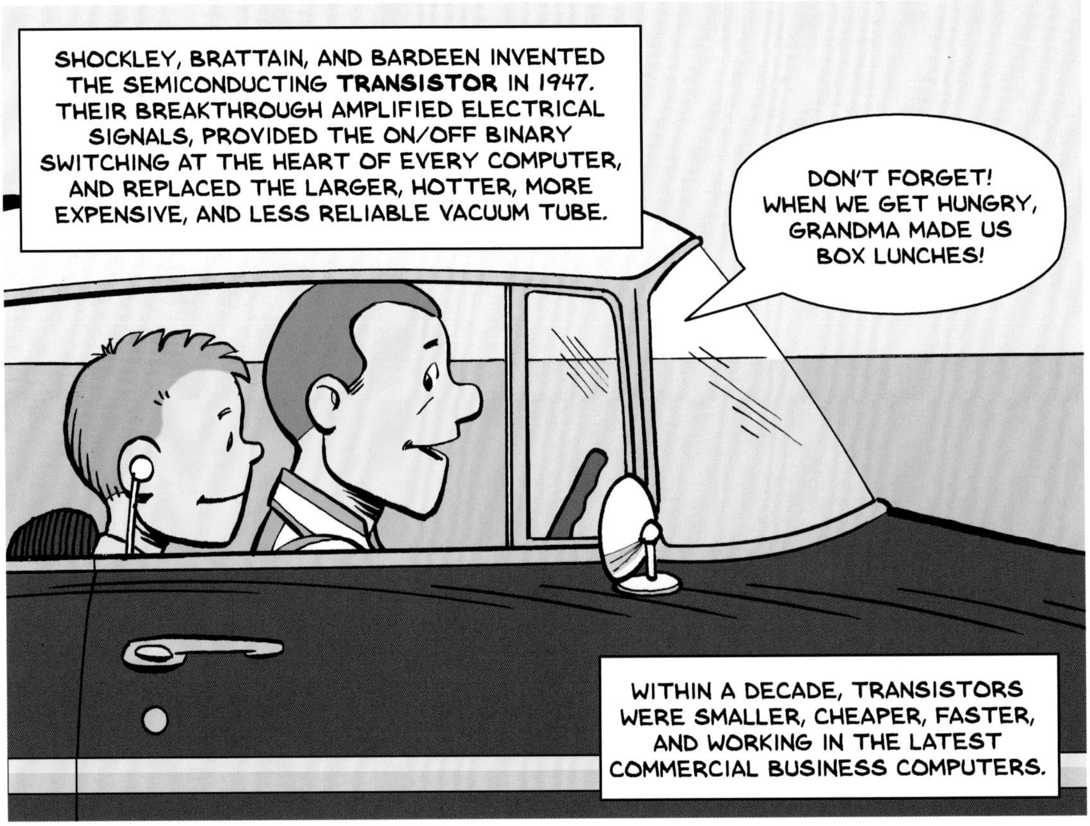
SHOCKLEY, BRATTAIN, AND BARDEEN INVENTED THE SEMICONDUCTING **TRANSISTOR** IN 1947. THEIR BREAKTHROUGH AMPLIFIED ELECTRICAL SIGNALS, PROVIDED THE ON/OFF BINARY SWITCHING AT THE HEART OF EVERY COMPUTER, AND REPLACED THE LARGER, HOTTER, MORE EXPENSIVE, AND LESS RELIABLE VACUUM TUBE.
DON'T FORGET! WHEN WE GET HUNGRY, GRANDMA MADE US BOX LUNCHES!
WITHIN A DECADE, TRANSISTORS WERE SMALLER, CHEAPER, FASTER, AND WORKING IN THE LATEST COMMERCIAL BUSINESS COMPUTERS.

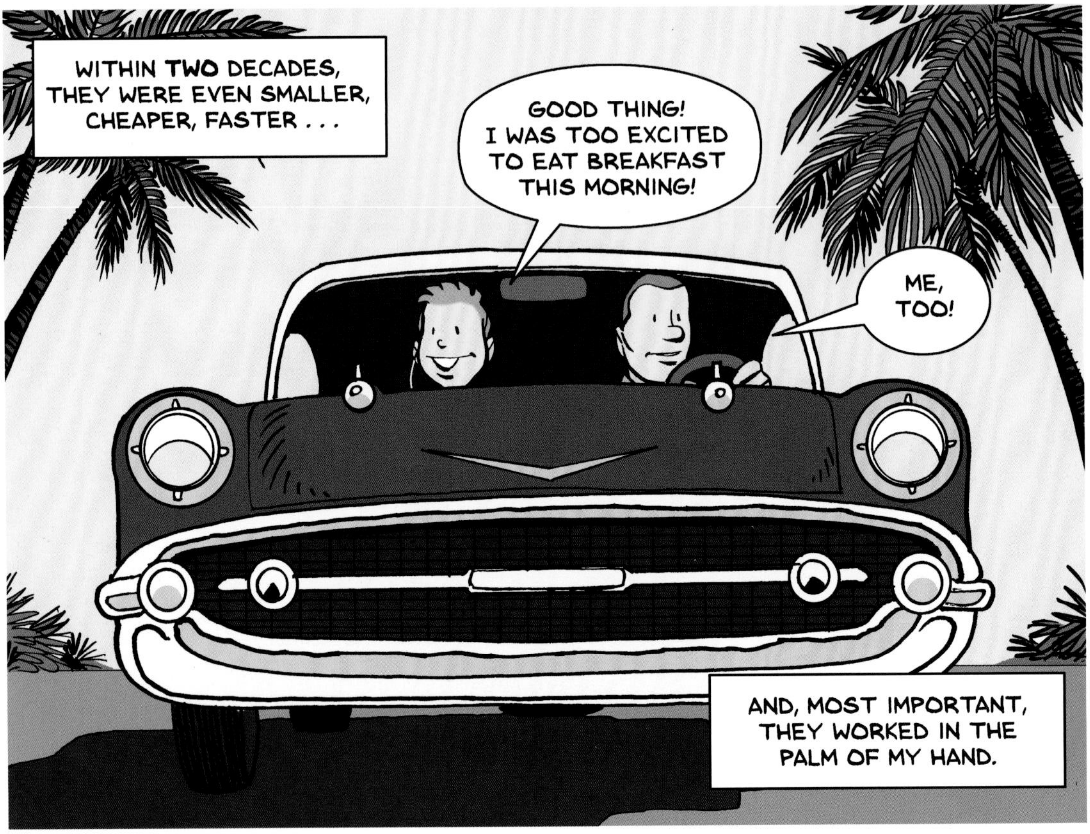
WITHIN **TWO** DECADES, THEY WERE EVEN SMALLER, CHEAPER, FASTER . . .
GOOD THING! I WAS TOO EXCITED TO EAT BREAKFAST THIS MORNING!
ME, TOO!
AND, MOST IMPORTANT, THEY WORKED IN THE PALM OF MY HAND.

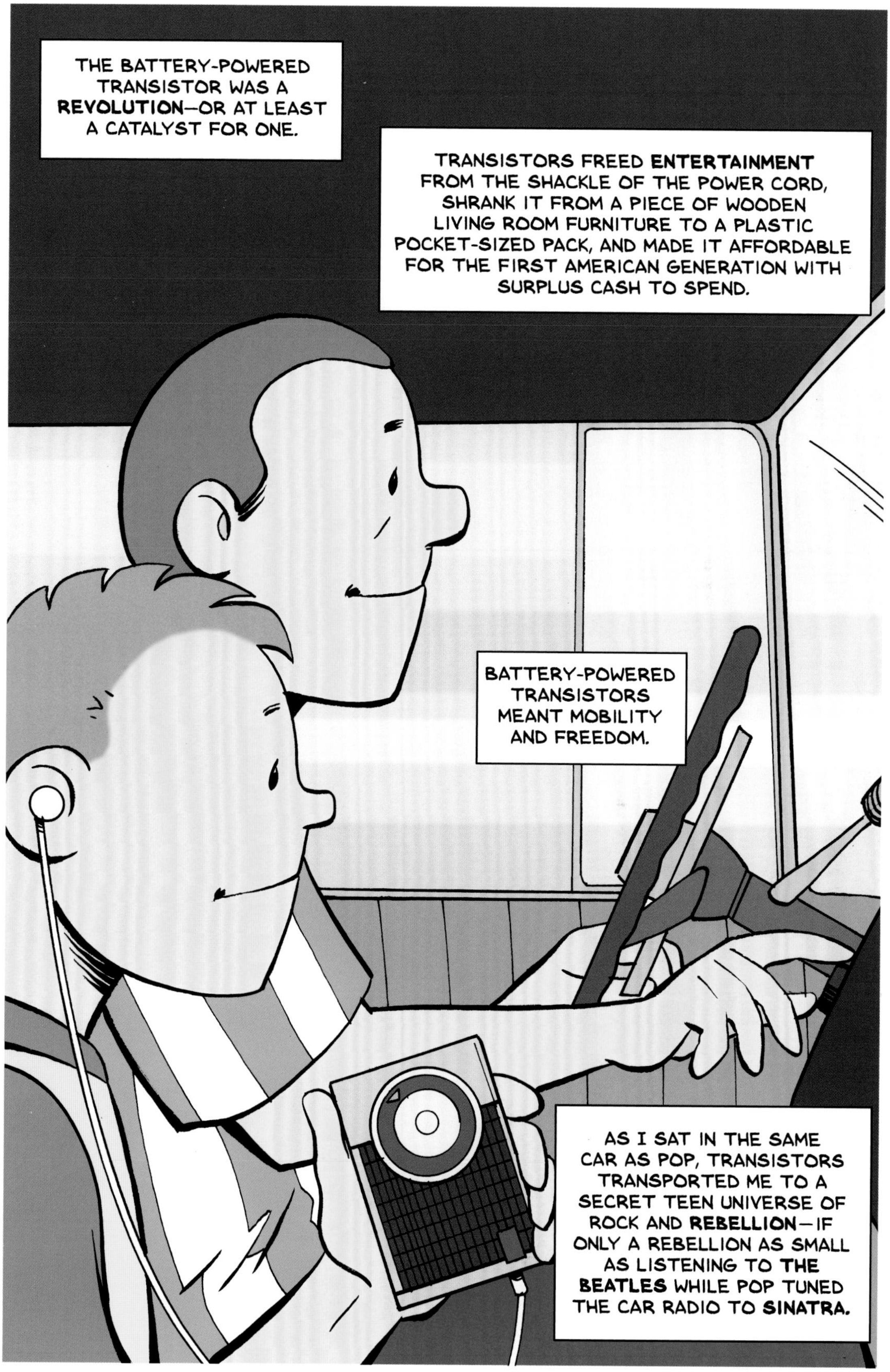
THE BATTERY-POWERED TRANSISTOR WAS A **REVOLUTION**—OR AT LEAST A CATALYST FOR ONE.
TRANSISTORS FREED **ENTERTAINMENT** FROM THE SHACKLE OF THE POWER CORD, SHRANK IT FROM A PIECE OF WOODEN LIVING ROOM FURNITURE TO A PLASTIC POCKET-SIZED PACK, AND MADE IT AFFORDABLE FOR THE FIRST AMERICAN GENERATION WITH SURPLUS CASH TO SPEND.
BATTERY-POWERED TRANSISTORS MEANT MOBILITY AND FREEDOM.
AS I SAT IN THE SAME CAR AS POP, TRANSISTORS TRANSPORTED ME TO A SECRET TEEN UNIVERSE OF ROCK AND **REBELLION**—IF ONLY A REBELLION AS SMALL AS LISTENING TO **THE BEATLES** WHILE POP TUNED THE CAR RADIO TO **SINATRA.**

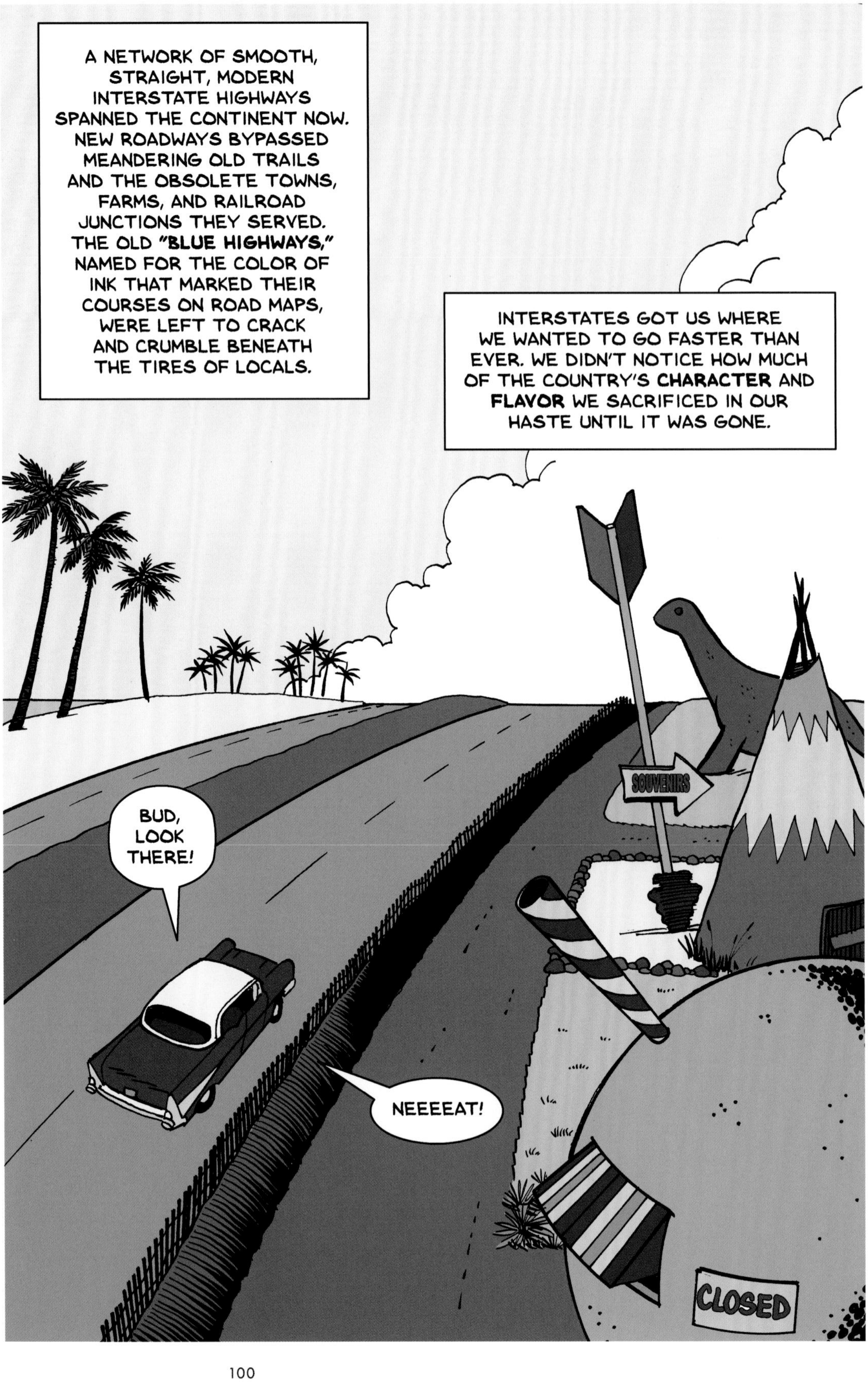
A NETWORK OF SMOOTH, STRAIGHT, MODERN INTERSTATE HIGHWAYS SPANNED THE CONTINENT NOW. NEW ROADWAYS BYPASSED MEANDERING OLD TRAILS AND THE OBSOLETE TOWNS, FARMS, AND RAILROAD JUNCTIONS THEY SERVED. THE OLD **"BLUE HIGHWAYS,"** NAMED FOR THE COLOR OF INK THAT MARKED THEIR COURSES ON ROAD MAPS, WERE LEFT TO CRACK AND CRUMBLE BENEATH THE TIRES OF LOCALS.
INTERSTATES GOT US WHERE WE WANTED TO GO FASTER THAN EVER. WE DIDN'T NOTICE HOW MUCH OF THE COUNTRY'S **CHARACTER** AND **FLAVOR** WE SACRIFICED IN OUR HASTE UNTIL IT WAS GONE.
SOUVENIRS
BUD, LOOK THERE!
NEEEEAT!
CLOSED

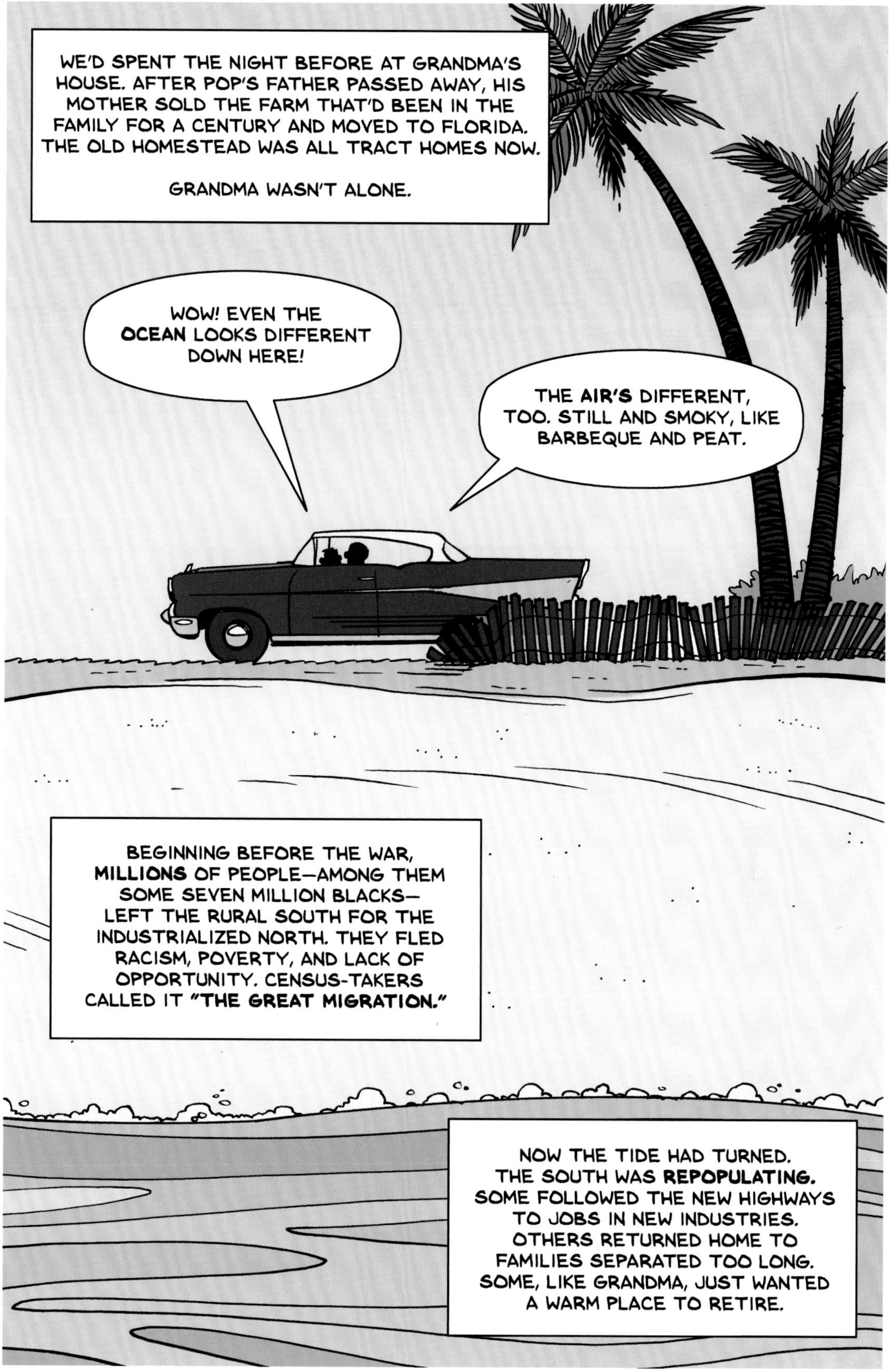
WE'D SPENT THE NIGHT BEFORE AT GRANDMA'S HOUSE. AFTER POP'S FATHER PASSED AWAY, HIS MOTHER SOLD THE FARM THAT'D BEEN IN THE FAMILY FOR A CENTURY AND MOVED TO FLORIDA. THE OLD HOMESTEAD WAS ALL TRACT HOMES NOW.
GRANDMA WASN'T ALONE.
WOW! EVEN THE **OCEAN** LOOKS DIFFERENT DOWN HERE!
THE **AIR'S** DIFFERENT, TOO. STILL AND SMOKY, LIKE BARBEQUE AND PEAT.
BEGINNING BEFORE THE WAR, **MILLIONS** OF PEOPLE—AMONG THEM SOME SEVEN MILLION BLACKS—LEFT THE RURAL SOUTH FOR THE INDUSTRIALIZED NORTH. THEY FLED RACISM, POVERTY, AND LACK OF OPPORTUNITY. CENSUS-TAKERS CALLED IT **"THE GREAT MIGRATION."**
NOW THE TIDE HAD TURNED. THE SOUTH WAS **REPOPULATING.** SOME FOLLOWED THE NEW HIGHWAYS TO JOBS IN NEW INDUSTRIES. OTHERS RETURNED HOME TO FAMILIES SEPARATED TOO LONG. SOME, LIKE GRANDMA, JUST WANTED A WARM PLACE TO RETIRE.

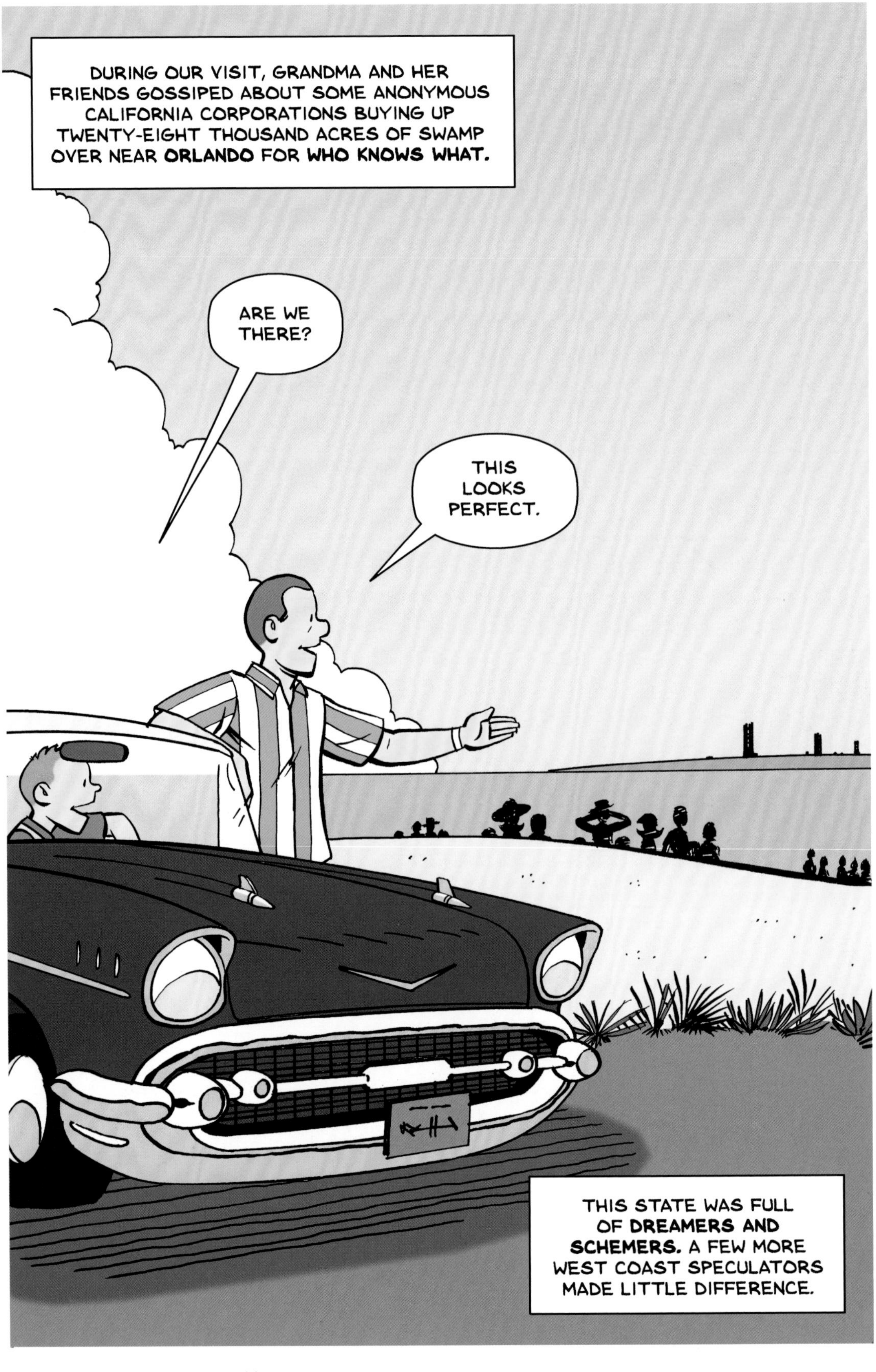
DURING OUR VISIT, GRANDMA AND HER FRIENDS GOSSIPED ABOUT SOME ANONYMOUS CALIFORNIA CORPORATIONS BUYING UP TWENTY-EIGHT THOUSAND ACRES OF SWAMP OVER NEAR **ORLANDO** FOR **WHO KNOWS WHAT.**
ARE WE THERE?
THIS LOOKS PERFECT.
THIS STATE WAS FULL OF **DREAMERS AND SCHEMERS.** A FEW MORE WEST COAST SPECULATORS MADE LITTLE DIFFERENCE.

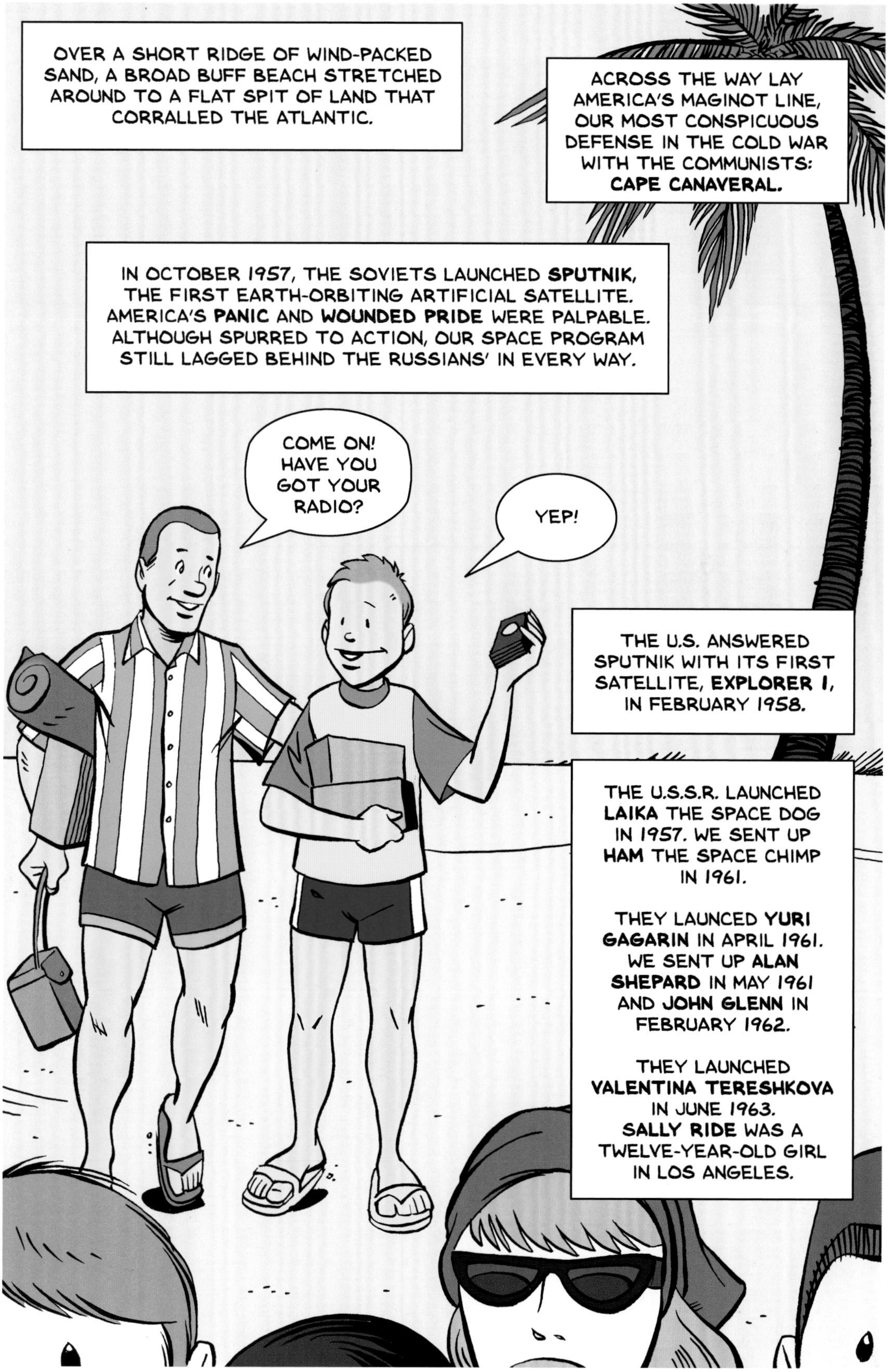
OVER A SHORT RIDGE OF WIND-PACKED SAND, A BROAD BUFF BEACH STRETCHED AROUND TO A FLAT SPIT OF LAND THAT CORRALLED THE ATLANTIC.
ACROSS THE WAY LAY AMERICA'S MAGINOT LINE, OUR MOST CONSPICUOUS DEFENSE IN THE COLD WAR WITH THE COMMUNISTS: **CAPE CANAVERAL.**
IN OCTOBER 1957, THE SOVIETS LAUNCHED **SPUTNIK,** THE FIRST EARTH-ORBITING ARTIFICIAL SATELLITE. AMERICA'S **PANIC** AND **WOUNDED PRIDE** WERE PALPABLE. ALTHOUGH SPURRED TO ACTION, OUR SPACE PROGRAM STILL LAGGED BEHIND THE RUSSIANS' IN EVERY WAY.
COME ON! HAVE YOU GOT YOUR RADIO?
YEP!
THE U.S. ANSWERED SPUTNIK WITH ITS FIRST SATELLITE, **EXPLORER I,** IN FEBRUARY 1958.
THE U.S.S.R. LAUNCHED **LAIKA** THE SPACE DOG IN 1957. WE SENT UP **HAM** THE SPACE CHIMP IN 1961.
THEY LAUNCED **YURI GAGARIN** IN APRIL 1961. WE SENT UP **ALAN SHEPARD** IN MAY 1961 AND **JOHN GLENN** IN FEBRUARY 1962.
THEY LAUNCHED **VALENTINA TERESHKOVA** IN JUNE 1963. **SALLY RIDE** WAS A TWELVE-YEAR-OLD GIRL IN LOS ANGELES.

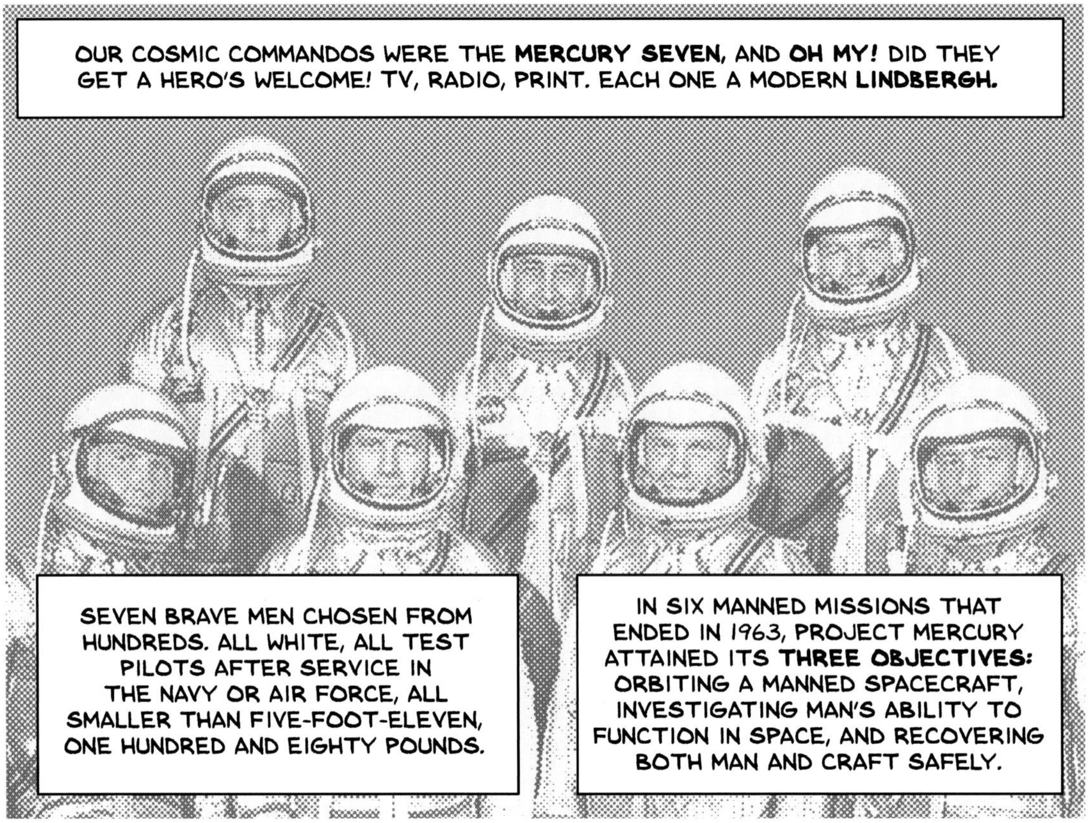
OUR COSMIC COMMANDOS WERE THE **MERCURY SEVEN**, AND **OH MY!** DID THEY GET A HERO'S WELCOME! TV, RADIO, PRINT. EACH ONE A MODERN **LINDBERGH.**
SEVEN BRAVE MEN CHOSEN FROM HUNDREDS. ALL WHITE, ALL TEST PILOTS AFTER SERVICE IN THE NAVY OR AIR FORCE, ALL SMALLER THAN FIVE-FOOT-ELEVEN, ONE HUNDRED AND EIGHTY POUNDS.
IN SIX MANNED MISSIONS THAT ENDED IN 1963, PROJECT MERCURY ATTAINED ITS **THREE OBJECTIVES:** ORBITING A MANNED SPACECRAFT, INVESTIGATING MAN'S ABILITY TO FUNCTION IN SPACE, AND RECOVERING BOTH MAN AND CRAFT SAFELY.

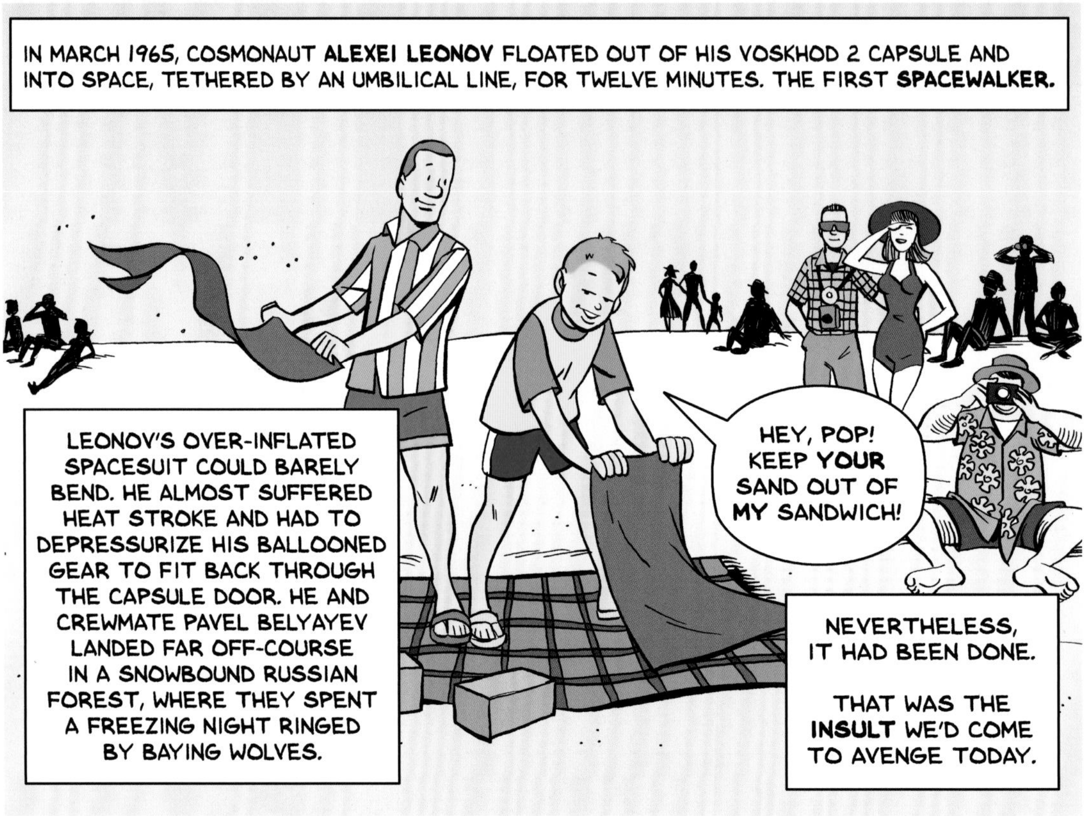
IN MARCH 1965, COSMONAUT **ALEXEI LEONOV** FLOATED OUT OF HIS VOSKHOD 2 CAPSULE AND INTO SPACE, TETHERED BY AN UMBILICAL LINE, FOR TWELVE MINUTES. THE FIRST **SPACEWALKER.**
LEONOV'S OVER-INFLATED SPACESUIT COULD BARELY BEND. HE ALMOST SUFFERED HEAT STROKE AND HAD TO DEPRESSURIZE HIS BALLOONED GEAR TO FIT BACK THROUGH THE CAPSULE DOOR. HE AND CREWMATE PAVEL BELYAYEV LANDED FAR OFF-COURSE IN A SNOWBOUND RUSSIAN FOREST, WHERE THEY SPENT A FREEZING NIGHT RINGED BY BAYING WOLVES.
HEY, POP! KEEP **YOUR** SAND OUT OF **MY** SANDWICH!
NEVERTHELESS, IT HAD BEEN DONE.
THAT WAS THE **INSULT** WE'D COME TO AVENGE TODAY.

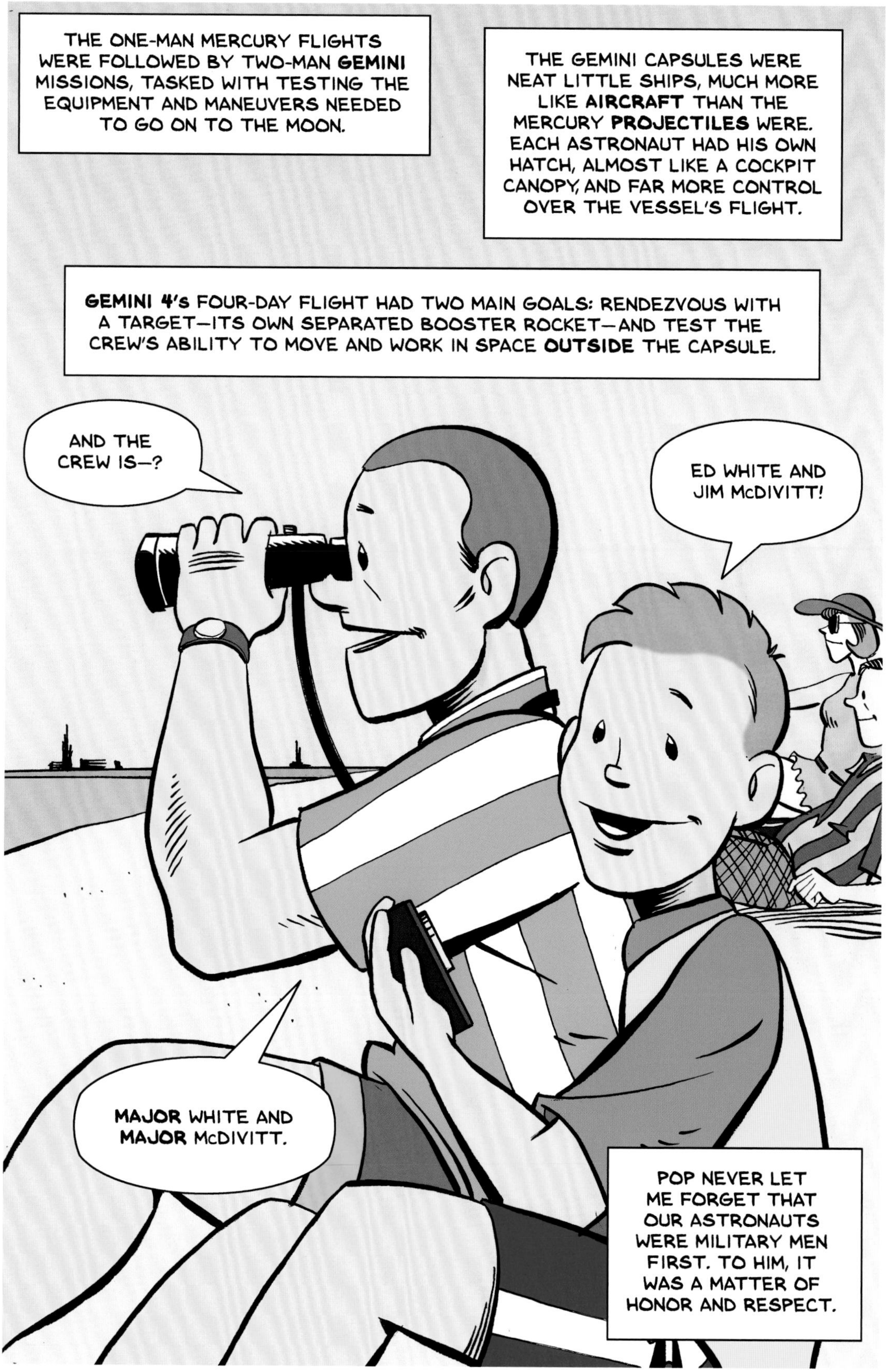
THE ONE-MAN MERCURY FLIGHTS WERE FOLLOWED BY TWO-MAN **GEMINI** MISSIONS, TASKED WITH TESTING THE EQUIPMENT AND MANEUVERS NEEDED TO GO ON TO THE MOON.
THE GEMINI CAPSULES WERE NEAT LITTLE SHIPS, MUCH MORE LIKE **AIRCRAFT** THAN THE MERCURY **PROJECTILES** WERE. EACH ASTRONAUT HAD HIS OWN HATCH, ALMOST LIKE A COCKPIT CANOPY, AND FAR MORE CONTROL OVER THE VESSEL'S FLIGHT.
**GEMINI 4's** FOUR-DAY FLIGHT HAD TWO MAIN GOALS: RENDEZVOUS WITH A TARGET—ITS OWN SEPARATED BOOSTER ROCKET—AND TEST THE CREW'S ABILITY TO MOVE AND WORK IN SPACE **OUTSIDE** THE CAPSULE.
AND THE CREW IS—?
ED WHITE AND JIM McDIVITT!
**MAJOR** WHITE AND **MAJOR** McDIVITT.
POP NEVER LET ME FORGET THAT OUR ASTRONAUTS WERE MILITARY MEN FIRST. TO HIM, IT WAS A MATTER OF HONOR AND RESPECT.

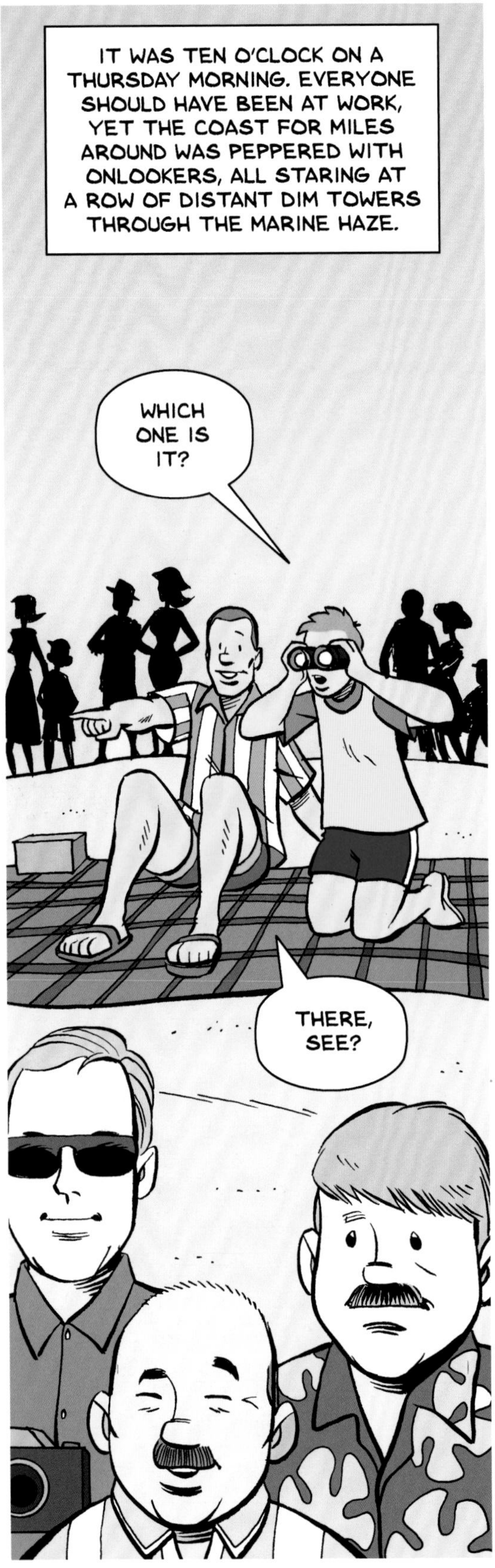
IT WAS TEN O'CLOCK ON A THURSDAY MORNING. EVERYONE SHOULD HAVE BEEN AT WORK, YET THE COAST FOR MILES AROUND WAS PEPPERED WITH ONLOOKERS, ALL STARING AT A ROW OF DISTANT DIM TOWERS THROUGH THE MARINE HAZE.
WHICH ONE IS IT?
THERE, SEE?

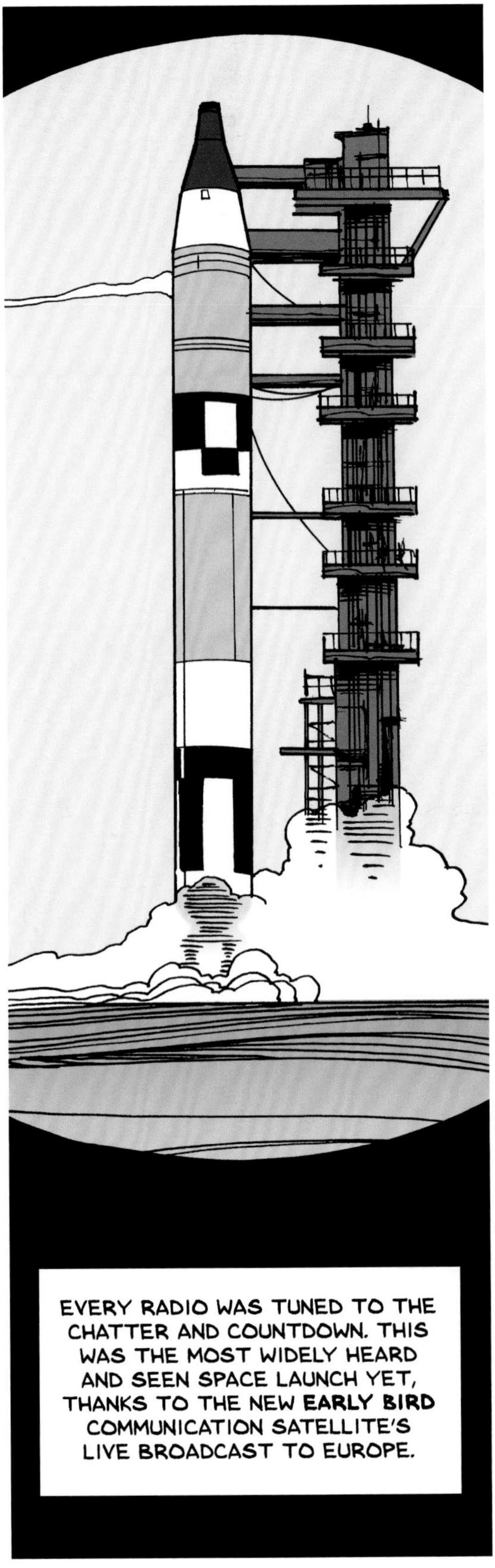
EVERY RADIO WAS TUNED TO THE CHATTER AND COUNTDOWN. THIS WAS THE MOST WIDELY HEARD AND SEEN SPACE LAUNCH YET, THANKS TO THE NEW **EARLY BIRD** COMMUNICATION SATELLITE'S LIVE BROADCAST TO EUROPE.

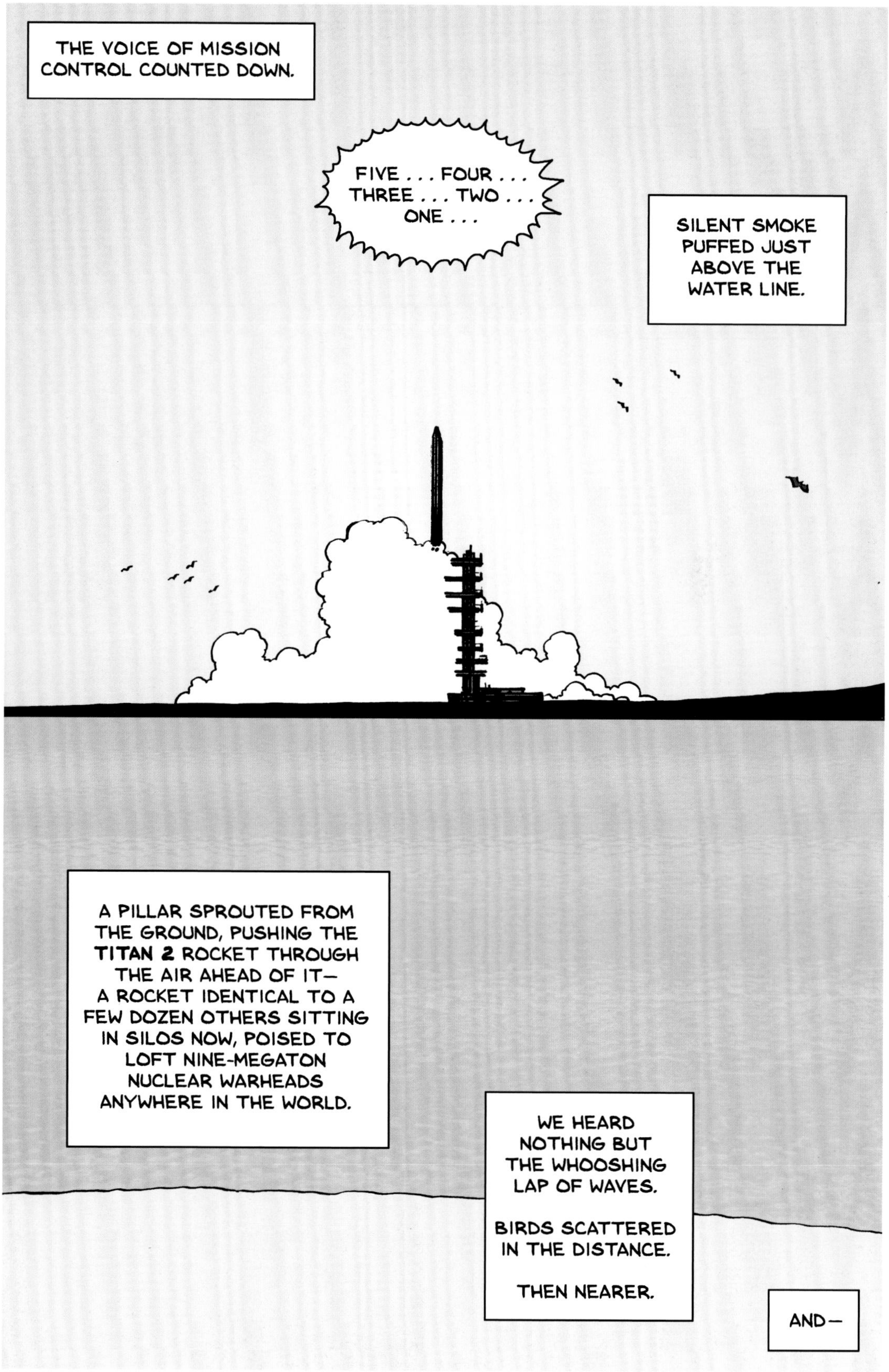
THE VOICE OF MISSION CONTROL COUNTED DOWN.
FIVE . . . FOUR . . . THREE . . . TWO . . . ONE . . .
SILENT SMOKE PUFFED JUST ABOVE THE WATER LINE.
A PILLAR SPROUTED FROM THE GROUND, PUSHING THE **TITAN 2** ROCKET THROUGH THE AIR AHEAD OF IT— A ROCKET IDENTICAL TO A FEW DOZEN OTHERS SITTING IN SILOS NOW, POISED TO LOFT NINE-MEGATON NUCLEAR WARHEADS ANYWHERE IN THE WORLD.
WE HEARD NOTHING BUT THE WHOOSHING LAP OF WAVES.
BIRDS SCATTERED IN THE DISTANCE.
THEN NEARER.
AND—

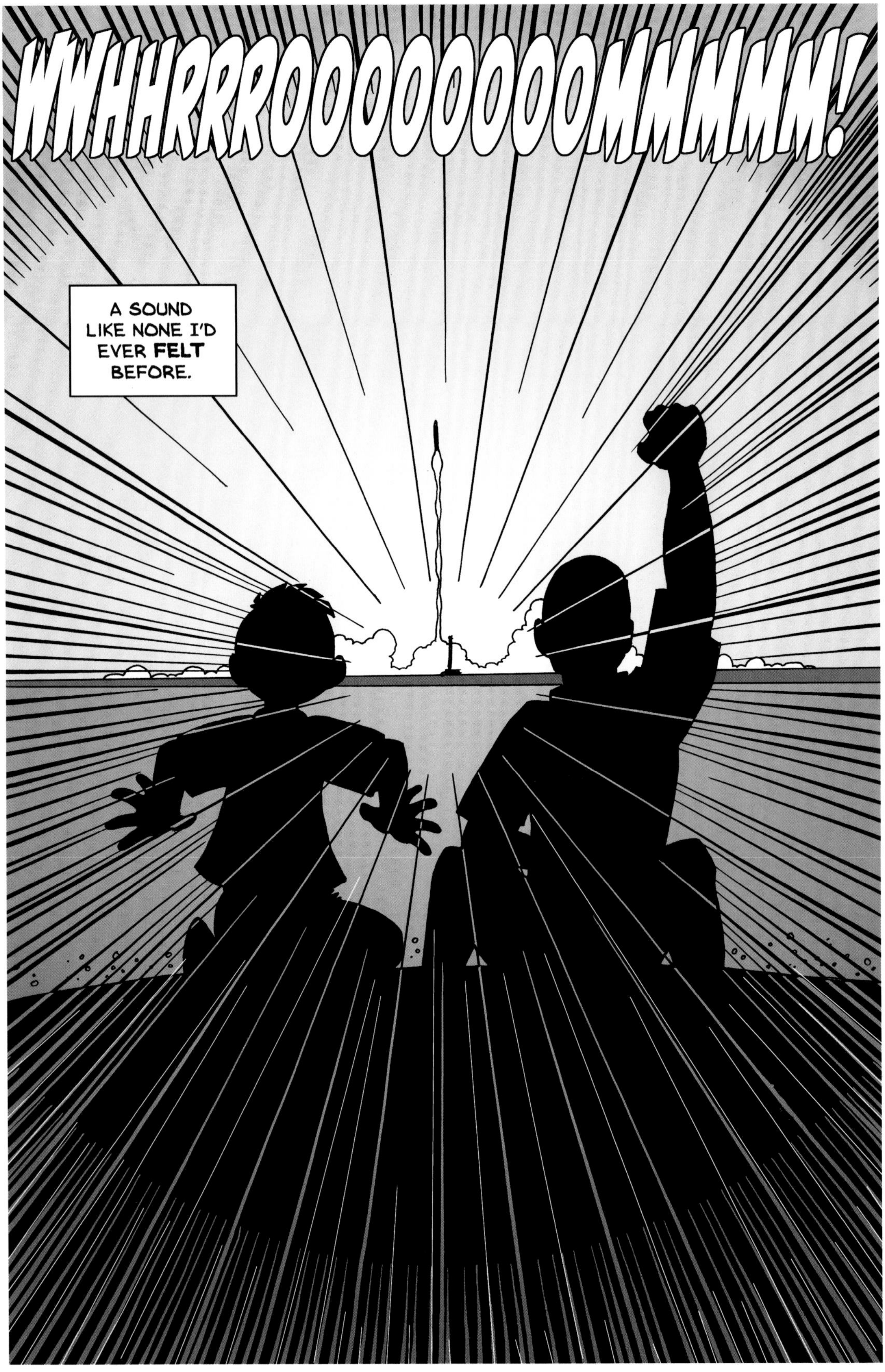
WWHHRRROOOOOOOOOMMMMMM!
A SOUND LIKE NONE I'D EVER **FELT** BEFORE.

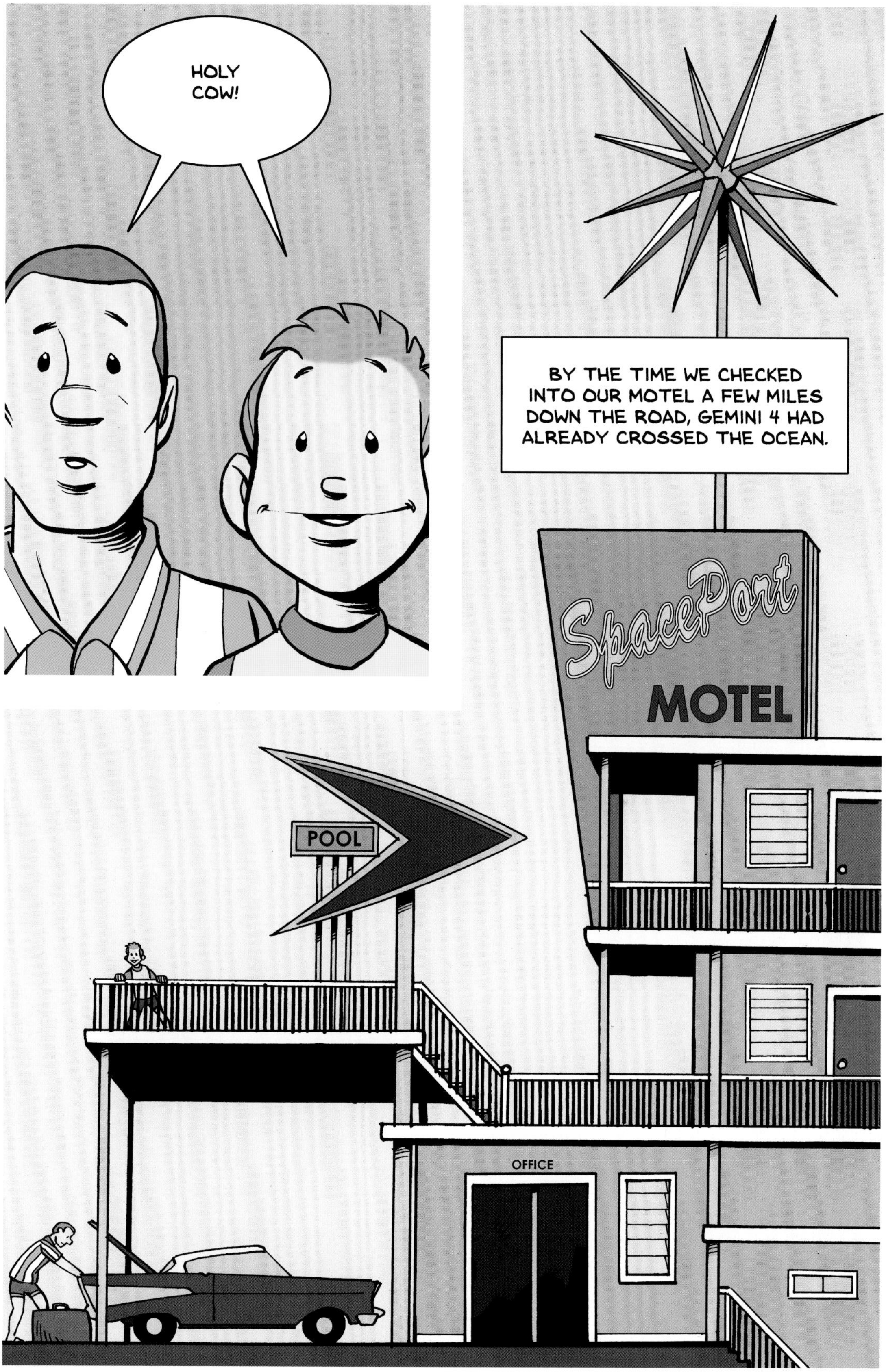
HOLY COW!
BY THE TIME WE CHECKED INTO OUR MOTEL A FEW MILES DOWN THE ROAD, GEMINI 4 HAD ALREADY CROSSED THE OCEAN.
SpacePort
MOTEL
POOL
OFFICE

FIVE AND A HALF HOURS AFTER LIFT-OFF, AND AFTER GEMINI FAILED TO RENDEZVOUS WITH ITS DISCARDED SECOND STAGE, ED WHITE POPPED OPEN HIS HATCH AND GENTLY STEPPED INTO NOTHING.

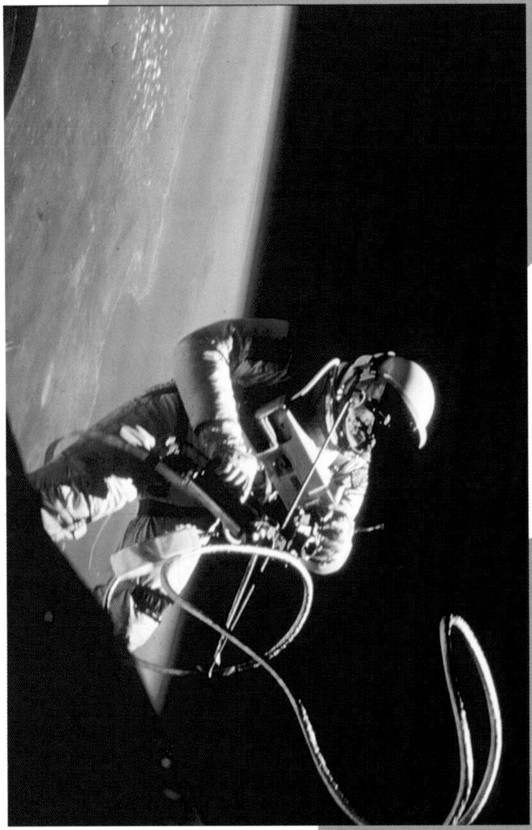

HE WAS ATTACHED TO THE SHIP BY A TWENTY-FIVE-FOOT TETHER, AND EQUIPPED WITH A CAMERA BOLTED TO A ZIP GUN— A PISTOL OF TUBES, NOZZLES, AND COMPRESSED OXYGEN THAT PROPELLED HIM THROUGH SPACE.

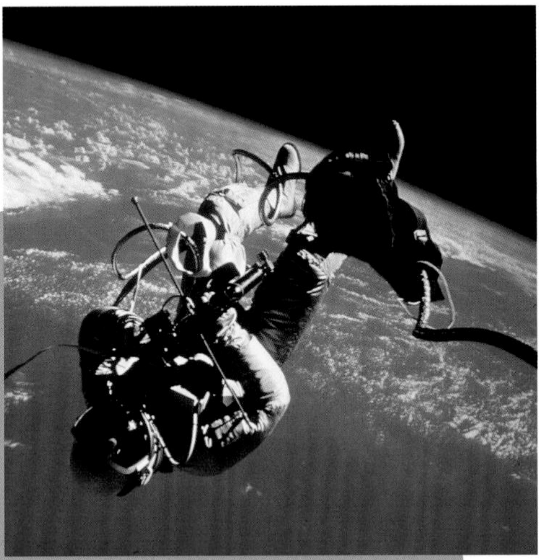

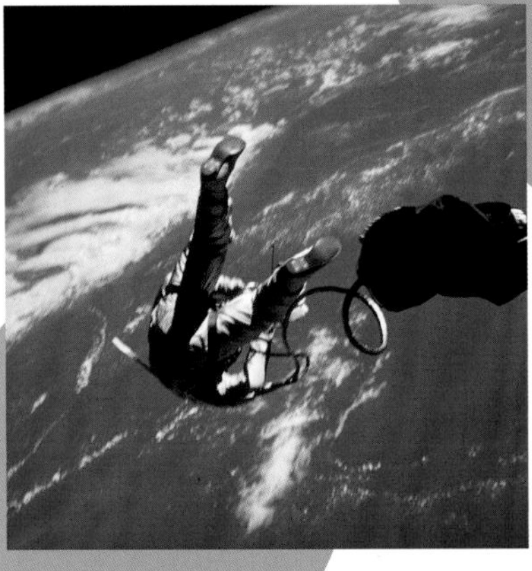

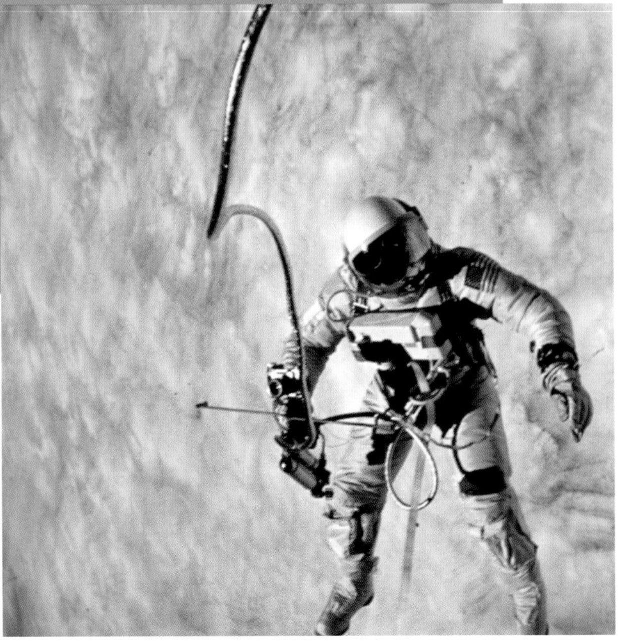

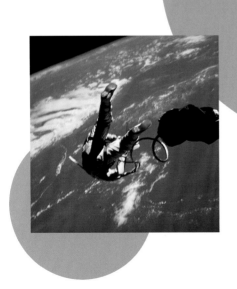

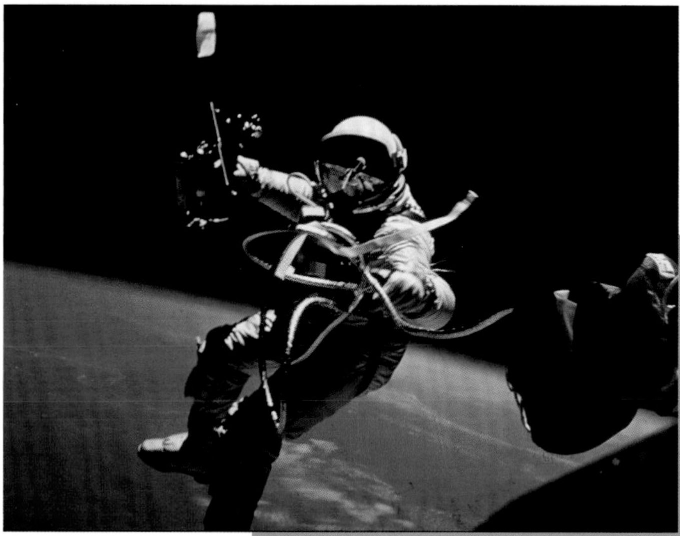

BACK IN THE SHIP, McDIVITT SHOT A SERIES OF PHOTOS THAT, WHEN RETURNED TO EARTH AND DEVELOPED DAYS LATER, WOULD BE CELEBRATED FOR YEARS AS SOME OF THE **MOST BEAUTIFUL** PICTURES EVER TAKEN OF MAN IN SPACE.

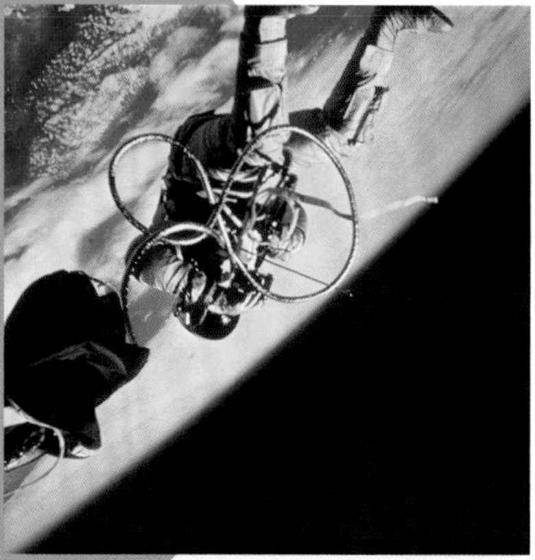

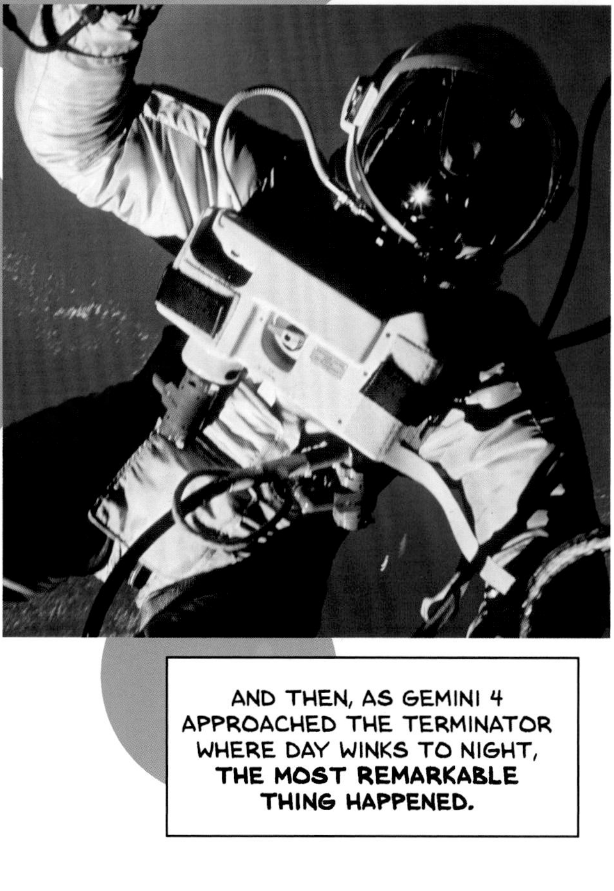

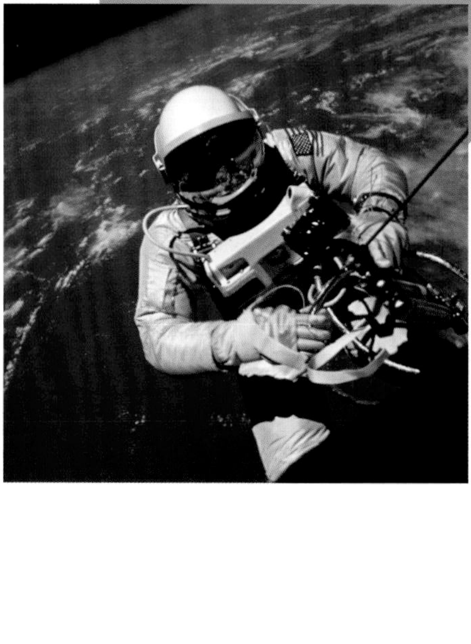

AND THEN, AS GEMINI 4 APPROACHED THE TERMINATOR WHERE DAY WINKS TO NIGHT, **THE MOST REMARKABLE THING HAPPENED.**

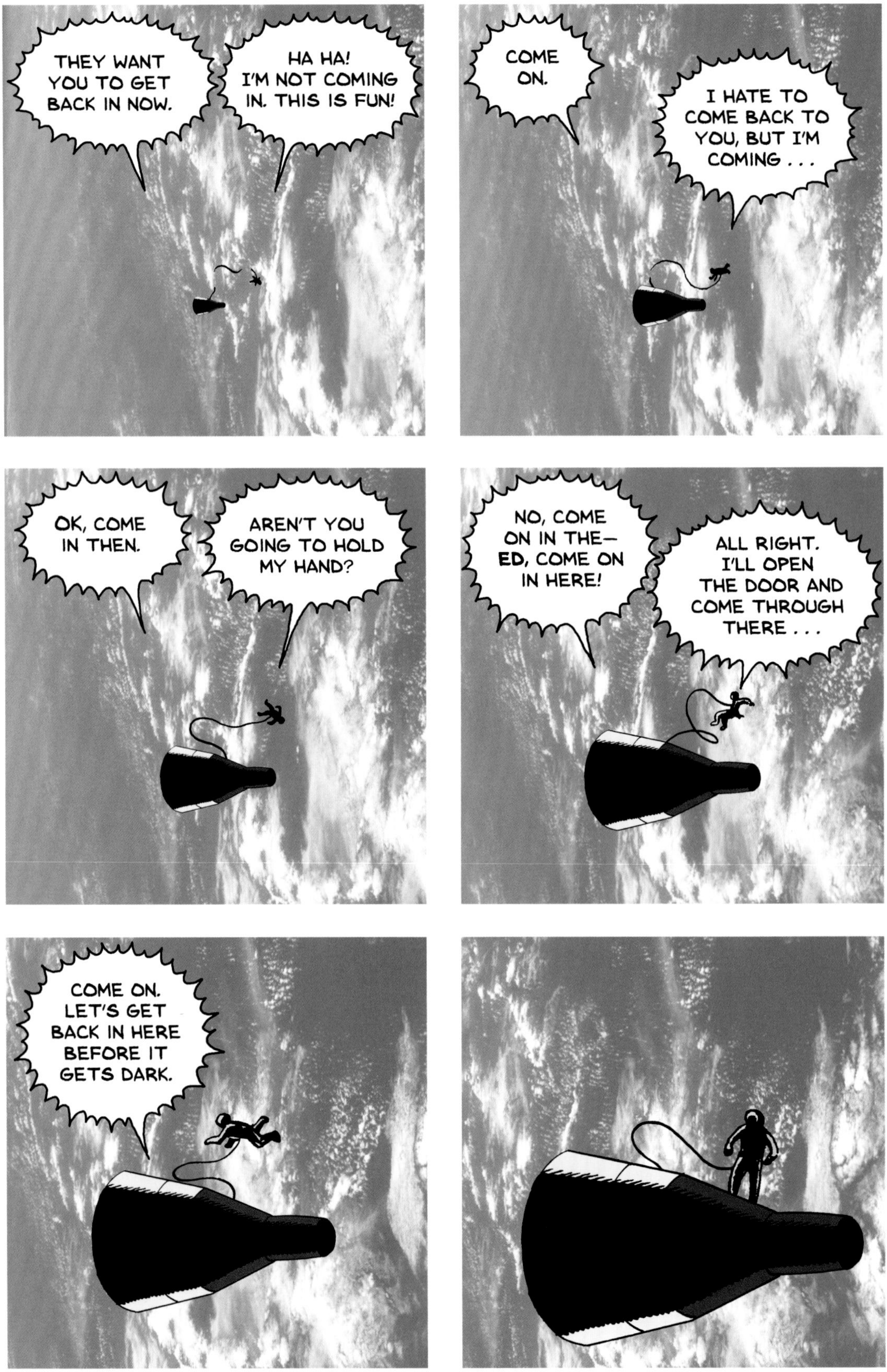
THEY WANT YOU TO GET BACK IN NOW.
HA HA! I'M NOT COMING IN. THIS IS FUN!
COME ON.
I HATE TO COME BACK TO YOU, BUT I'M COMING . . .
OK, COME IN THEN.
AREN'T YOU GOING TO HOLD MY HAND?
NO, COME ON IN THE— **ED**, COME ON IN HERE!
ALL RIGHT. I'LL OPEN THE DOOR AND COME THROUGH THERE . . .
COME ON. LET'S GET BACK IN HERE BEFORE IT GETS DARK.

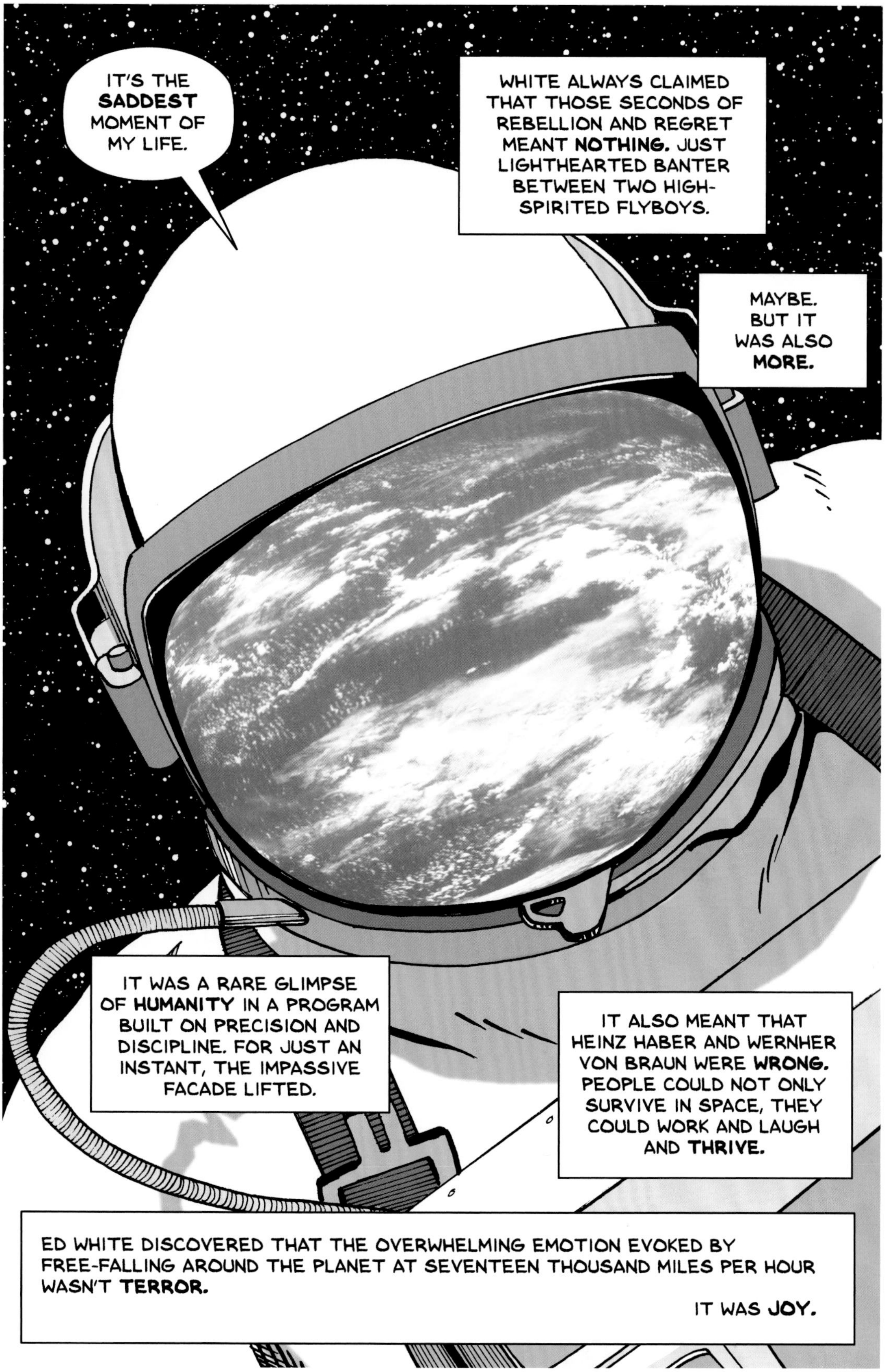

IT'S THE SADDEST MOMENT OF MY LIFE.
WHITE ALWAYS CLAIMED THAT THOSE SECONDS OF REBELLION AND REGRET MEANT NOTHING. JUST LIGHTHEARTED BANTER BETWEEN TWO HIGH-SPIRITED FLYBOYS.
MAYBE. BUT IT WAS ALSO MORE.
IT WAS A RARE GLIMPSE OF HUMANITY IN A PROGRAM BUILT ON PRECISION AND DISCIPLINE. FOR JUST AN INSTANT, THE IMPASSIVE FACADE LIFTED.
IT ALSO MEANT THAT HEINZ HABER AND WERNHER VON BRAUN WERE WRONG. PEOPLE COULD NOT ONLY SURVIVE IN SPACE, THEY COULD WORK AND LAUGH AND THRIVE.
ED WHITE DISCOVERED THAT THE OVERWHELMING EMOTION EVOKED BY FREE-FALLING AROUND THE PLANET AT SEVENTEEN THOUSAND MILES PER HOUR WASN'T TERROR.
IT WAS JOY.

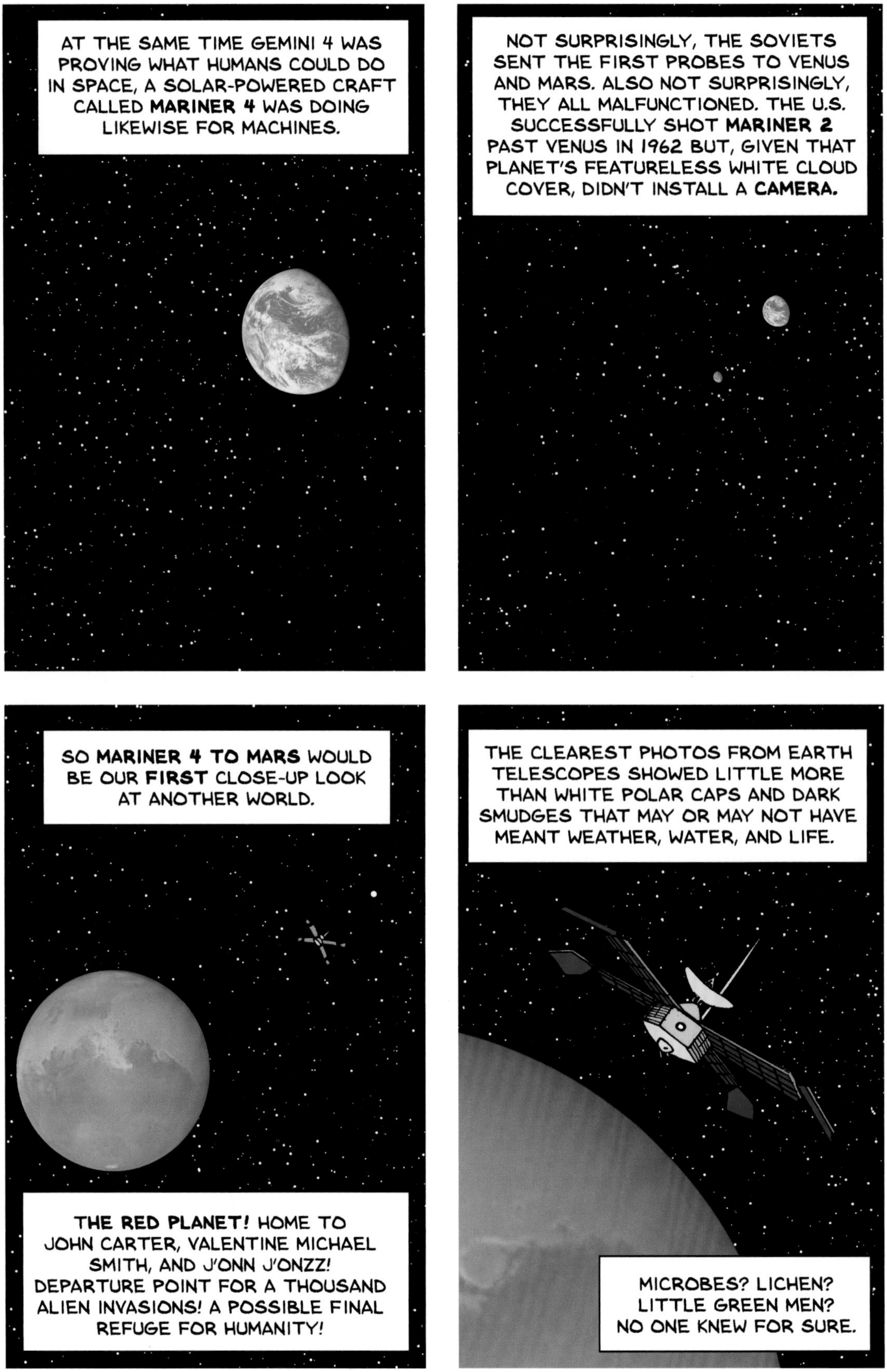
AT THE SAME TIME GEMINI 4 WAS PROVING WHAT HUMANS COULD DO IN SPACE, A SOLAR-POWERED CRAFT CALLED MARINER 4 WAS DOING LIKEWISE FOR MACHINES.
NOT SURPRISINGLY, THE SOVIETS SENT THE FIRST PROBES TO VENUS AND MARS. ALSO NOT SURPRISINGLY, THEY ALL MALFUNCTIONED. THE U.S. SUCCESSFULLY SHOT MARINER 2 PAST VENUS IN 1962 BUT, GIVEN THAT PLANET'S FEATURELESS WHITE CLOUD COVER, DIDN'T INSTALL A CAMERA.
SO MARINER 4 TO MARS WOULD BE OUR FIRST CLOSE-UP LOOK AT ANOTHER WORLD.
THE RED PLANET! HOME TO JOHN CARTER, VALENTINE MICHAEL SMITH, AND J'ONN J'ONZZ! DEPARTURE POINT FOR A THOUSAND ALIEN INVASIONS! A POSSIBLE FINAL REFUGE FOR HUMANITY!
THE CLEAREST PHOTOS FROM EARTH TELESCOPES SHOWED LITTLE MORE THAN WHITE POLAR CAPS AND DARK SMUDGES THAT MAY OR MAY NOT HAVE MEANT WEATHER, WATER, AND LIFE.
MICROBES? LICHEN? LITTLE GREEN MEN? NO ONE KNEW FOR SURE.

IN 1877, ITALIAN ASTRONOMER GIOVANNI SCHIAPARELLI CHARTED MARTIAN FEATURES HE CALLED **"CANALI"**—IN ENGLISH, "CHANNELS." SOME, INCLUDING AMERICAN ASTRONOMER PERCIVAL LOWELL, TOOK THE WORD TO MEAN **"CANALS,"** AND DEDUCED A HEROIC FEAT OF PLANETARY ENGINEERING BY AN ANCIENT CIVILIZATION. LOWELL AND OTHERS SOON MAPPED HUNDREDS OF ELABORATELY LACED CANALS KNOTTED WITH ROUND OASES THAT FLOURISHED WHERE THE WATERWAYS MET.

IN HIS 1908 BOOK "MARS AS THE ABODE OF LIFE," LOWELL WROTE: "PECULIARLY IMPRESSIVE IS THE THOUGHT THAT LIFE ON ANOTHER WORLD SHOULD THUS HAVE MADE ITS PRESENCE KNOWN BY ITS **EXERCISE OF MIND.**

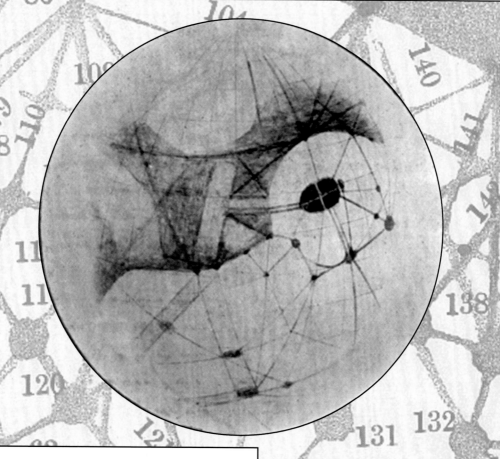

"NOT ONLY DO THE OBSERVATIONS SCANNED LEAD US TO THE CONCLUSION THAT MARS AT THIS MOMENT IS **INHABITED,** BUT THEY LAND US AT THE FURTHER ONE THAT THESE DENIZENS ARE OF AN ORDER WHOSE ACQUAINTANCE WAS WORTH THE MAKING . . . THEIR PRESENCE CERTAINLY **OUSTS US** FROM ANY UNIQUE OR SELF-CENTERED POSITION IN THE SOLAR SYSTEM."

ORSON WELLES'S INFAMOUS 1938 "WAR OF THE WORLDS" RADIO PROGRAM HAD THE POWER TO PANIC LISTENERS BECAUSE THE BEST SCIENCE OF THE DAY MADE ITS TALE OF MARTIAN INVASION ENTIRELY TOO **PLAUSIBLE.**

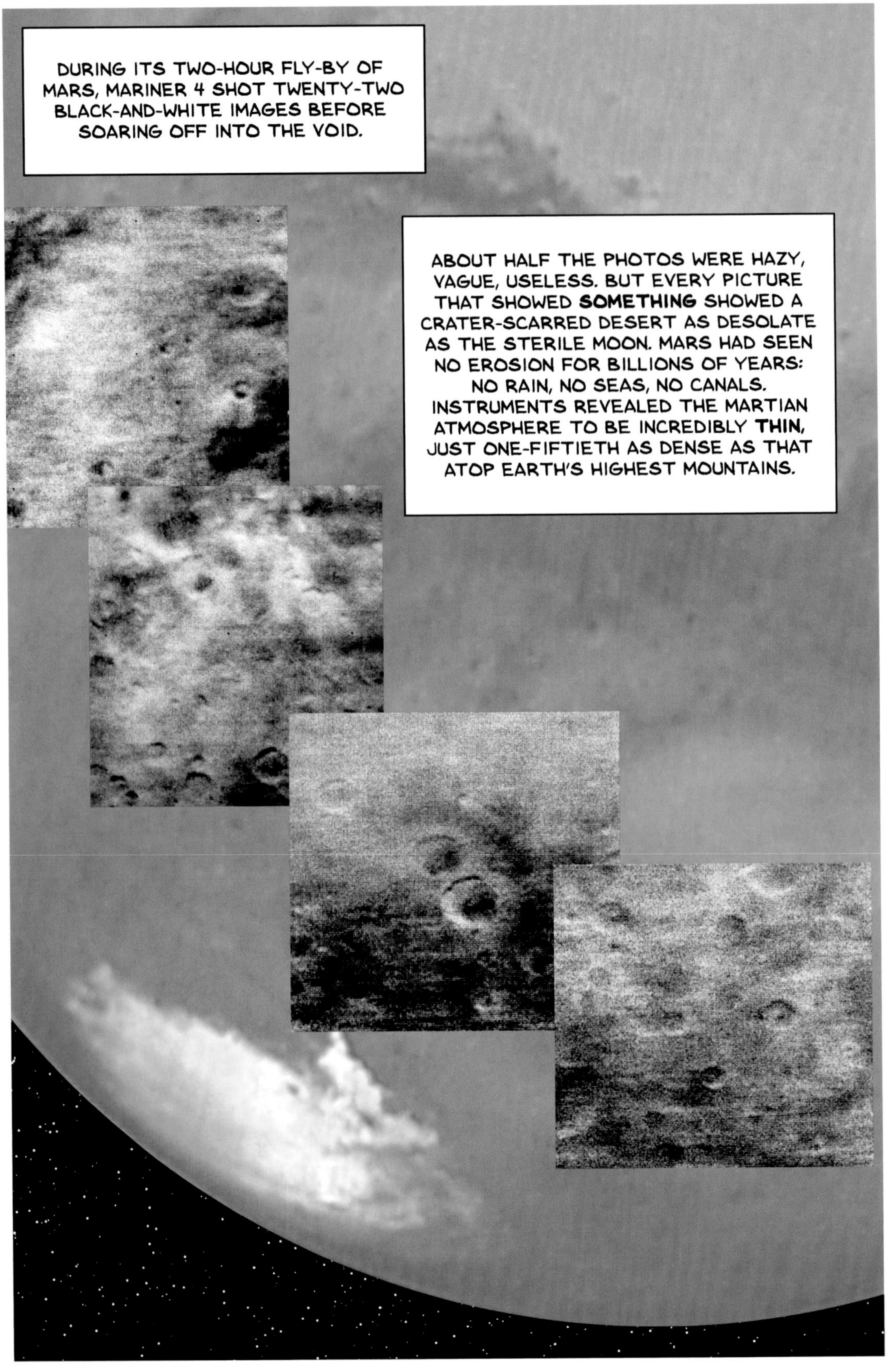
DURING ITS TWO-HOUR FLY-BY OF MARS, MARINER 4 SHOT TWENTY-TWO BLACK-AND-WHITE IMAGES BEFORE SOARING OFF INTO THE VOID.
ABOUT HALF THE PHOTOS WERE HAZY, VAGUE, USELESS. BUT EVERY PICTURE THAT SHOWED **SOMETHING** SHOWED A CRATER-SCARRED DESERT AS DESOLATE AS THE STERILE MOON. MARS HAD SEEN NO EROSION FOR BILLIONS OF YEARS: NO RAIN, NO SEAS, NO CANALS. INSTRUMENTS REVEALED THE MARTIAN ATMOSPHERE TO BE INCREDIBLY **THIN**, JUST ONE-FIFTIETH AS DENSE AS THAT ATOP EARTH'S HIGHEST MOUNTAINS.

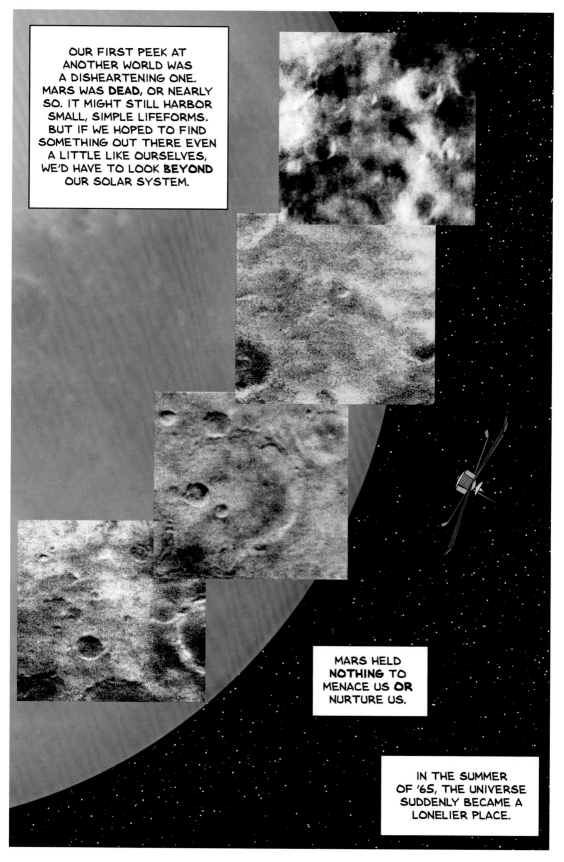

OUR FIRST PEEK AT ANOTHER WORLD WAS A DISHEARTENING ONE. MARS WAS **DEAD**, OR NEARLY SO. IT MIGHT STILL HARBOR SMALL, SIMPLE LIFEFORMS. BUT IF WE HOPED TO FIND SOMETHING OUT THERE EVEN A LITTLE LIKE OURSELVES, WE'D HAVE TO LOOK **BEYOND** OUR SOLAR SYSTEM.

MARS HELD **NOTHING TO** MENACE US **OR** NURTURE US.

IN THE SUMMER OF '65, THE UNIVERSE SUDDENLY BECAME A LONELIER PLACE.

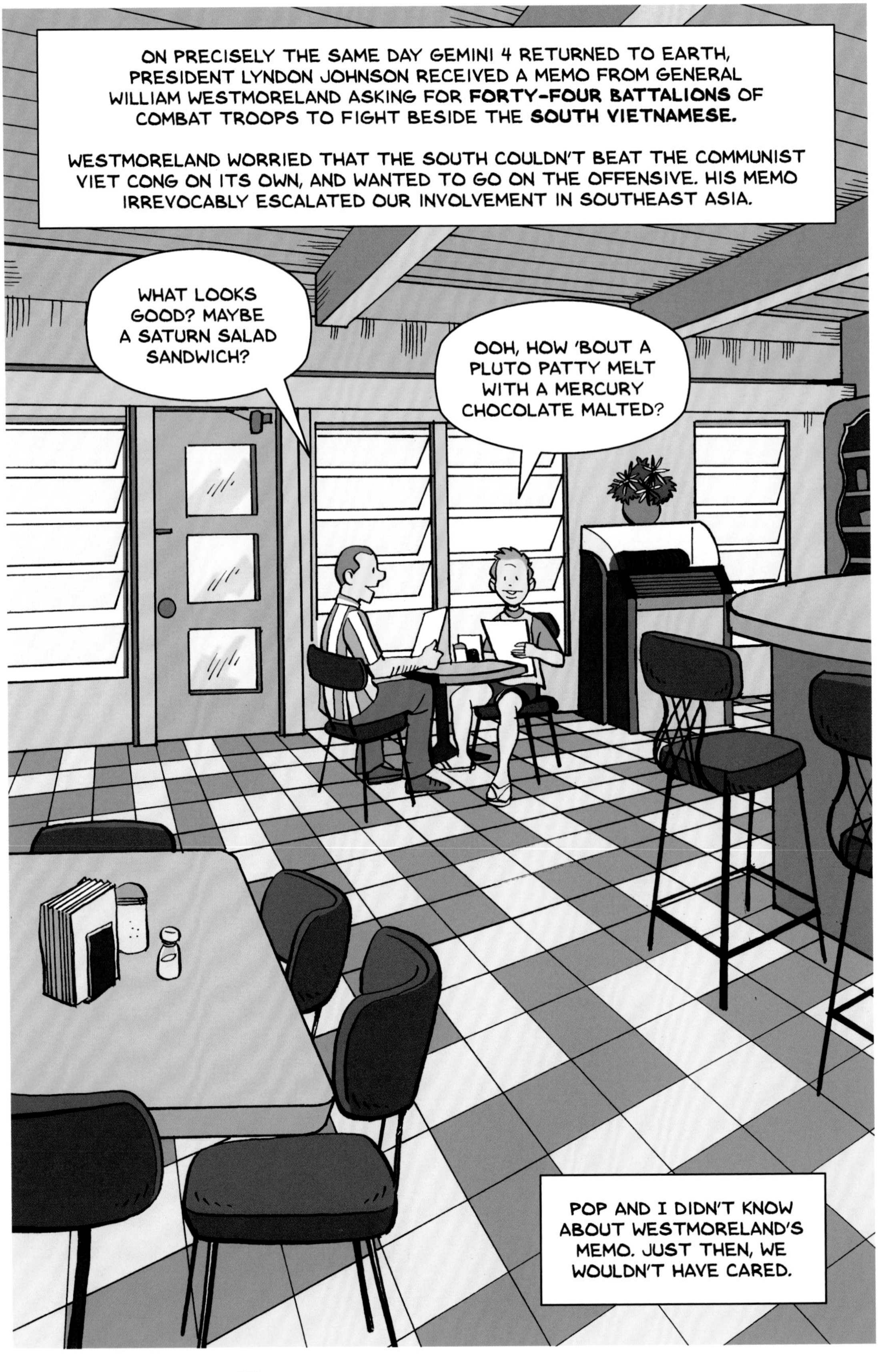
ON PRECISELY THE SAME DAY GEMINI 4 RETURNED TO EARTH, PRESIDENT LYNDON JOHNSON RECEIVED A MEMO FROM GENERAL WILLIAM WESTMORELAND ASKING FOR **FORTY-FOUR BATTALIONS** OF COMBAT TROOPS TO FIGHT BESIDE THE **SOUTH VIETNAMESE.**
WESTMORELAND WORRIED THAT THE SOUTH COULDN'T BEAT THE COMMUNIST VIET CONG ON ITS OWN, AND WANTED TO GO ON THE OFFENSIVE. HIS MEMO IRREVOCABLY ESCALATED OUR INVOLVEMENT IN SOUTHEAST ASIA.
WHAT LOOKS GOOD? MAYBE A SATURN SALAD SANDWICH?
OOH, HOW 'BOUT A PLUTO PATTY MELT WITH A MERCURY CHOCOLATE MALTED?
POP AND I DIDN'T KNOW ABOUT WESTMORELAND'S MEMO. JUST THEN, WE WOULDN'T HAVE CARED.

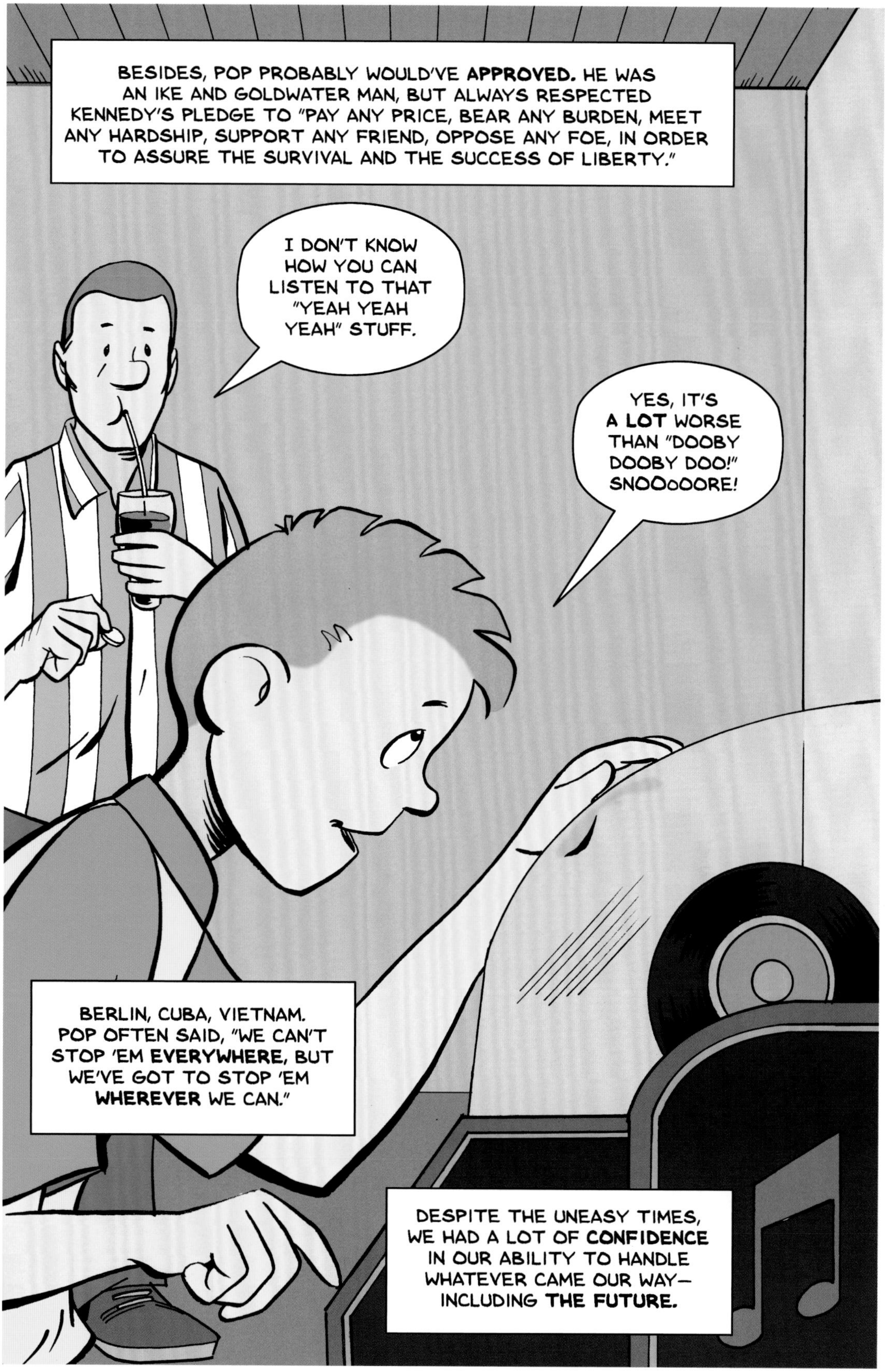
BESIDES, POP PROBABLY WOULD'VE **APPROVED.** HE WAS AN IKE AND GOLDWATER MAN, BUT ALWAYS RESPECTED KENNEDY'S PLEDGE TO "PAY ANY PRICE, BEAR ANY BURDEN, MEET ANY HARDSHIP, SUPPORT ANY FRIEND, OPPOSE ANY FOE, IN ORDER TO ASSURE THE SURVIVAL AND THE SUCCESS OF LIBERTY."
I DON'T KNOW HOW YOU CAN LISTEN TO THAT "YEAH YEAH YEAH" STUFF.
YES, IT'S A **LOT** WORSE THAN "DOOBY DOOBY DOO!" SNOOoOORE!
BERLIN, CUBA, VIETNAM. POP OFTEN SAID, "WE CAN'T STOP 'EM **EVERYWHERE,** BUT WE'VE GOT TO STOP 'EM **WHEREVER** WE CAN."
DESPITE THE UNEASY TIMES, WE HAD A LOT OF **CONFIDENCE** IN OUR ABILITY TO HANDLE WHATEVER CAME OUR WAY— INCLUDING **THE FUTURE.**

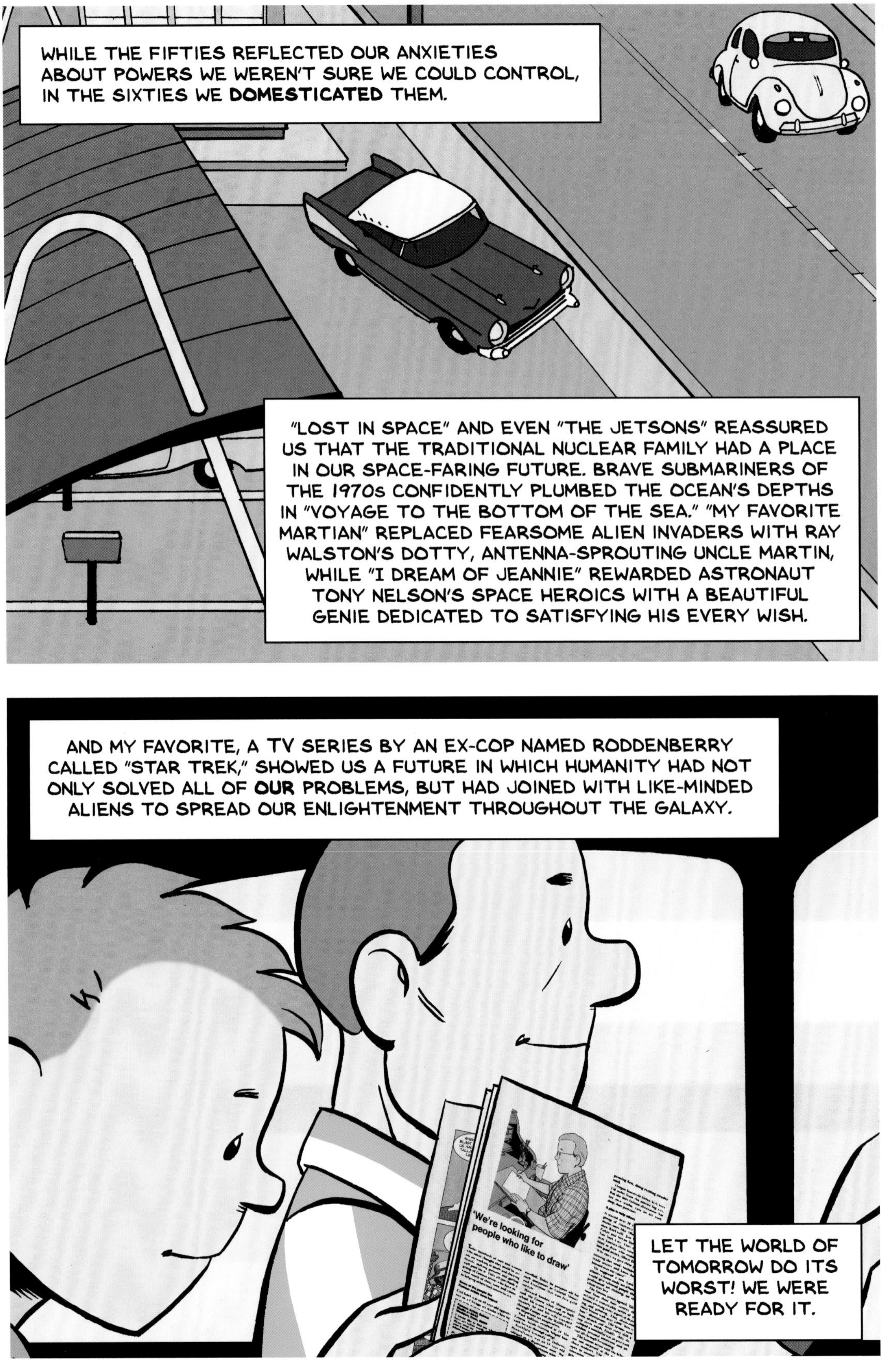
WHILE THE FIFTIES REFLECTED OUR ANXIETIES ABOUT POWERS WE WEREN'T SURE WE COULD CONTROL, IN THE SIXTIES WE **DOMESTICATED** THEM.
"LOST IN SPACE" AND EVEN "THE JETSONS" REASSURED US THAT THE TRADITIONAL NUCLEAR FAMILY HAD A PLACE IN OUR SPACE-FARING FUTURE. BRAVE SUBMARINERS OF THE 1970s CONFIDENTLY PLUMBED THE OCEAN'S DEPTHS IN "VOYAGE TO THE BOTTOM OF THE SEA." "MY FAVORITE MARTIAN" REPLACED FEARSOME ALIEN INVADERS WITH RAY WALSTON'S DOTTY, ANTENNA-SPROUTING UNCLE MARTIN, WHILE "I DREAM OF JEANNIE" REWARDED ASTRONAUT TONY NELSON'S SPACE HEROICS WITH A BEAUTIFUL GENIE DEDICATED TO SATISFYING HIS EVERY WISH.
AND MY FAVORITE, A TV SERIES BY AN EX-COP NAMED RODDENBERRY CALLED "STAR TREK," SHOWED US A FUTURE IN WHICH HUMANITY HAD NOT ONLY SOLVED ALL OF **OUR** PROBLEMS, BUT HAD JOINED WITH LIKE-MINDED ALIENS TO SPREAD OUR ENLIGHTENMENT THROUGHOUT THE GALAXY.
'We're looking for people who like to draw'
LET THE WORLD OF TOMORROW DO ITS WORST! WE WERE READY FOR IT.

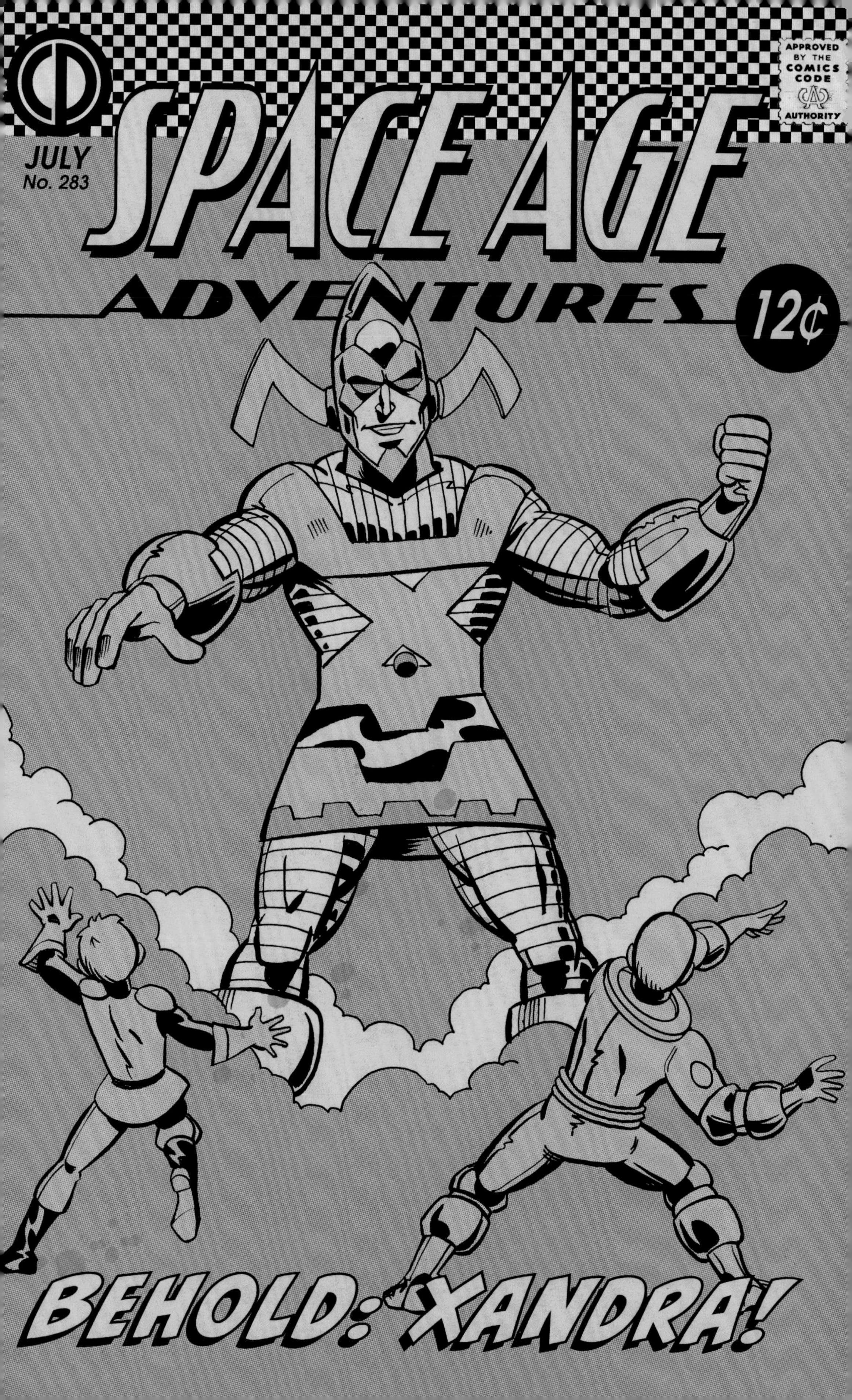
APPROVED BY THE COMICS CODE AUTHORITY
SPACE AGE ADVENTURES
JULY
No. 283
12¢
BEHOLD: XANDRA!

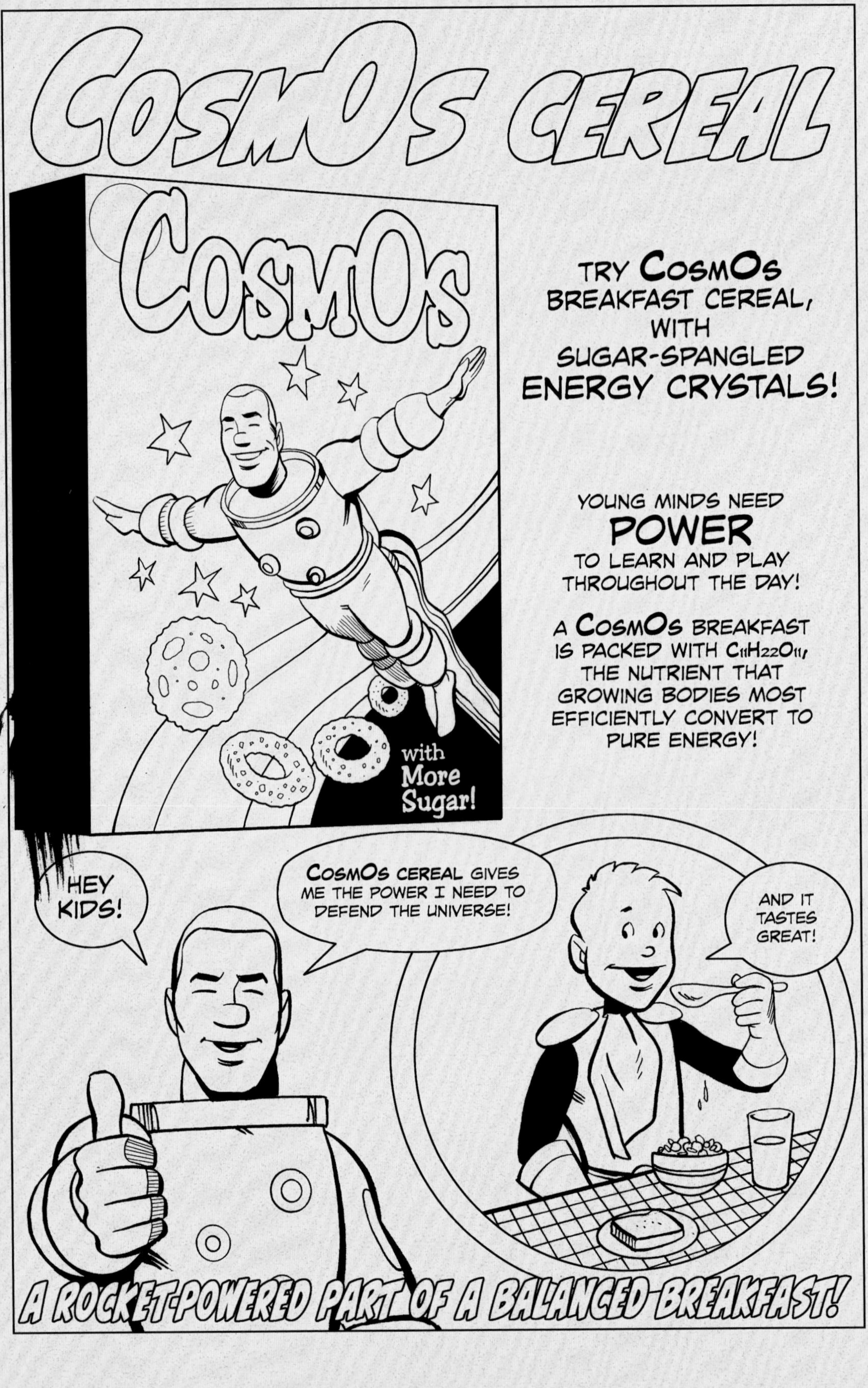
COSMOS CEREAL
COSMOS
with More Sugar!
TRY COSMOS BREAKFAST CEREAL, WITH SUGAR-SPANGLED ENERGY CRYSTALS!
YOUNG MINDS NEED POWER TO LEARN AND PLAY THROUGHOUT THE DAY!
A COSMOS BREAKFAST IS PACKED WITH $C_{11}H_{22}O_{11}$, THE NUTRIENT THAT GROWING BODIES MOST EFFICIENTLY CONVERT TO PURE ENERGY!
HEY KIDS!
COSMOS CEREAL GIVES ME THE POWER I NEED TO DEFEND THE UNIVERSE!
AND IT TASTES GREAT!
A ROCKET-POWERED PART OF A BALANCED BREAKFAST!

SPACE AGE ADVENTURES, No. 283, July 1965. Published monthly by CAPITAL PERIODICALS, INC., 115 W. 18th St., New York 11, N.Y. SECOND CLASS POSTAGE PAID AT NEW YORK, N.Y. under the act of March 3, 1879. Yearly subscription in the U.S., $1.40 including postage. Foreign, $2.80 in American funds. Canada, $1.70 in American funds. Copyright Capital Periodicals, Inc., 1965. All rights reserved under International and Pan-American Copyright Conventions. The stories, characters, and incidents mentioned in this magazine are entirely fictional. No actual persons, living or dead, are intended or should be inferred.

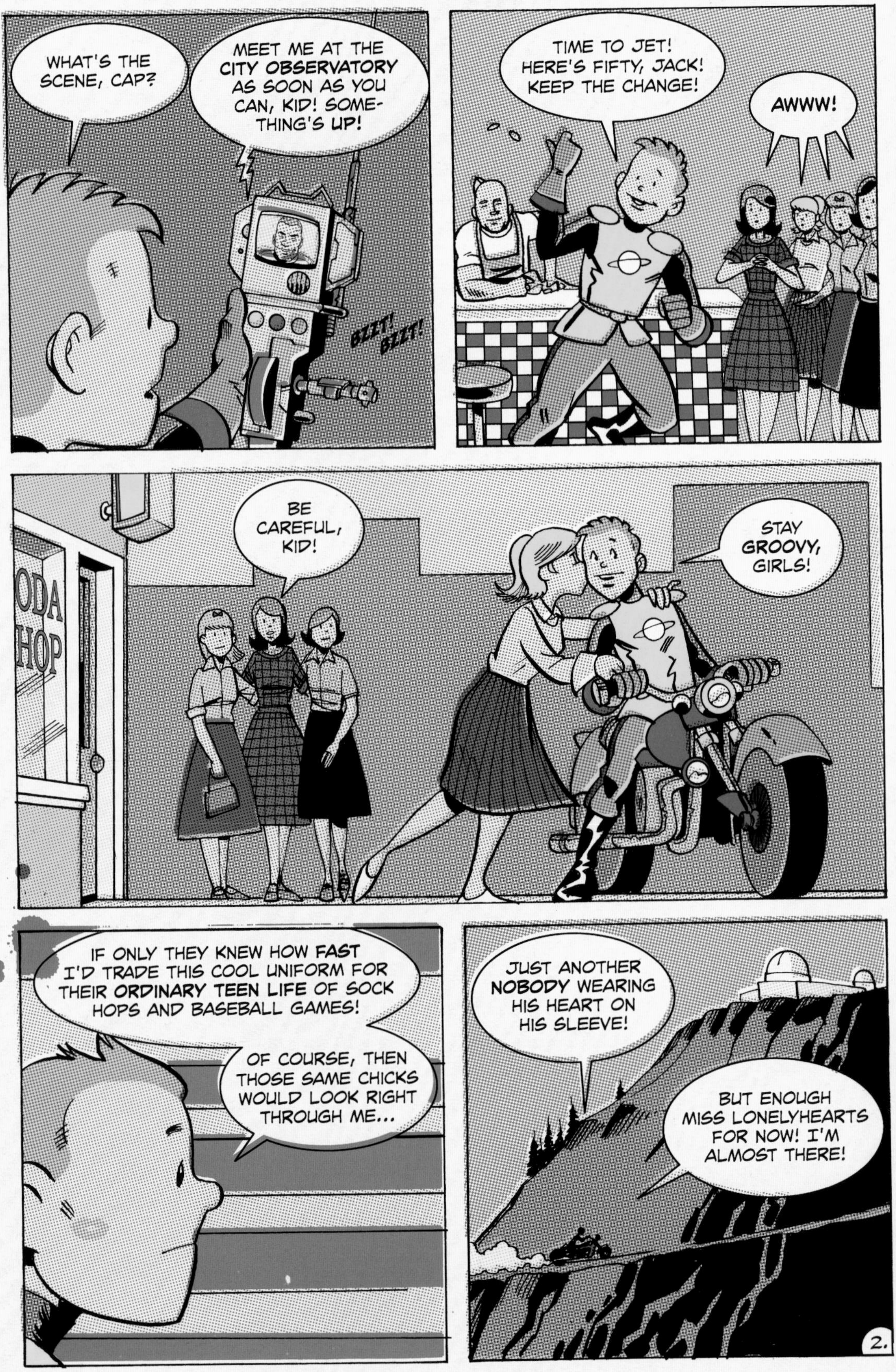
WHAT'S THE SCENE, CAP?
MEET ME AT THE CITY OBSERVATORY AS SOON AS YOU CAN, KID! SOMETHING'S UP!
BZZT! BZZT!
TIME TO JET! HERE'S FIFTY, JACK! KEEP THE CHANGE!
AWWW!
ODA
HOP
BE CAREFUL, KID!
STAY GROOVY, GIRLS!
IF ONLY THEY KNEW HOW FAST I'D TRADE THIS COOL UNIFORM FOR THEIR ORDINARY TEEN LIFE OF SOCK HOPS AND BASEBALL GAMES!
OF COURSE, THEN THOSE SAME CHICKS WOULD LOOK RIGHT THROUGH ME...
JUST ANOTHER NOBODY WEARING HIS HEART ON HIS SLEEVE!
BUT ENOUGH MISS LONELYHEARTS FOR NOW! I'M ALMOST THERE!

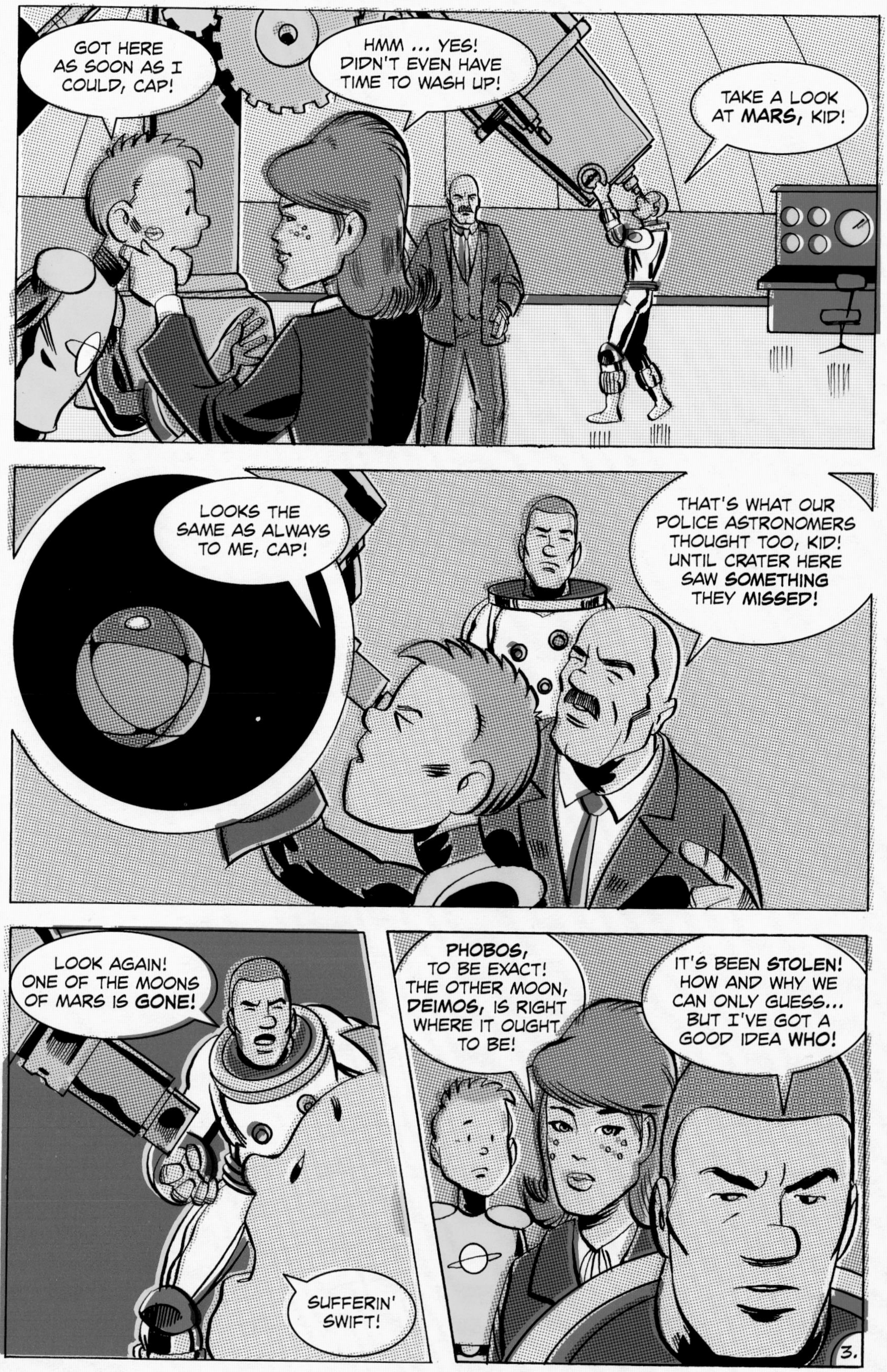
GOT HERE AS SOON AS I COULD, CAP!
HMM ... YES! DIDN'T EVEN HAVE TIME TO WASH UP!
TAKE A LOOK AT MARS, KID!
LOOKS THE SAME AS ALWAYS TO ME, CAP!
THAT'S WHAT OUR POLICE ASTRONOMERS THOUGHT TOO, KID! UNTIL CRATER HERE SAW SOMETHING THEY MISSED!
LOOK AGAIN! ONE OF THE MOONS OF MARS IS GONE!
SUFFERIN' SWIFT!
PHOBOS, TO BE EXACT! THE OTHER MOON, DEIMOS, IS RIGHT WHERE IT OUGHT TO BE!
IT'S BEEN STOLEN! HOW AND WHY WE CAN ONLY GUESS... BUT I'VE GOT A GOOD IDEA WHO!

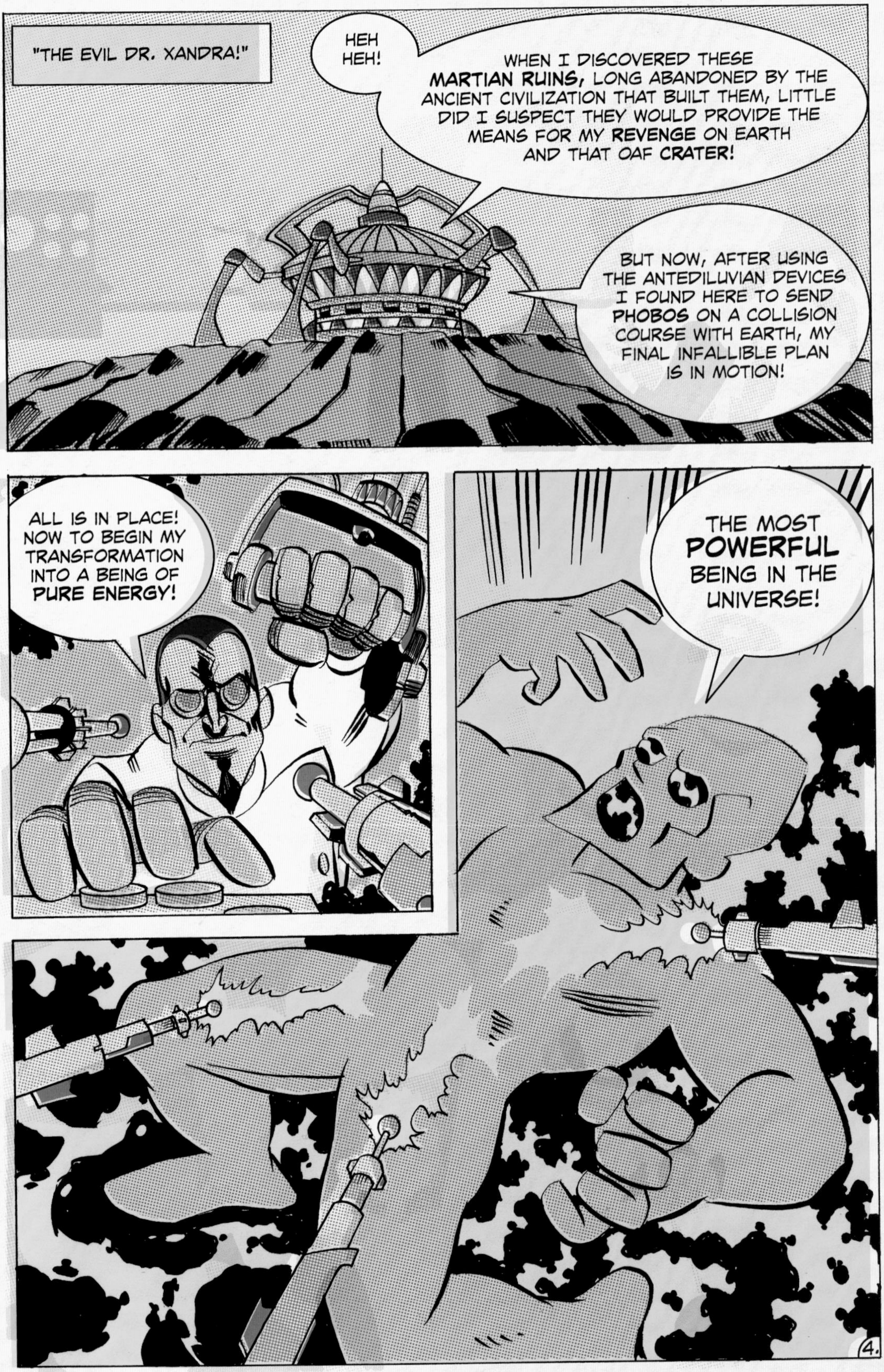

"THE EVIL DR. XANDRA!"
HEH HEH!
WHEN I DISCOVERED THESE MARTIAN RUINS, LONG ABANDONED BY THE ANCIENT CIVILIZATION THAT BUILT THEM, LITTLE DID I SUSPECT THEY WOULD PROVIDE THE MEANS FOR MY REVENGE ON EARTH AND THAT OAF CRATER!
BUT NOW, AFTER USING THE ANTEDILUVIAN DEVICES I FOUND HERE TO SEND PHOBOS ON A COLLISION COURSE WITH EARTH, MY FINAL INFALLIBLE PLAN IS IN MOTION!
ALL IS IN PLACE! NOW TO BEGIN MY TRANSFORMATION INTO A BEING OF PURE ENERGY!
THE MOST POWERFUL BEING IN THE UNIVERSE!
4.

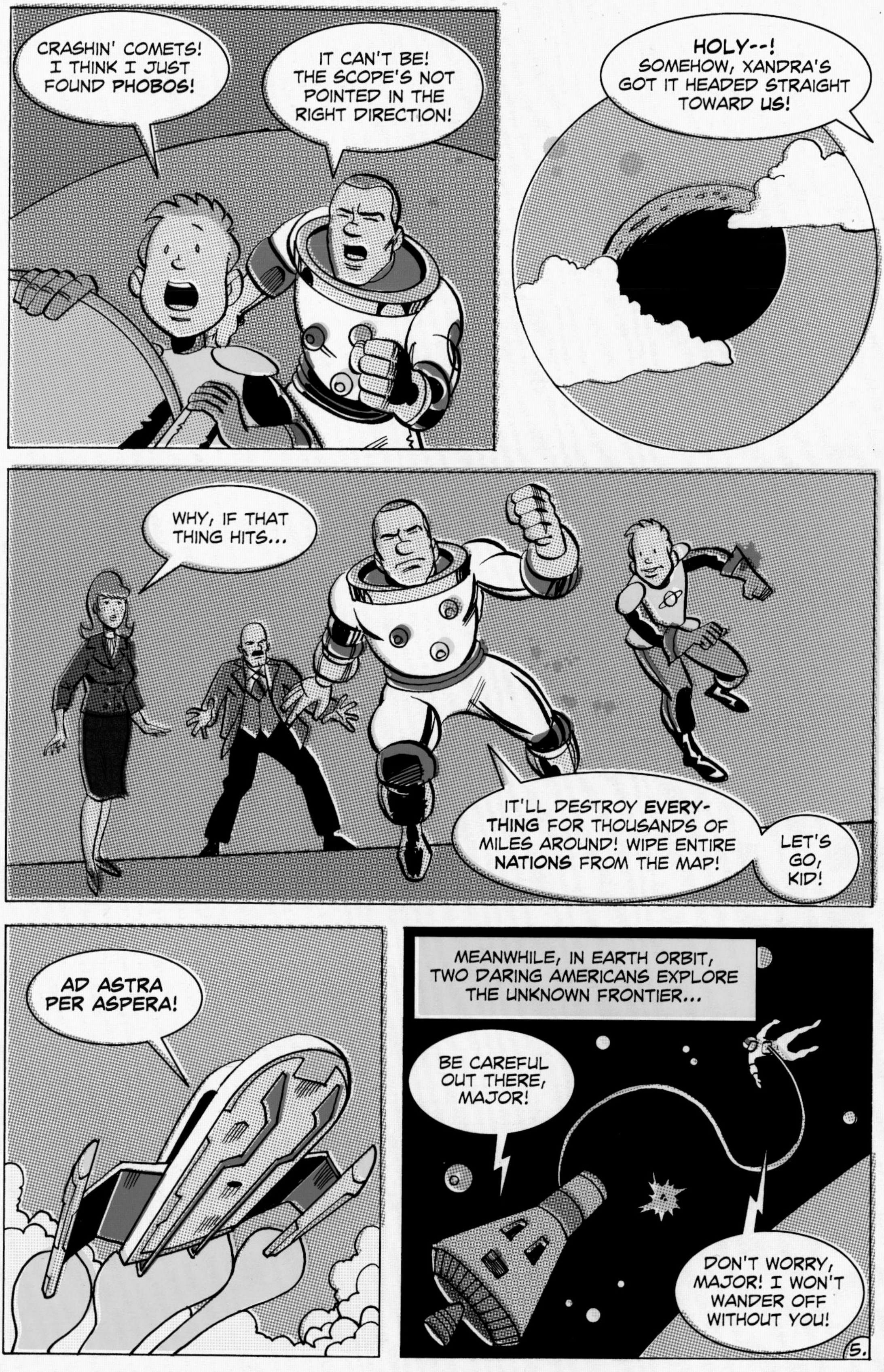
CRASHIN' COMETS! I THINK I JUST FOUND PHOBOS!
IT CAN'T BE! THE SCOPE'S NOT POINTED IN THE RIGHT DIRECTION!
HOLY--! SOMEHOW, XANDRA'S GOT IT HEADED STRAIGHT TOWARD US!
WHY, IF THAT THING HITS...
IT'LL DESTROY EVERY-THING FOR THOUSANDS OF MILES AROUND! WIPE ENTIRE NATIONS FROM THE MAP!
LET'S GO, KID!
AD ASTRA PER ASPERA!
MEANWHILE, IN EARTH ORBIT, TWO DARING AMERICANS EXPLORE THE UNKNOWN FRONTIER...
BE CAREFUL OUT THERE, MAJOR!
DON'T WORRY, MAJOR! I WON'T WANDER OFF WITHOUT YOU!
5.

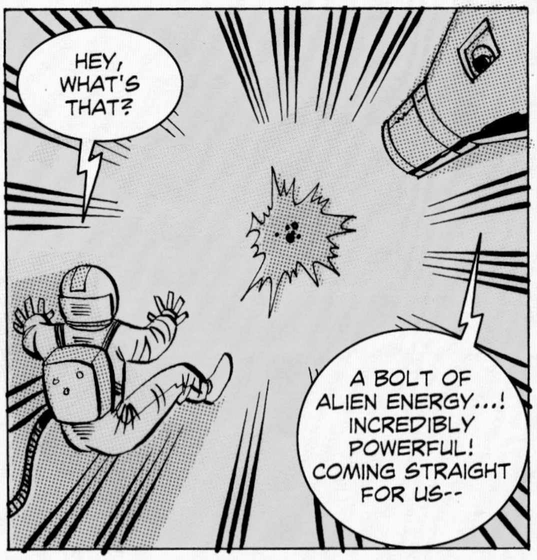
HEY, WHAT'S THAT?
A BOLT OF ALIEN ENERGY...! INCREDIBLY POWERFUL! COMING STRAIGHT FOR US--

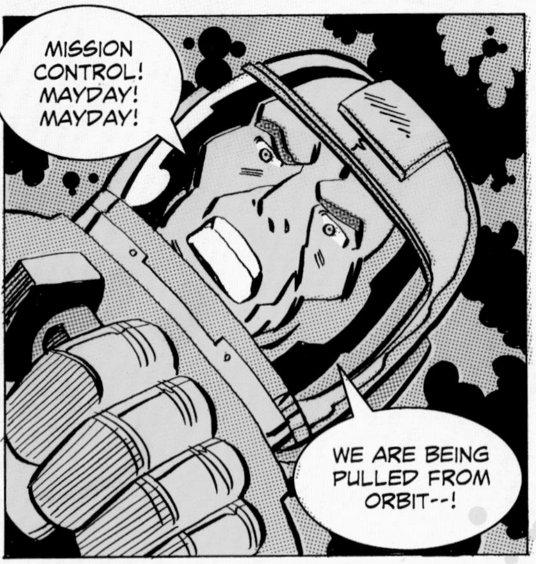
MISSION CONTROL! MAYDAY! MAYDAY!
WE ARE BEING PULLED FROM ORBIT--!

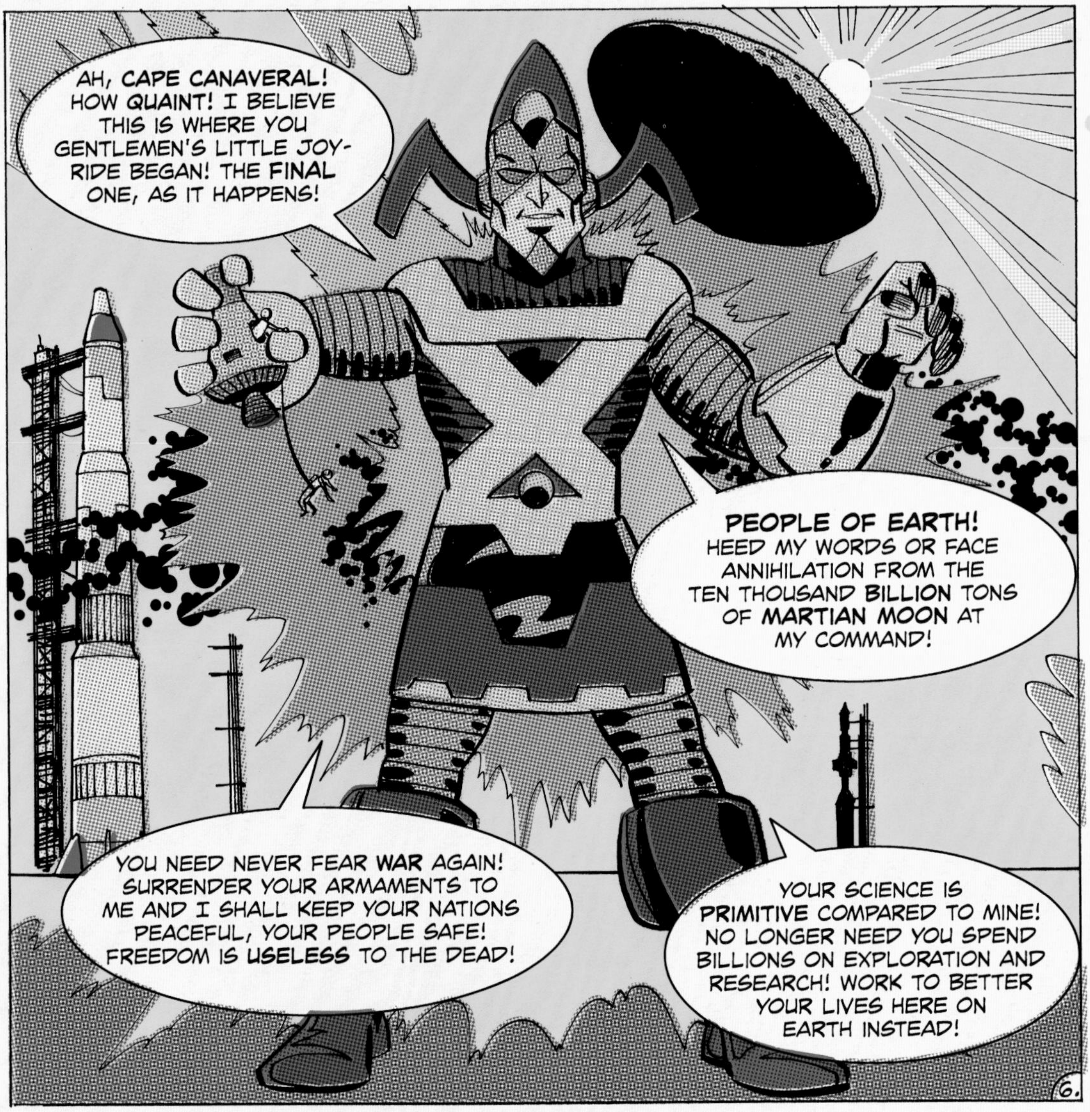
AH, CAPE CANAVERAL! HOW QUAINT! I BELIEVE THIS IS WHERE YOU GENTLEMEN'S LITTLE JOY-RIDE BEGAN! THE FINAL ONE, AS IT HAPPENS!
PEOPLE OF EARTH! HEED MY WORDS OR FACE ANNIHILATION FROM THE TEN THOUSAND BILLION TONS OF MARTIAN MOON AT MY COMMAND!
YOU NEED NEVER FEAR WAR AGAIN! SURRENDER YOUR ARMAMENTS TO ME AND I SHALL KEEP YOUR NATIONS PEACEFUL, YOUR PEOPLE SAFE! FREEDOM IS USELESS TO THE DEAD!
YOUR SCIENCE IS PRIMITIVE COMPARED TO MINE! NO LONGER NEED YOU SPEND BILLIONS ON EXPLORATION AND RESEARCH! WORK TO BETTER YOUR LIVES HERE ON EARTH INSTEAD!
6.

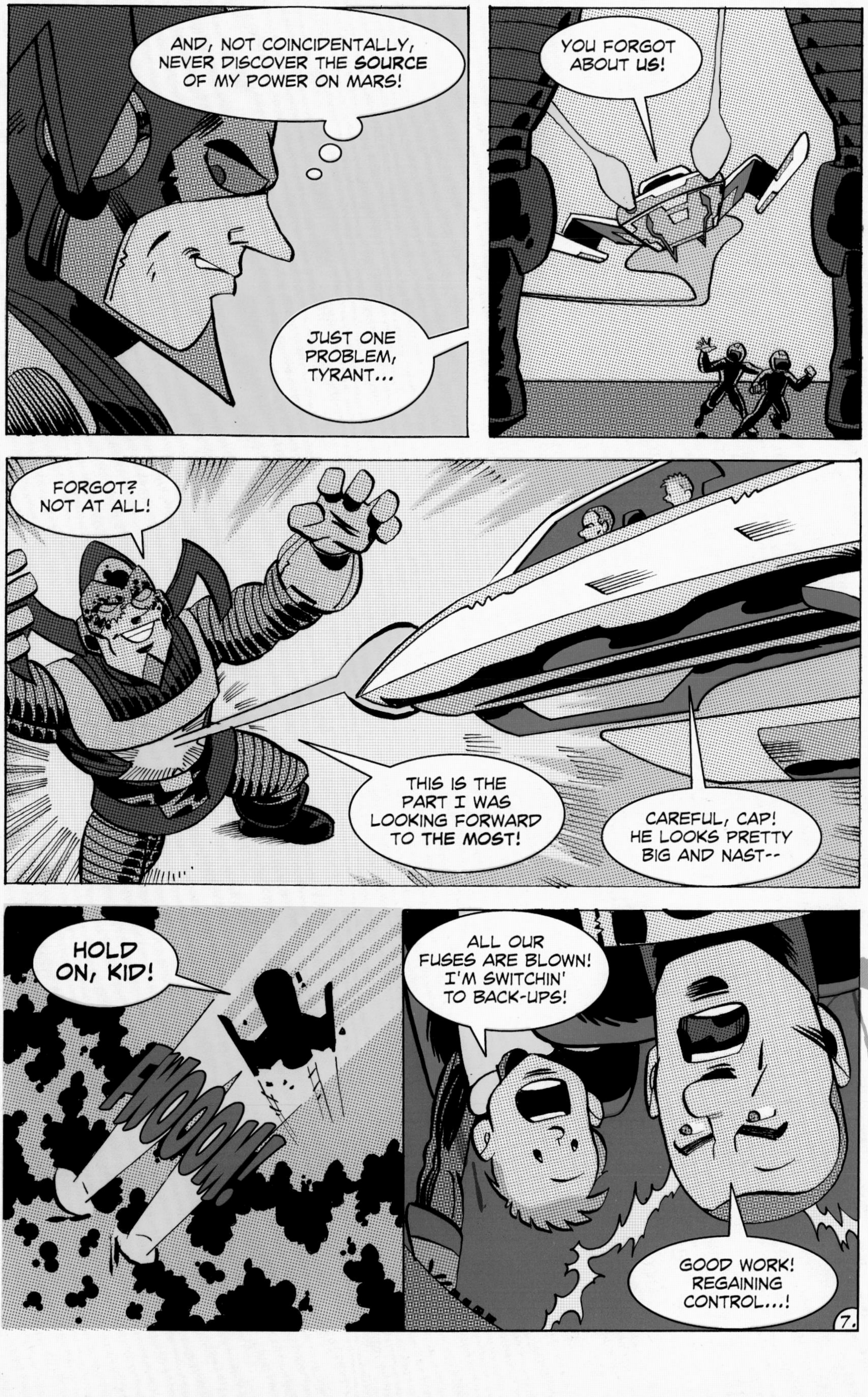
AND, NOT COINCIDENTALLY, NEVER DISCOVER THE SOURCE OF MY POWER ON MARS!
JUST ONE PROBLEM, TYRANT...
YOU FORGOT ABOUT US!
FORGOT? NOT AT ALL!
THIS IS THE PART I WAS LOOKING FORWARD TO THE MOST!
CAREFUL, CAP! HE LOOKS PRETTY BIG AND NAST--
HOLD ON, KID!
FWOOM!
ALL OUR FUSES ARE BLOWN! I'M SWITCHIN' TO BACK-UPS!
GOOD WORK! REGAINING CONTROL...!
7.

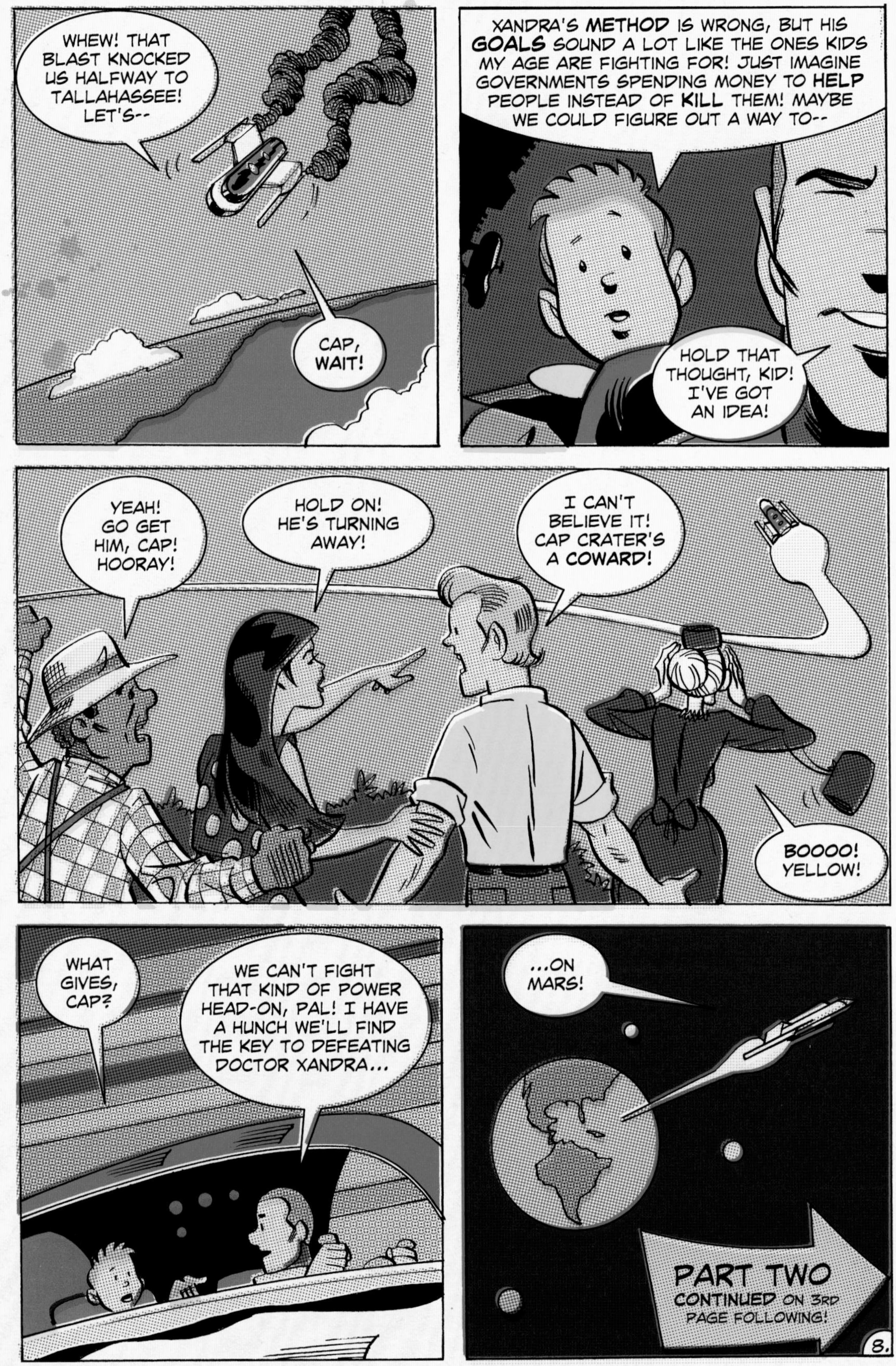
WHEW! THAT BLAST KNOCKED US HALFWAY TO TALLAHASSEE! LET'S--
CAP, WAIT!
XANDRA'S METHOD IS WRONG, BUT HIS GOALS SOUND A LOT LIKE THE ONES KIDS MY AGE ARE FIGHTING FOR! JUST IMAGINE GOVERNMENTS SPENDING MONEY TO HELP PEOPLE INSTEAD OF KILL THEM! MAYBE WE COULD FIGURE OUT A WAY TO--
HOLD THAT THOUGHT, KID! I'VE GOT AN IDEA!
YEAH! GO GET HIM, CAP! HOORAY!
HOLD ON! HE'S TURNING AWAY!
I CAN'T BELIEVE IT! CAP CRATER'S A COWARD!
BOOOO! YELLOW!
WHAT GIVES, CAP?
WE CAN'T FIGHT THAT KIND OF POWER HEAD-ON, PAL! I HAVE A HUNCH WE'LL FIND THE KEY TO DEFEATING DOCTOR XANDRA...
...ON MARS!
PART TWO CONTINUED ON 3RD PAGE FOLLOWING!
8.

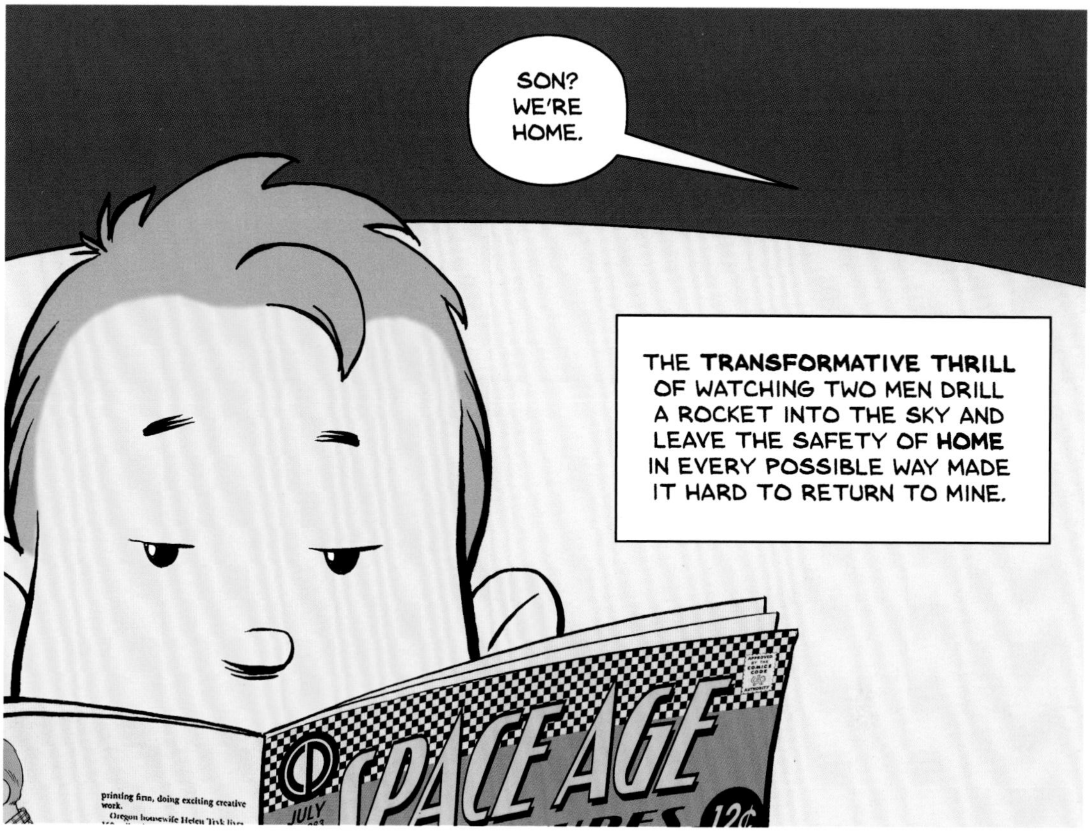
SON? WE'RE HOME.
THE **TRANSFORMATIVE THRILL** OF WATCHING TWO MEN DRILL A ROCKET INTO THE SKY AND LEAVE THE SAFETY OF **HOME** IN EVERY POSSIBLE WAY MADE IT HARD TO RETURN TO MINE.
SPACE AGE
JULY
12¢
printing firm, doing exciting creative work.

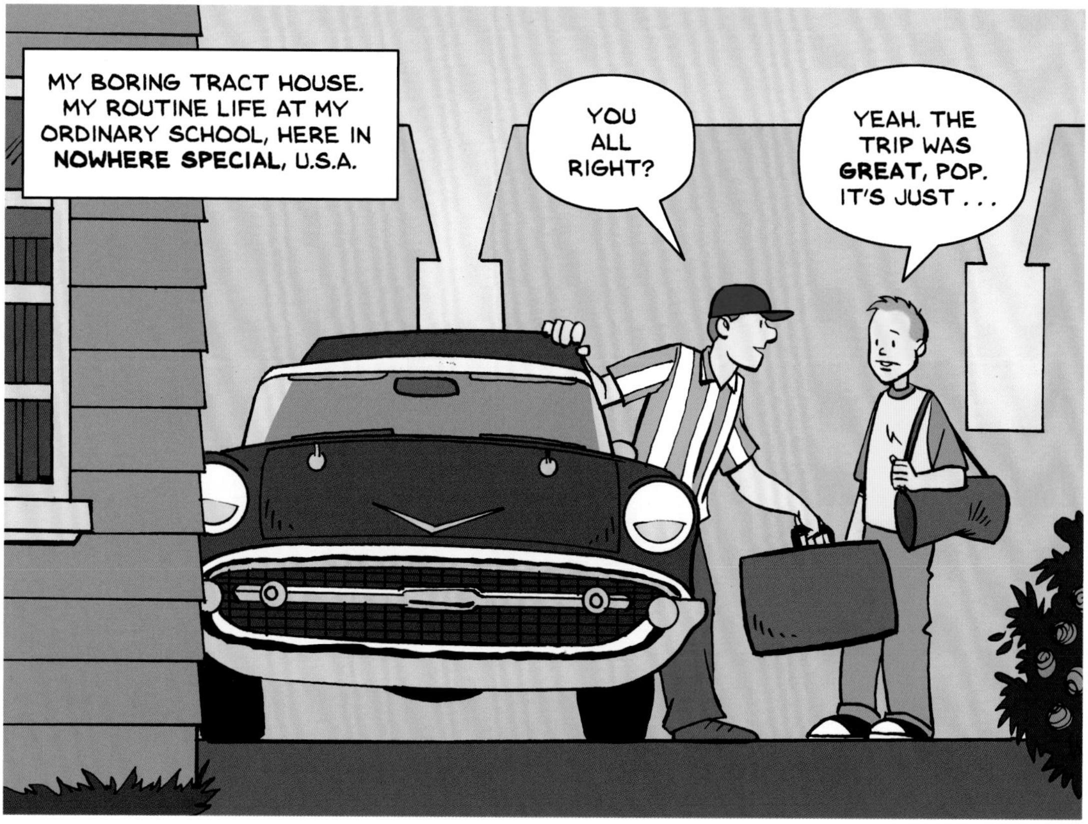
MY BORING TRACT HOUSE. MY ROUTINE LIFE AT MY ORDINARY SCHOOL, HERE IN **NOWHERE SPECIAL**, U.S.A.
YOU ALL RIGHT?
YEAH. THE TRIP WAS **GREAT**, POP. IT'S JUST . . .

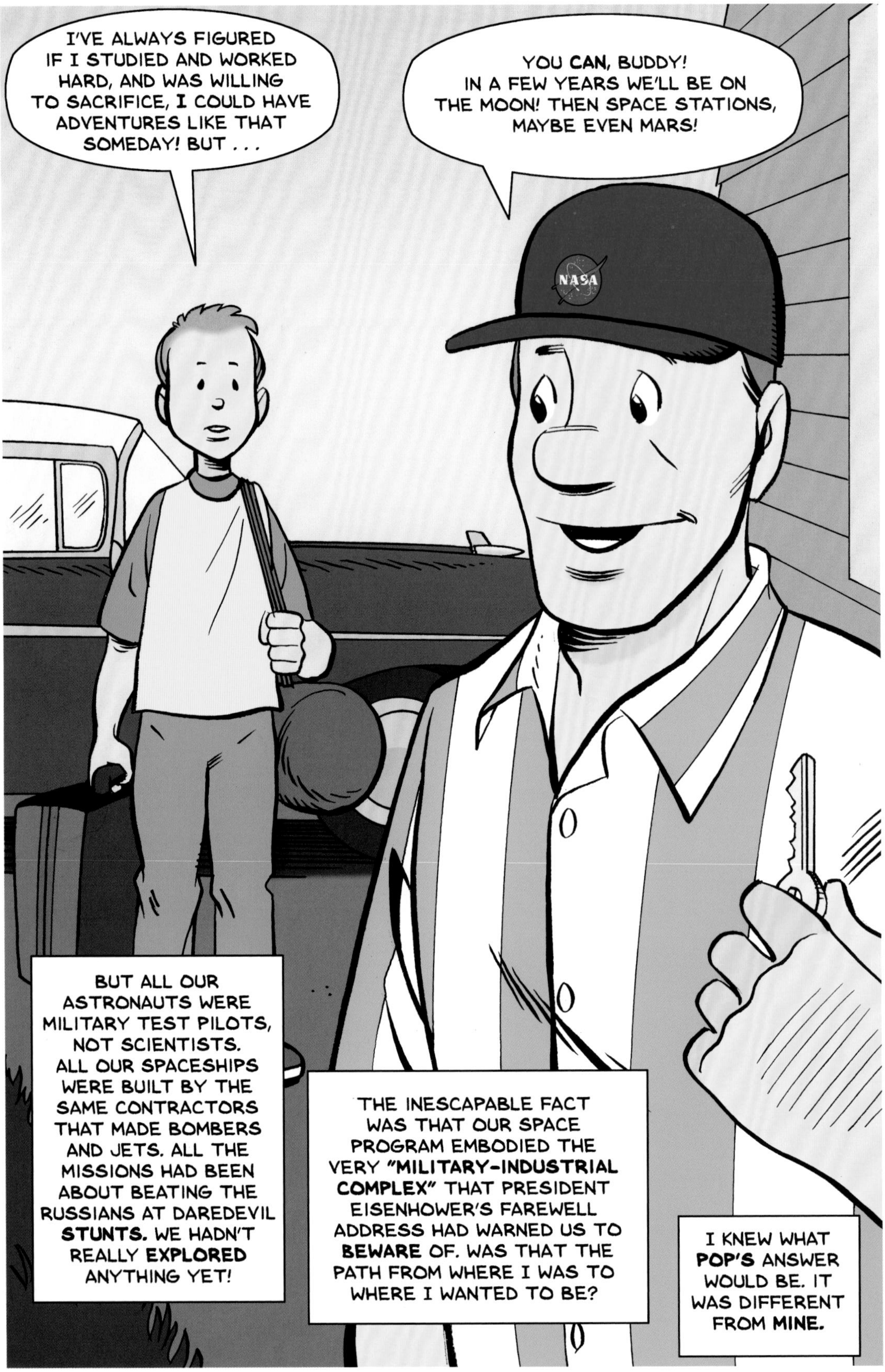
I'VE ALWAYS FIGURED IF I STUDIED AND WORKED HARD, AND WAS WILLING TO SACRIFICE, I COULD HAVE ADVENTURES LIKE THAT SOMEDAY! BUT . . .
YOU **CAN**, BUDDY! IN A FEW YEARS WE'LL BE ON THE MOON! THEN SPACE STATIONS, MAYBE EVEN MARS!
NASA
BUT ALL OUR ASTRONAUTS WERE MILITARY TEST PILOTS, NOT SCIENTISTS. ALL OUR SPACESHIPS WERE BUILT BY THE SAME CONTRACTORS THAT MADE BOMBERS AND JETS. ALL THE MISSIONS HAD BEEN ABOUT BEATING THE RUSSIANS AT DAREDEVIL **STUNTS.** WE HADN'T REALLY **EXPLORED** ANYTHING YET!
THE INESCAPABLE FACT WAS THAT OUR SPACE PROGRAM EMBODIED THE VERY **"MILITARY-INDUSTRIAL COMPLEX"** THAT PRESIDENT EISENHOWER'S FAREWELL ADDRESS HAD WARNED US TO **BEWARE** OF. WAS THAT THE PATH FROM WHERE I WAS TO WHERE I WANTED TO BE?
I KNEW WHAT **POP'S** ANSWER WOULD BE. IT WAS DIFFERENT FROM **MINE.**

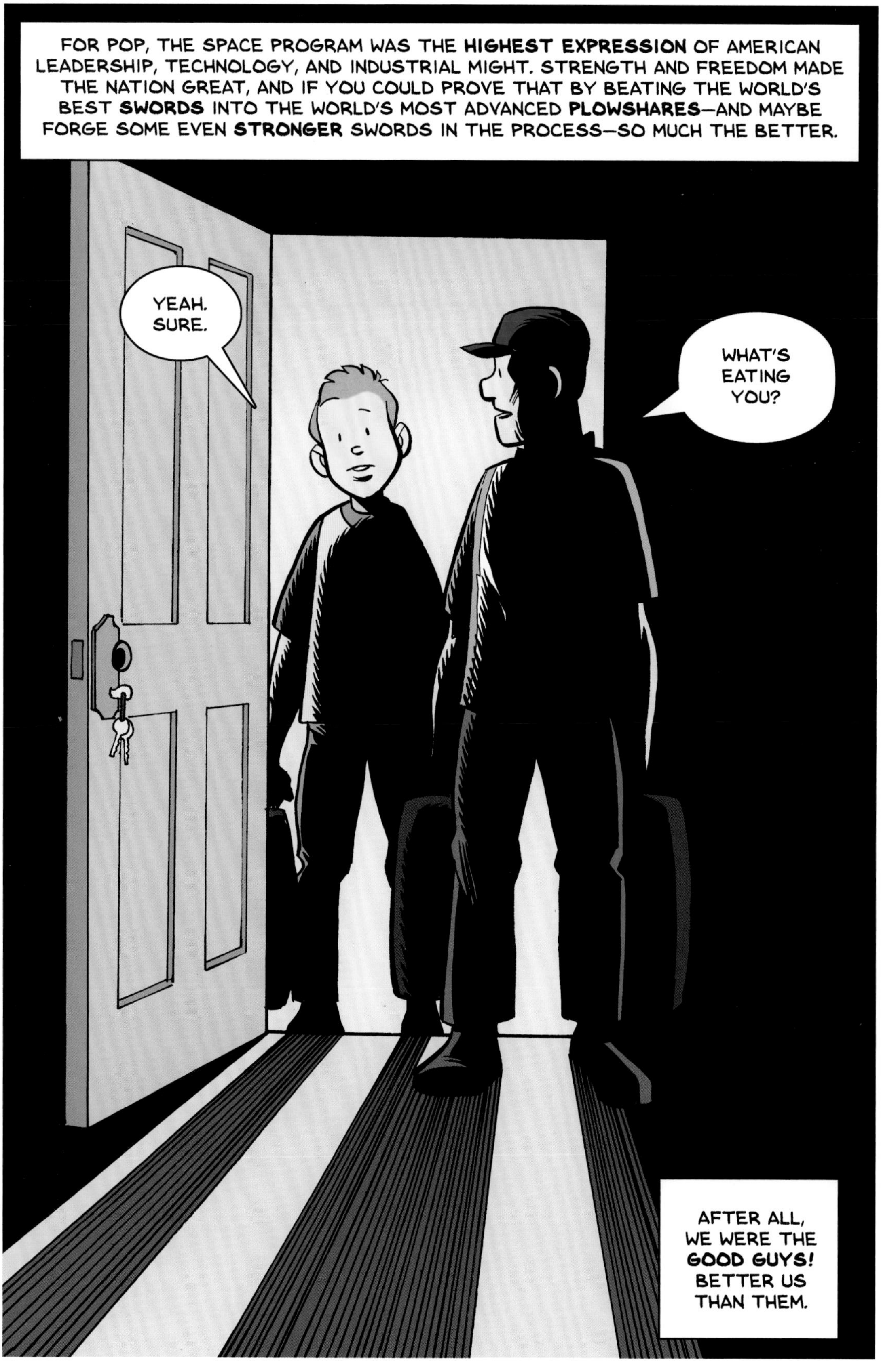
FOR POP, THE SPACE PROGRAM WAS THE **HIGHEST EXPRESSION** OF AMERICAN LEADERSHIP, TECHNOLOGY, AND INDUSTRIAL MIGHT. STRENGTH AND FREEDOM MADE THE NATION GREAT, AND IF YOU COULD PROVE THAT BY BEATING THE WORLD'S BEST **SWORDS** INTO THE WORLD'S MOST ADVANCED **PLOWSHARES**—AND MAYBE FORGE SOME EVEN **STRONGER** SWORDS IN THE PROCESS—SO MUCH THE BETTER.
WHAT'S EATING YOU?
YEAH. SURE.
AFTER ALL, WE WERE THE **GOOD GUYS!** BETTER US THAN THEM.

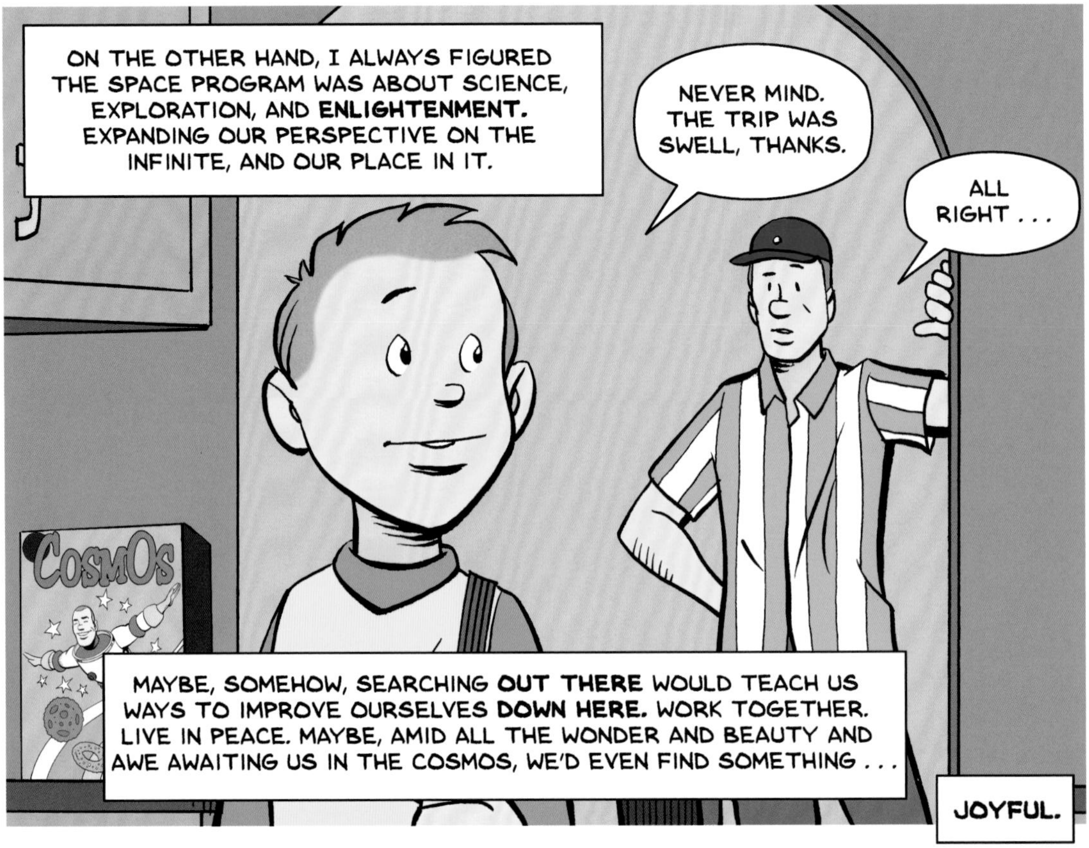
ON THE OTHER HAND, I ALWAYS FIGURED THE SPACE PROGRAM WAS ABOUT SCIENCE, EXPLORATION, AND **ENLIGHTENMENT.** EXPANDING OUR PERSPECTIVE ON THE INFINITE, AND OUR PLACE IN IT.
NEVER MIND. THE TRIP WAS SWELL, THANKS.
ALL RIGHT . . .
COSMOS
MAYBE, SOMEHOW, SEARCHING **OUT THERE** WOULD TEACH US WAYS TO IMPROVE OURSELVES **DOWN HERE.** WORK TOGETHER. LIVE IN PEACE. MAYBE, AMID ALL THE WONDER AND BEAUTY AND AWE AWAITING US IN THE COSMOS, WE'D EVEN FIND SOMETHING . . .
**JOYFUL.**

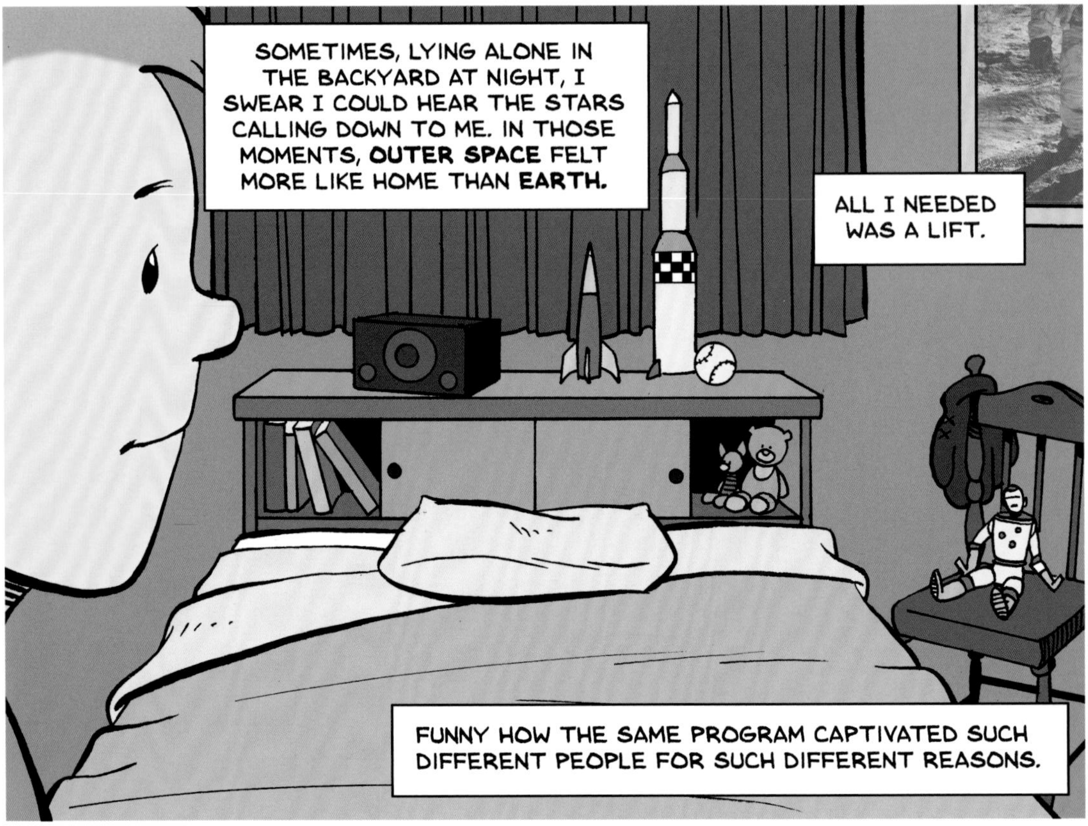
SOMETIMES, LYING ALONE IN THE BACKYARD AT NIGHT, I SWEAR I COULD HEAR THE STARS CALLING DOWN TO ME. IN THOSE MOMENTS, **OUTER SPACE** FELT MORE LIKE HOME THAN **EARTH.**
ALL I NEEDED WAS A LIFT.
FUNNY HOW THE SAME PROGRAM CAPTIVATED SUCH DIFFERENT PEOPLE FOR SUCH DIFFERENT REASONS.

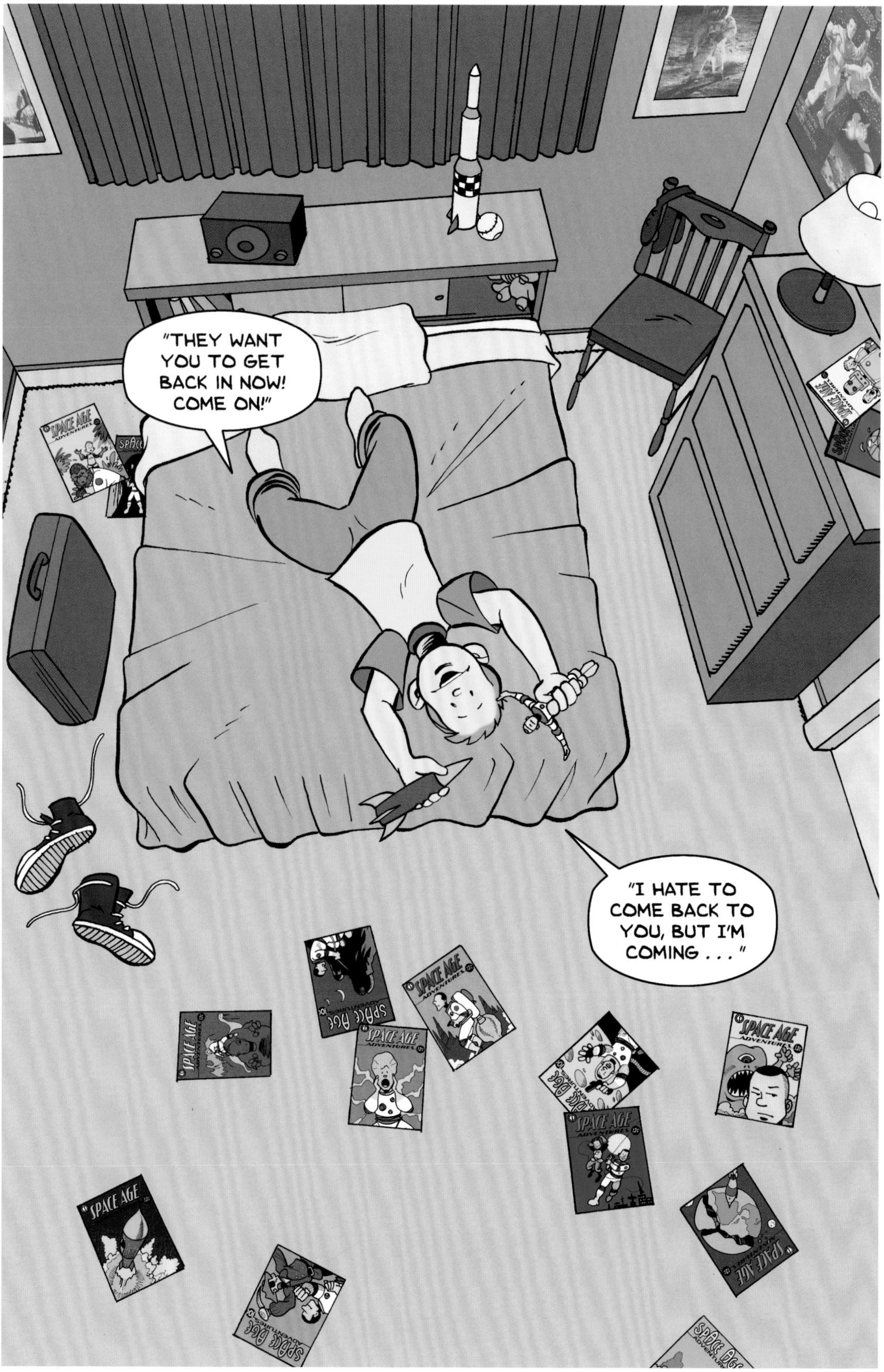
"THEY WANT YOU TO GET BACK IN NOW! COME ON!"
"I HATE TO COME BACK TO YOU, BUT I'M COMING . . ."

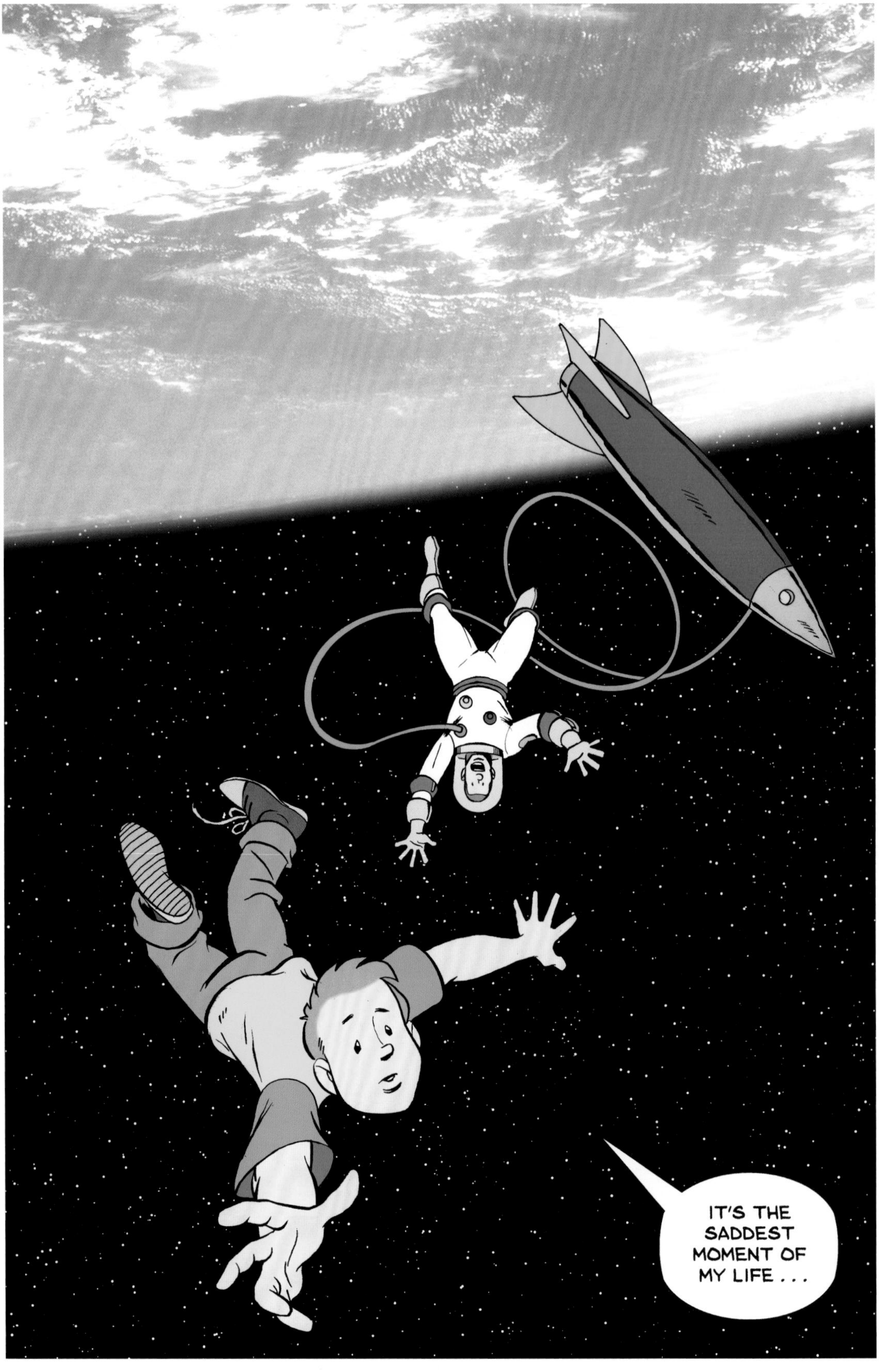
IT'S THE SADDEST MOMENT OF MY LIFE . . .

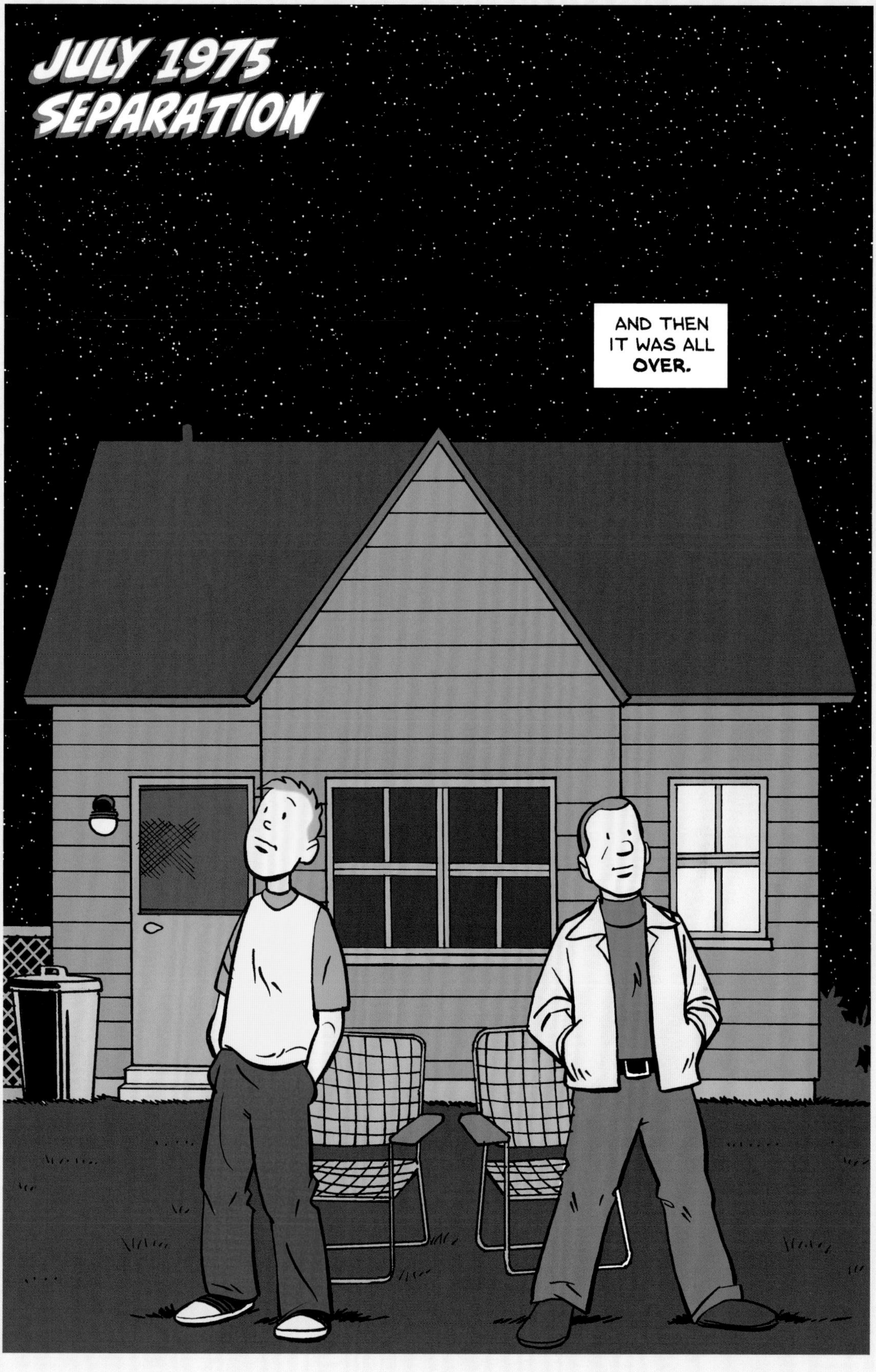
JULY 1975
SEPARATION
AND THEN IT WAS ALL OVER.

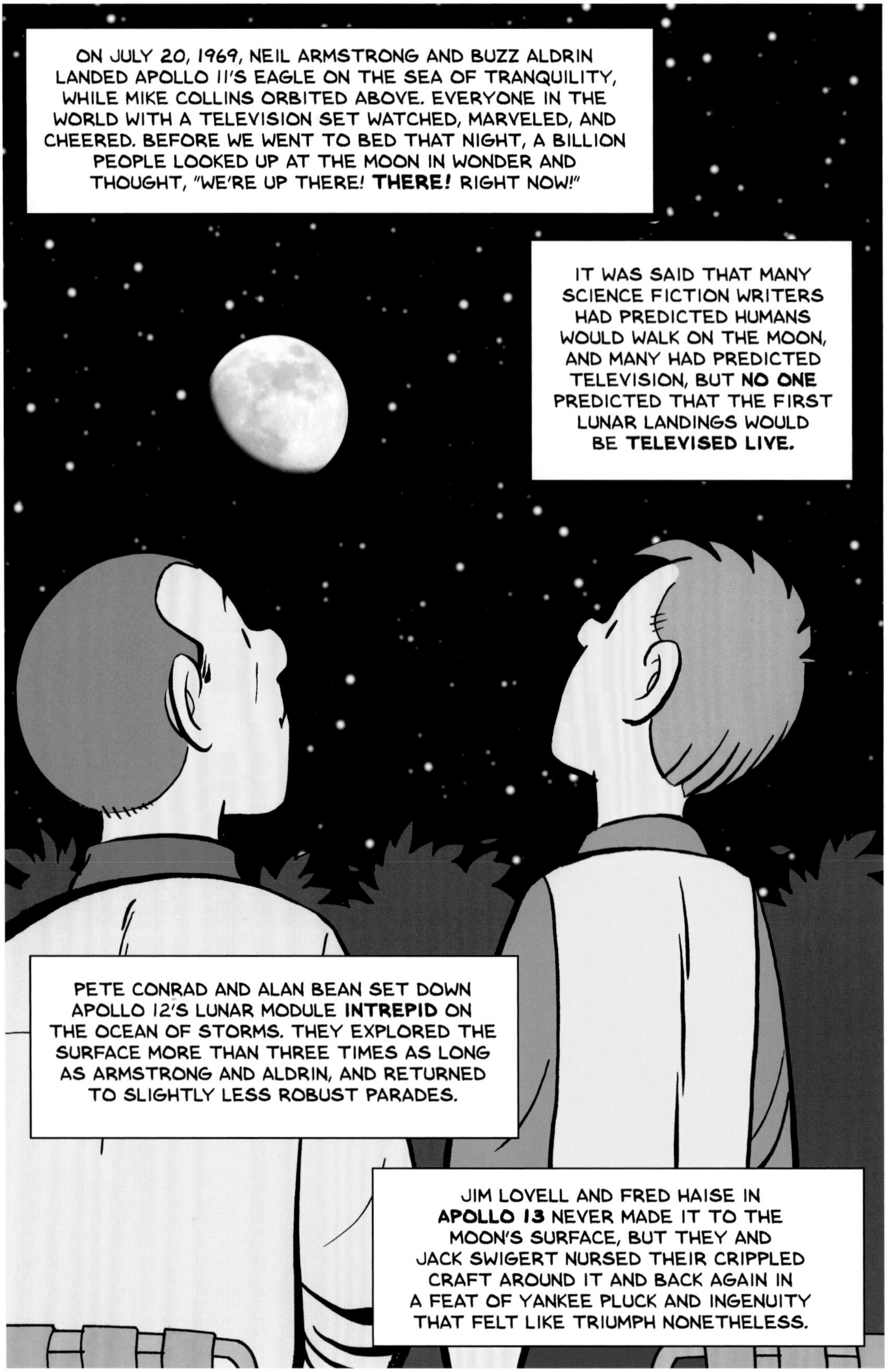
ON JULY 20, 1969, NEIL ARMSTRONG AND BUZZ ALDRIN LANDED APOLLO 11'S EAGLE ON THE SEA OF TRANQUILITY, WHILE MIKE COLLINS ORBITED ABOVE. EVERYONE IN THE WORLD WITH A TELEVISION SET WATCHED, MARVELED, AND CHEERED. BEFORE WE WENT TO BED THAT NIGHT, A BILLION PEOPLE LOOKED UP AT THE MOON IN WONDER AND THOUGHT, "WE'RE UP THERE! **THERE!** RIGHT NOW!"
IT WAS SAID THAT MANY SCIENCE FICTION WRITERS HAD PREDICTED HUMANS WOULD WALK ON THE MOON, AND MANY HAD PREDICTED TELEVISION, BUT **NO ONE** PREDICTED THAT THE FIRST LUNAR LANDINGS WOULD BE **TELEVISED LIVE.**
PETE CONRAD AND ALAN BEAN SET DOWN APOLLO 12'S LUNAR MODULE **INTREPID** ON THE OCEAN OF STORMS. THEY EXPLORED THE SURFACE MORE THAN THREE TIMES AS LONG AS ARMSTRONG AND ALDRIN, AND RETURNED TO SLIGHTLY LESS ROBUST PARADES.
JIM LOVELL AND FRED HAISE IN **APOLLO 13** NEVER MADE IT TO THE MOON'S SURFACE, BUT THEY AND JACK SWIGERT NURSED THEIR CRIPPLED CRAFT AROUND IT AND BACK AGAIN IN A FEAT OF YANKEE PLUCK AND INGENUITY THAT FELT LIKE TRIUMPH NONETHELESS.

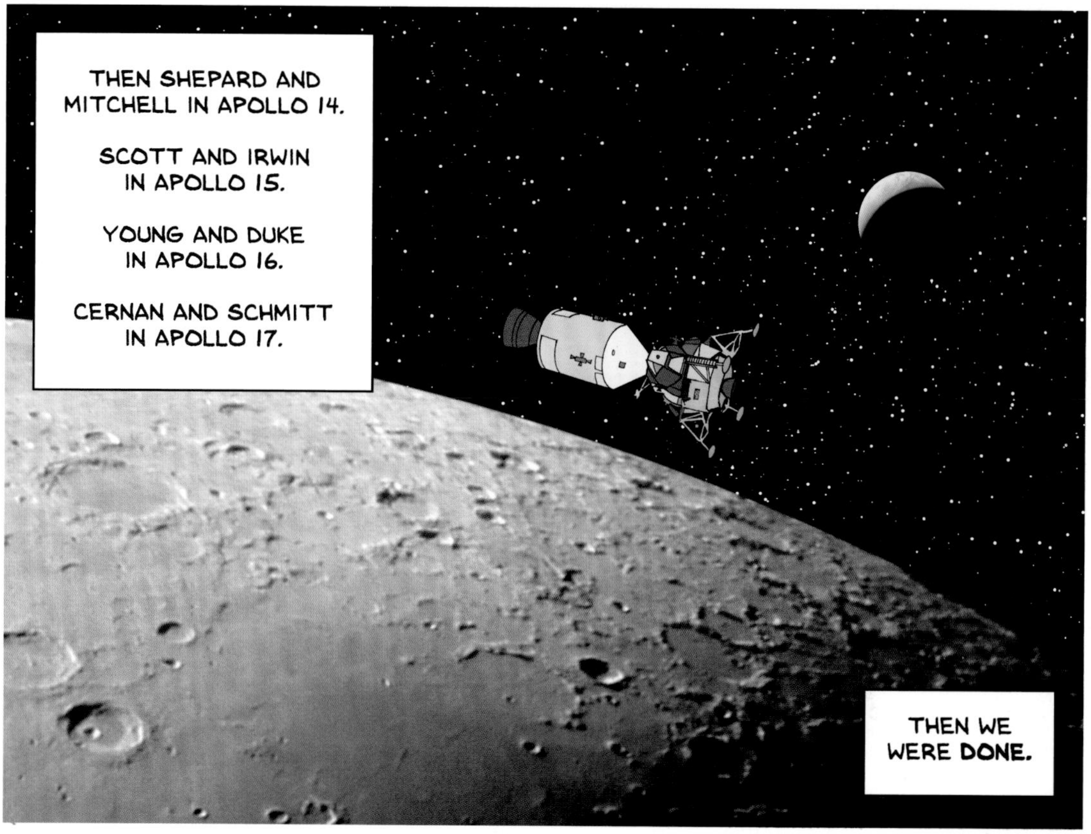
THEN SHEPARD AND MITCHELL IN APOLLO 14.
SCOTT AND IRWIN IN APOLLO 15.
YOUNG AND DUKE IN APOLLO 16.
CERNAN AND SCHMITT IN APOLLO 17.
THEN WE WERE **DONE.**

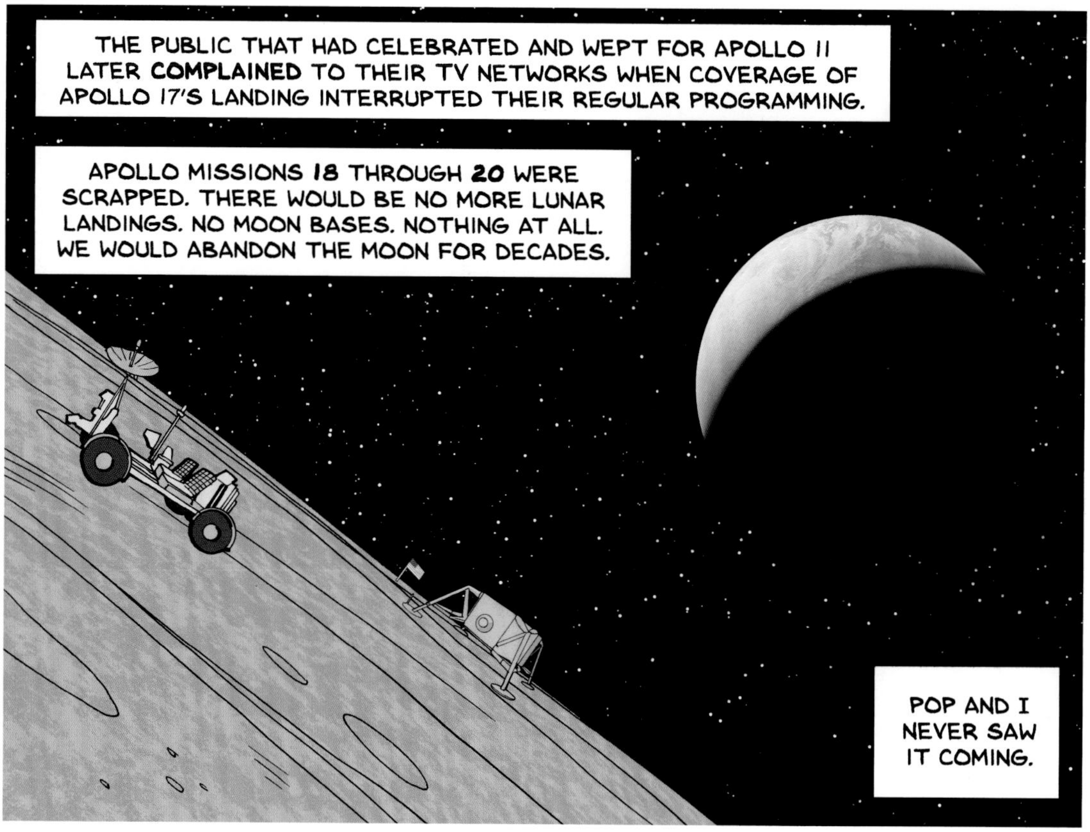
THE PUBLIC THAT HAD CELEBRATED AND WEPT FOR APOLLO 11 LATER **COMPLAINED** TO THEIR TV NETWORKS WHEN COVERAGE OF APOLLO 17'S LANDING INTERRUPTED THEIR REGULAR PROGRAMMING.
APOLLO MISSIONS **18** THROUGH **20** WERE SCRAPPED. THERE WOULD BE NO MORE LUNAR LANDINGS. NO MOON BASES. NOTHING AT ALL. WE WOULD ABANDON THE MOON FOR DECADES.
POP AND I NEVER SAW IT COMING.

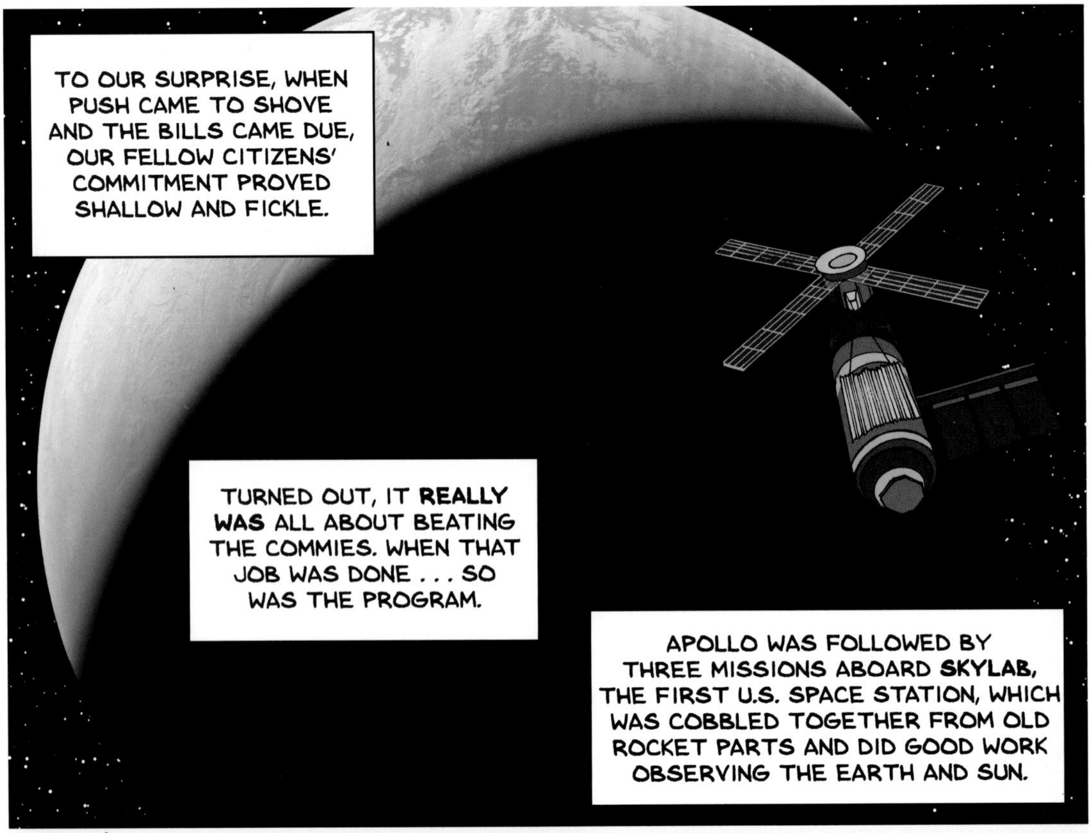
TO OUR SURPRISE, WHEN PUSH CAME TO SHOVE AND THE BILLS CAME DUE, OUR FELLOW CITIZENS' COMMITMENT PROVED SHALLOW AND FICKLE.
TURNED OUT, IT **REALLY WAS** ALL ABOUT BEATING THE COMMIES. WHEN THAT JOB WAS DONE . . . SO WAS THE PROGRAM.
APOLLO WAS FOLLOWED BY THREE MISSIONS ABOARD **SKYLAB,** THE FIRST U.S. SPACE STATION, WHICH WAS COBBLED TOGETHER FROM OLD ROCKET PARTS AND DID GOOD WORK OBSERVING THE EARTH AND SUN.

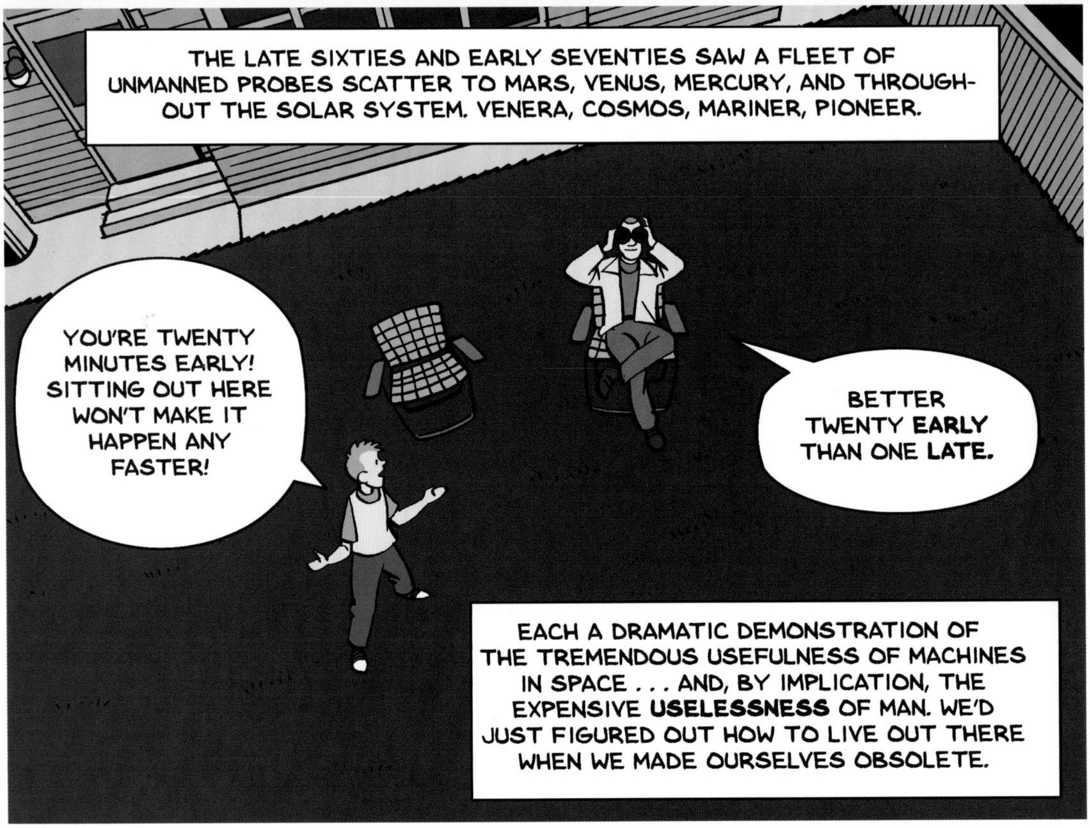
THE LATE SIXTIES AND EARLY SEVENTIES SAW A FLEET OF UNMANNED PROBES SCATTER TO MARS, VENUS, MERCURY, AND THROUGHOUT THE SOLAR SYSTEM. VENERA, COSMOS, MARINER, PIONEER.
YOU'RE TWENTY MINUTES EARLY! SITTING OUT HERE WON'T MAKE IT HAPPEN ANY FASTER!
BETTER TWENTY **EARLY** THAN ONE **LATE.**
EACH A DRAMATIC DEMONSTRATION OF THE TREMENDOUS USEFULNESS OF MACHINES IN SPACE . . . AND, BY IMPLICATION, THE EXPENSIVE **USELESSNESS** OF MAN. WE'D JUST FIGURED OUT HOW TO LIVE OUT THERE WHEN WE MADE OURSELVES OBSOLETE.

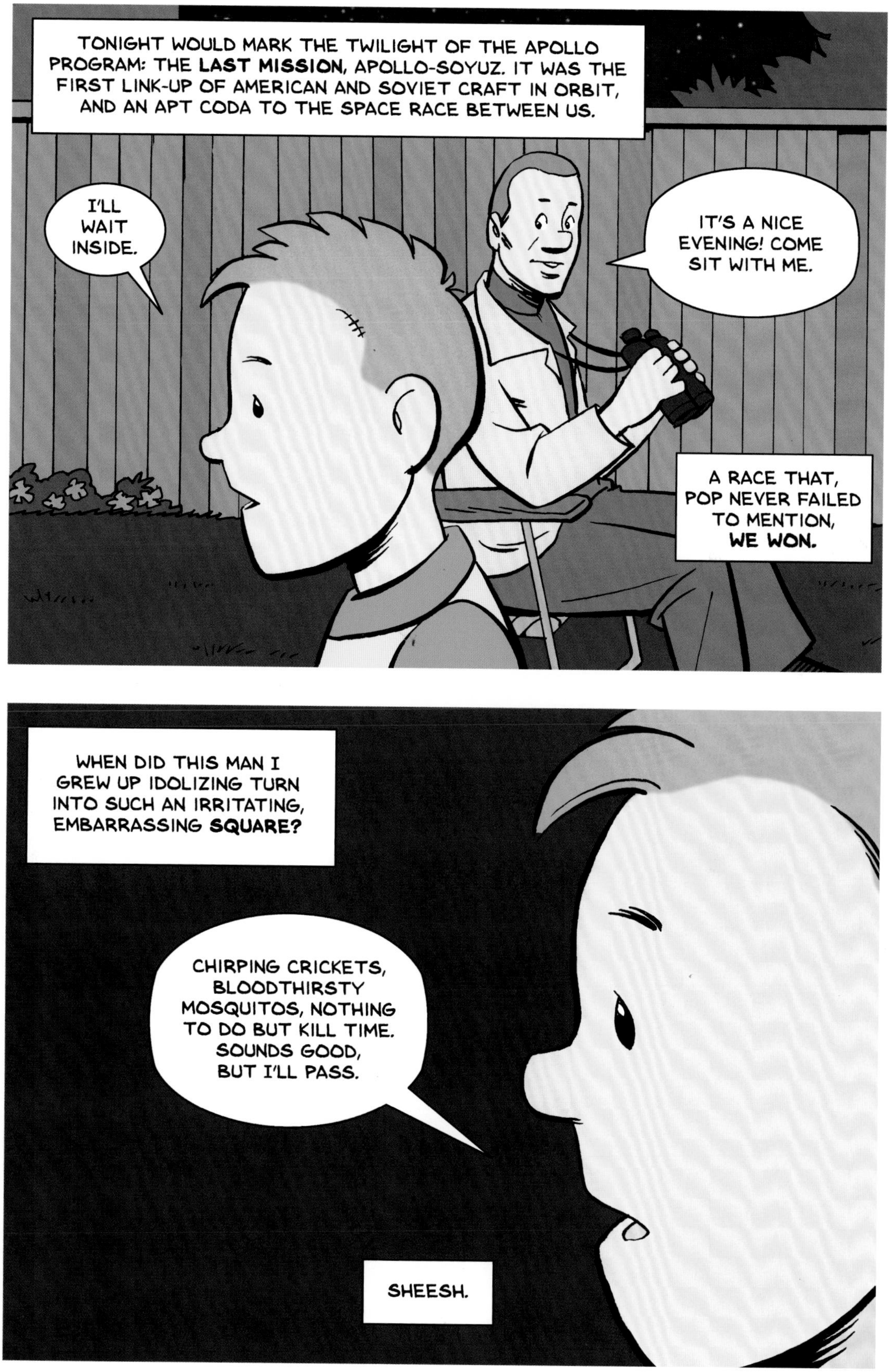
TONIGHT WOULD MARK THE TWILIGHT OF THE APOLLO PROGRAM: THE **LAST MISSION**, APOLLO-SOYUZ. IT WAS THE FIRST LINK-UP OF AMERICAN AND SOVIET CRAFT IN ORBIT, AND AN APT CODA TO THE SPACE RACE BETWEEN US.
I'LL WAIT INSIDE.
IT'S A NICE EVENING! COME SIT WITH ME.
A RACE THAT, POP NEVER FAILED TO MENTION, **WE WON.**
WHEN DID THIS MAN I GREW UP IDOLIZING TURN INTO SUCH AN IRRITATING, EMBARRASSING **SQUARE?**
CHIRPING CRICKETS, BLOODTHIRSTY MOSQUITOS, NOTHING TO DO BUT KILL TIME. SOUNDS GOOD, BUT I'LL PASS.
SHEESH.

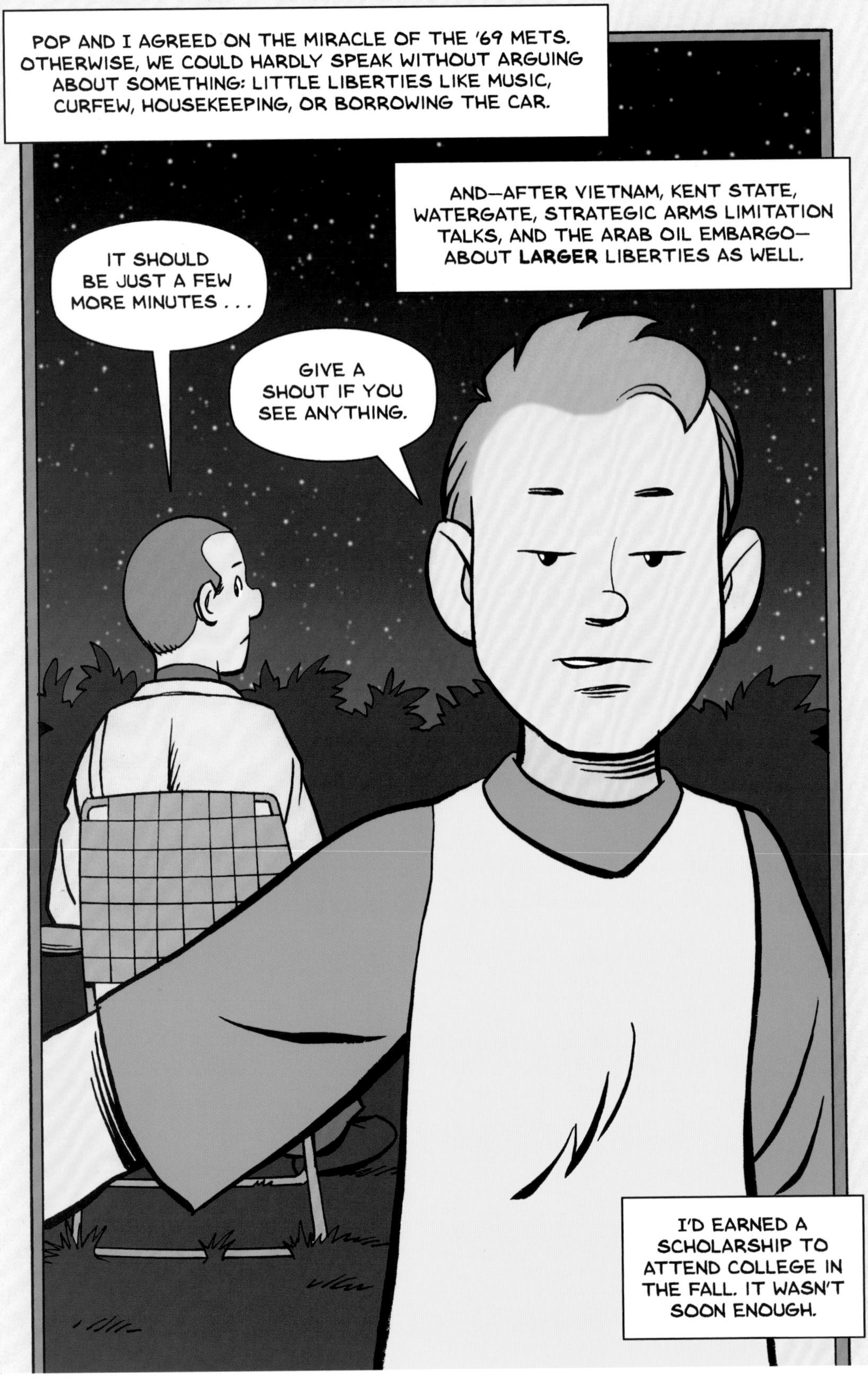
POP AND I AGREED ON THE MIRACLE OF THE '69 METS. OTHERWISE, WE COULD HARDLY SPEAK WITHOUT ARGUING ABOUT SOMETHING: LITTLE LIBERTIES LIKE MUSIC, CURFEW, HOUSEKEEPING, OR BORROWING THE CAR.
AND—AFTER VIETNAM, KENT STATE, WATERGATE, STRATEGIC ARMS LIMITATION TALKS, AND THE ARAB OIL EMBARGO—ABOUT **LARGER** LIBERTIES AS WELL.
IT SHOULD BE JUST A FEW MORE MINUTES . . .
GIVE A SHOUT IF YOU SEE ANYTHING.
I'D EARNED A SCHOLARSHIP TO ATTEND COLLEGE IN THE FALL. IT WASN'T SOON ENOUGH.

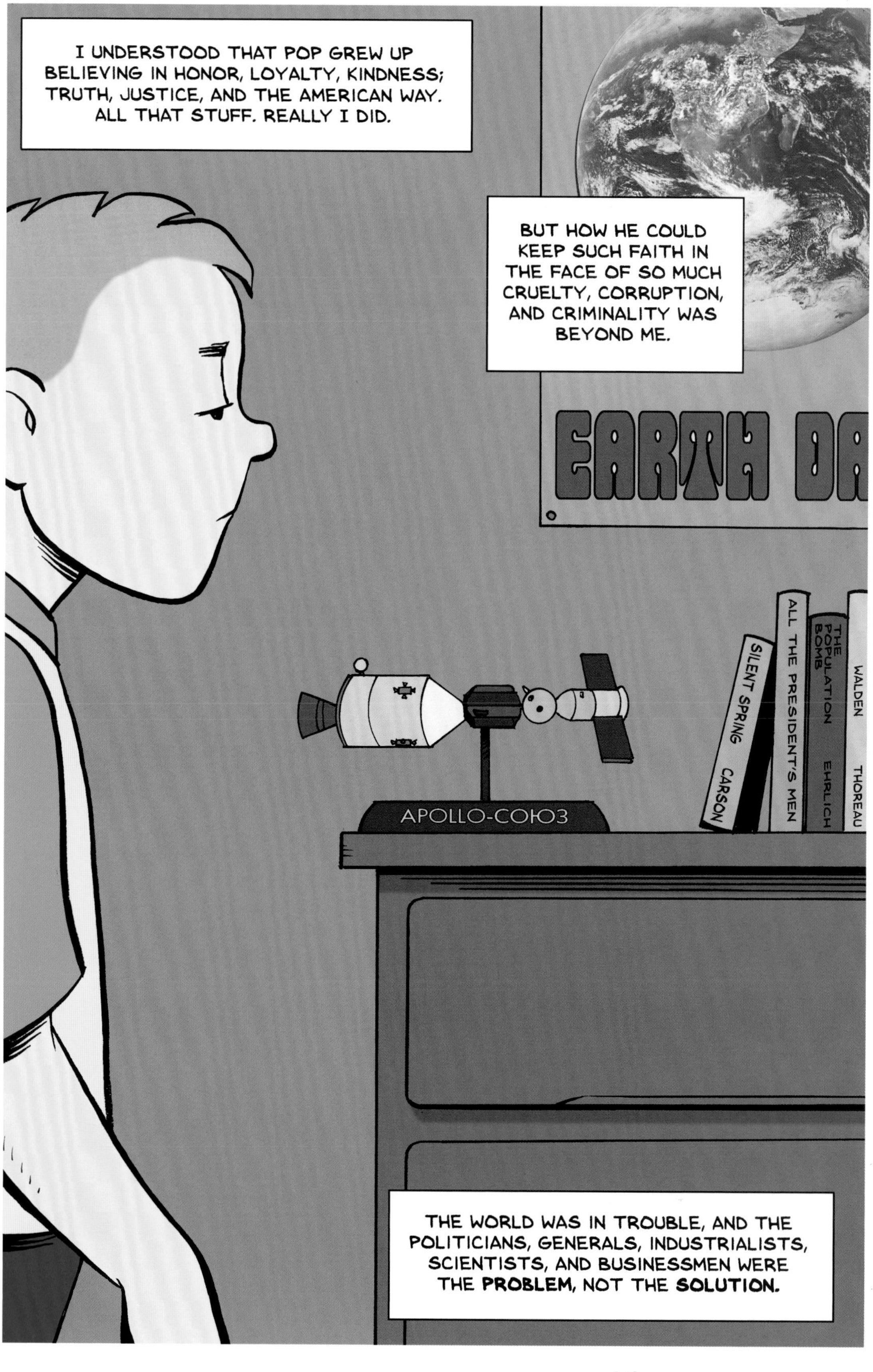
I UNDERSTOOD THAT POP GREW UP BELIEVING IN HONOR, LOYALTY, KINDNESS; TRUTH, JUSTICE, AND THE AMERICAN WAY. ALL THAT STUFF. REALLY I DID.
BUT HOW HE COULD KEEP SUCH FAITH IN THE FACE OF SO MUCH CRUELTY, CORRUPTION, AND CRIMINALITY WAS BEYOND ME.
EARTH DA
APOLLO-СОЮЗ
SILENT SPRING CARSON
ALL THE PRESIDENT'S MEN
THE POPULATION BOMB EHRLICH
WALDEN THOREAU
THE WORLD WAS IN TROUBLE, AND THE POLITICIANS, GENERALS, INDUSTRIALISTS, SCIENTISTS, AND BUSINESSMEN WERE THE **PROBLEM**, NOT THE **SOLUTION**.

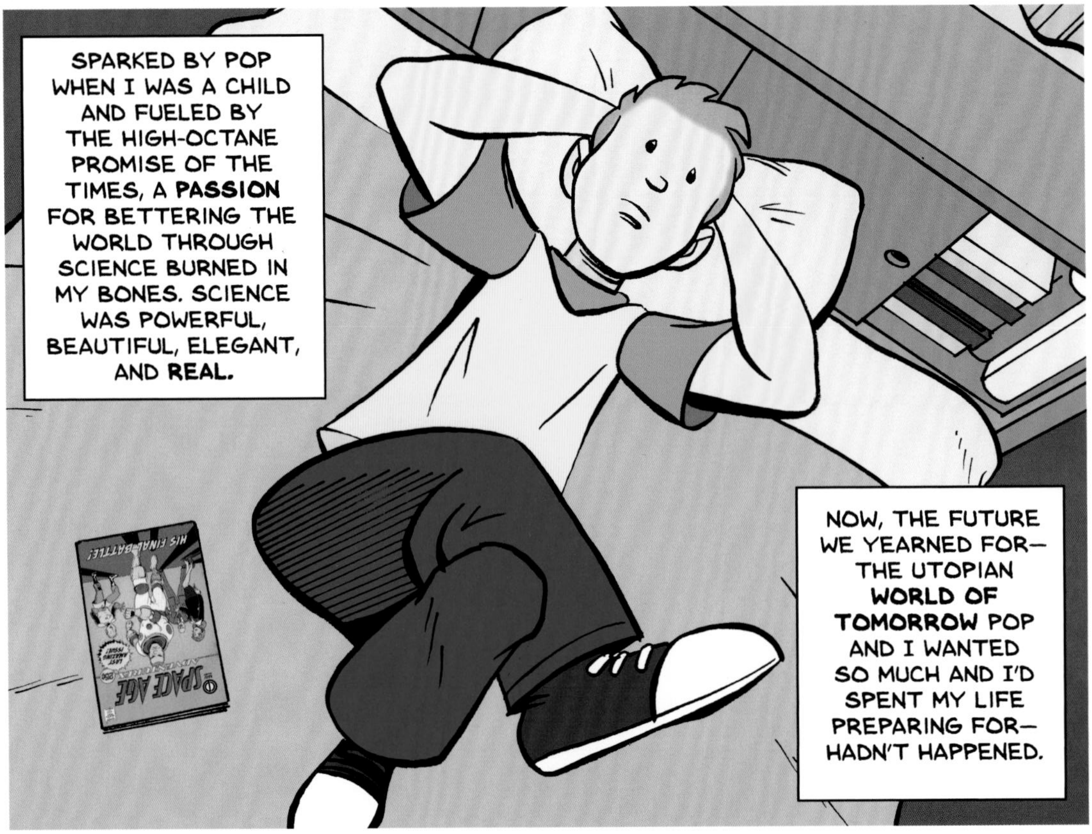
SPARKED BY POP WHEN I WAS A CHILD AND FUELED BY THE HIGH-OCTANE PROMISE OF THE TIMES, A **PASSION** FOR BETTERING THE WORLD THROUGH SCIENCE BURNED IN MY BONES. SCIENCE WAS POWERFUL, BEAUTIFUL, ELEGANT, AND **REAL.**
NOW, THE FUTURE WE YEARNED FOR—THE UTOPIAN **WORLD OF TOMORROW** POP AND I WANTED SO MUCH AND I'D SPENT MY LIFE PREPARING FOR—HADN'T HAPPENED.

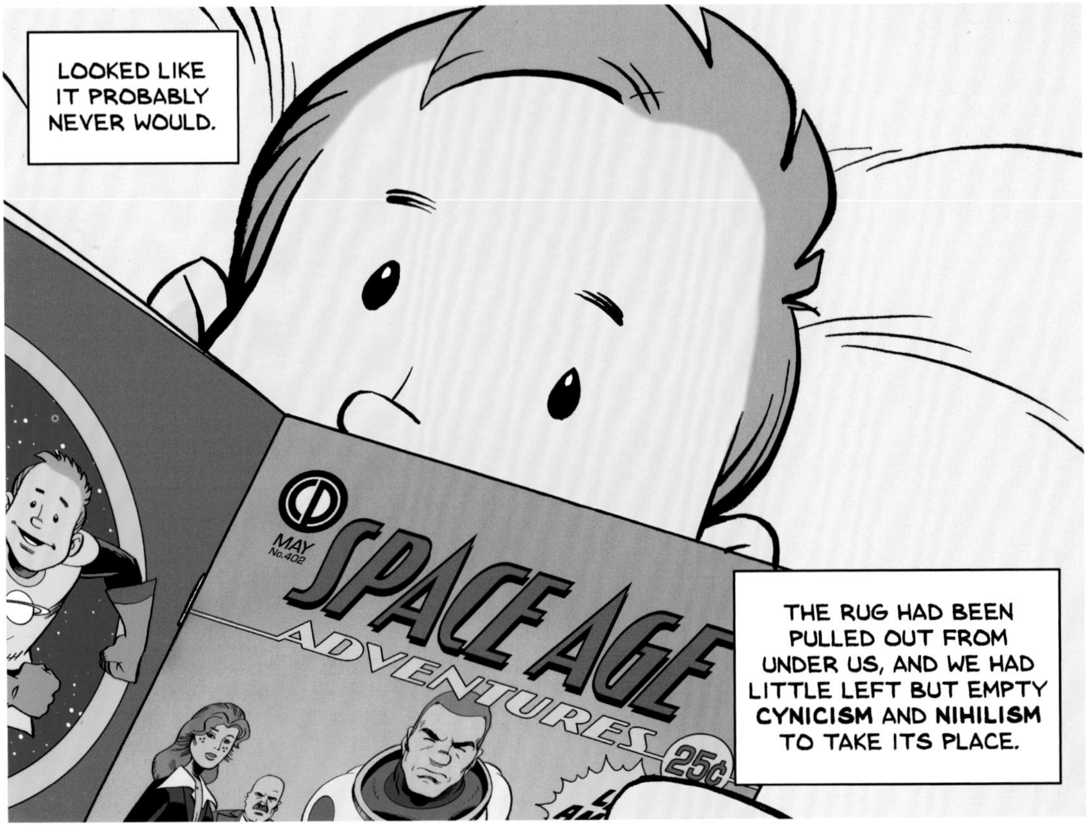
LOOKED LIKE IT PROBABLY NEVER WOULD.
MAY
No.402
SPACE AGE
ADVENTURES
25¢
THE RUG HAD BEEN PULLED OUT FROM UNDER US, AND WE HAD LITTLE LEFT BUT EMPTY **CYNICISM** AND **NIHILISM** TO TAKE ITS PLACE.

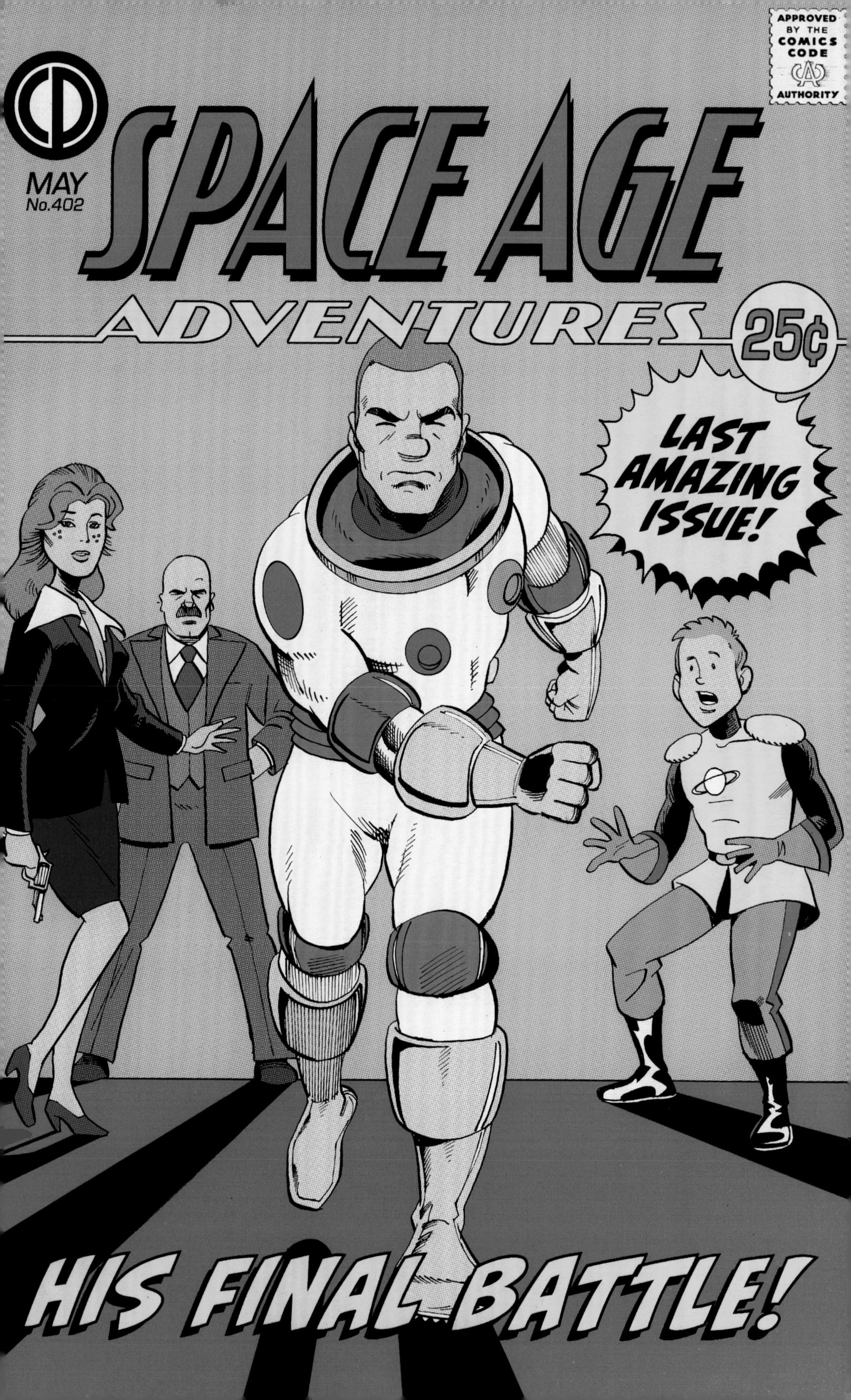
APPROVED BY THE COMICS CODE AUTHORITY
MAY
No.402
SPACE AGE
ADVENTURES
25¢
LAST AMAZING ISSUE!
HIS FINAL BATTLE!

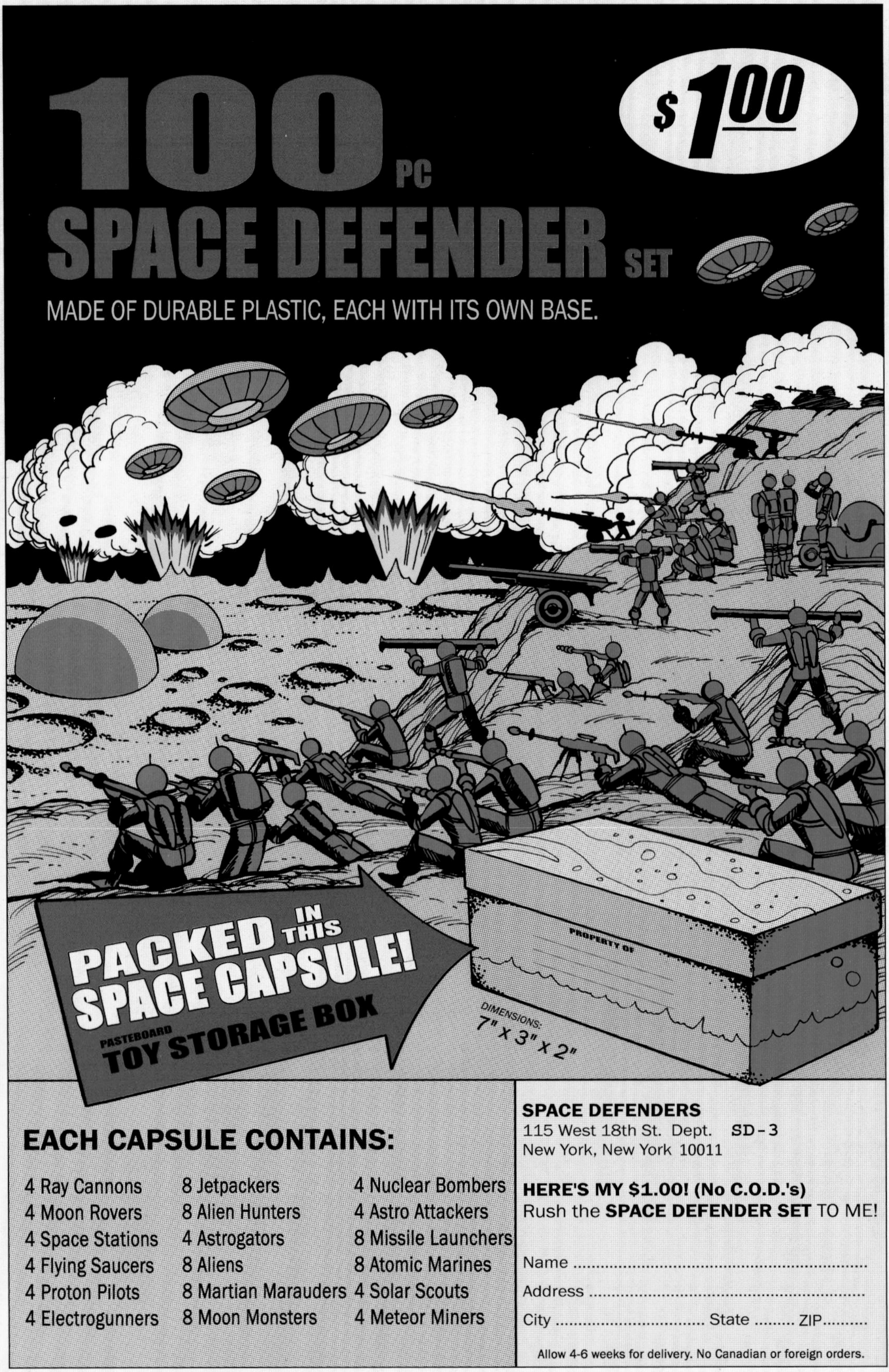
100 PC
$1.00
SPACE DEFENDER SET
MADE OF DURABLE PLASTIC, EACH WITH ITS OWN BASE.
PACKED IN THIS SPACE CAPSULE!
PASTEBOARD TOY STORAGE BOX
PROPERTY OF
DIMENSIONS: 7" x 3" x 2"

## EACH CAPSULE CONTAINS:

| | | |
|---|---|---|
| 4 Ray Cannons | 8 Jetpackers | 4 Nuclear Bombers |
| 4 Moon Rovers | 8 Alien Hunters | 4 Astro Attackers |
| 4 Space Stations | 4 Astrogators | 8 Missile Launchers |
| 4 Flying Saucers | 8 Aliens | 8 Atomic Marines |
| 4 Proton Pilots | 8 Martian Marauders | 4 Solar Scouts |
| 4 Electrogunners | 8 Moon Monsters | 4 Meteor Miners |

**SPACE DEFENDERS**
115 West 18th St. Dept. SD-3
New York, New York 10011

**HERE'S MY $1.00! (No C.O.D.'s)**
Rush the **SPACE DEFENDER SET** TO ME!

Name ..........................................................

Address ......................................................

City ............................... State ......... ZIP..........

Allow 4-6 weeks for delivery. No Canadian or foreign orders.

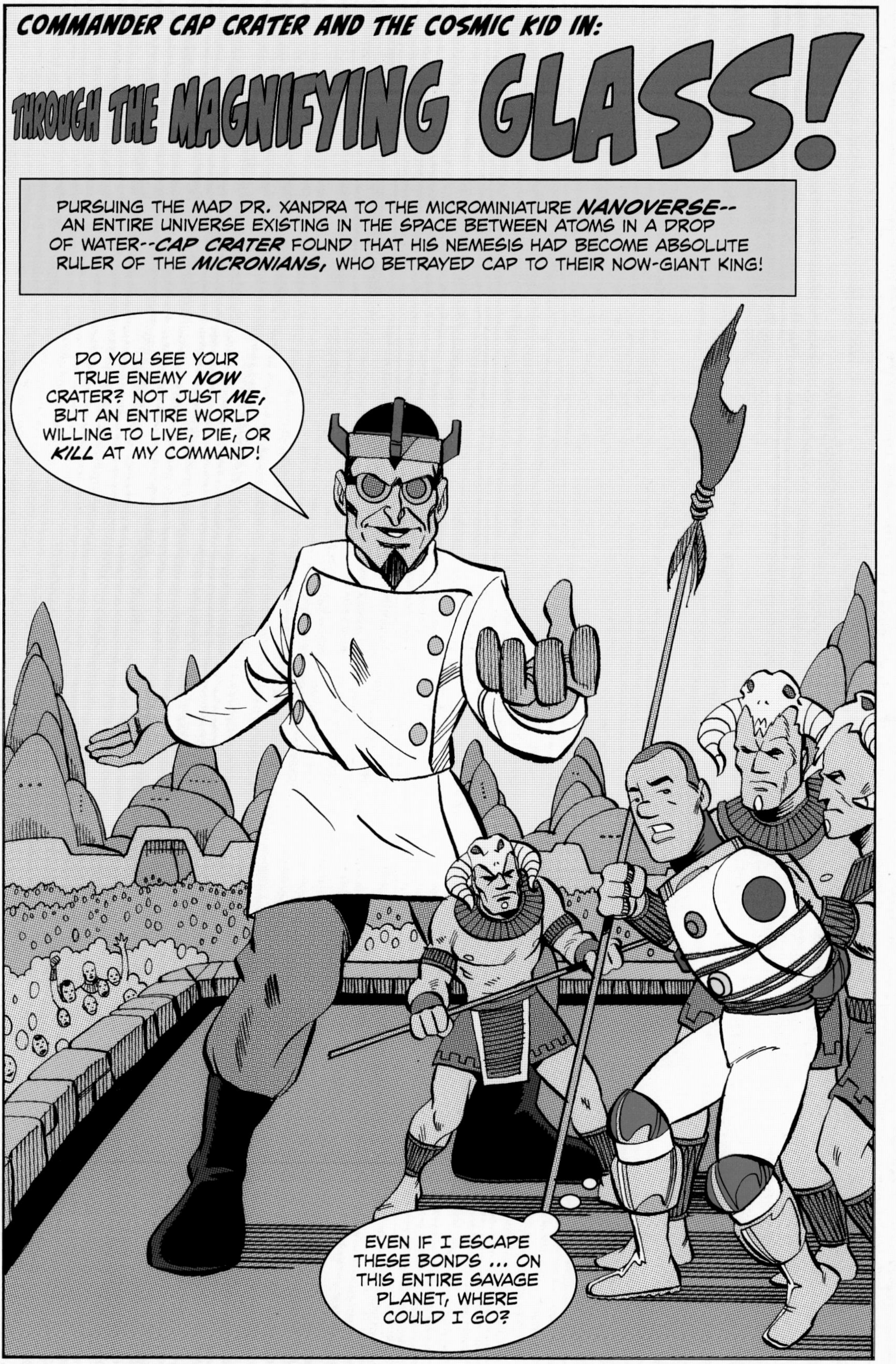
COMMANDER CAP CRATER AND THE COSMIC KID IN:
THROUGH THE MAGNIFYING GLASS!
PURSUING THE MAD DR. XANDRA TO THE MICROMINIATURE NANOVERSE-- AN ENTIRE UNIVERSE EXISTING IN THE SPACE BETWEEN ATOMS IN A DROP OF WATER--CAP CRATER FOUND THAT HIS NEMESIS HAD BECOME ABSOLUTE RULER OF THE MICRONIANS, WHO BETRAYED CAP TO THEIR NOW-GIANT KING!
DO YOU SEE YOUR TRUE ENEMY NOW CRATER? NOT JUST ME, BUT AN ENTIRE WORLD WILLING TO LIVE, DIE, OR KILL AT MY COMMAND!
EVEN IF I ESCAPE THESE BONDS ... ON THIS ENTIRE SAVAGE PLANET, WHERE COULD I GO?

SPACE AGE ADVENTURES is published by CAPITAL PERIODICALS CO., INC. OFFICE OF PUBLICATION: 115 W. 18th ST., NEW YORK, N.Y. 10011. SECOND CLASS POSTAGE PAID AT NEW YORK, N.Y., AND AT ADDITIONAL MAILING OFFICES. Published monthly. Copyright 1975 by Capital Periodicals Co., Inc., all rights reserved. Vol. 1, No. 402, May 1975 issue. Price 25 cents per copy. No similarity between any of the names, characters, persons, and/or instititutions in this magazine with those of any living or dead person or institution is intended, and any such similarity which may exist is purely coincidental. Printed in the U.S.A. Subscription rate $3.75 for 13 issues including King Size Special. Canada $4.50. Foreign $6.00.

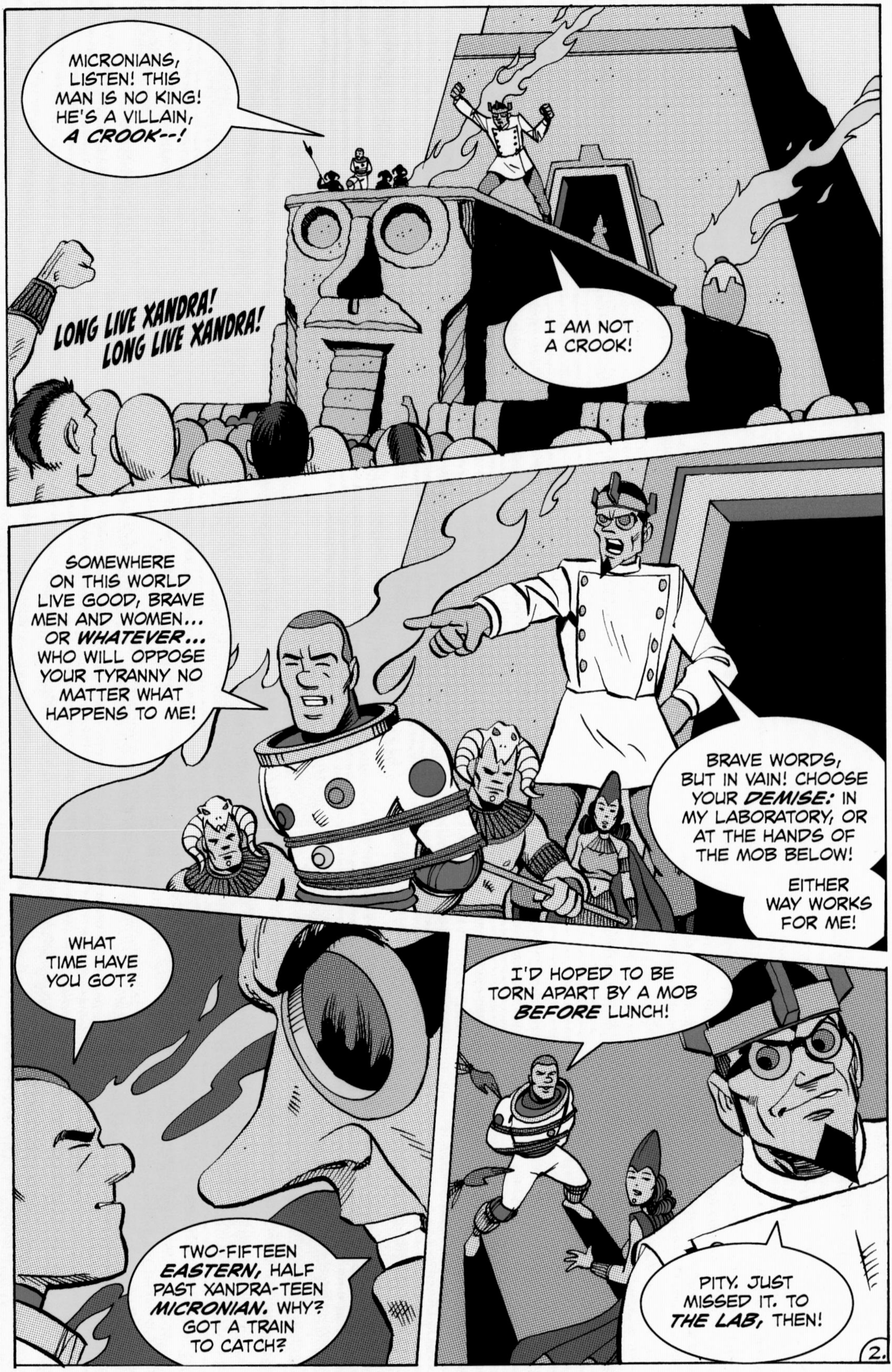
MICRONIANS, LISTEN! THIS MAN IS NO KING! HE'S A VILLAIN, A CROOK--!
LONG LIVE XANDRA! LONG LIVE XANDRA!
I AM NOT A CROOK!
SOMEWHERE ON THIS WORLD LIVE GOOD, BRAVE MEN AND WOMEN... OR WHATEVER... WHO WILL OPPOSE YOUR TYRANNY NO MATTER WHAT HAPPENS TO ME!
BRAVE WORDS, BUT IN VAIN! CHOOSE YOUR DEMISE: IN MY LABORATORY, OR AT THE HANDS OF THE MOB BELOW!
EITHER WAY WORKS FOR ME!
WHAT TIME HAVE YOU GOT?
TWO-FIFTEEN EASTERN, HALF PAST XANDRA-TEEN MICRONIAN. WHY? GOT A TRAIN TO CATCH?
I'D HOPED TO BE TORN APART BY A MOB BEFORE LUNCH!
PITY. JUST MISSED IT. TO THE LAB, THEN!

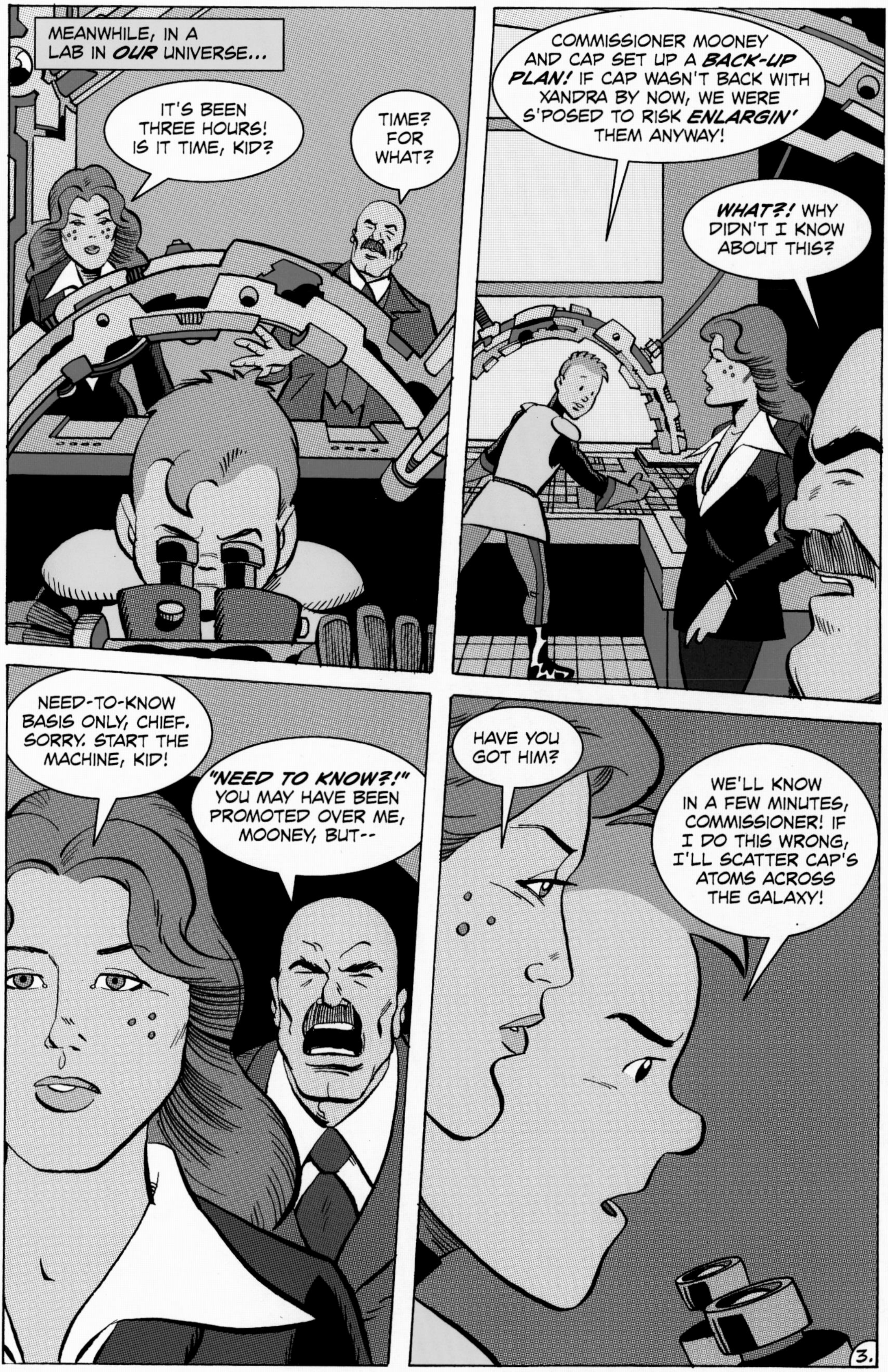
MEANWHILE, IN A LAB IN OUR UNIVERSE...
IT'S BEEN THREE HOURS! IS IT TIME, KID?
TIME? FOR WHAT?
COMMISSIONER MOONEY AND CAP SET UP A BACK-UP PLAN! IF CAP WASN'T BACK WITH XANDRA BY NOW, WE WERE S'POSED TO RISK ENLARGIN' THEM ANYWAY!
WHAT?! WHY DIDN'T I KNOW ABOUT THIS?
NEED-TO-KNOW BASIS ONLY, CHIEF. SORRY. START THE MACHINE, KID!
"NEED TO KNOW?!" YOU MAY HAVE BEEN PROMOTED OVER ME, MOONEY, BUT--
HAVE YOU GOT HIM?
WE'LL KNOW IN A FEW MINUTES, COMMISSIONER! IF I DO THIS WRONG, I'LL SCATTER CAP'S ATOMS ACROSS THE GALAXY!
3.

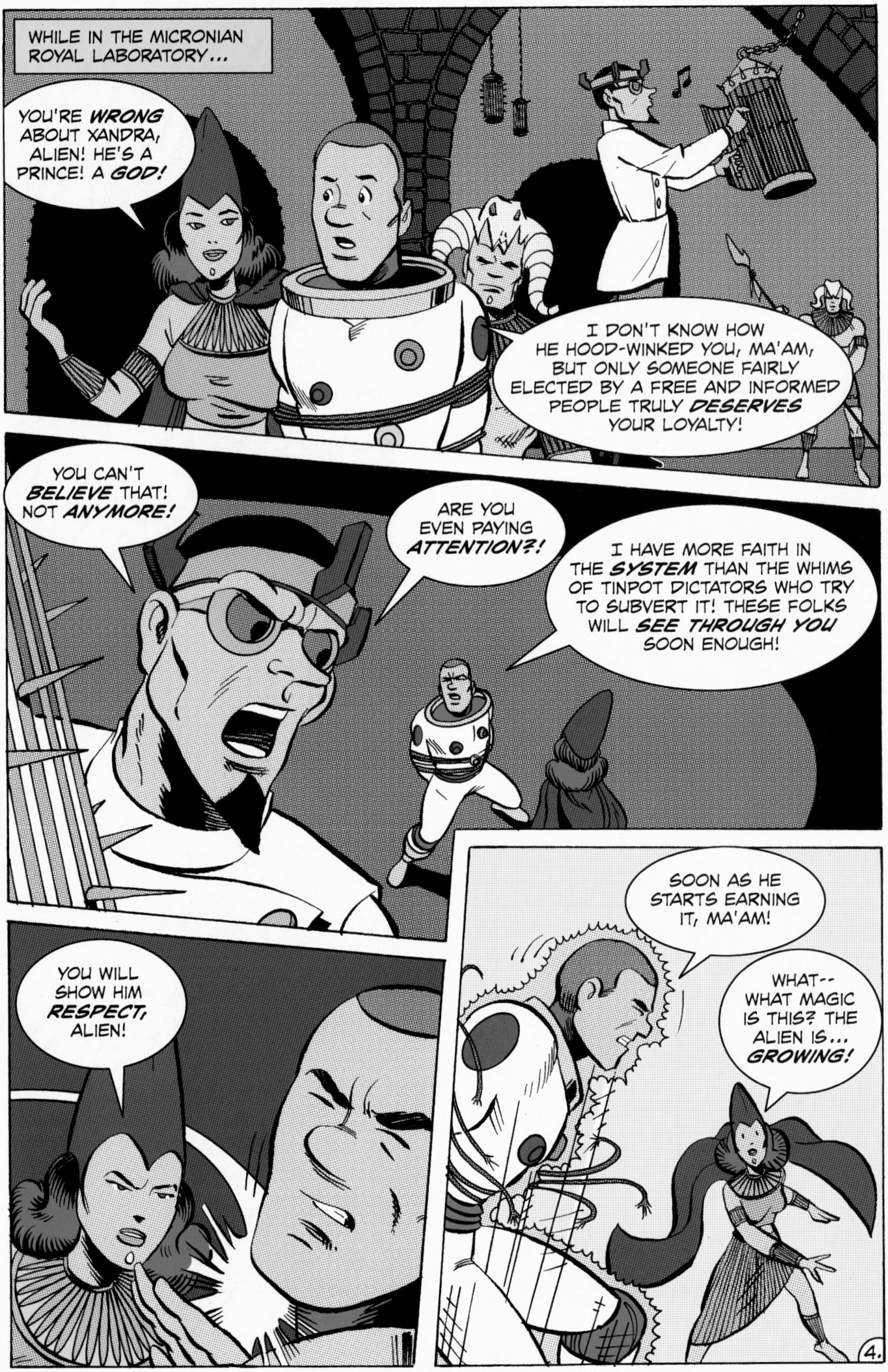
WHILE IN THE MICRONIAN ROYAL LABORATORY...
YOU'RE WRONG ABOUT XANDRA, ALIEN! HE'S A PRINCE! A GOD!
I DON'T KNOW HOW HE HOOD-WINKED YOU, MA'AM, BUT ONLY SOMEONE FAIRLY ELECTED BY A FREE AND INFORMED PEOPLE TRULY DESERVES YOUR LOYALTY!
YOU CAN'T BELIEVE THAT! NOT ANYMORE!
ARE YOU EVEN PAYING ATTENTION?!
I HAVE MORE FAITH IN THE SYSTEM THAN THE WHIMS OF TINPOT DICTATORS WHO TRY TO SUBVERT IT! THESE FOLKS WILL SEE THROUGH YOU SOON ENOUGH!
YOU WILL SHOW HIM RESPECT, ALIEN!
SOON AS HE STARTS EARNING IT, MA'AM!
WHAT-- WHAT MAGIC IS THIS? THE ALIEN IS... GROWING!
4.

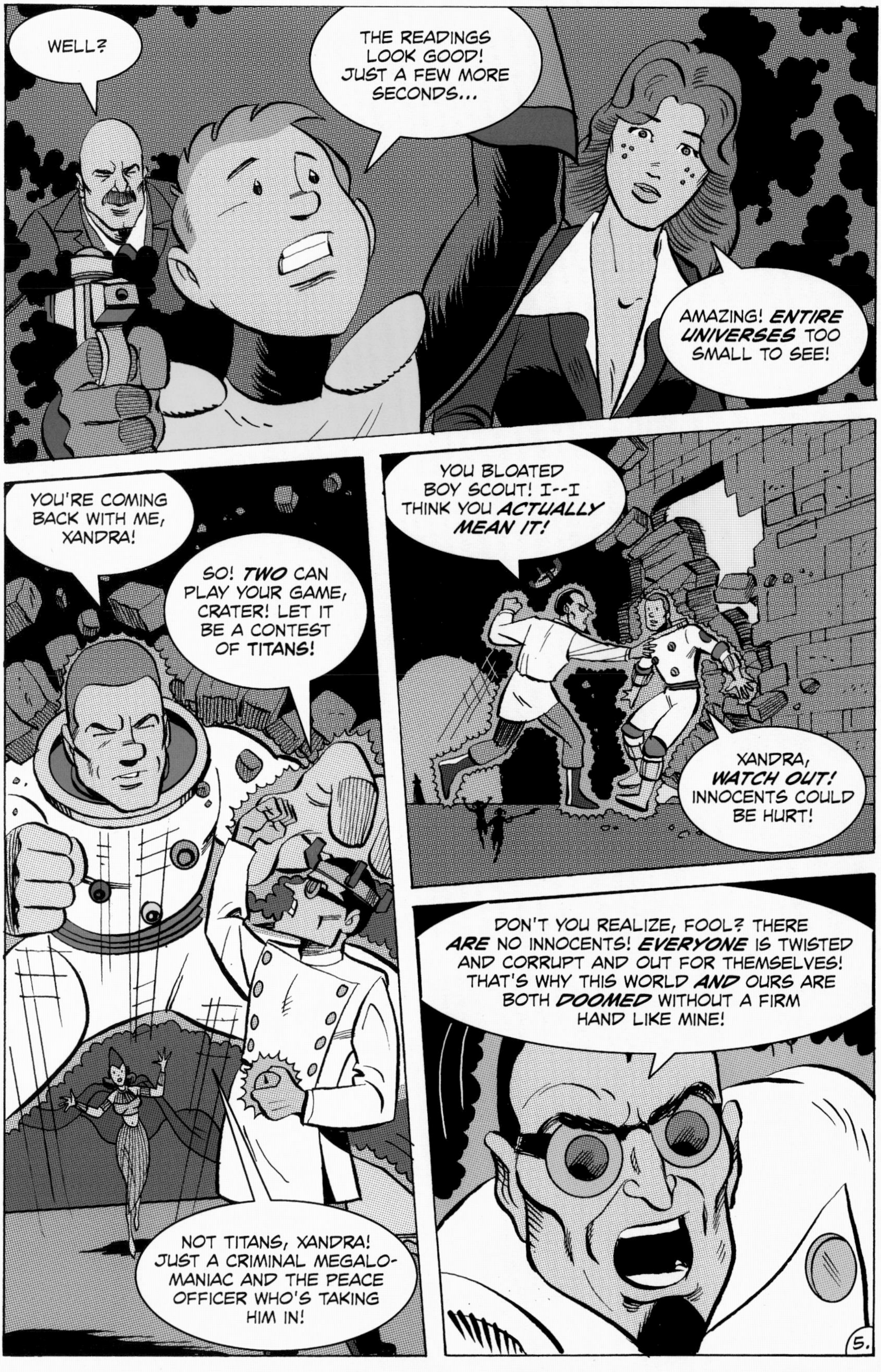
WELL?
THE READINGS LOOK GOOD! JUST A FEW MORE SECONDS...
AMAZING! ENTIRE UNIVERSES TOO SMALL TO SEE!
YOU'RE COMING BACK WITH ME, XANDRA!
SO! TWO CAN PLAY YOUR GAME, CRATER! LET IT BE A CONTEST OF TITANS!
NOT TITANS, XANDRA! JUST A CRIMINAL MEGALO-MANIAC AND THE PEACE OFFICER WHO'S TAKING HIM IN!
YOU BLOATED BOY SCOUT! I--I THINK YOU ACTUALLY MEAN IT!
XANDRA, WATCH OUT! INNOCENTS COULD BE HURT!
DON'T YOU REALIZE, FOOL? THERE ARE NO INNOCENTS! EVERYONE IS TWISTED AND CORRUPT AND OUT FOR THEMSELVES! THAT'S WHY THIS WORLD AND OURS ARE BOTH DOOMED WITHOUT A FIRM HAND LIKE MINE!
5.

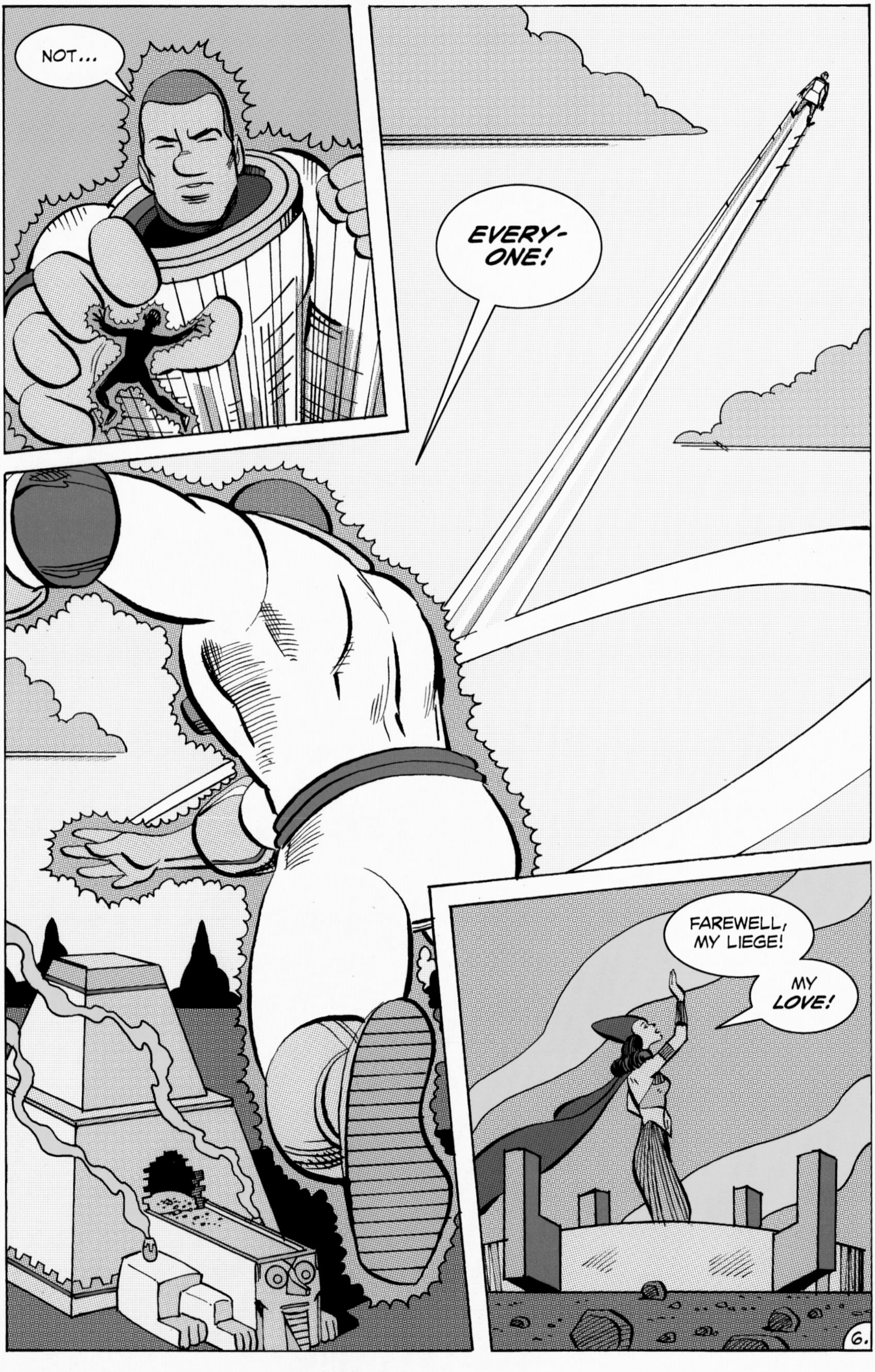
NOT...
EVERY-ONE!
FAREWELL, MY LIEGE!
MY LOVE!
6.

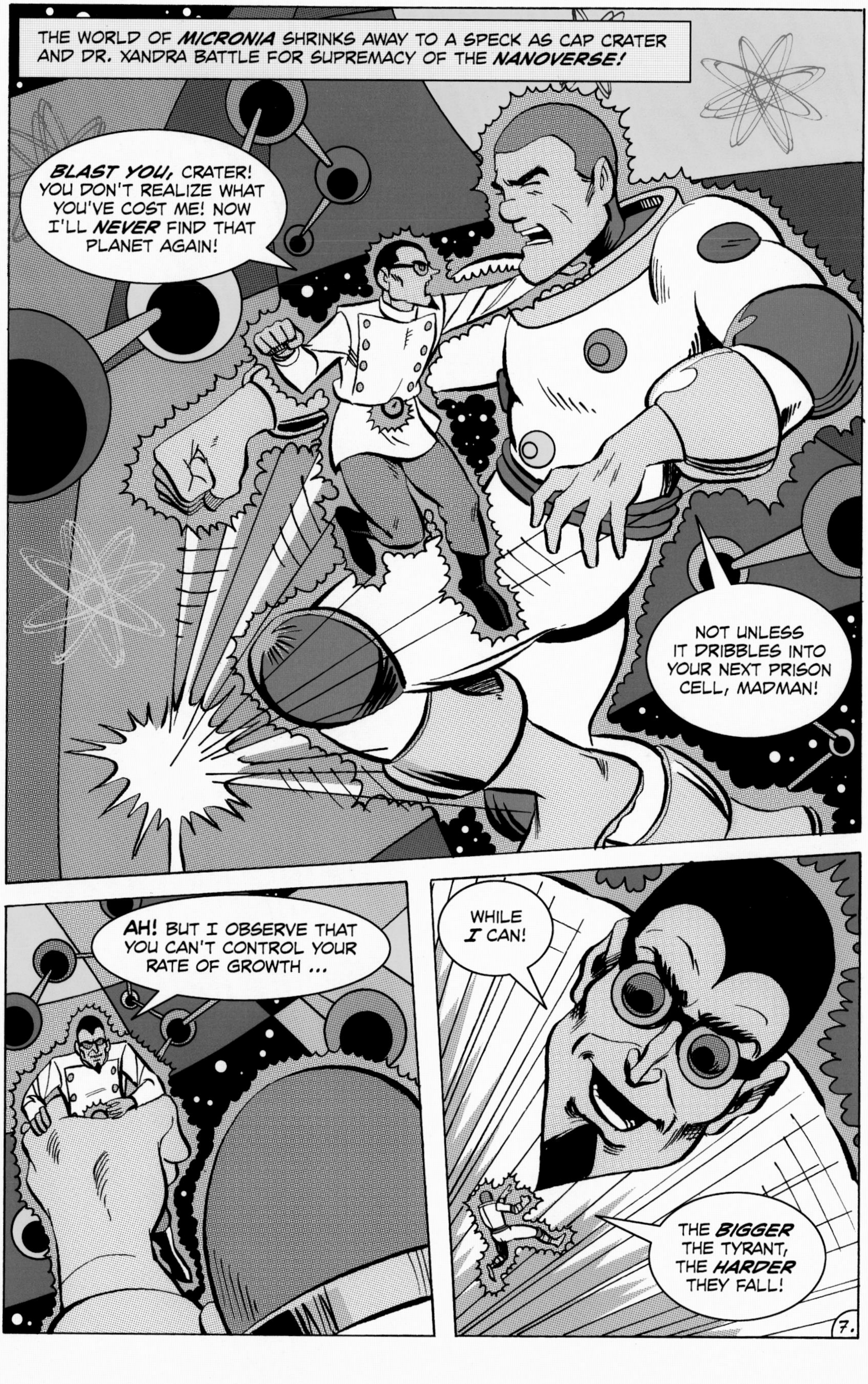
THE WORLD OF *MICRONIA* SHRINKS AWAY TO A SPECK AS CAP CRATER AND DR. XANDRA BATTLE FOR SUPREMACY OF THE *NANOVERSE!*
*BLAST YOU,* CRATER! YOU DON'T REALIZE WHAT YOU'VE COST ME! NOW I'LL *NEVER* FIND THAT PLANET AGAIN!
NOT UNLESS IT DRIBBLES INTO YOUR NEXT PRISON CELL, MADMAN!
*AH!* BUT I OBSERVE THAT YOU CAN'T CONTROL YOUR RATE OF GROWTH ...
WHILE *I* CAN!
THE *BIGGER* THE TYRANT, THE *HARDER* THEY FALL!

DO YOU SAY ANYTHING THAT ISN'T A CLICHE?
BLAST YOU! HOLD STILL!
GAAAH! GET OFF, YOU SANCTIMONIOUS INSECT!
USUALLY WHEN YOU CALL ME "INSECT" IT'S HYPERBOLE! BUT THIS TIME...
I'D SAY YOU WERE JUST ABOUT RIGHT!
TIME TO ROCK THE BOAT!

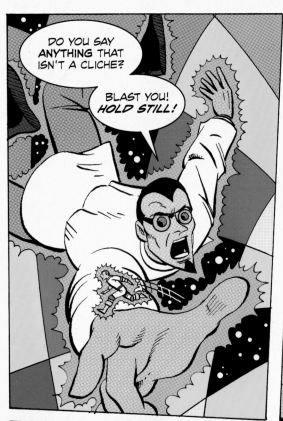

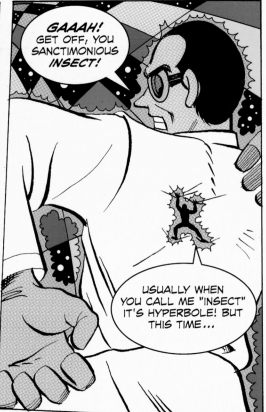

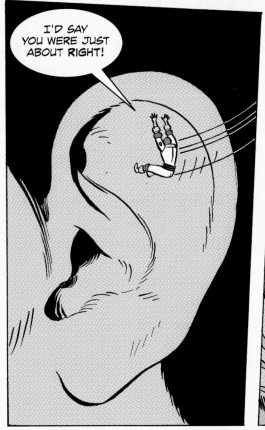

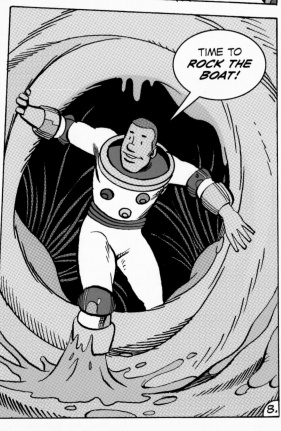

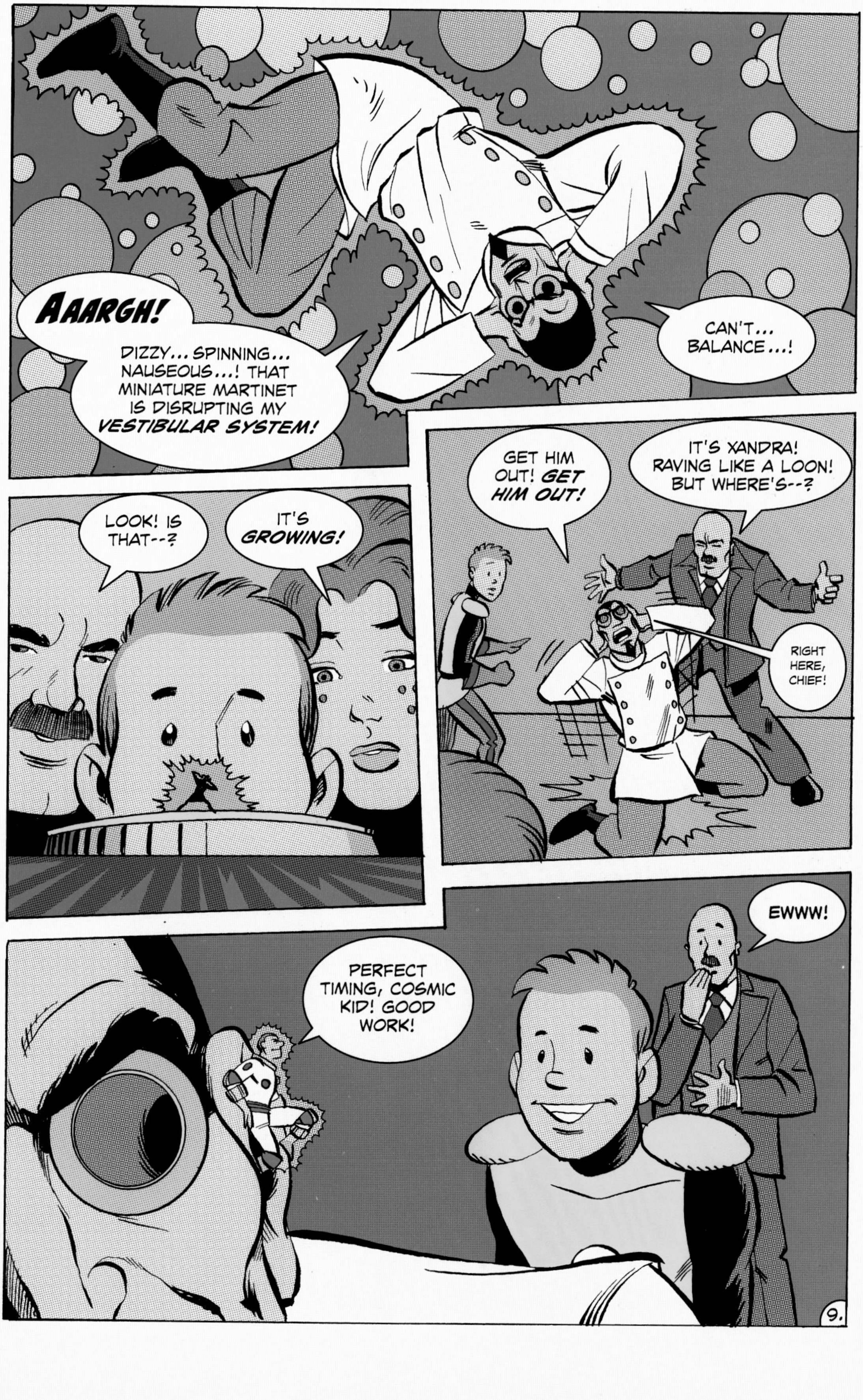
AAARGH!
DIZZY... SPINNING... NAUSEOUS...! THAT MINIATURE MARTINET IS DISRUPTING MY VESTIBULAR SYSTEM!
CAN'T... BALANCE...!
LOOK! IS THAT--?
IT'S GROWING!
GET HIM OUT! GET HIM OUT!
IT'S XANDRA! RAVING LIKE A LOON! BUT WHERE'S--?
RIGHT HERE, CHIEF!
PERFECT TIMING, COSMIC KID! GOOD WORK!
EWWW!

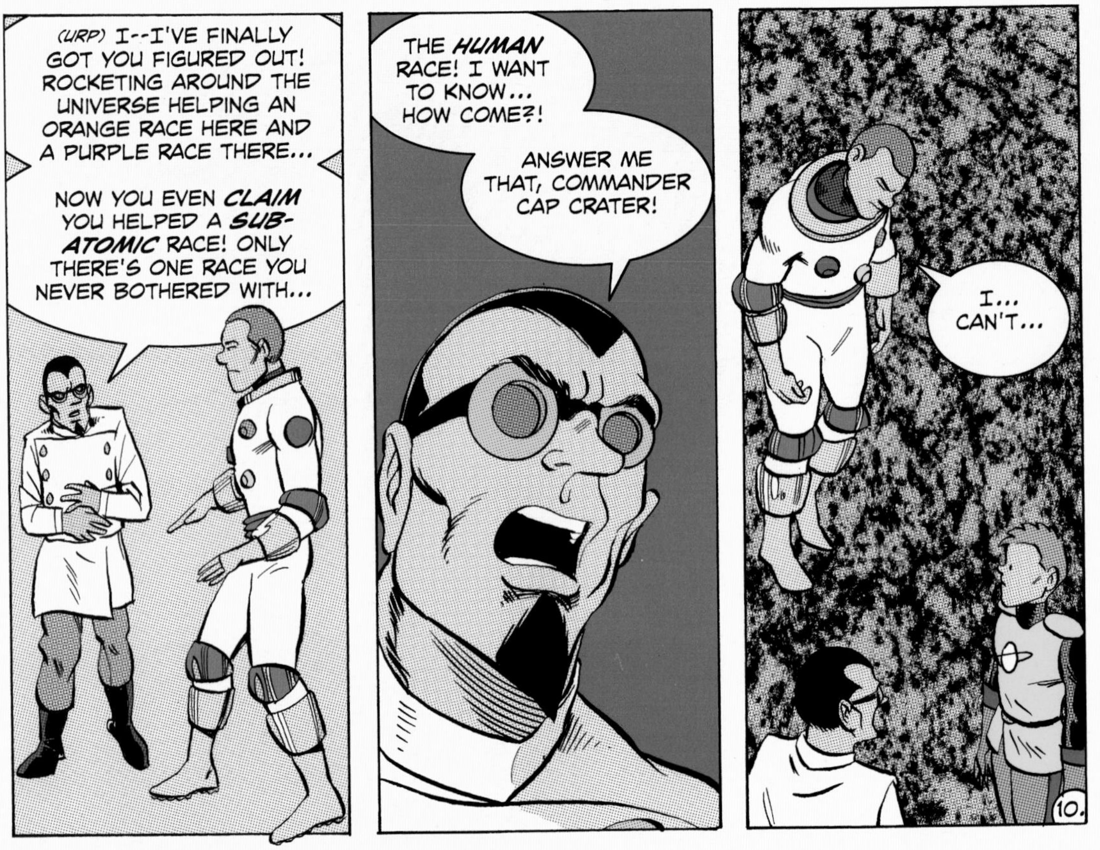

(URP) I--I'VE FINALLY GOT YOU FIGURED OUT! ROCKETING AROUND THE UNIVERSE HELPING AN ORANGE RACE HERE AND A PURPLE RACE THERE...
NOW YOU EVEN CLAIM YOU HELPED A SUB-ATOMIC RACE! ONLY THERE'S ONE RACE YOU NEVER BOTHERED WITH...
THE HUMAN RACE! I WANT TO KNOW... HOW COME?!
ANSWER ME THAT, COMMANDER CAP CRATER!
I... CAN'T...
10.


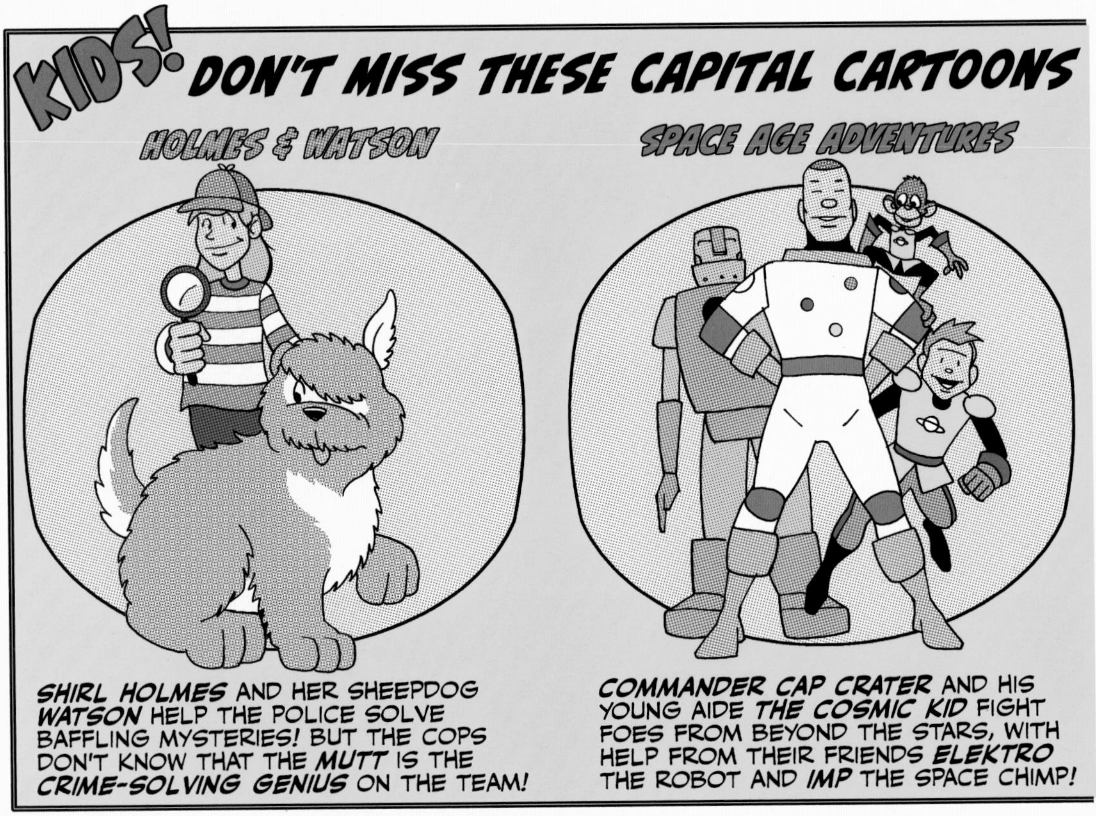

KIDS! DON'T MISS THESE CAPITAL CARTOONS
HOLMES & WATSON
SPACE AGE ADVENTURES
SHIRL HOLMES AND HER SHEEPDOG WATSON HELP THE POLICE SOLVE BAFFLING MYSTERIES! BUT THE COPS DON'T KNOW THAT THE MUTT IS THE CRIME-SOLVING GENIUS ON THE TEAM!
COMMANDER CAP CRATER AND HIS YOUNG AIDE THE COSMIC KID FIGHT FOES FROM BEYOND THE STARS, WITH HELP FROM THEIR FRIENDS ELEKTRO THE ROBOT AND IMP THE SPACE CHIMP!

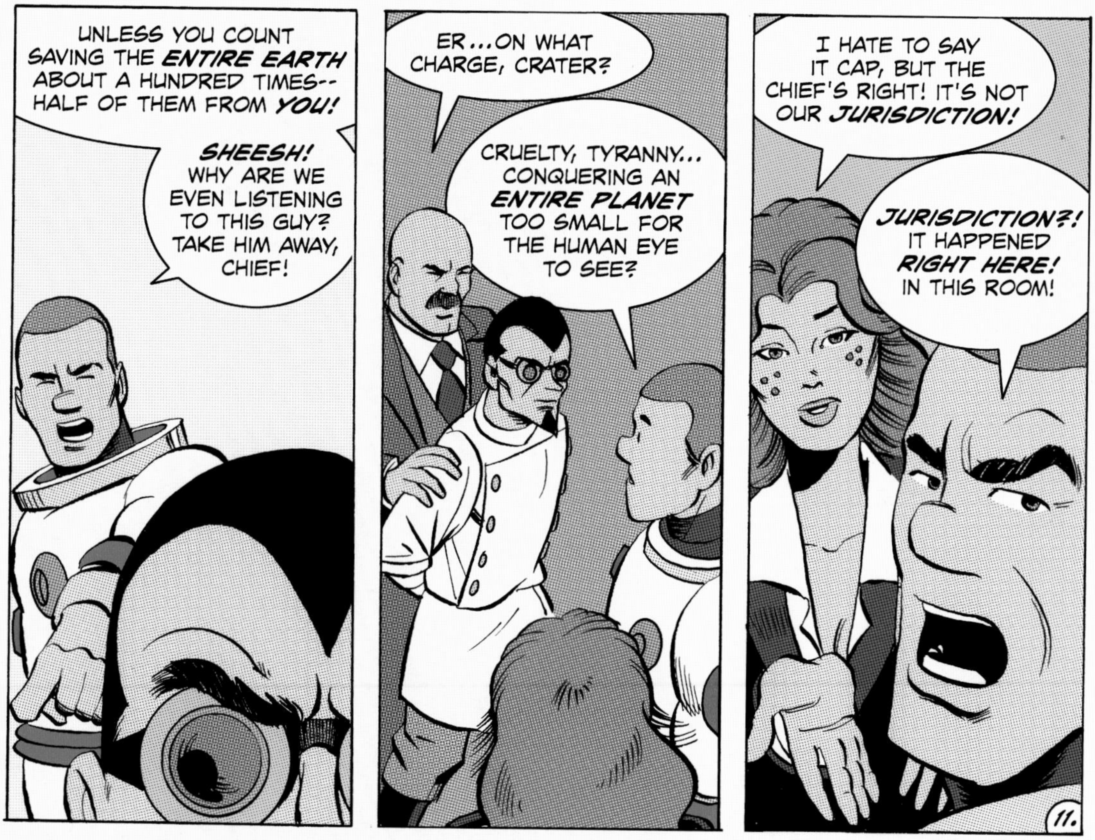
UNLESS YOU COUNT SAVING THE ENTIRE EARTH ABOUT A HUNDRED TIMES-- HALF OF THEM FROM YOU!
SHEESH! WHY ARE WE EVEN LISTENING TO THIS GUY? TAKE HIM AWAY, CHIEF!
ER...ON WHAT CHARGE, CRATER?
CRUELTY, TYRANNY... CONQUERING AN ENTIRE PLANET TOO SMALL FOR THE HUMAN EYE TO SEE?
I HATE TO SAY IT CAP, BUT THE CHIEF'S RIGHT! IT'S NOT OUR JURISDICTION!
JURISDICTION?! IT HAPPENED RIGHT HERE! IN THIS ROOM!
11.

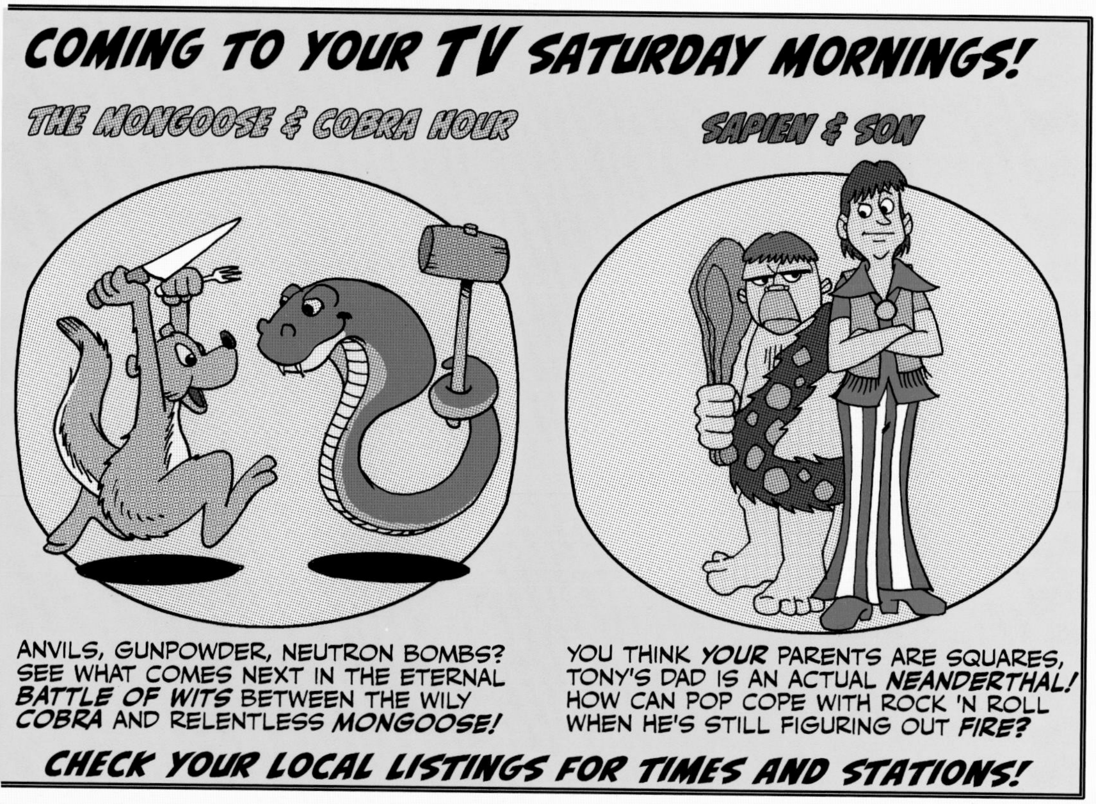
COMING TO YOUR TV SATURDAY MORNINGS!
THE MONGOOSE & COBRA HOUR
SAPIEN & SON
ANVILS, GUNPOWDER, NEUTRON BOMBS? SEE WHAT COMES NEXT IN THE ETERNAL BATTLE OF WITS BETWEEN THE WILY COBRA AND RELENTLESS MONGOOSE!
YOU THINK YOUR PARENTS ARE SQUARES, TONY'S DAD IS AN ACTUAL NEANDERTHAL! HOW CAN POP COPE WITH ROCK 'N ROLL WHEN HE'S STILL FIGURING OUT FIRE?
CHECK YOUR LOCAL LISTINGS FOR TIMES AND STATIONS!

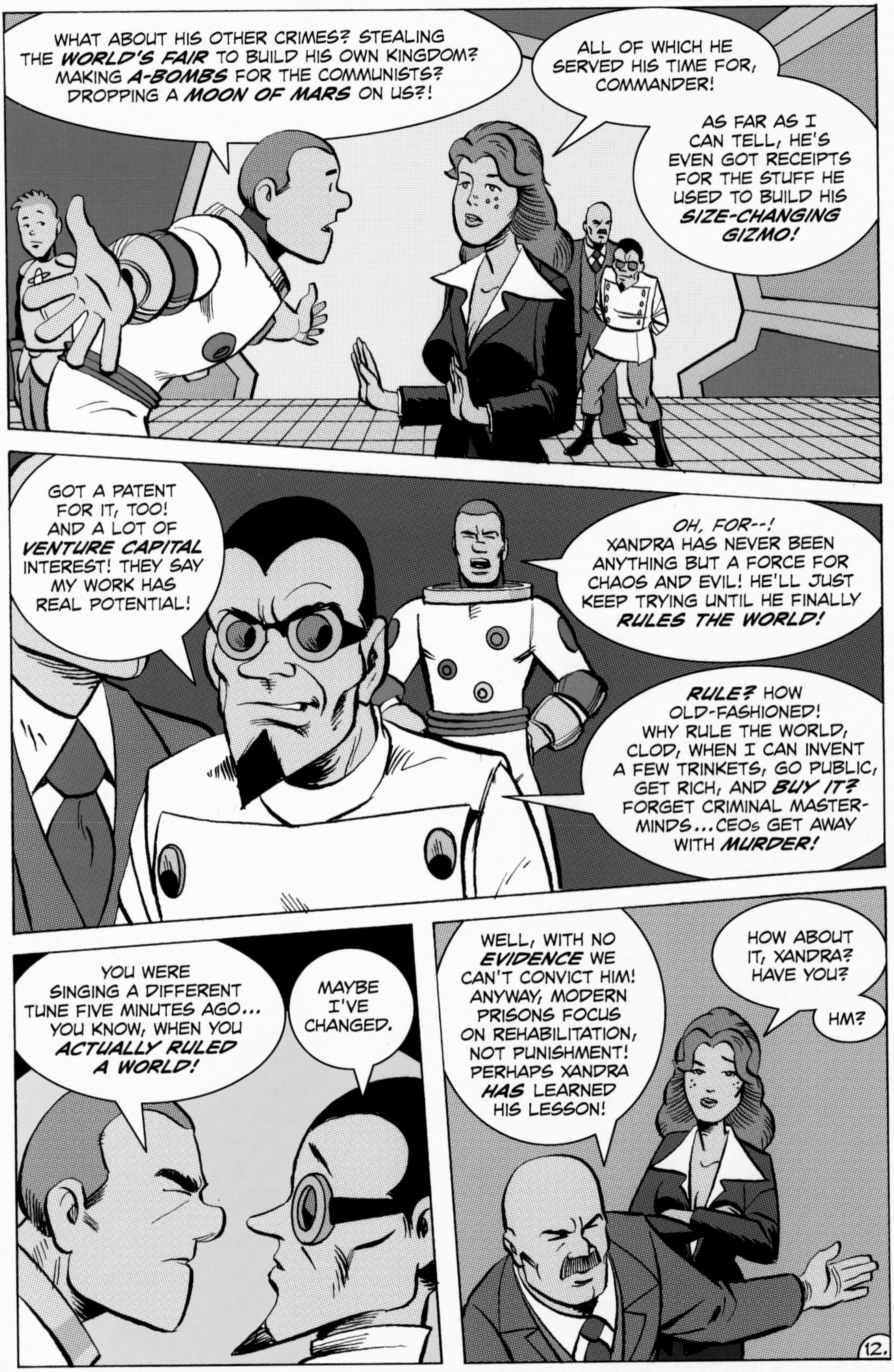
WHAT ABOUT HIS OTHER CRIMES? STEALING THE WORLD'S FAIR TO BUILD HIS OWN KINGDOM? MAKING A-BOMBS FOR THE COMMUNISTS? DROPPING A MOON OF MARS ON US?!
ALL OF WHICH HE SERVED HIS TIME FOR, COMMANDER!
AS FAR AS I CAN TELL, HE'S EVEN GOT RECEIPTS FOR THE STUFF HE USED TO BUILD HIS SIZE-CHANGING GIZMO!
GOT A PATENT FOR IT, TOO! AND A LOT OF VENTURE CAPITAL INTEREST! THEY SAY MY WORK HAS REAL POTENTIAL!
OH, FOR--! XANDRA HAS NEVER BEEN ANYTHING BUT A FORCE FOR CHAOS AND EVIL! HE'LL JUST KEEP TRYING UNTIL HE FINALLY RULES THE WORLD!
RULE? HOW OLD-FASHIONED! WHY RULE THE WORLD, CLOD, WHEN I CAN INVENT A FEW TRINKETS, GO PUBLIC, GET RICH, AND BUY IT? FORGET CRIMINAL MASTER-MINDS...CEOs GET AWAY WITH MURDER!
YOU WERE SINGING A DIFFERENT TUNE FIVE MINUTES AGO... YOU KNOW, WHEN YOU ACTUALLY RULED A WORLD!
MAYBE I'VE CHANGED.
WELL, WITH NO EVIDENCE WE CAN'T CONVICT HIM! ANYWAY, MODERN PRISONS FOCUS ON REHABILITATION, NOT PUNISHMENT! PERHAPS XANDRA HAS LEARNED HIS LESSON!
HOW ABOUT IT, XANDRA? HAVE YOU?
HM?

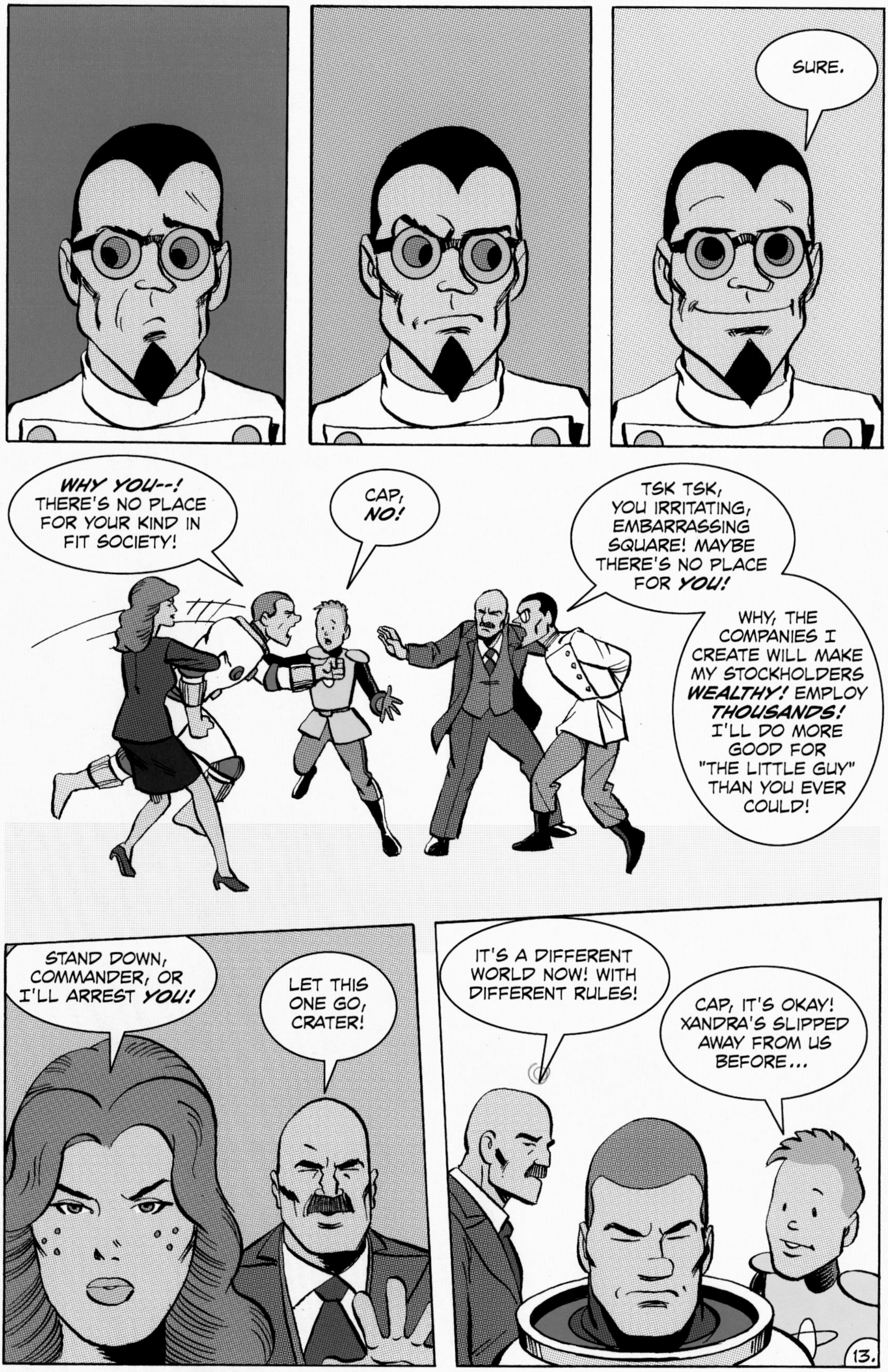
SURE.
WHY YOU--! THERE'S NO PLACE FOR YOUR KIND IN FIT SOCIETY!
CAP, NO!
TSK TSK, YOU IRRITATING, EMBARRASSING SQUARE! MAYBE THERE'S NO PLACE FOR YOU!
WHY, THE COMPANIES I CREATE WILL MAKE MY STOCKHOLDERS WEALTHY! EMPLOY THOUSANDS! I'LL DO MORE GOOD FOR "THE LITTLE GUY" THAN YOU EVER COULD!
STAND DOWN, COMMANDER, OR I'LL ARREST YOU!
LET THIS ONE GO, CRATER!
IT'S A DIFFERENT WORLD NOW! WITH DIFFERENT RULES!
CAP, IT'S OKAY! XANDRA'S SLIPPED AWAY FROM US BEFORE...
13.

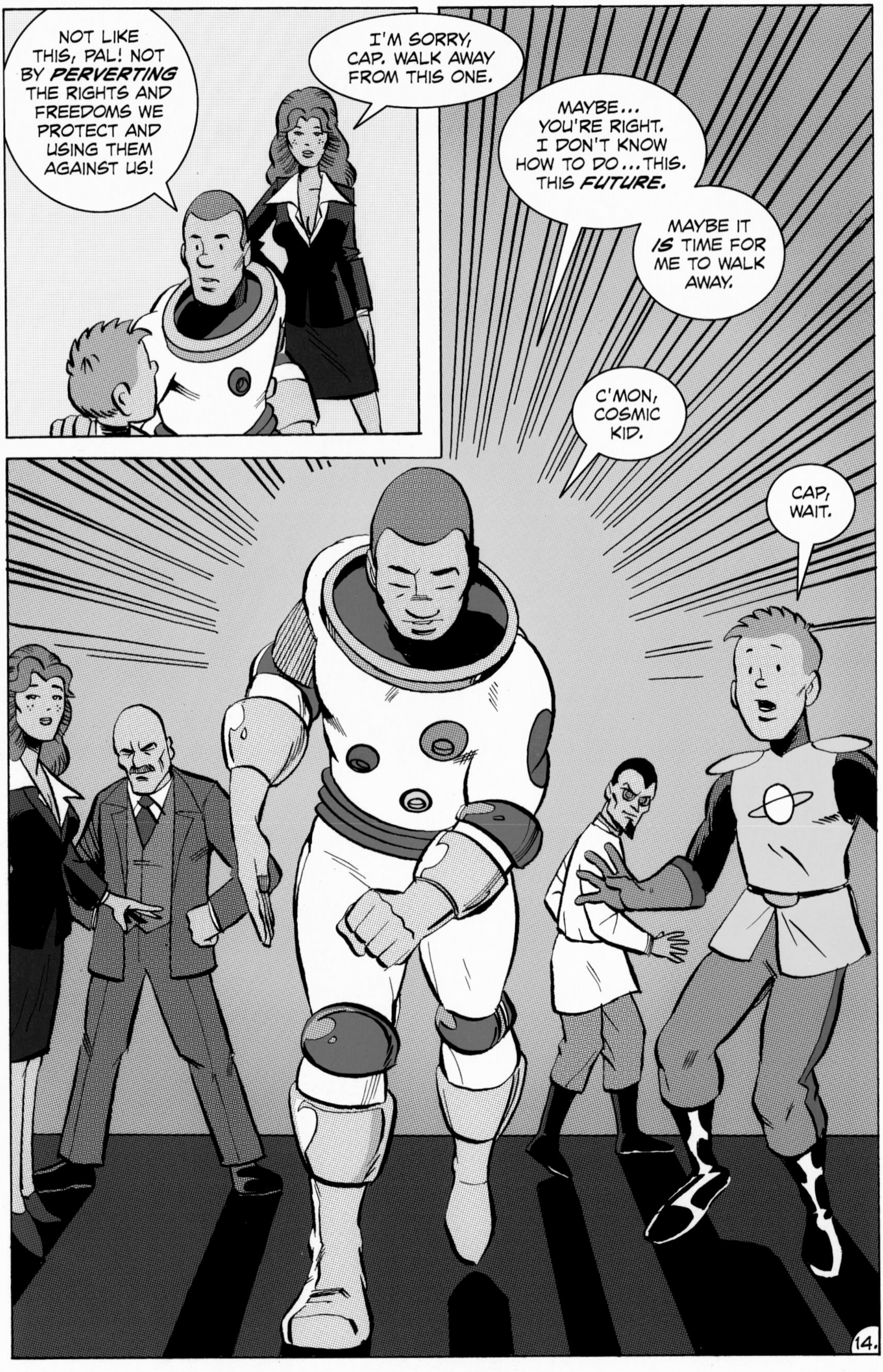
NOT LIKE THIS, PAL! NOT BY PERVERTING THE RIGHTS AND FREEDOMS WE PROTECT AND USING THEM AGAINST US!
I'M SORRY, CAP. WALK AWAY FROM THIS ONE.
MAYBE... YOU'RE RIGHT. I DON'T KNOW HOW TO DO... THIS. THIS FUTURE.
MAYBE IT IS TIME FOR ME TO WALK AWAY.
C'MON, COSMIC KID.
CAP, WAIT.

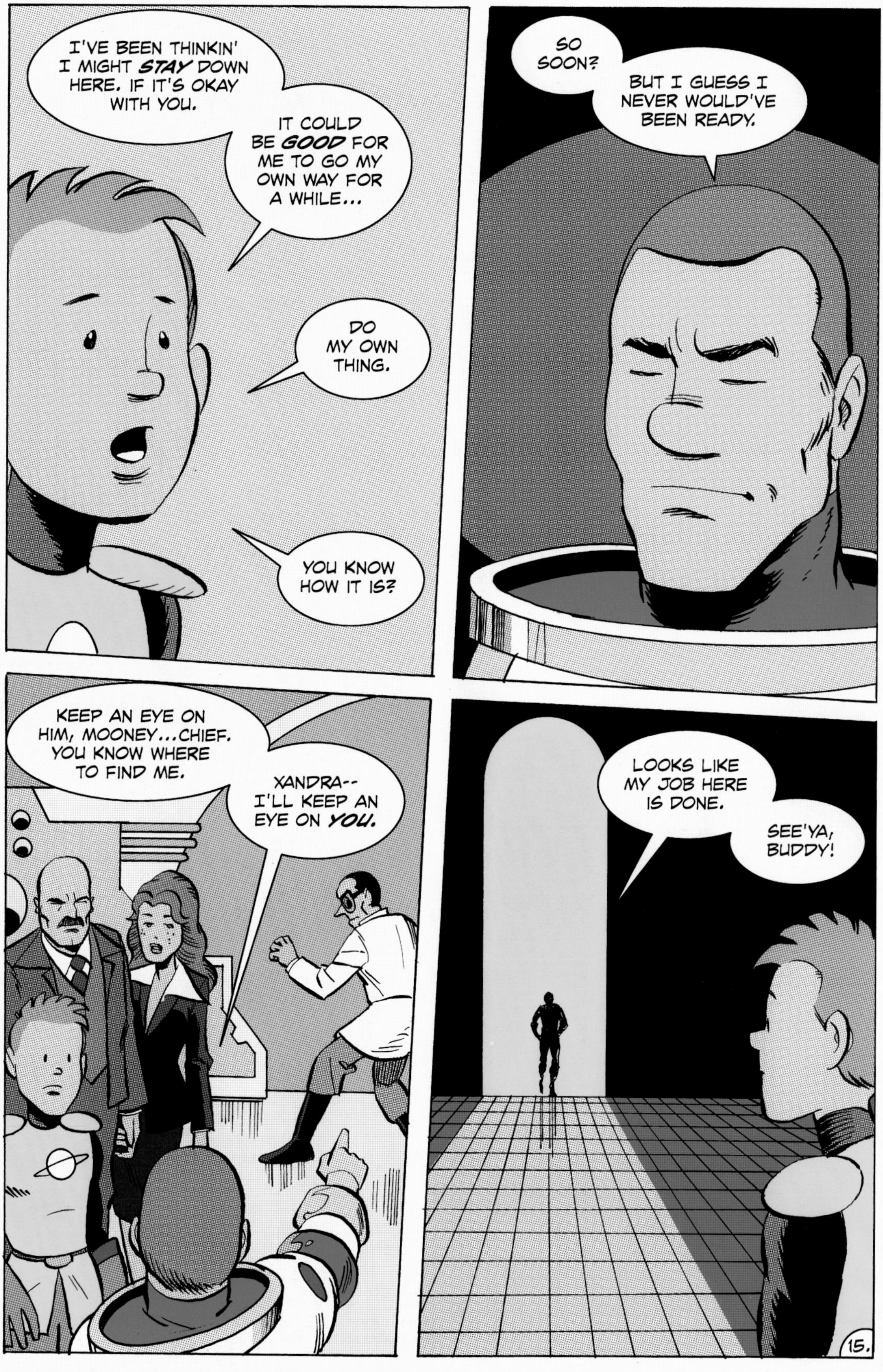

I'VE BEEN THINKIN' I MIGHT *STAY* DOWN HERE. IF IT'S OKAY WITH YOU.
IT COULD BE *GOOD* FOR ME TO GO MY OWN WAY FOR A WHILE...
DO MY OWN THING.
YOU KNOW HOW IT IS?
SO SOON?
BUT I GUESS I NEVER WOULD'VE BEEN READY.
KEEP AN EYE ON HIM, MOONEY...CHIEF. YOU KNOW WHERE TO FIND ME.
XANDRA-- I'LL KEEP AN EYE ON *YOU.*
LOOKS LIKE MY JOB HERE IS DONE.
SEE'YA, BUDDY!

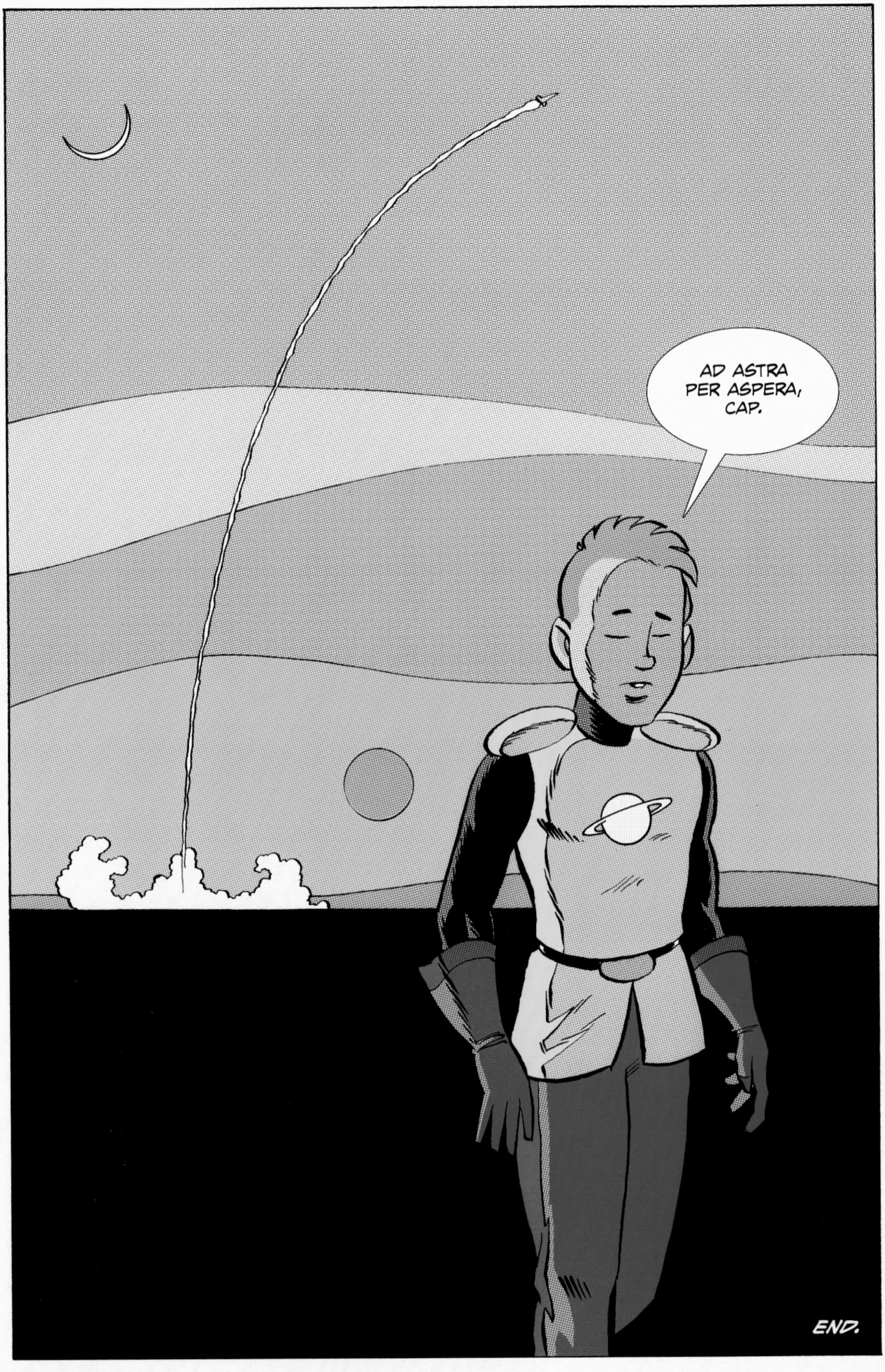
AD ASTRA
PER ASPERA,
CAP.
END.

# COMMANDER'S COMMUNIQUES

Dear Readers,

This is the final issue of the exploits of Cap Crater and the Cosmic Kid in *Space Age Adventures*. More than four hundred issues is a good run for any comic book, and we're proud of the stories we told over all these years.

But the hard fact is that Cap Crater and his cast are simpler characters for simpler times. Attempts to update them for the modern day didn't really satisfy us or you, our readers, as proven by declining circulation. During World War II, *Space Age Adventures* and comics like it sold millions of copies each month, many to young men taking their first trips overseas to fight for the ideals they espoused. To borrow a phrase from our Distinguished Competition, there was a time when "Truth, Justice, and the American Way" didn't sound corny or naive. But changing tastes and new entertainments slowly whittled our readership to numbers too small to maintain.

In our era of rocket ships to the Moon, it is also increasingly hard to keep our *Space Age Adventures* ahead of the real ones. Neil Armstrong didn't find Cap Crater's secret Lunar Outpost, nor did Mariner's cameras detect Dr. Xandra's Forbidden Martian Fortress. But their days were clearly numbered. Technologies that seemed like the most outlandish science fiction we could conceive of ten years ago are nearly commonplace today. In many ways, the World of Tomorrow we imagined for the Commander and his cohorts in the earliest tales of *Space Age Adventures* has arrived.

And so we retire Cap Crater to his Selene Sanctum, knowing he'll always be overhead watching us and roaring to our rescue if we need him. Perhaps new generations of writers and artists will find fresh stories to tell, or perhaps we'll return to the Moon someday and meet ol' Cap there. Either way, we suspect that the *Space Age Adventures* of Cap Crater and the Cosmic Kid are far from finished.

**The Editors**

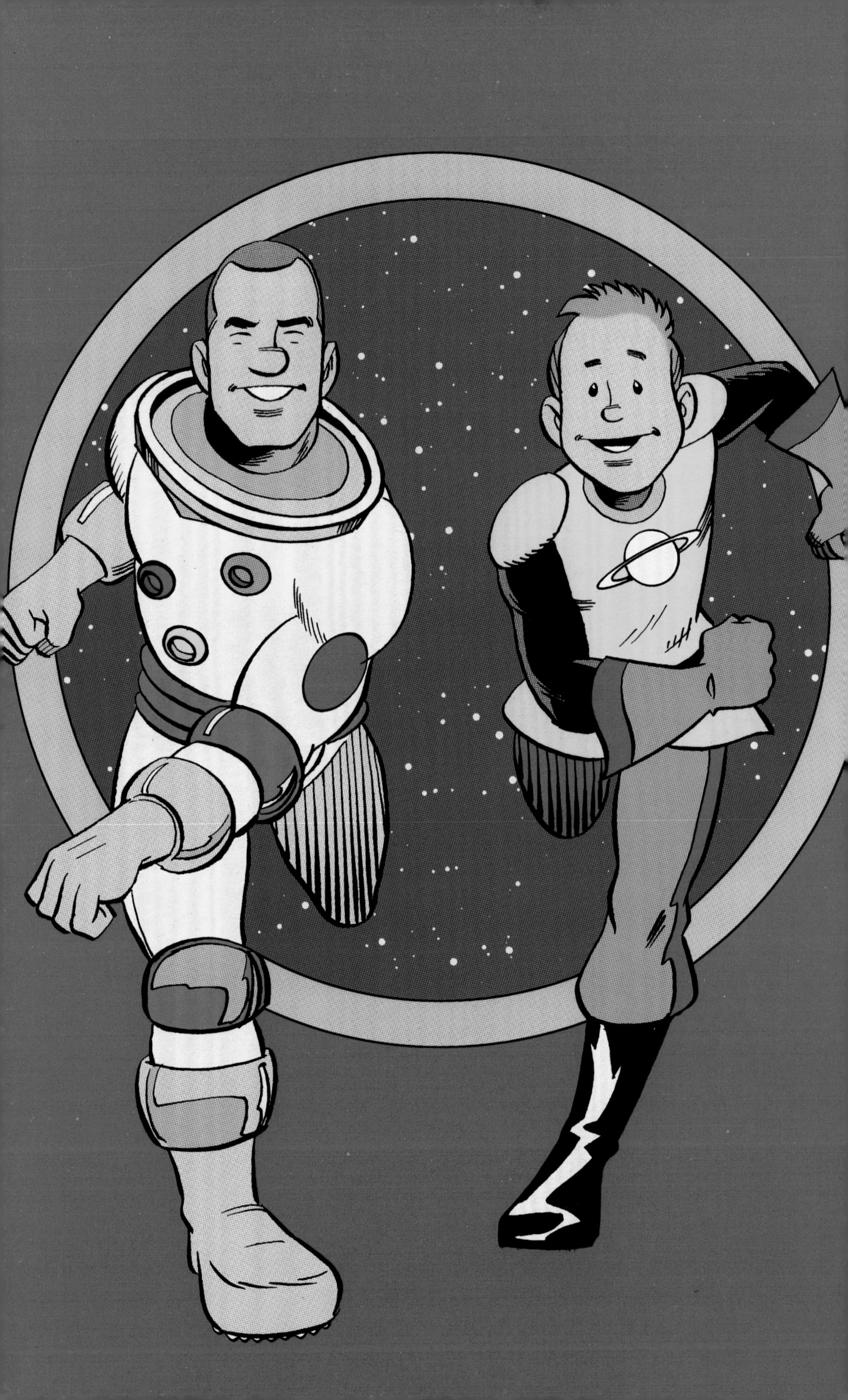

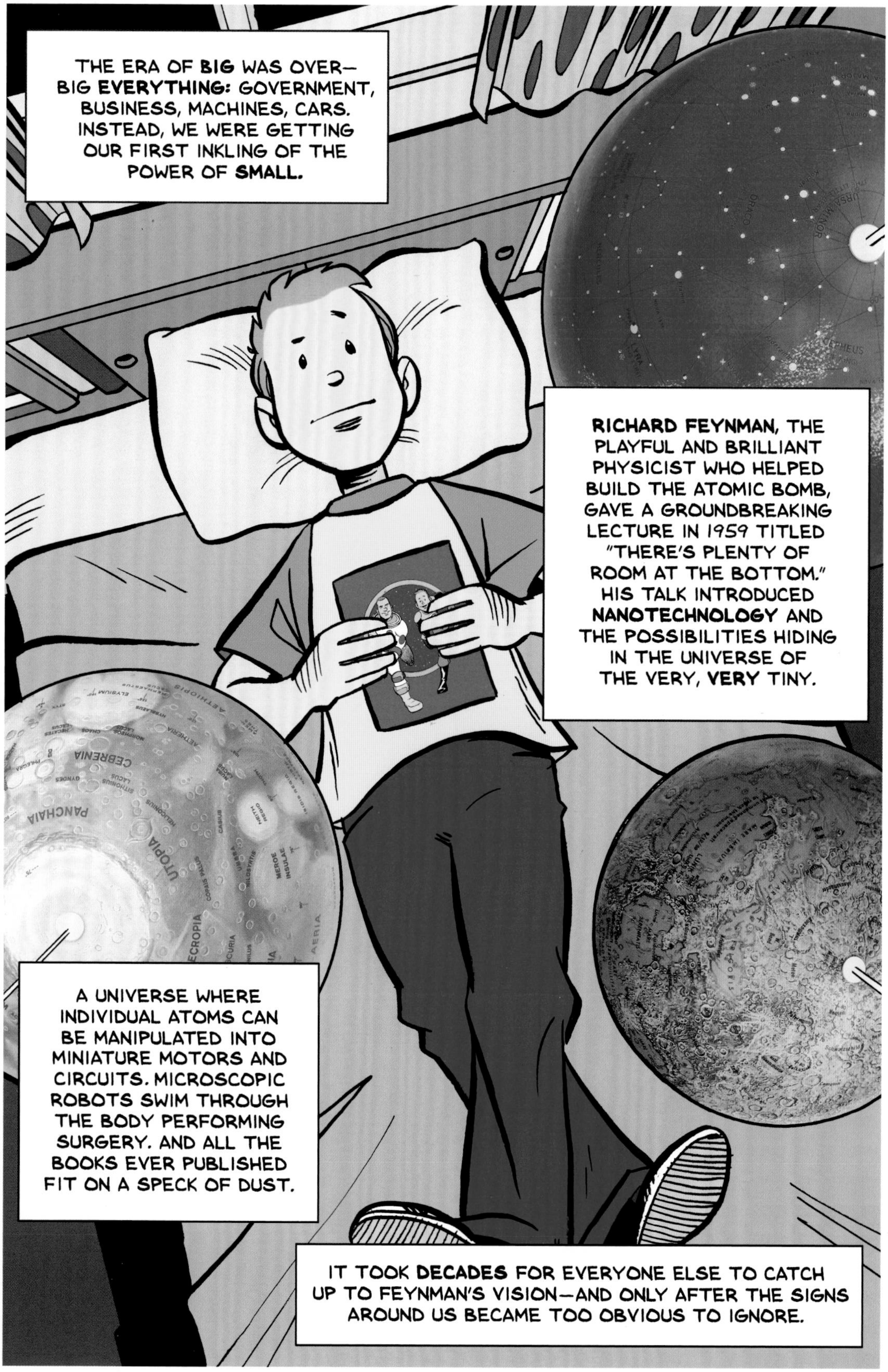
THE ERA OF **BIG** WAS OVER— BIG **EVERYTHING:** GOVERNMENT, BUSINESS, MACHINES, CARS. INSTEAD, WE WERE GETTING OUR FIRST INKLING OF THE POWER OF **SMALL.**
**RICHARD FEYNMAN**, THE PLAYFUL AND BRILLIANT PHYSICIST WHO HELPED BUILD THE ATOMIC BOMB, GAVE A GROUNDBREAKING LECTURE IN 1959 TITLED "THERE'S PLENTY OF ROOM AT THE BOTTOM." HIS TALK INTRODUCED **NANOTECHNOLOGY** AND THE POSSIBILITIES HIDING IN THE UNIVERSE OF THE VERY, **VERY** TINY.
A UNIVERSE WHERE INDIVIDUAL ATOMS CAN BE MANIPULATED INTO MINIATURE MOTORS AND CIRCUITS. MICROSCOPIC ROBOTS SWIM THROUGH THE BODY PERFORMING SURGERY. AND ALL THE BOOKS EVER PUBLISHED FIT ON A SPECK OF DUST.
IT TOOK **DECADES** FOR EVERYONE ELSE TO CATCH UP TO FEYNMAN'S VISION—AND ONLY AFTER THE SIGNS AROUND US BECAME TOO OBVIOUS TO IGNORE.

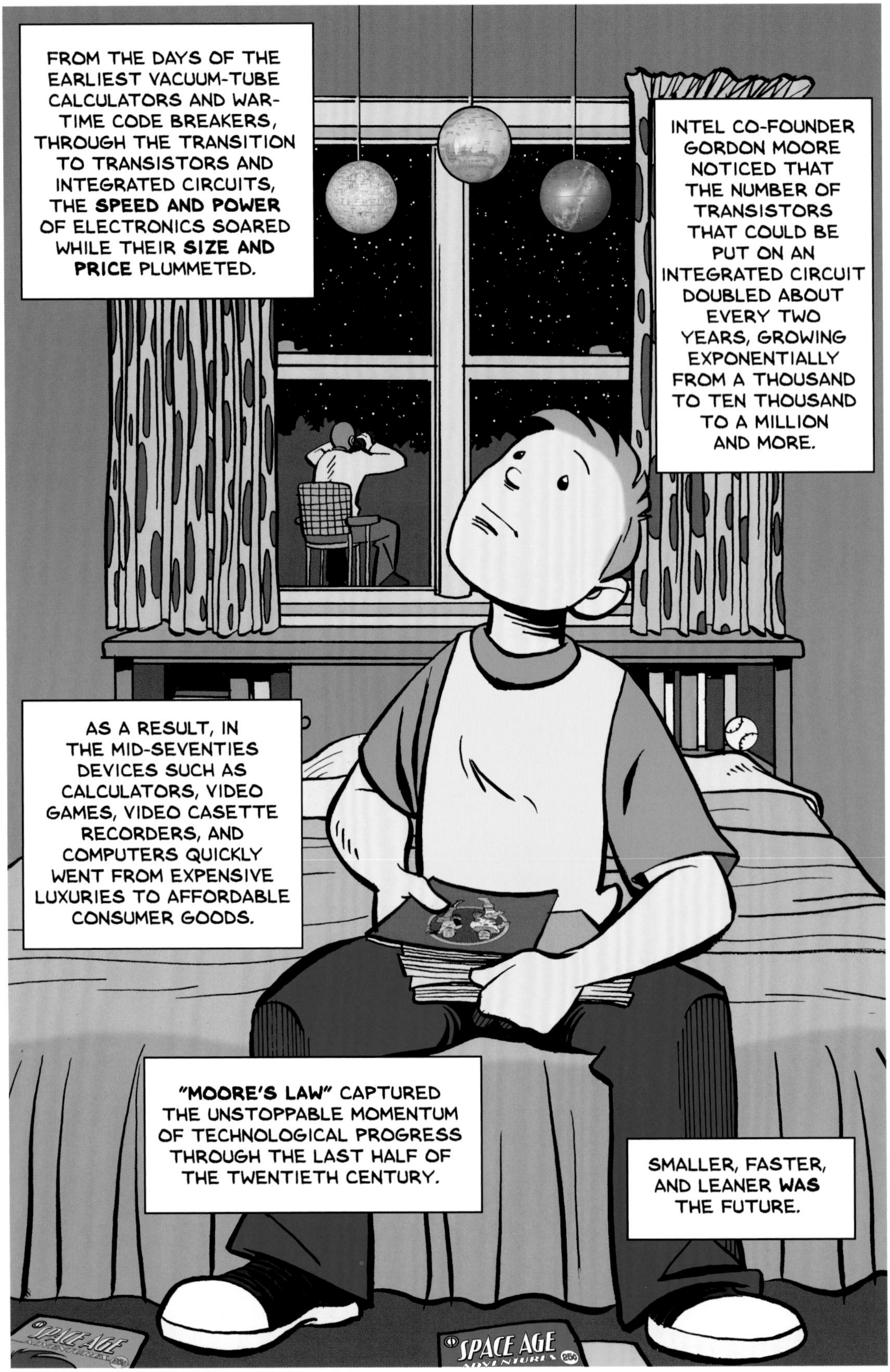
FROM THE DAYS OF THE EARLIEST VACUUM-TUBE CALCULATORS AND WAR-TIME CODE BREAKERS, THROUGH THE TRANSITION TO TRANSISTORS AND INTEGRATED CIRCUITS, THE **SPEED AND POWER** OF ELECTRONICS SOARED WHILE THEIR **SIZE AND PRICE** PLUMMETED.
INTEL CO-FOUNDER GORDON MOORE NOTICED THAT THE NUMBER OF TRANSISTORS THAT COULD BE PUT ON AN INTEGRATED CIRCUIT DOUBLED ABOUT EVERY TWO YEARS, GROWING EXPONENTIALLY FROM A THOUSAND TO TEN THOUSAND TO A MILLION AND MORE.
AS A RESULT, IN THE MID-SEVENTIES DEVICES SUCH AS CALCULATORS, VIDEO GAMES, VIDEO CASETTE RECORDERS, AND COMPUTERS QUICKLY WENT FROM EXPENSIVE LUXURIES TO AFFORDABLE CONSUMER GOODS.
**"MOORE'S LAW"** CAPTURED THE UNSTOPPABLE MOMENTUM OF TECHNOLOGICAL PROGRESS THROUGH THE LAST HALF OF THE TWENTIETH CENTURY.
SMALLER, FASTER, AND LEANER **WAS** THE FUTURE.
SPACE AGE ADVENTURES
SPACE AGE ADVENTURES

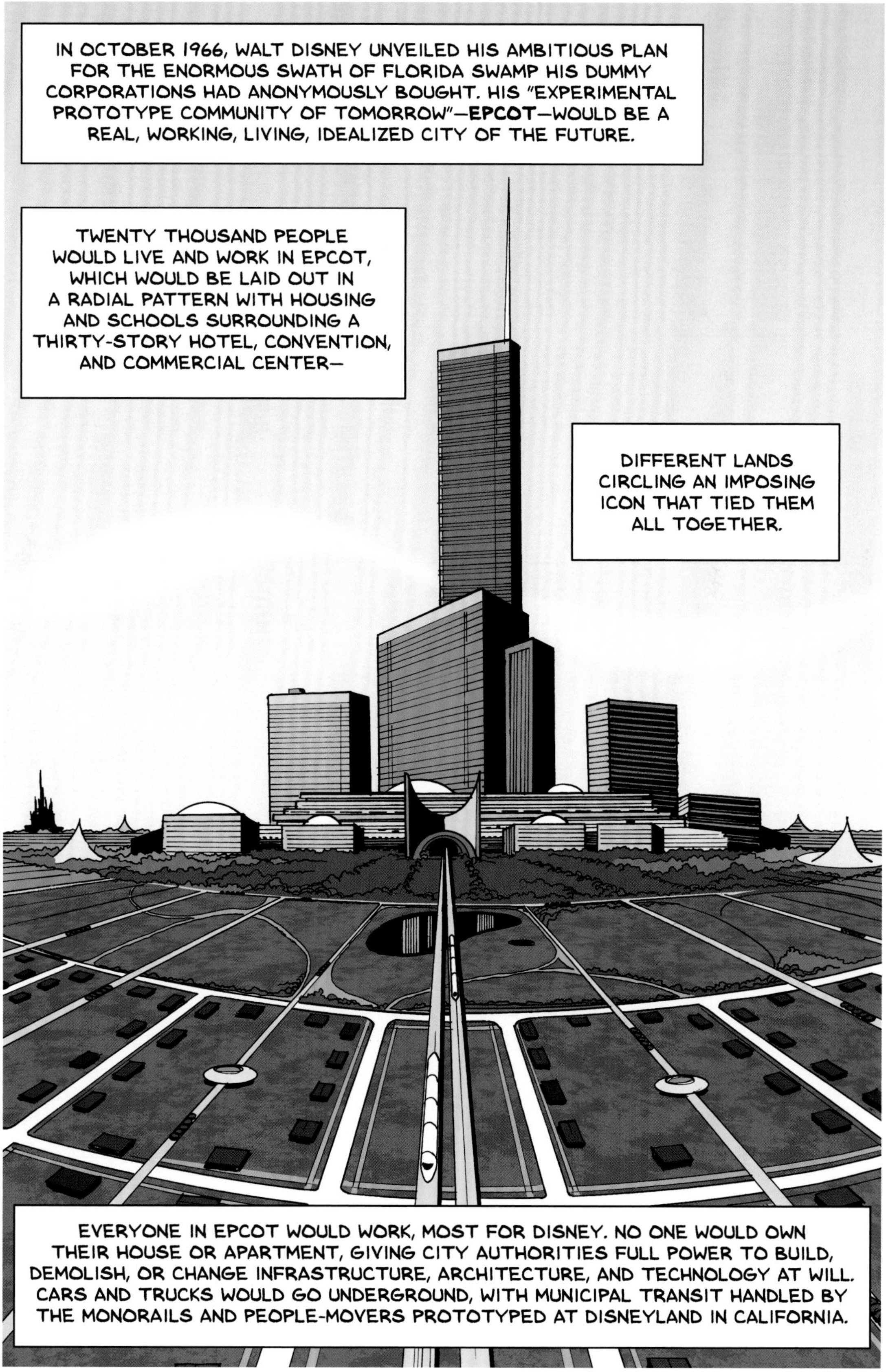
IN OCTOBER 1966, WALT DISNEY UNVEILED HIS AMBITIOUS PLAN FOR THE ENORMOUS SWATH OF FLORIDA SWAMP HIS DUMMY CORPORATIONS HAD ANONYMOUSLY BOUGHT. HIS "EXPERIMENTAL PROTOTYPE COMMUNITY OF TOMORROW"—**EPCOT**—WOULD BE A REAL, WORKING, LIVING, IDEALIZED CITY OF THE FUTURE.
TWENTY THOUSAND PEOPLE WOULD LIVE AND WORK IN EPCOT, WHICH WOULD BE LAID OUT IN A RADIAL PATTERN WITH HOUSING AND SCHOOLS SURROUNDING A THIRTY-STORY HOTEL, CONVENTION, AND COMMERCIAL CENTER—
DIFFERENT LANDS CIRCLING AN IMPOSING ICON THAT TIED THEM ALL TOGETHER.
EVERYONE IN EPCOT WOULD WORK, MOST FOR DISNEY. NO ONE WOULD OWN THEIR HOUSE OR APARTMENT, GIVING CITY AUTHORITIES FULL POWER TO BUILD, DEMOLISH, OR CHANGE INFRASTRUCTURE, ARCHITECTURE, AND TECHNOLOGY AT WILL. CARS AND TRUCKS WOULD GO UNDERGROUND, WITH MUNICIPAL TRANSIT HANDLED BY THE MONORAILS AND PEOPLE-MOVERS PROTOTYPED AT DISNEYLAND IN CALIFORNIA.

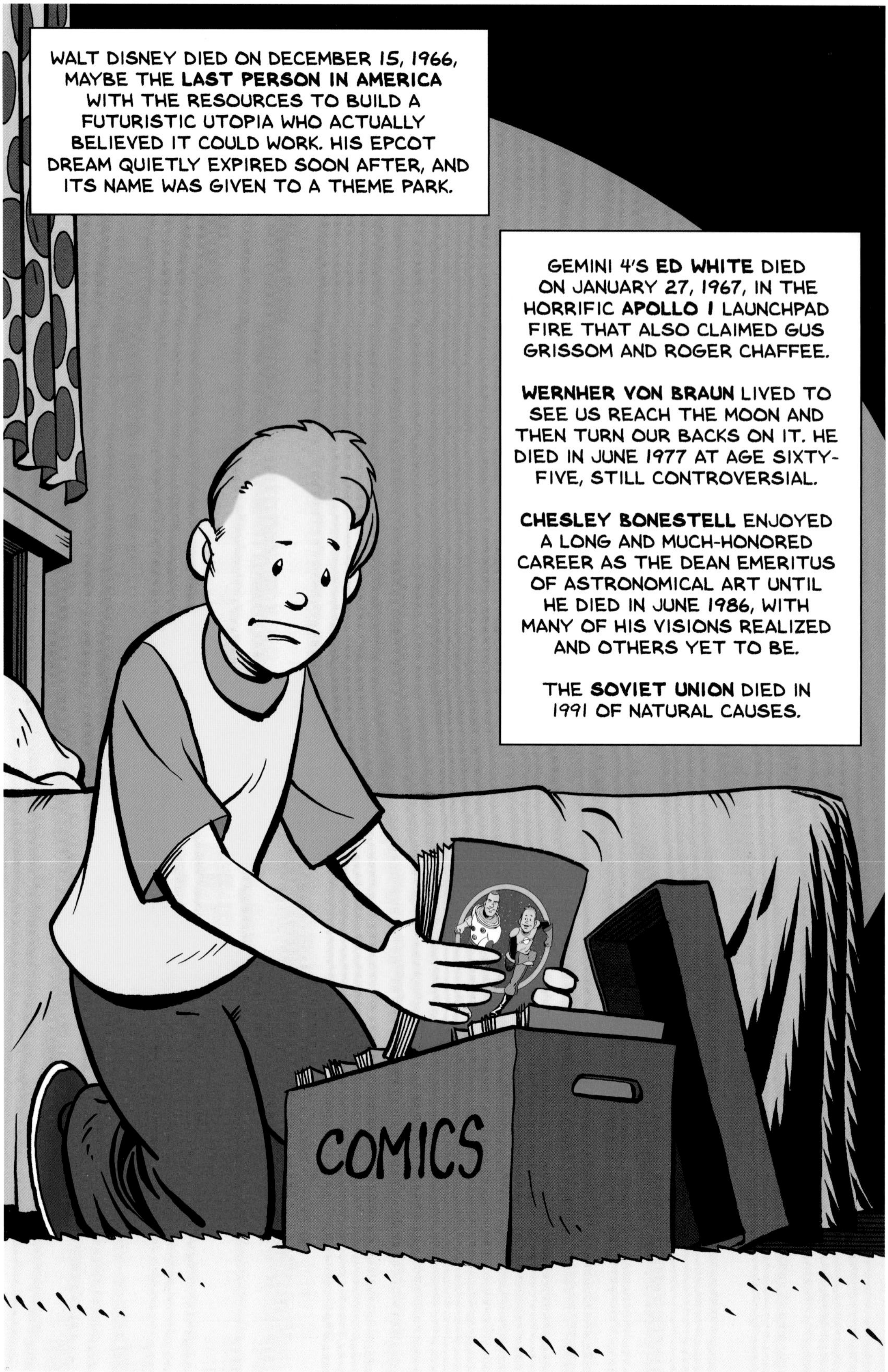
WALT DISNEY DIED ON DECEMBER 15, 1966, MAYBE THE **LAST PERSON IN AMERICA** WITH THE RESOURCES TO BUILD A FUTURISTIC UTOPIA WHO ACTUALLY BELIEVED IT COULD WORK. HIS EPCOT DREAM QUIETLY EXPIRED SOON AFTER, AND ITS NAME WAS GIVEN TO A THEME PARK.
GEMINI 4'S **ED WHITE** DIED ON JANUARY 27, 1967, IN THE HORRIFIC **APOLLO I** LAUNCHPAD FIRE THAT ALSO CLAIMED GUS GRISSOM AND ROGER CHAFFEE.
**WERNHER VON BRAUN** LIVED TO SEE US REACH THE MOON AND THEN TURN OUR BACKS ON IT. HE DIED IN JUNE 1977 AT AGE SIXTY-FIVE, STILL CONTROVERSIAL.
**CHESLEY BONESTELL** ENJOYED A LONG AND MUCH-HONORED CAREER AS THE DEAN EMERITUS OF ASTRONOMICAL ART UNTIL HE DIED IN JUNE 1986, WITH MANY OF HIS VISIONS REALIZED AND OTHERS YET TO BE.
THE **SOVIET UNION** DIED IN 1991 OF NATURAL CAUSES.
COMICS

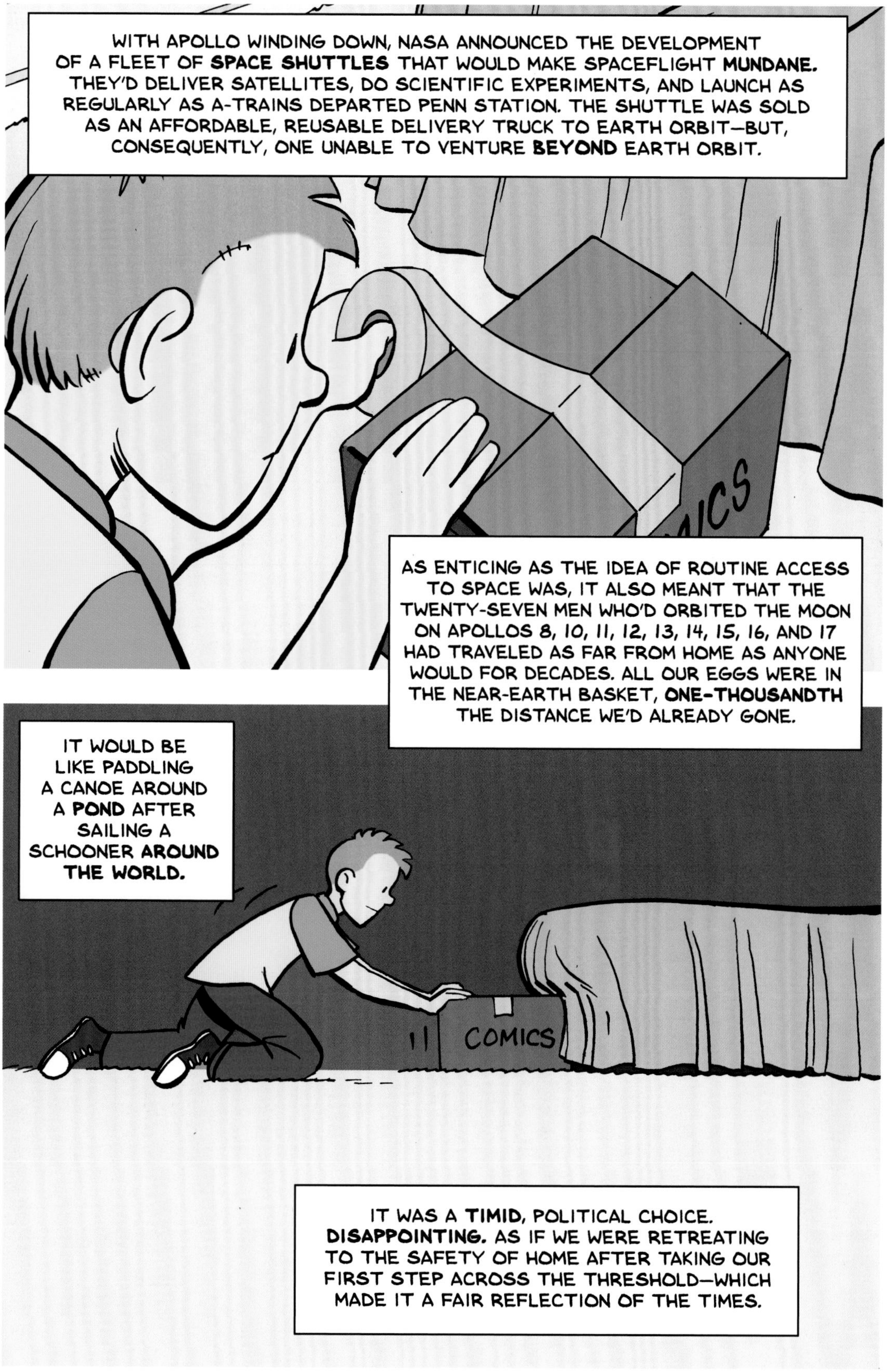
WITH APOLLO WINDING DOWN, NASA ANNOUNCED THE DEVELOPMENT OF A FLEET OF **SPACE SHUTTLES** THAT WOULD MAKE SPACEFLIGHT **MUNDANE.** THEY'D DELIVER SATELLITES, DO SCIENTIFIC EXPERIMENTS, AND LAUNCH AS REGULARLY AS A-TRAINS DEPARTED PENN STATION. THE SHUTTLE WAS SOLD AS AN AFFORDABLE, REUSABLE DELIVERY TRUCK TO EARTH ORBIT—BUT, CONSEQUENTLY, ONE UNABLE TO VENTURE **BEYOND** EARTH ORBIT.
AS ENTICING AS THE IDEA OF ROUTINE ACCESS TO SPACE WAS, IT ALSO MEANT THAT THE TWENTY-SEVEN MEN WHO'D ORBITED THE MOON ON APOLLOS 8, 10, 11, 12, 13, 14, 15, 16, AND 17 HAD TRAVELED AS FAR FROM HOME AS ANYONE WOULD FOR DECADES. ALL OUR EGGS WERE IN THE NEAR-EARTH BASKET, **ONE-THOUSANDTH** THE DISTANCE WE'D ALREADY GONE.
IT WOULD BE LIKE PADDLING A CANOE AROUND A **POND** AFTER SAILING A SCHOONER **AROUND THE WORLD.**
COMICS
IT WAS A **TIMID**, POLITICAL CHOICE. **DISAPPOINTING.** AS IF WE WERE RETREATING TO THE SAFETY OF HOME AFTER TAKING OUR FIRST STEP ACROSS THE THRESHOLD—WHICH MADE IT A FAIR REFLECTION OF THE TIMES.

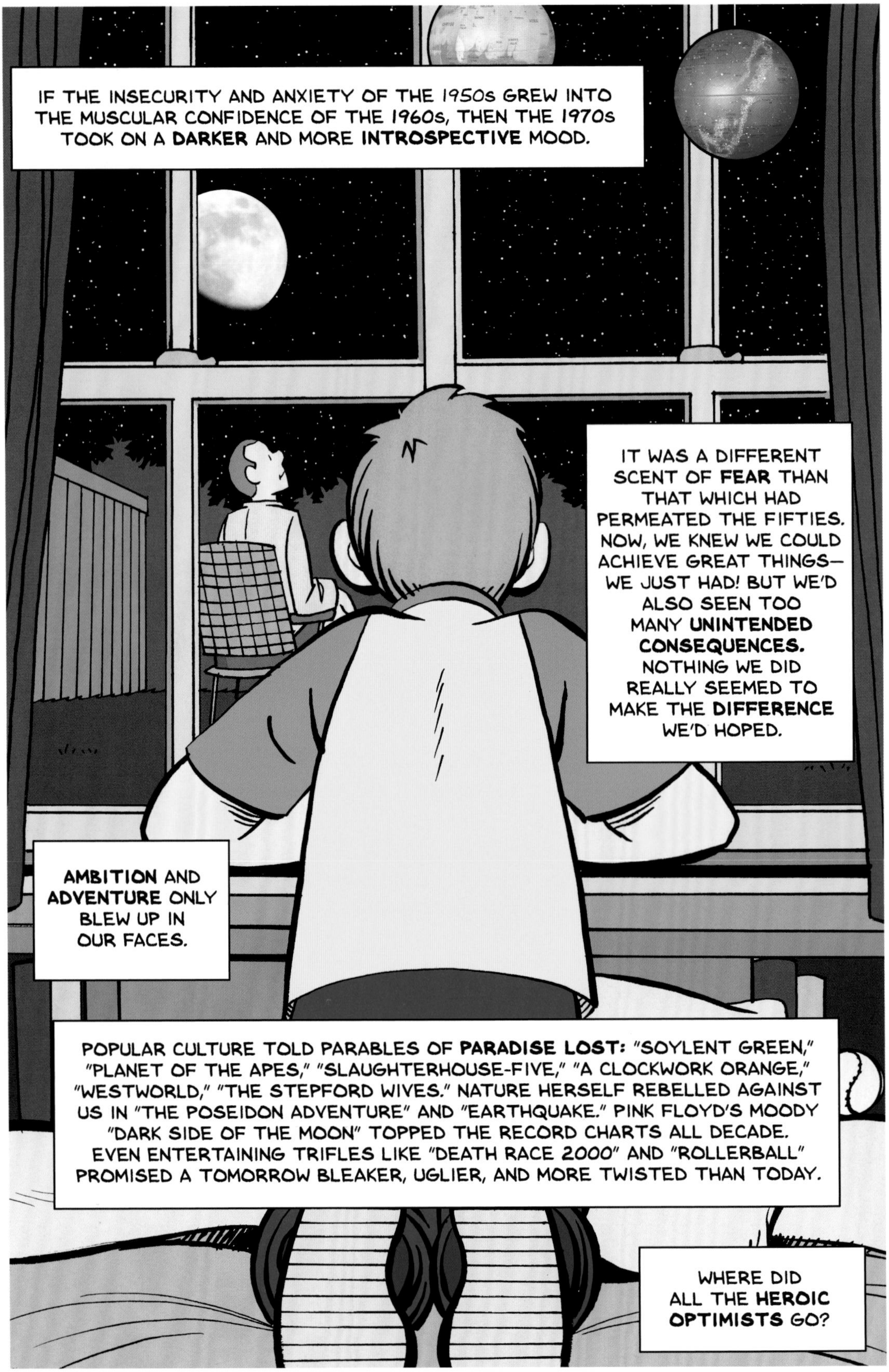
IF THE INSECURITY AND ANXIETY OF THE 1950s GREW INTO THE MUSCULAR CONFIDENCE OF THE 1960s, THEN THE 1970s TOOK ON A DARKER AND MORE INTROSPECTIVE MOOD.
IT WAS A DIFFERENT SCENT OF FEAR THAN THAT WHICH HAD PERMEATED THE FIFTIES. NOW, WE KNEW WE COULD ACHIEVE GREAT THINGS— WE JUST HAD! BUT WE'D ALSO SEEN TOO MANY UNINTENDED CONSEQUENCES. NOTHING WE DID REALLY SEEMED TO MAKE THE DIFFERENCE WE'D HOPED.
AMBITION AND ADVENTURE ONLY BLEW UP IN OUR FACES.
POPULAR CULTURE TOLD PARABLES OF PARADISE LOST: "SOYLENT GREEN," "PLANET OF THE APES," "SLAUGHTERHOUSE-FIVE," "A CLOCKWORK ORANGE," "WESTWORLD," "THE STEPFORD WIVES." NATURE HERSELF REBELLED AGAINST US IN "THE POSEIDON ADVENTURE" AND "EARTHQUAKE." PINK FLOYD'S MOODY "DARK SIDE OF THE MOON" TOPPED THE RECORD CHARTS ALL DECADE. EVEN ENTERTAINING TRIFLES LIKE "DEATH RACE 2000" AND "ROLLERBALL" PROMISED A TOMORROW BLEAKER, UGLIER, AND MORE TWISTED THAN TODAY.
WHERE DID ALL THE HEROIC OPTIMISTS GO?

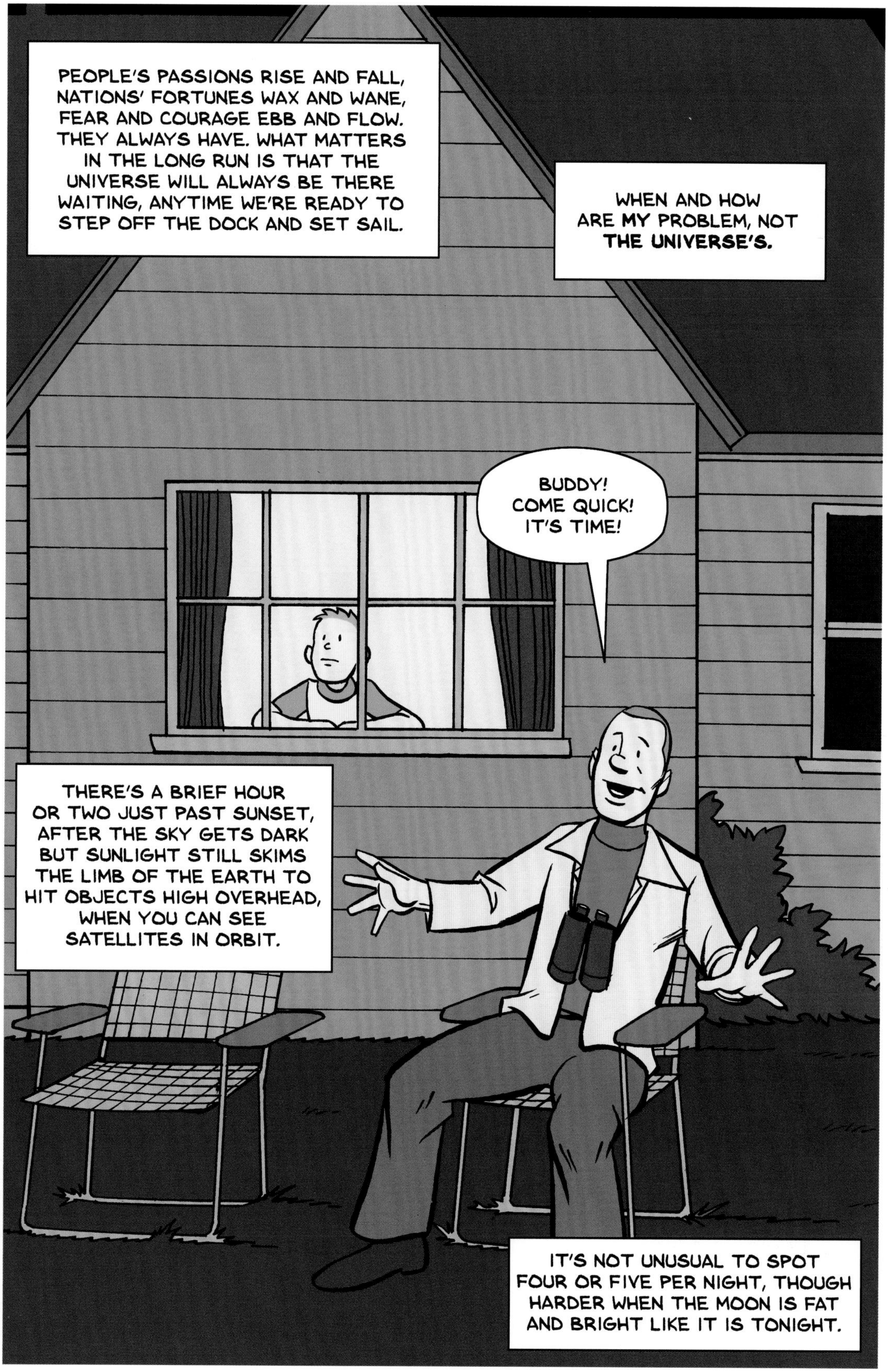
PEOPLE'S PASSIONS RISE AND FALL, NATIONS' FORTUNES WAX AND WANE, FEAR AND COURAGE EBB AND FLOW. THEY ALWAYS HAVE. WHAT MATTERS IN THE LONG RUN IS THAT THE UNIVERSE WILL ALWAYS BE THERE WAITING, ANYTIME WE'RE READY TO STEP OFF THE DOCK AND SET SAIL.
WHEN AND HOW ARE MY PROBLEM, NOT **THE UNIVERSE'S.**
BUDDY! COME QUICK! IT'S TIME!
THERE'S A BRIEF HOUR OR TWO JUST PAST SUNSET, AFTER THE SKY GETS DARK BUT SUNLIGHT STILL SKIMS THE LIMB OF THE EARTH TO HIT OBJECTS HIGH OVERHEAD, WHEN YOU CAN SEE SATELLITES IN ORBIT.
IT'S NOT UNUSUAL TO SPOT FOUR OR FIVE PER NIGHT, THOUGH HARDER WHEN THE MOON IS FAT AND BRIGHT LIKE IT IS TONIGHT.

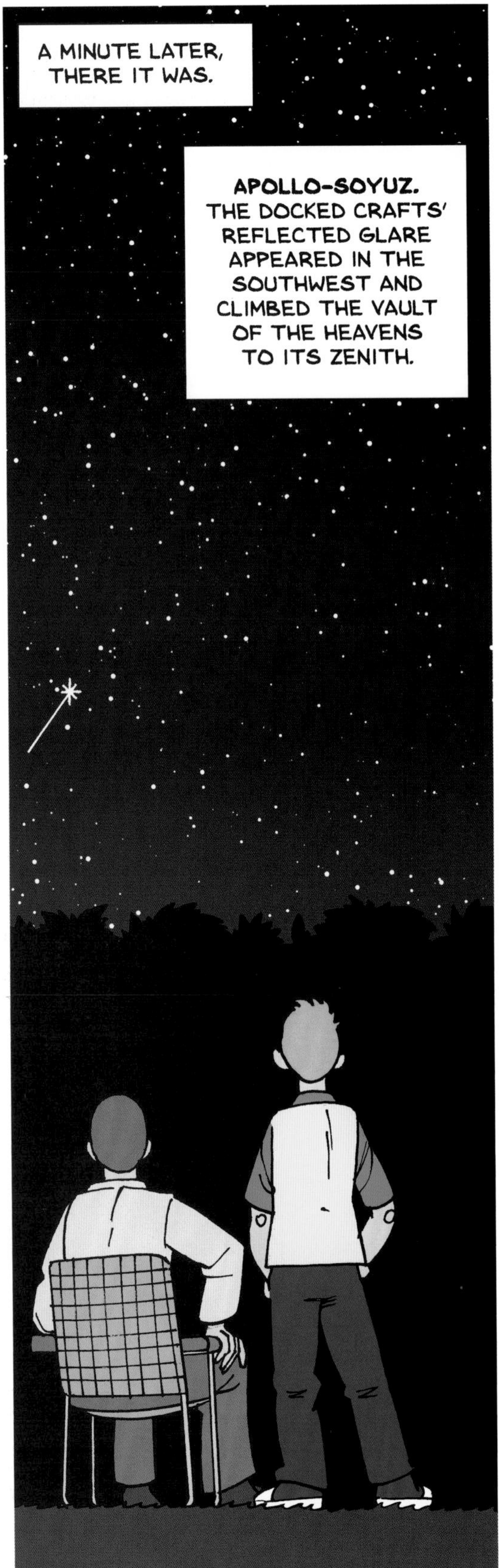
A MINUTE LATER, THERE IT WAS.
APOLLO-SOYUZ. THE DOCKED CRAFTS' REFLECTED GLARE APPEARED IN THE SOUTHWEST AND CLIMBED THE VAULT OF THE HEAVENS TO ITS ZENITH.

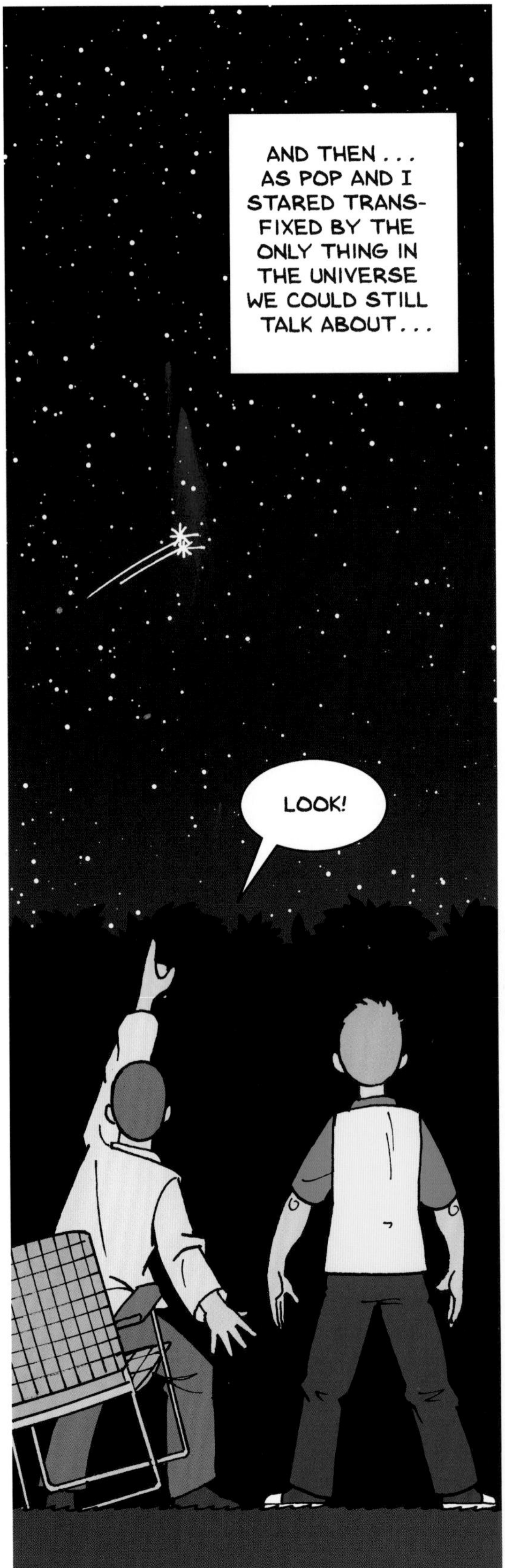
AND THEN . . . AS POP AND I STARED TRANS-FIXED BY THE ONLY THING IN THE UNIVERSE WE COULD STILL TALK ABOUT . . .
LOOK!

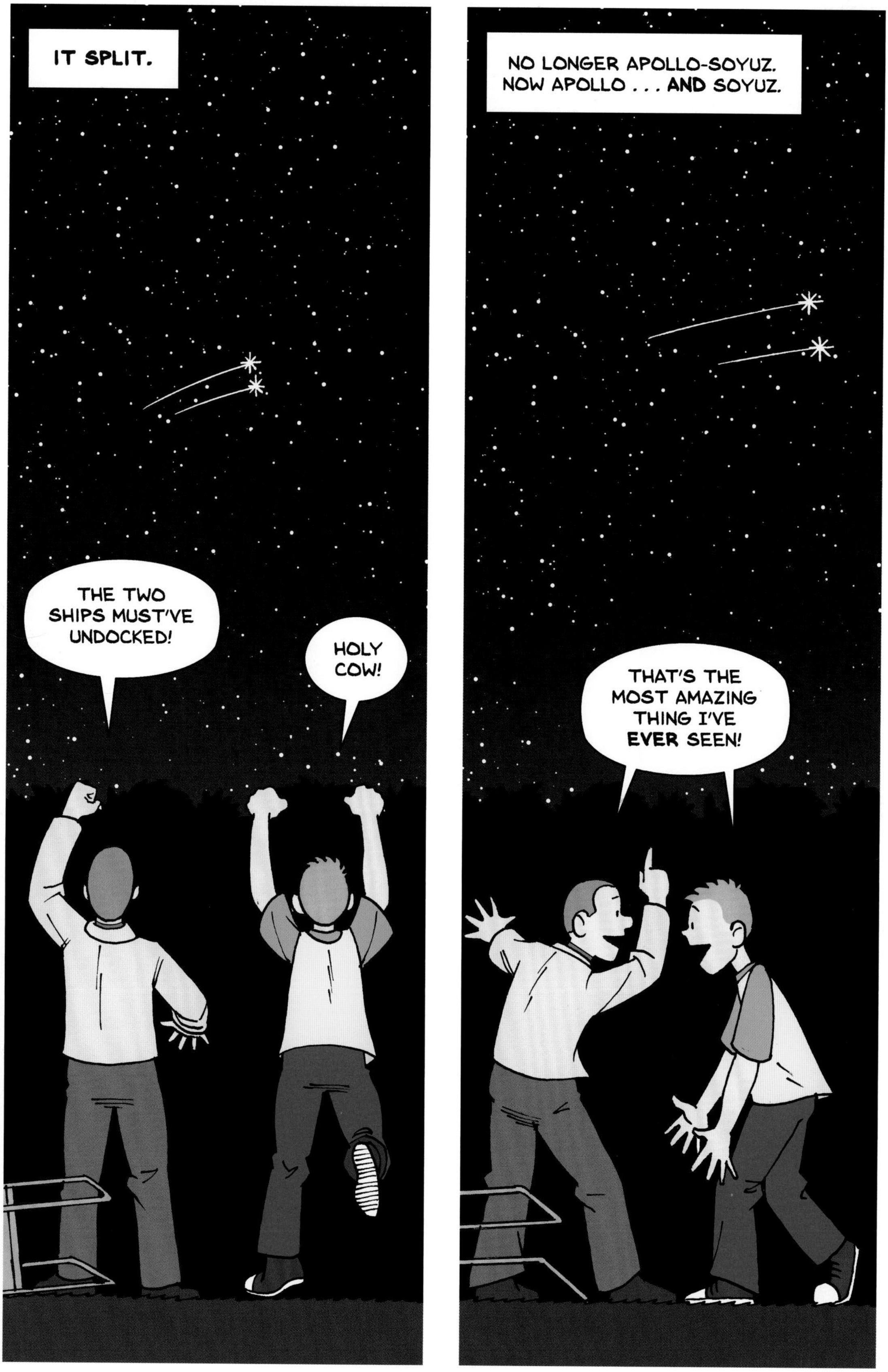
IT SPLIT.
THE TWO SHIPS MUST'VE UNDOCKED!
HOLY COW!
NO LONGER APOLLO-SOYUZ. NOW APOLLO . . . AND SOYUZ.
THAT'S THE MOST AMAZING THING I'VE **EVER** SEEN!

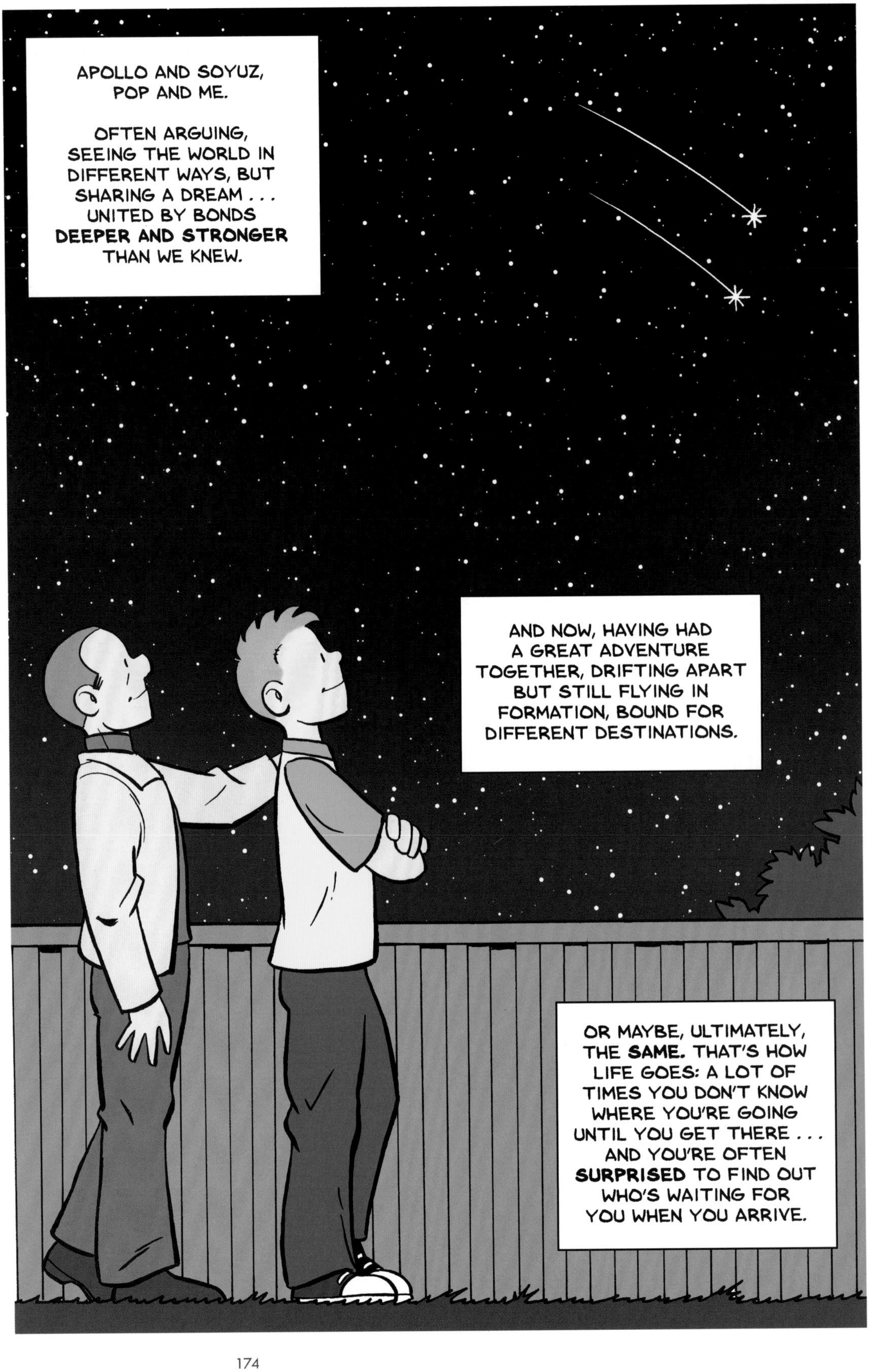
APOLLO AND SOYUZ, POP AND ME.
OFTEN ARGUING, SEEING THE WORLD IN DIFFERENT WAYS, BUT SHARING A DREAM . . . UNITED BY BONDS **DEEPER AND STRONGER** THAN WE KNEW.
AND NOW, HAVING HAD A GREAT ADVENTURE TOGETHER, DRIFTING APART BUT STILL FLYING IN FORMATION, BOUND FOR DIFFERENT DESTINATIONS.
OR MAYBE, ULTIMATELY, THE **SAME.** THAT'S HOW LIFE GOES: A LOT OF TIMES YOU DON'T KNOW WHERE YOU'RE GOING UNTIL YOU GET THERE . . . AND YOU'RE OFTEN **SURPRISED** TO FIND OUT WHO'S WAITING FOR YOU WHEN YOU ARRIVE.

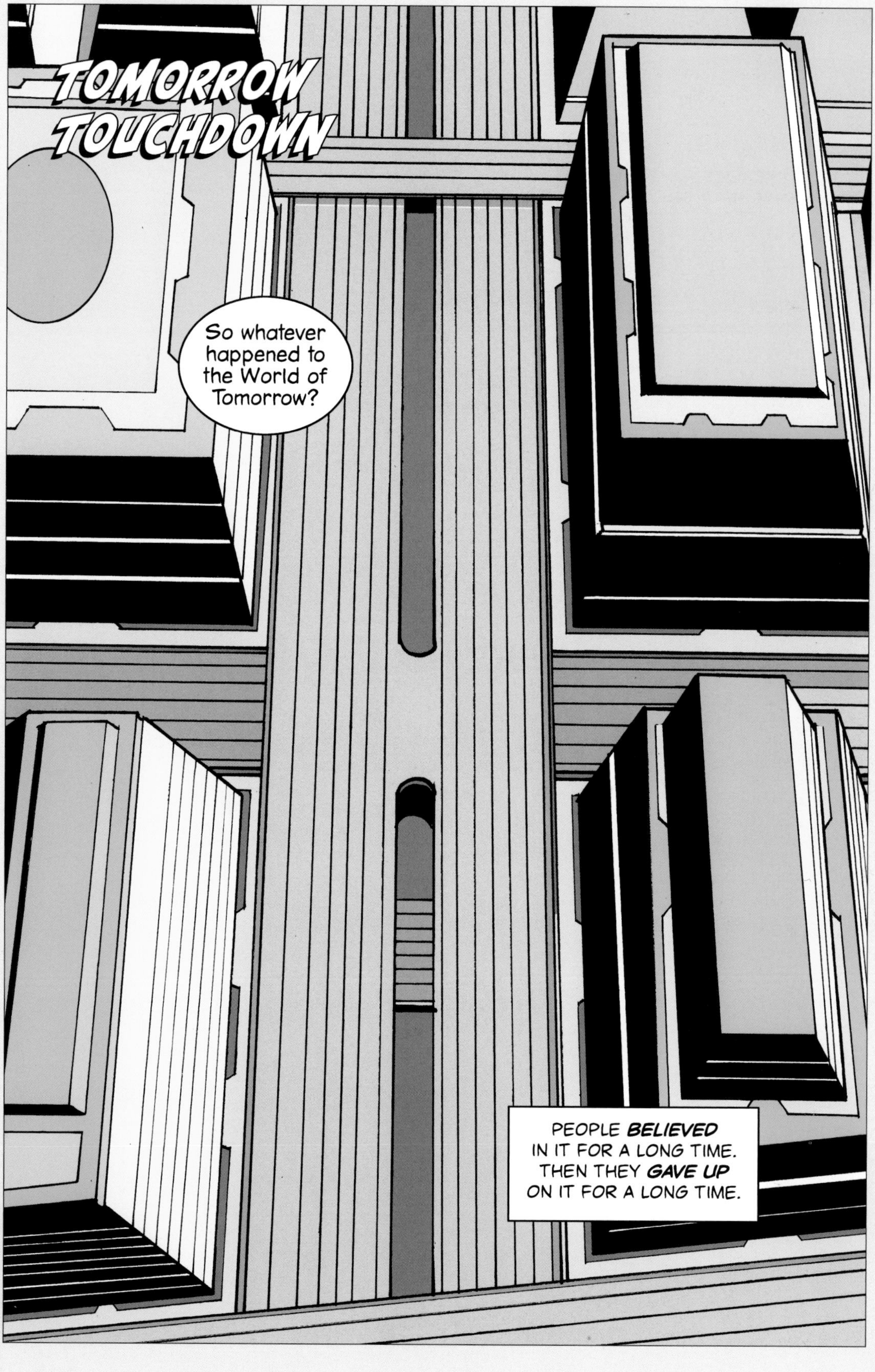
TOMORROW TOUCHDOWN
So whatever happened to the World of Tomorrow?
PEOPLE BELIEVED IN IT FOR A LONG TIME. THEN THEY GAVE UP ON IT FOR A LONG TIME.

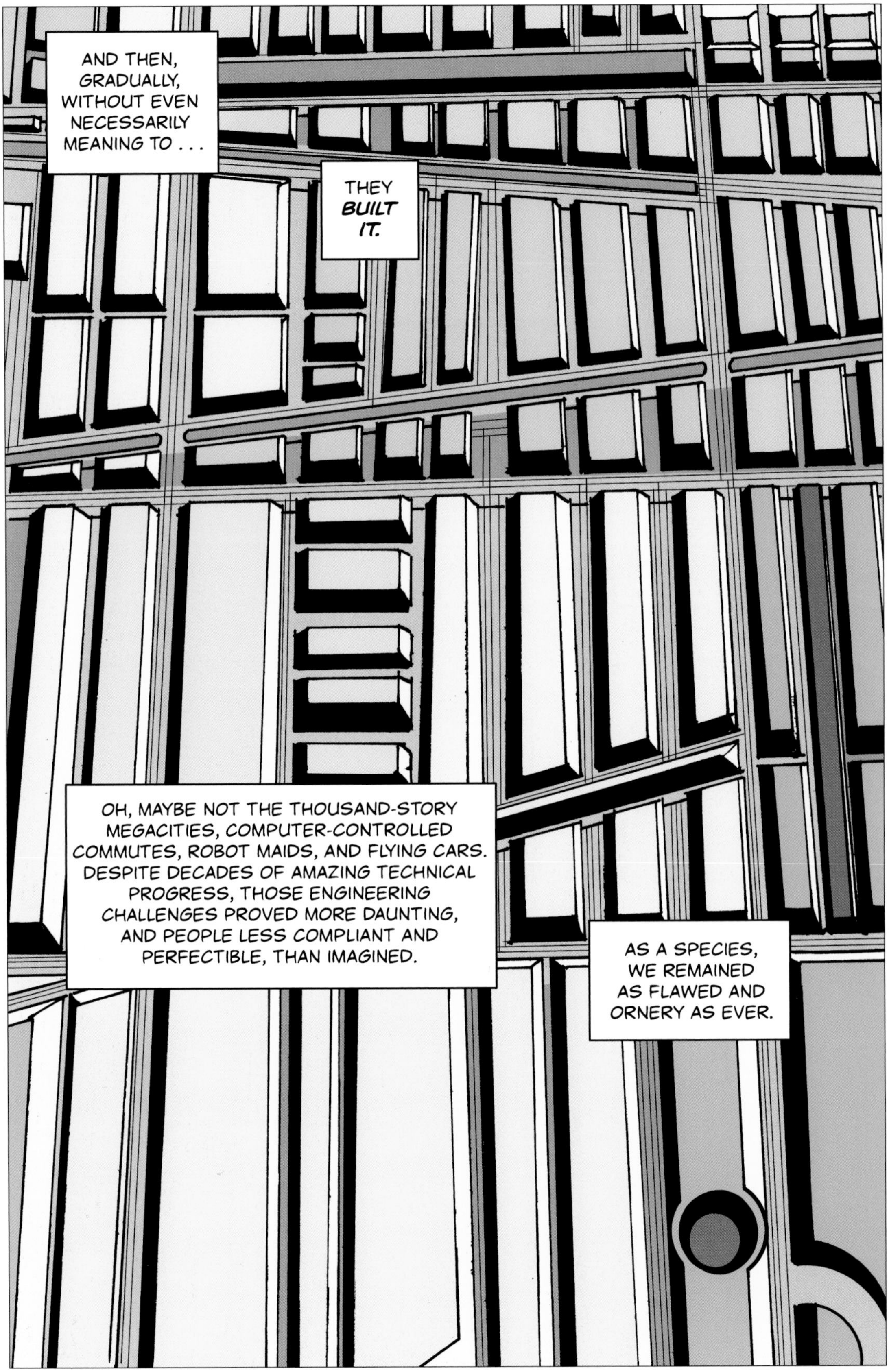
AND THEN, GRADUALLY, WITHOUT EVEN NECESSARILY MEANING TO . . .
THEY *BUILT IT.*
OH, MAYBE NOT THE THOUSAND-STORY MEGACITIES, COMPUTER-CONTROLLED COMMUTES, ROBOT MAIDS, AND FLYING CARS. DESPITE DECADES OF AMAZING TECHNICAL PROGRESS, THOSE ENGINEERING CHALLENGES PROVED MORE DAUNTING, AND PEOPLE LESS COMPLIANT AND PERFECTIBLE, THAN IMAGINED.
AS A SPECIES, WE REMAINED AS FLAWED AND ORNERY AS EVER.

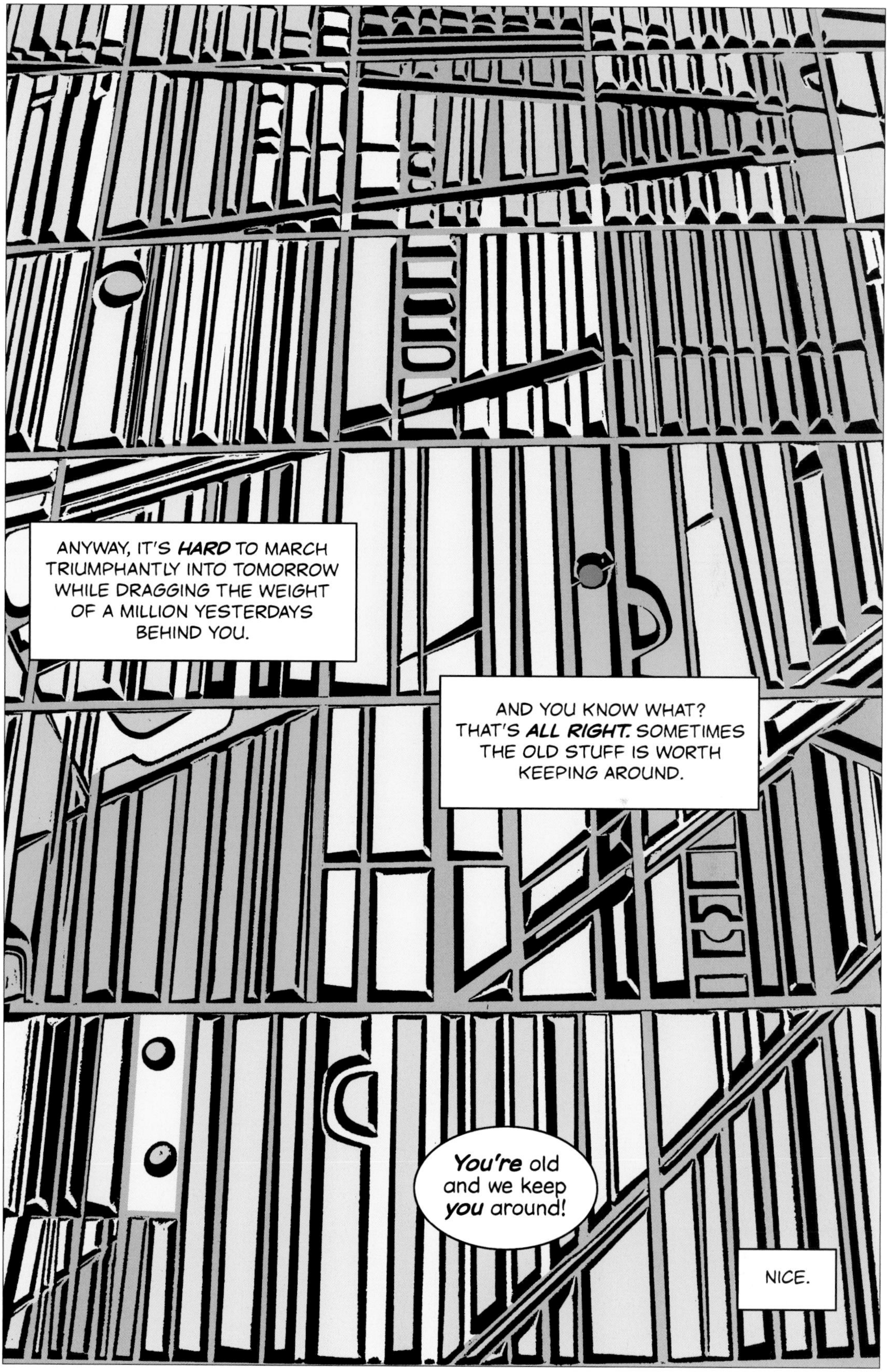
ANYWAY, IT'S HARD TO MARCH TRIUMPHANTLY INTO TOMORROW WHILE DRAGGING THE WEIGHT OF A MILLION YESTERDAYS BEHIND YOU.
AND YOU KNOW WHAT? THAT'S ALL RIGHT. SOMETIMES THE OLD STUFF IS WORTH KEEPING AROUND.
You're old and we keep you around!
NICE.

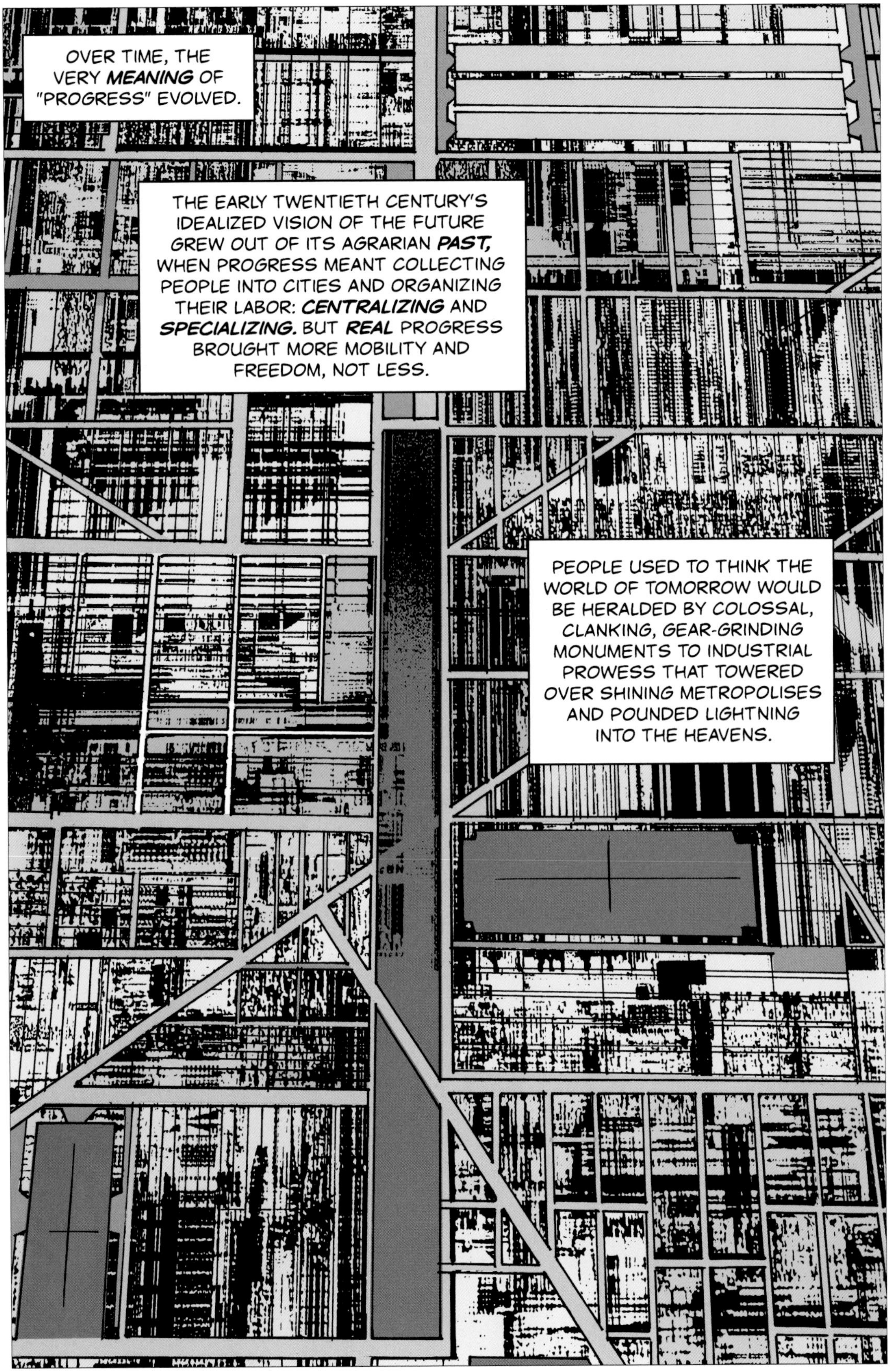
OVER TIME, THE VERY ***MEANING*** OF "PROGRESS" EVOLVED.
THE EARLY TWENTIETH CENTURY'S IDEALIZED VISION OF THE FUTURE GREW OUT OF ITS AGRARIAN ***PAST,*** WHEN PROGRESS MEANT COLLECTING PEOPLE INTO CITIES AND ORGANIZING THEIR LABOR: ***CENTRALIZING*** AND ***SPECIALIZING.*** BUT ***REAL*** PROGRESS BROUGHT MORE MOBILITY AND FREEDOM, NOT LESS.
PEOPLE USED TO THINK THE WORLD OF TOMORROW WOULD BE HERALDED BY COLOSSAL, CLANKING, GEAR-GRINDING MONUMENTS TO INDUSTRIAL PROWESS THAT TOWERED OVER SHINING METROPOLISES AND POUNDED LIGHTNING INTO THE HEAVENS.

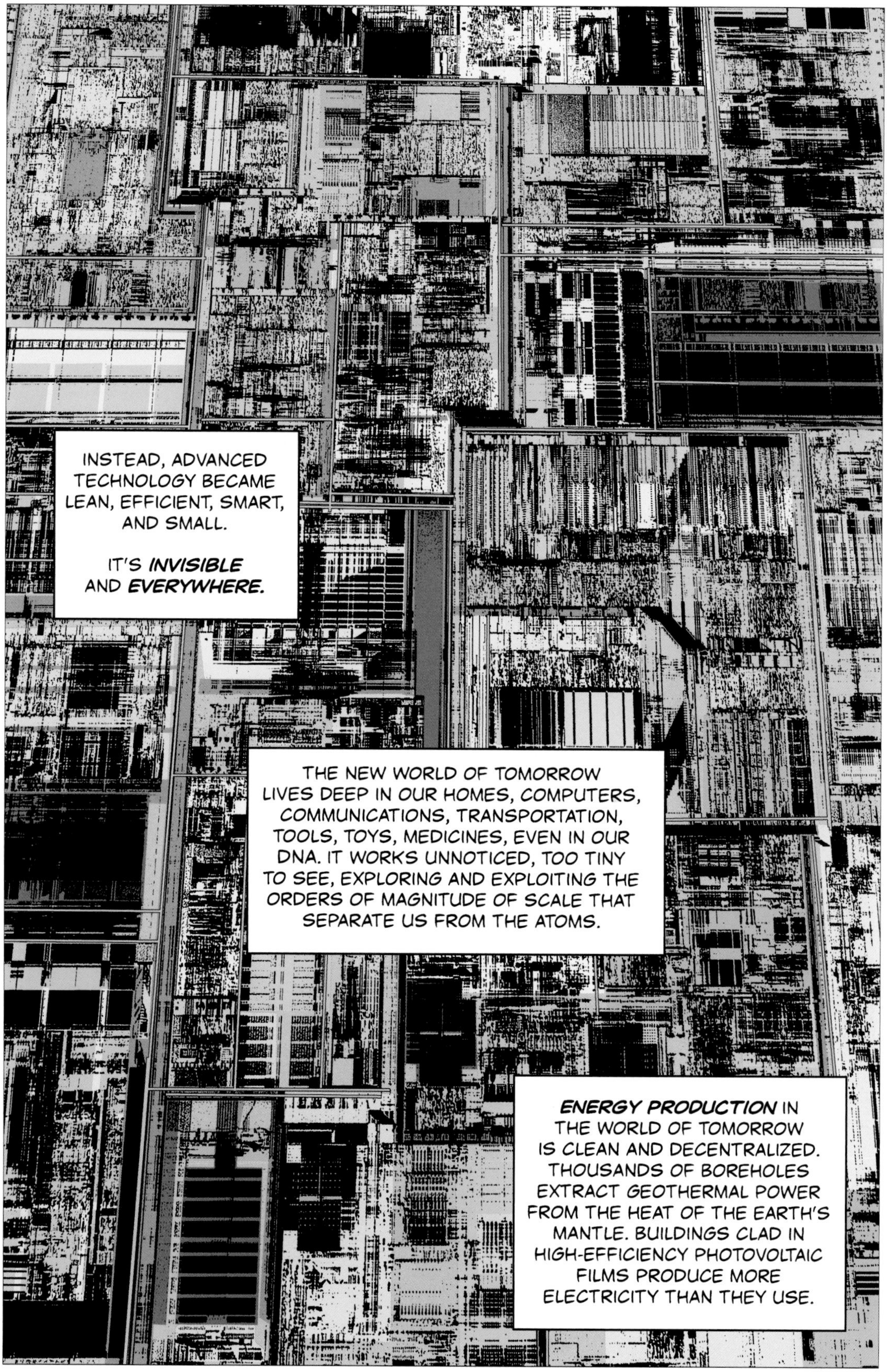
INSTEAD, ADVANCED TECHNOLOGY BECAME LEAN, EFFICIENT, SMART, AND SMALL.
IT'S *INVISIBLE* AND *EVERYWHERE.*
THE NEW WORLD OF TOMORROW LIVES DEEP IN OUR HOMES, COMPUTERS, COMMUNICATIONS, TRANSPORTATION, TOOLS, TOYS, MEDICINES, EVEN IN OUR DNA. IT WORKS UNNOTICED, TOO TINY TO SEE, EXPLORING AND EXPLOITING THE ORDERS OF MAGNITUDE OF SCALE THAT SEPARATE US FROM THE ATOMS.
*ENERGY PRODUCTION* IN THE WORLD OF TOMORROW IS CLEAN AND DECENTRALIZED. THOUSANDS OF BOREHOLES EXTRACT GEOTHERMAL POWER FROM THE HEAT OF THE EARTH'S MANTLE. BUILDINGS CLAD IN HIGH-EFFICIENCY PHOTOVOLTAIC FILMS PRODUCE MORE ELECTRICITY THAN THEY USE.

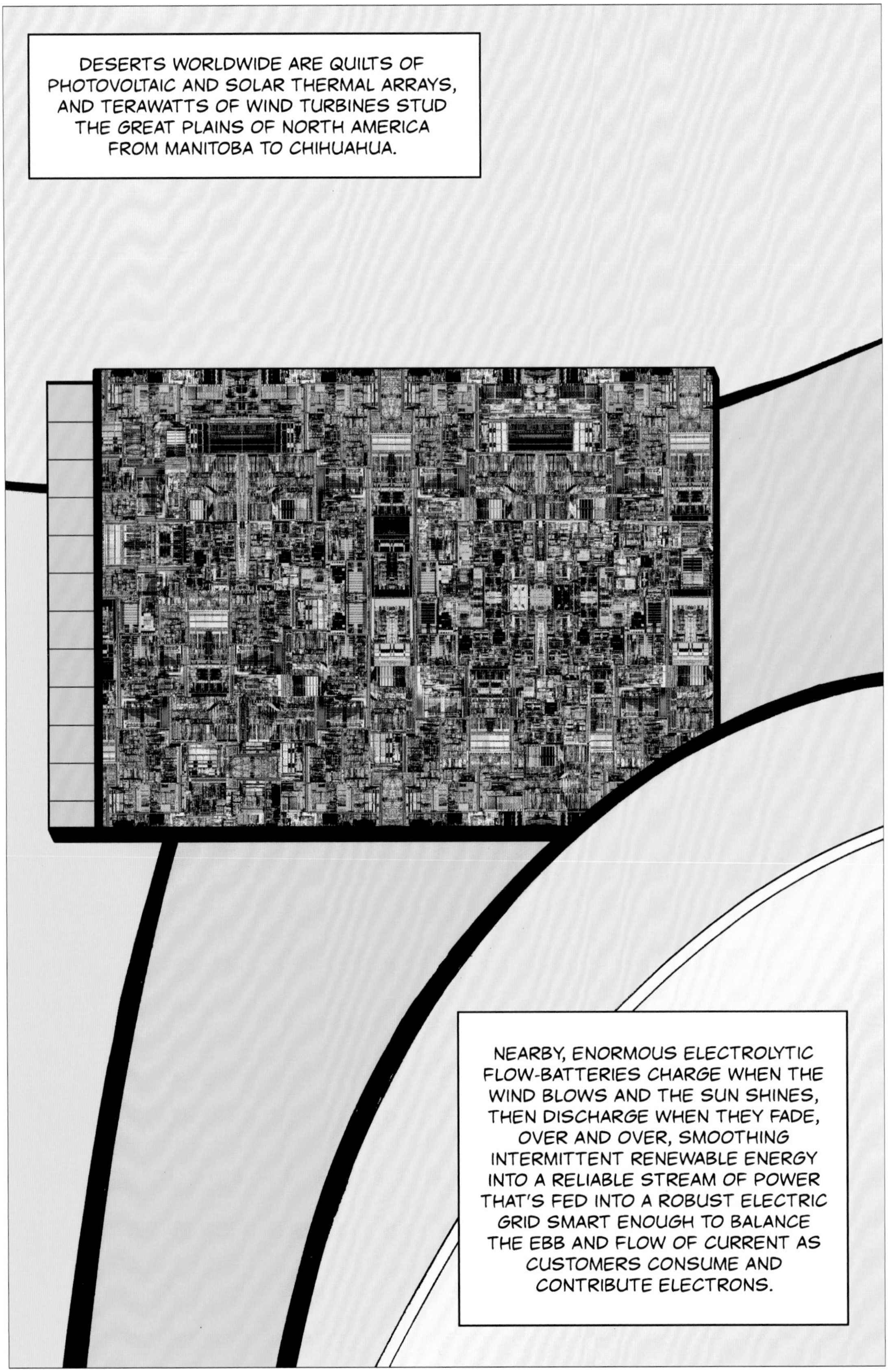

DESERTS WORLDWIDE ARE QUILTS OF PHOTOVOLTAIC AND SOLAR THERMAL ARRAYS, AND TERAWATTS OF WIND TURBINES STUD THE GREAT PLAINS OF NORTH AMERICA FROM MANITOBA TO CHIHUAHUA.

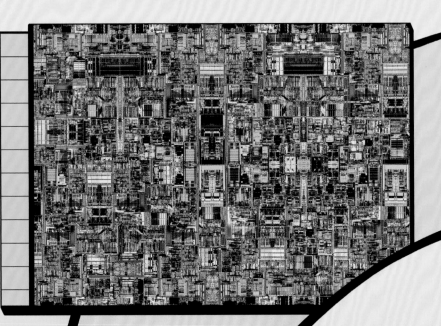

NEARBY, ENORMOUS ELECTROLYTIC FLOW-BATTERIES CHARGE WHEN THE WIND BLOWS AND THE SUN SHINES, THEN DISCHARGE WHEN THEY FADE, OVER AND OVER, SMOOTHING INTERMITTENT RENEWABLE ENERGY INTO A RELIABLE STREAM OF POWER THAT'S FED INTO A ROBUST ELECTRIC GRID SMART ENOUGH TO BALANCE THE EBB AND FLOW OF CURRENT AS CUSTOMERS CONSUME AND CONTRIBUTE ELECTRONS.

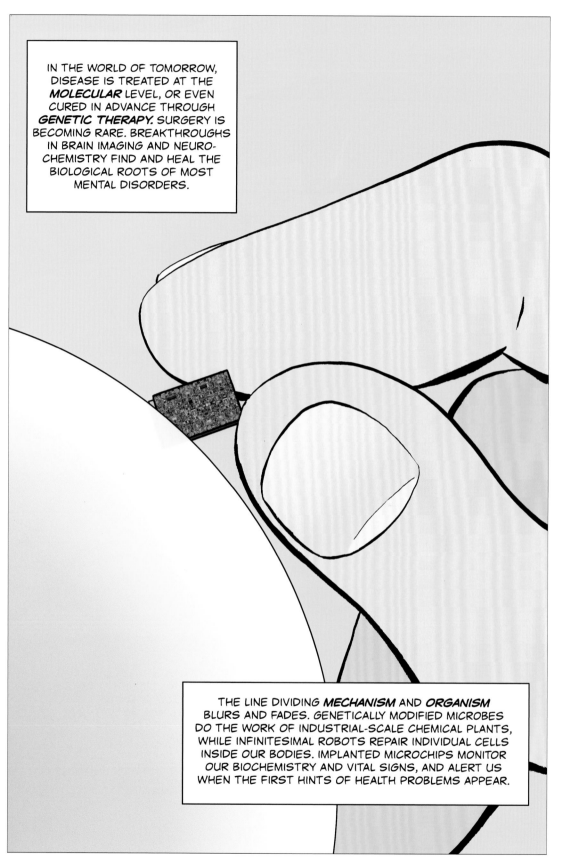

IN THE WORLD OF TOMORROW, DISEASE IS TREATED AT THE **MOLECULAR** LEVEL, OR EVEN CURED IN ADVANCE THROUGH **GENETIC THERAPY.** SURGERY IS BECOMING RARE. BREAKTHROUGHS IN BRAIN IMAGING AND NEURO-CHEMISTRY FIND AND HEAL THE BIOLOGICAL ROOTS OF MOST MENTAL DISORDERS.

THE LINE DIVIDING **MECHANISM** AND **ORGANISM** BLURS AND FADES. GENETICALLY MODIFIED MICROBES DO THE WORK OF INDUSTRIAL-SCALE CHEMICAL PLANTS, WHILE INFINITESIMAL ROBOTS REPAIR INDIVIDUAL CELLS INSIDE OUR BODIES. IMPLANTED MICROCHIPS MONITOR OUR BIOCHEMISTRY AND VITAL SIGNS, AND ALERT US WHEN THE FIRST HINTS OF HEALTH PROBLEMS APPEAR.

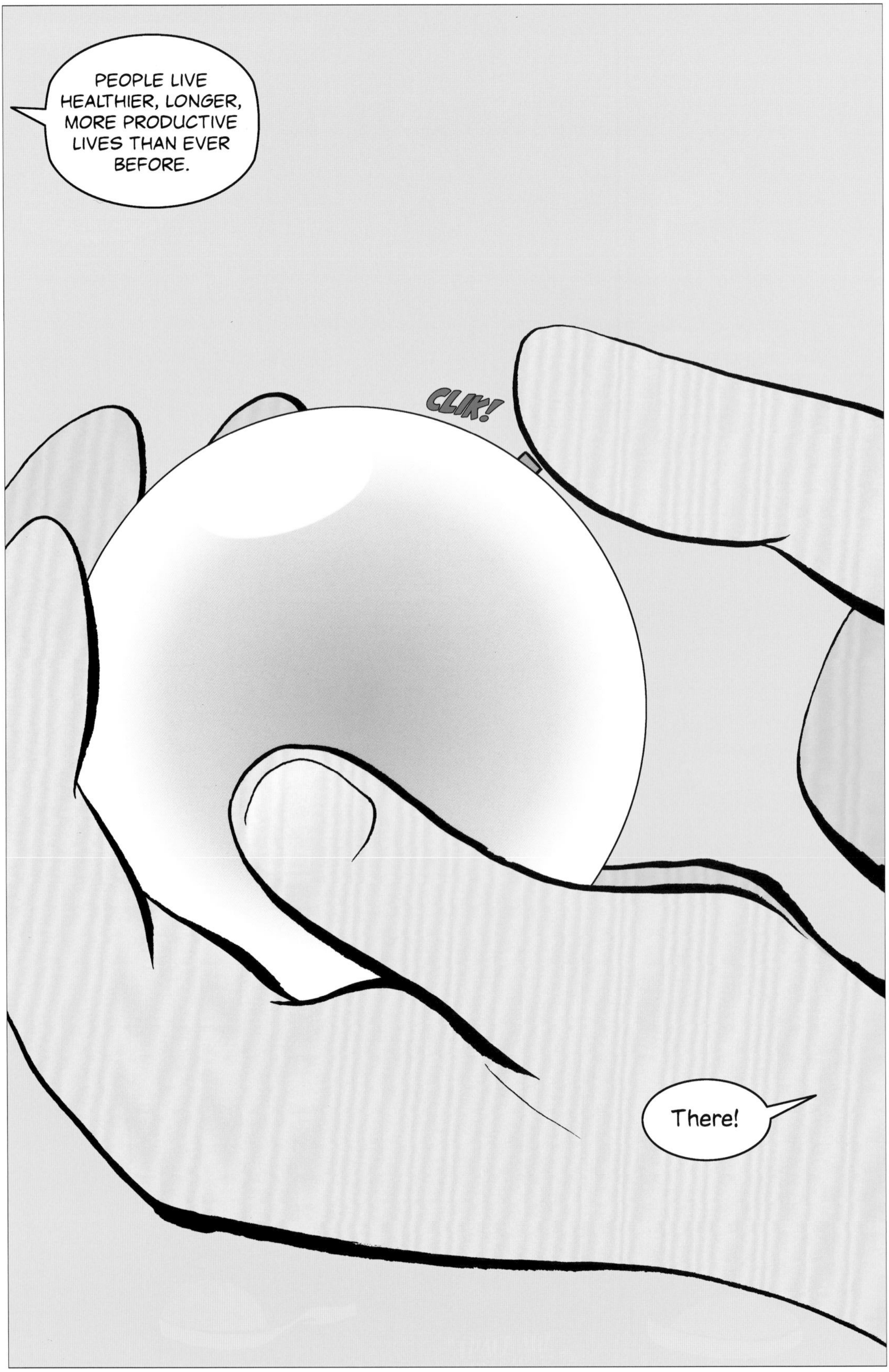
PEOPLE LIVE HEALTHIER, LONGER, MORE PRODUCTIVE LIVES THAN EVER BEFORE.
CLIK!
There!

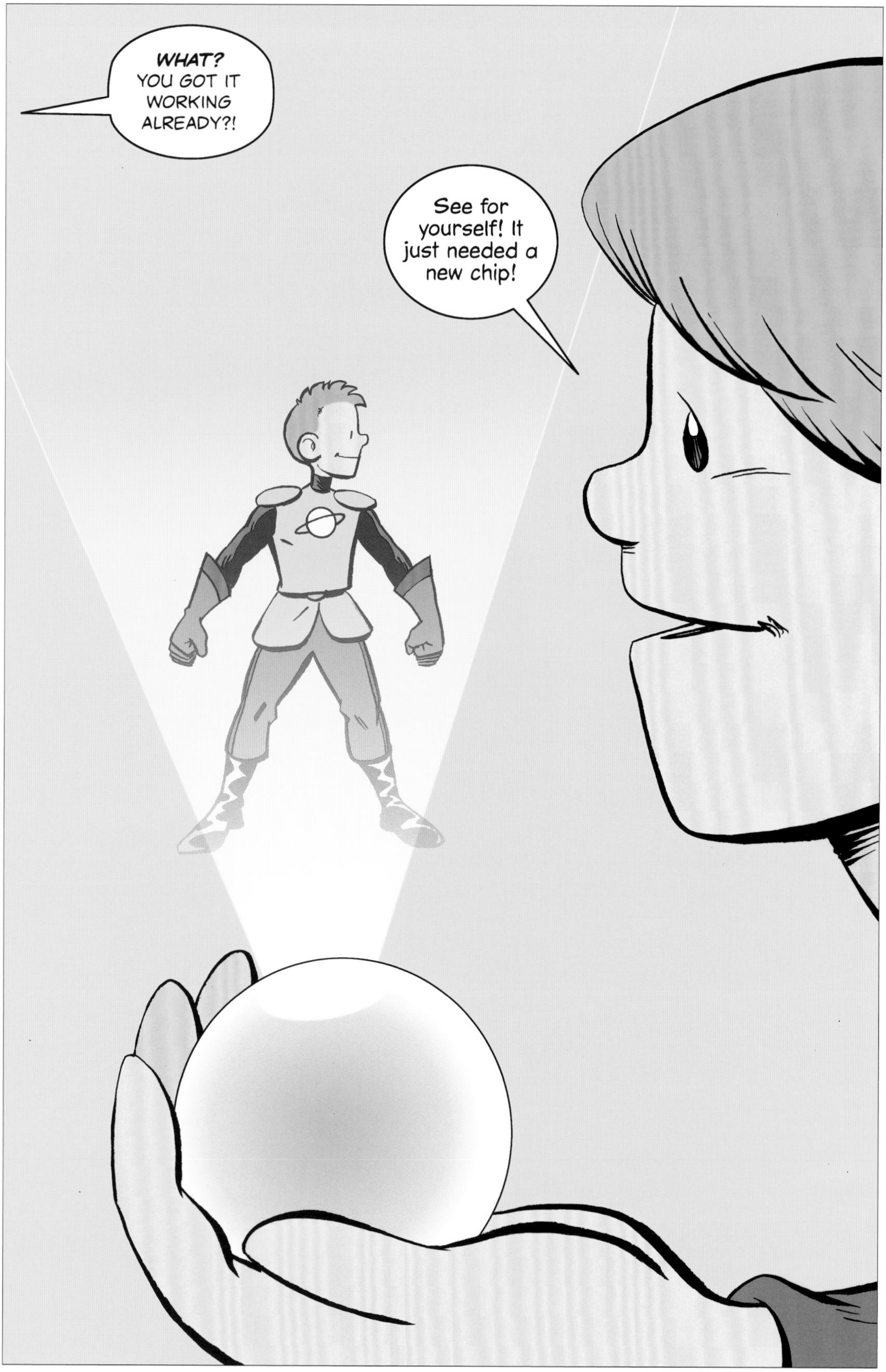
WHAT? YOU GOT IT WORKING ALREADY?!
See for yourself! It just needed a new chip!

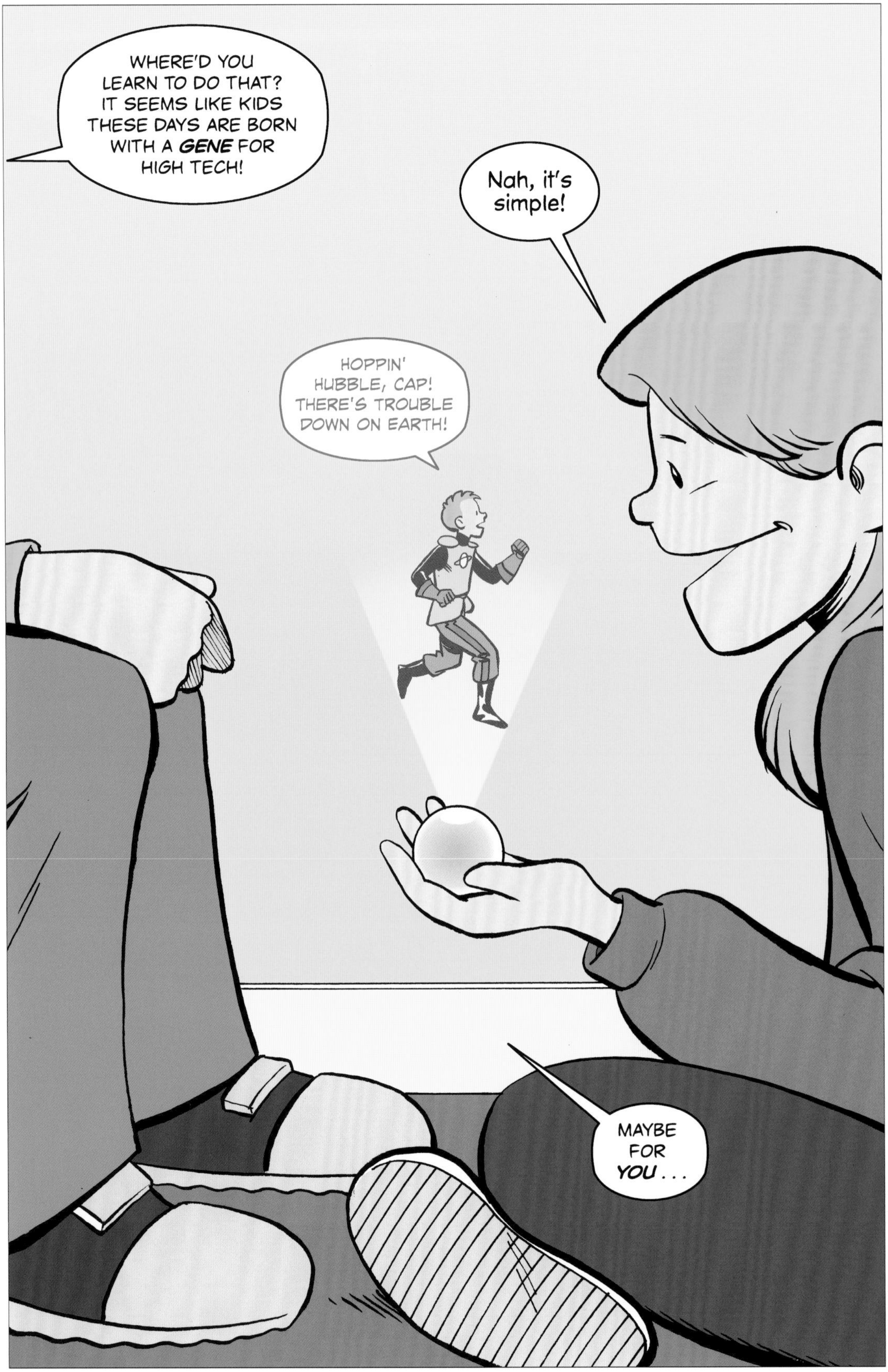
WHERE'D YOU LEARN TO DO THAT? IT SEEMS LIKE KIDS THESE DAYS ARE BORN WITH A GENE FOR HIGH TECH!
Nah, it's simple!
HOPPIN' HUBBLE, CAP! THERE'S TROUBLE DOWN ON EARTH!
MAYBE FOR YOU . . .

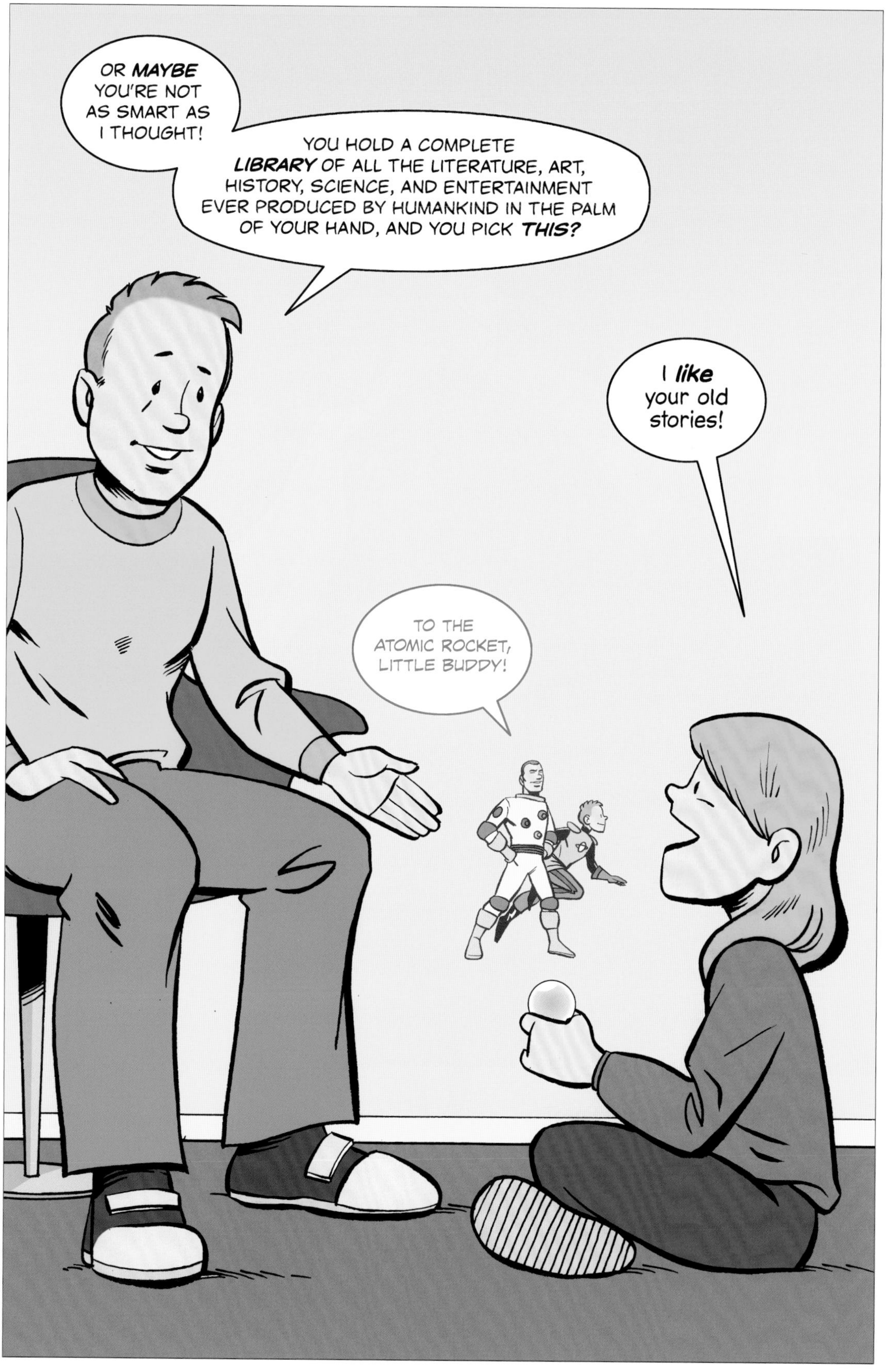
OR MAYBE YOU'RE NOT AS SMART AS I THOUGHT!
YOU HOLD A COMPLETE LIBRARY OF ALL THE LITERATURE, ART, HISTORY, SCIENCE, AND ENTERTAINMENT EVER PRODUCED BY HUMANKIND IN THE PALM OF YOUR HAND, AND YOU PICK THIS?
I like your old stories!
TO THE ATOMIC ROCKET, LITTLE BUDDY!

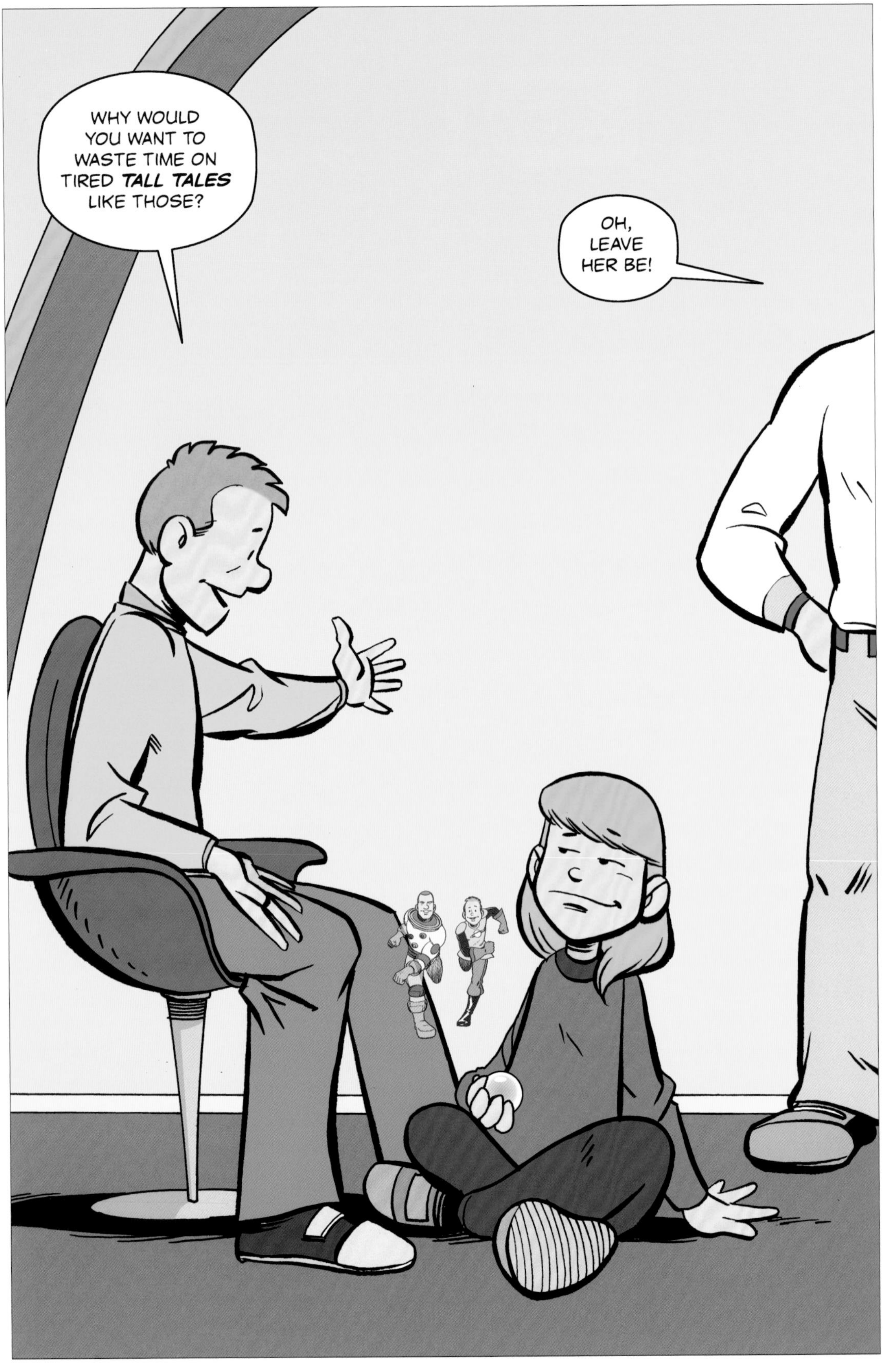
WHY WOULD YOU WANT TO WASTE TIME ON TIRED **TALL TALES** LIKE THOSE?
OH, LEAVE HER BE!

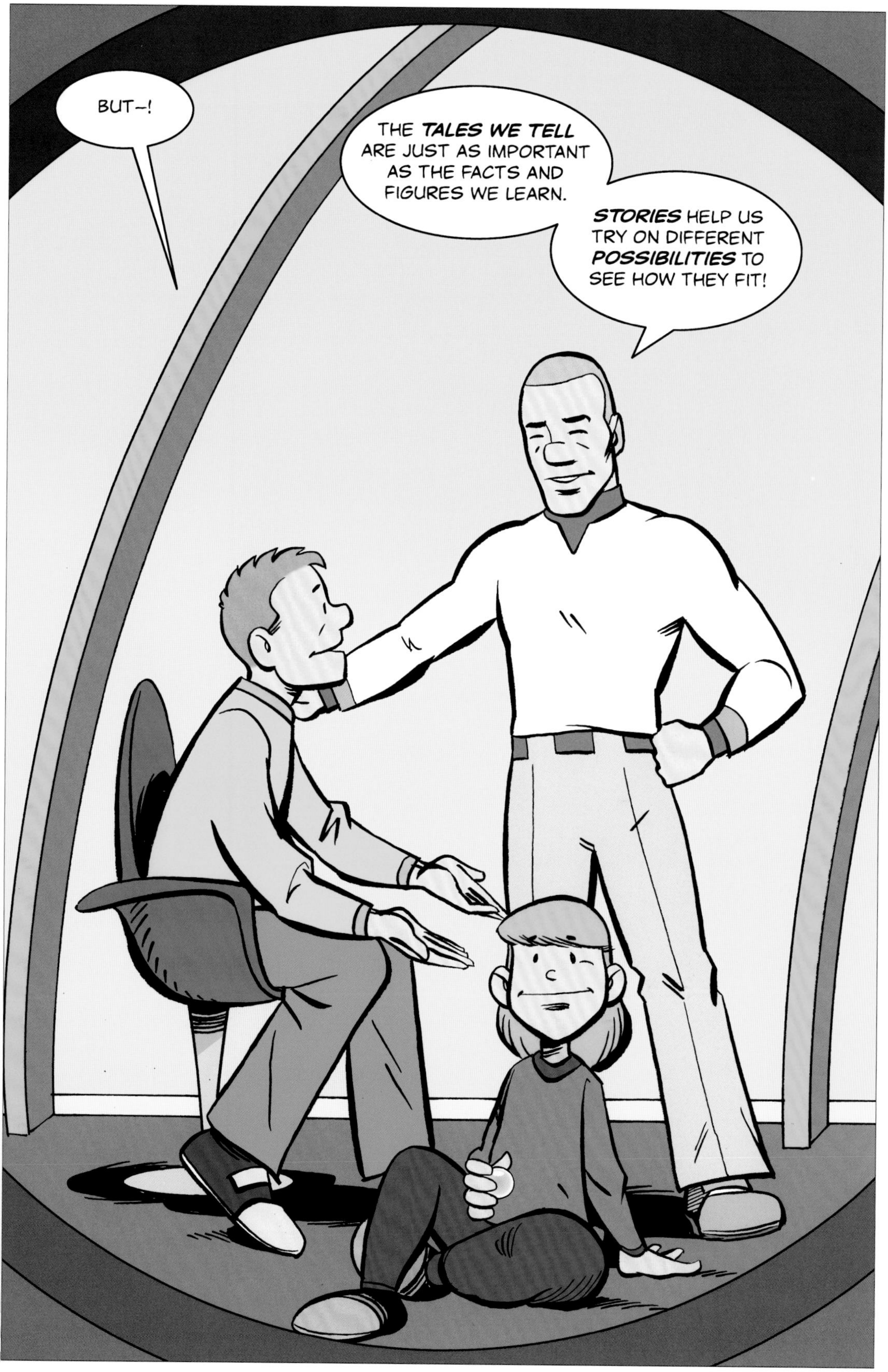
BUT--!
THE **TALES WE TELL** ARE JUST AS IMPORTANT AS THE FACTS AND FIGURES WE LEARN.
**STORIES** HELP US TRY ON DIFFERENT **POSSIBILITIES** TO SEE HOW THEY FIT!

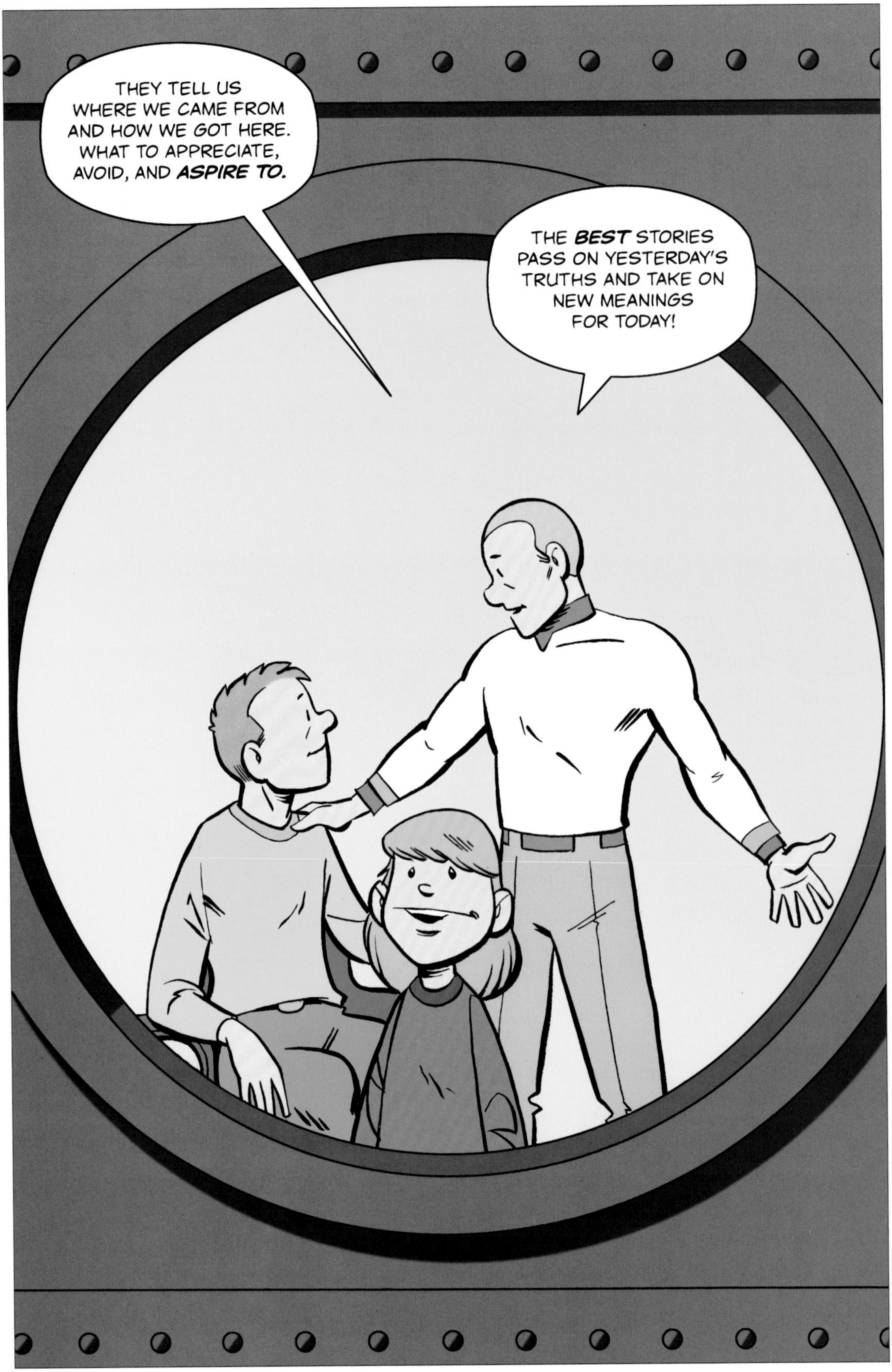
THEY TELL US WHERE WE CAME FROM AND HOW WE GOT HERE. WHAT TO APPRECIATE, AVOID, AND **ASPIRE TO.**
THE **BEST** STORIES PASS ON YESTERDAY'S TRUTHS AND TAKE ON NEW MEANINGS FOR TODAY!

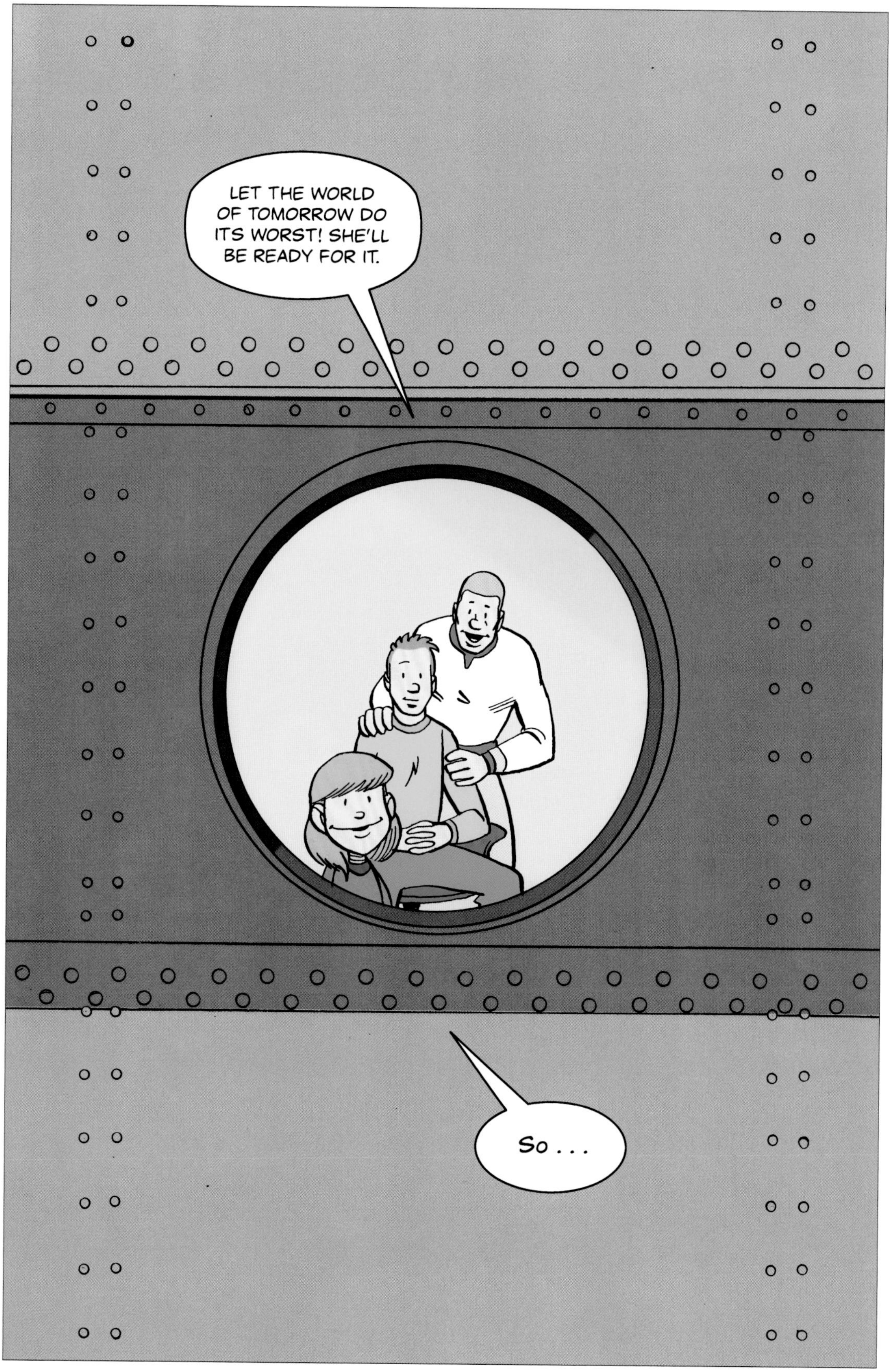
LET THE WORLD OF TOMORROW DO ITS WORST! SHE'LL BE READY FOR IT.
So . . .

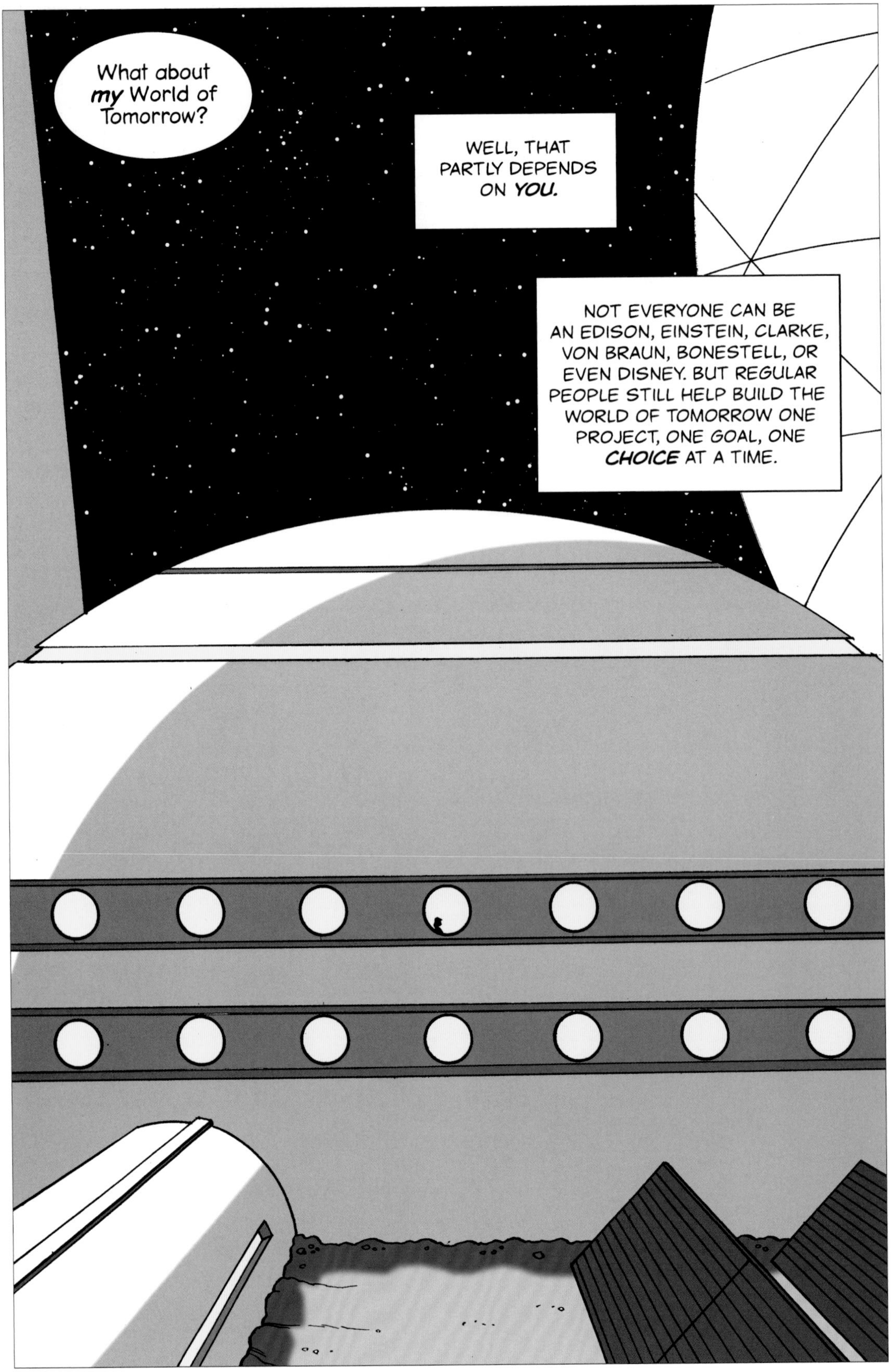
What about *my* World of Tomorrow?
WELL, THAT PARTLY DEPENDS ON *YOU.*
NOT EVERYONE CAN BE AN EDISON, EINSTEIN, CLARKE, VON BRAUN, BONESTELL, OR EVEN DISNEY. BUT REGULAR PEOPLE STILL HELP BUILD THE WORLD OF TOMORROW ONE PROJECT, ONE GOAL, ONE *CHOICE* AT A TIME.

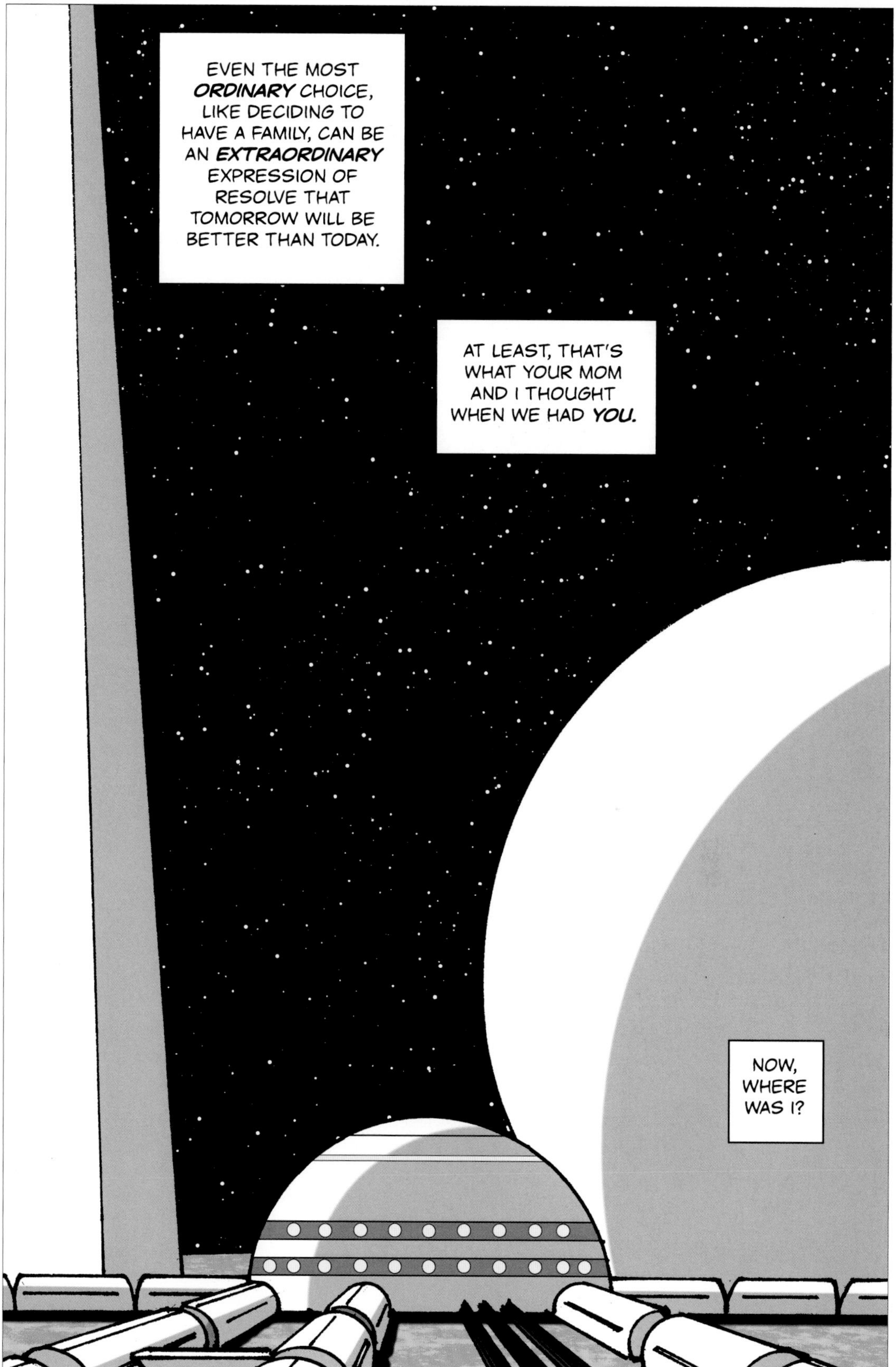
EVEN THE MOST ORDINARY CHOICE, LIKE DECIDING TO HAVE A FAMILY, CAN BE AN EXTRAORDINARY EXPRESSION OF RESOLVE THAT TOMORROW WILL BE BETTER THAN TODAY.
AT LEAST, THAT'S WHAT YOUR MOM AND I THOUGHT WHEN WE HAD YOU.
NOW, WHERE WAS I?

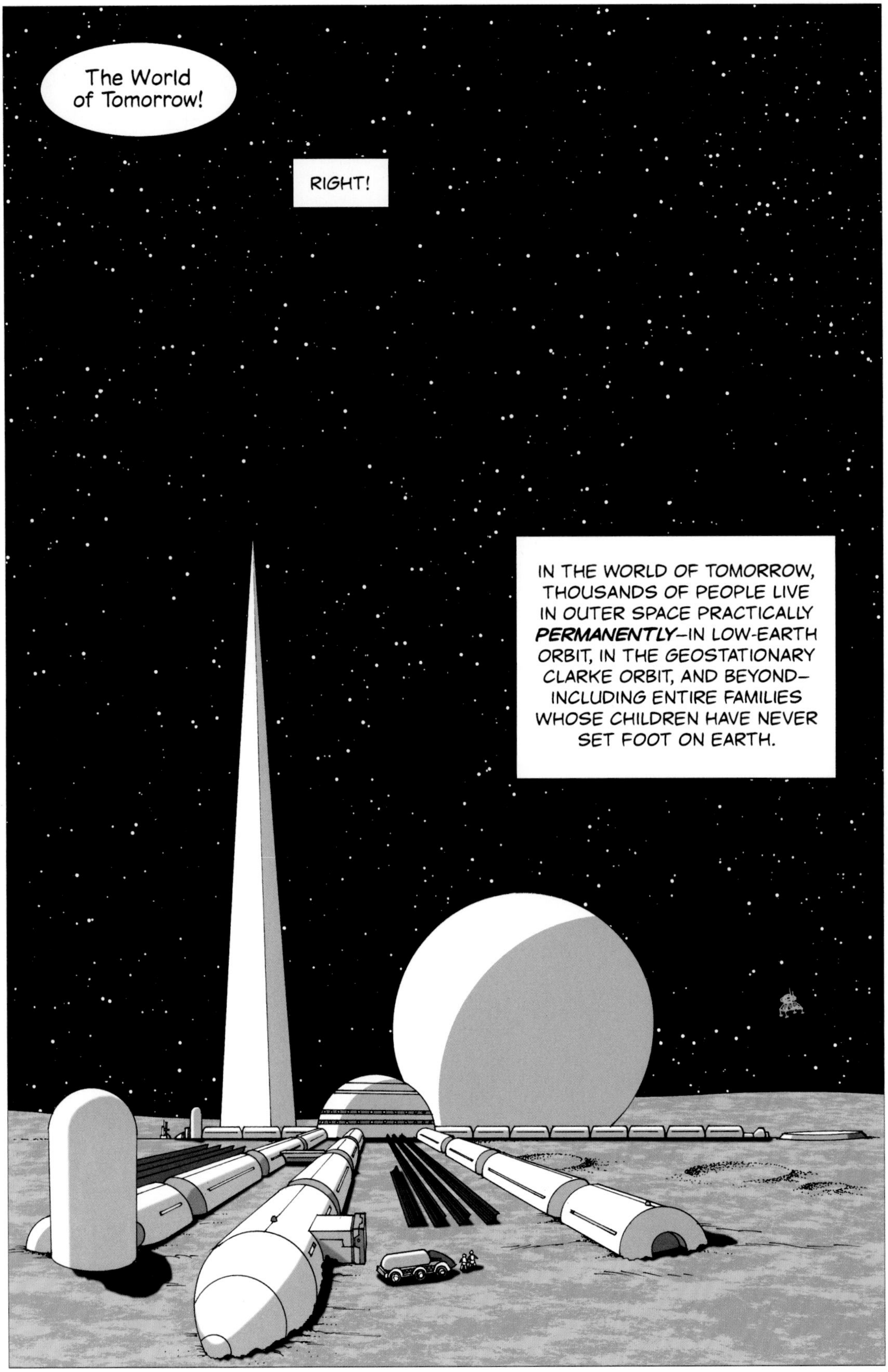
The World of Tomorrow!
RIGHT!
IN THE WORLD OF TOMORROW, THOUSANDS OF PEOPLE LIVE IN OUTER SPACE PRACTICALLY *PERMANENTLY*—IN LOW-EARTH ORBIT, IN THE GEOSTATIONARY CLARKE ORBIT, AND BEYOND—INCLUDING ENTIRE FAMILIES WHOSE CHILDREN HAVE NEVER SET FOOT ON EARTH.

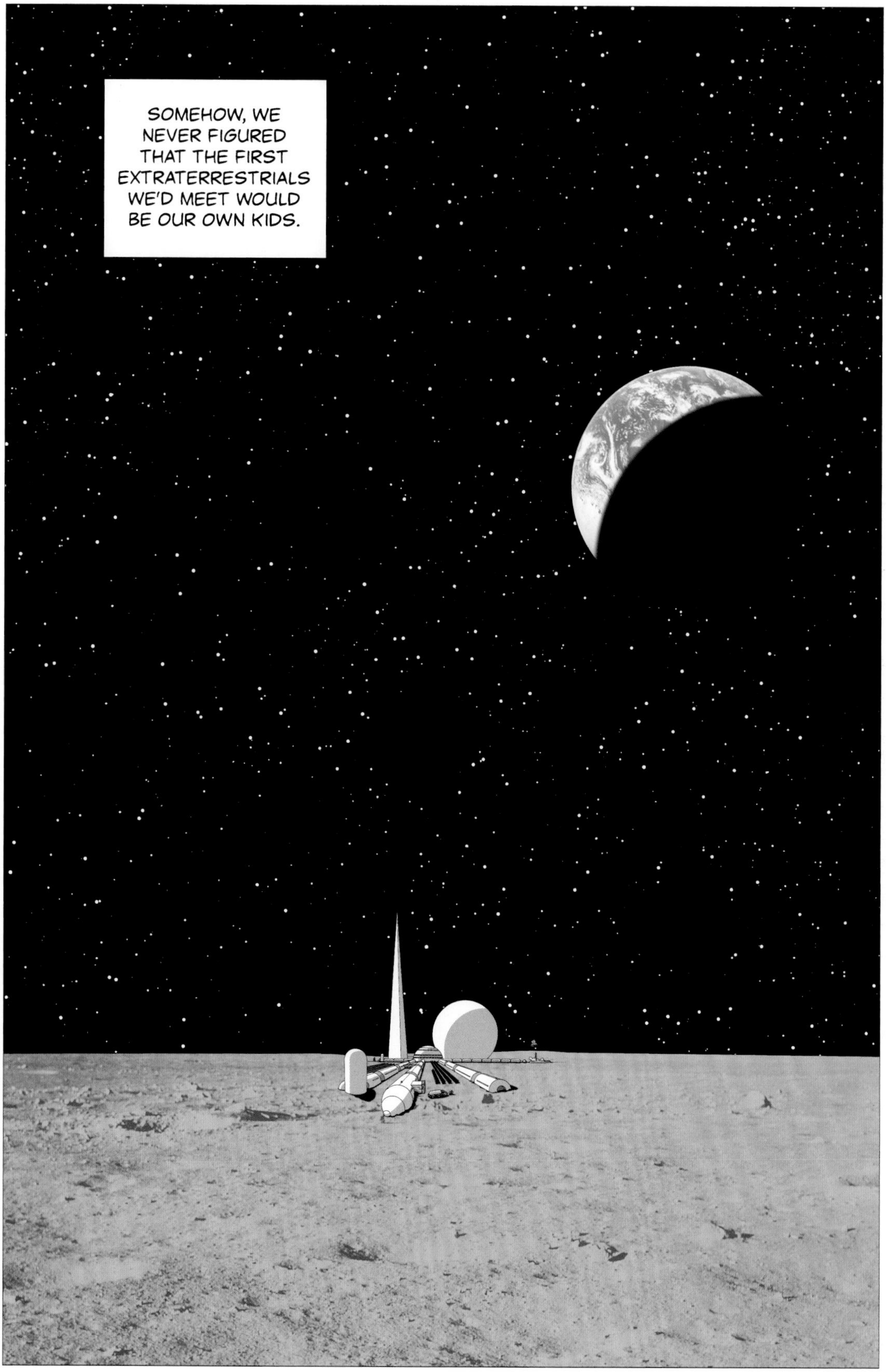
SOMEHOW, WE NEVER FIGURED THAT THE FIRST EXTRATERRESTRIALS WE'D MEET WOULD BE OUR OWN KIDS.

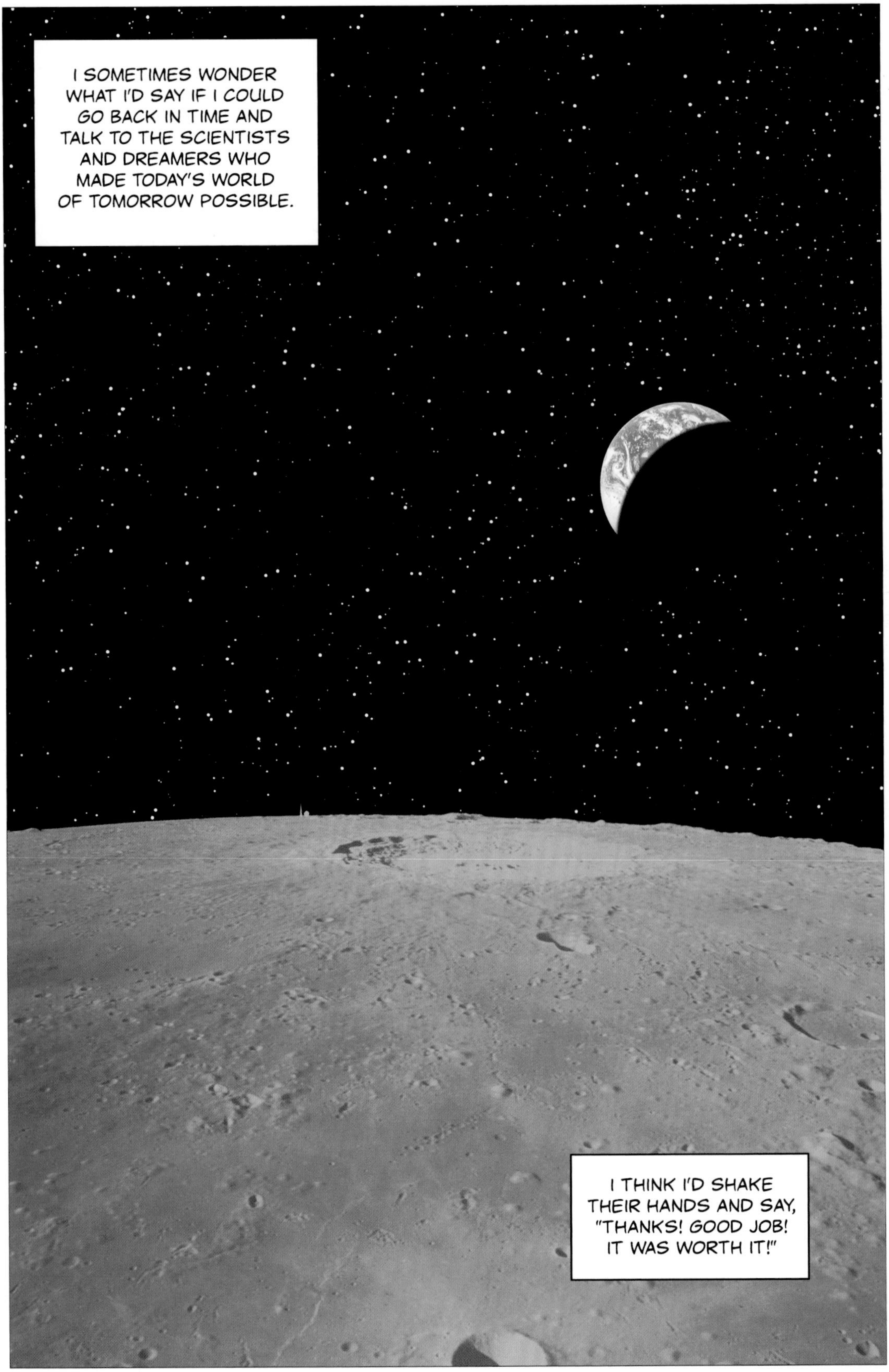
I SOMETIMES WONDER WHAT I'D SAY IF I COULD GO BACK IN TIME AND TALK TO THE SCIENTISTS AND DREAMERS WHO MADE TODAY'S WORLD OF TOMORROW POSSIBLE.
I THINK I'D SHAKE THEIR HANDS AND SAY, "THANKS! GOOD JOB! IT WAS WORTH IT!"

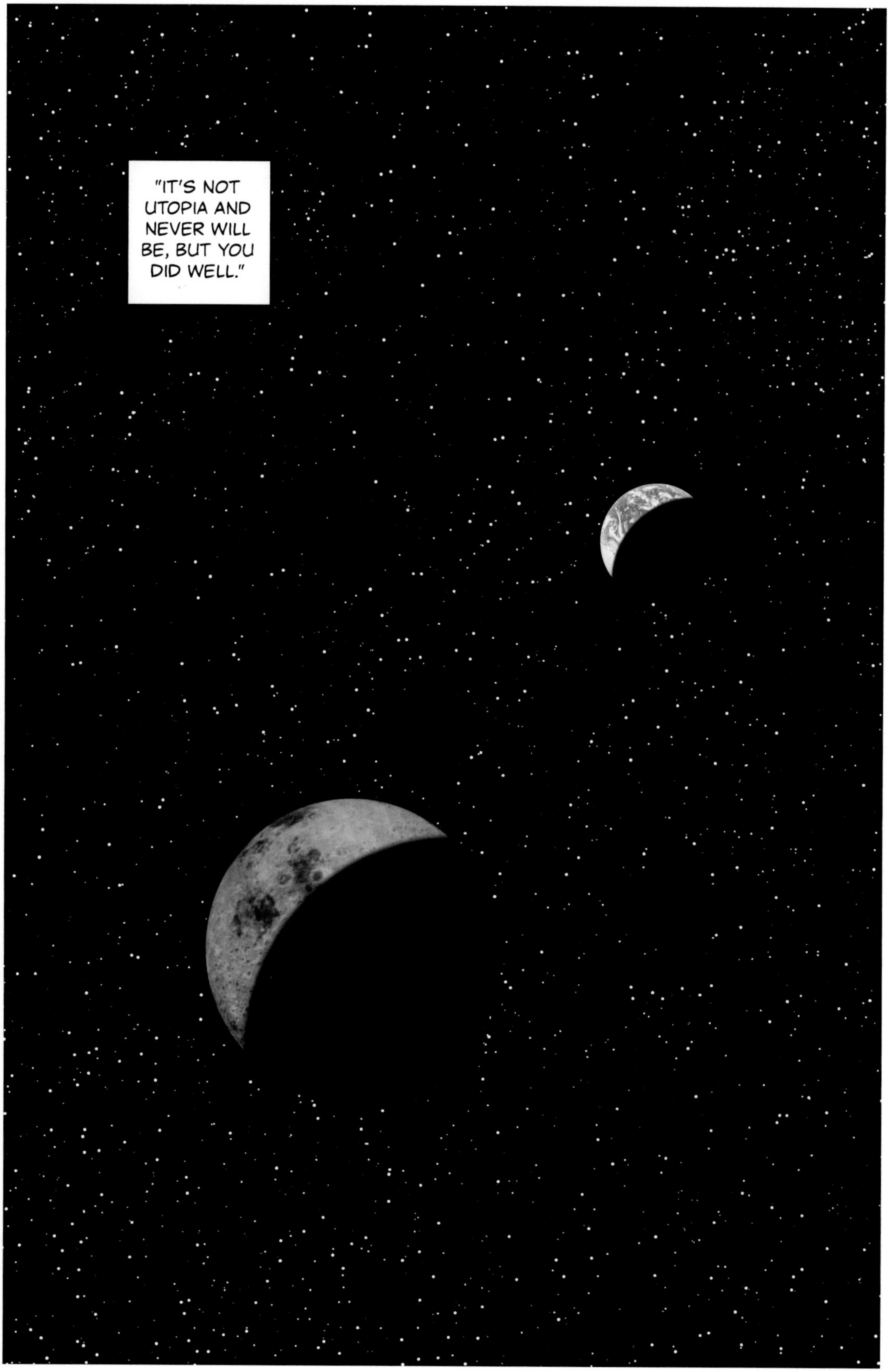
"IT'S NOT UTOPIA AND NEVER WILL BE, BUT YOU DID WELL."

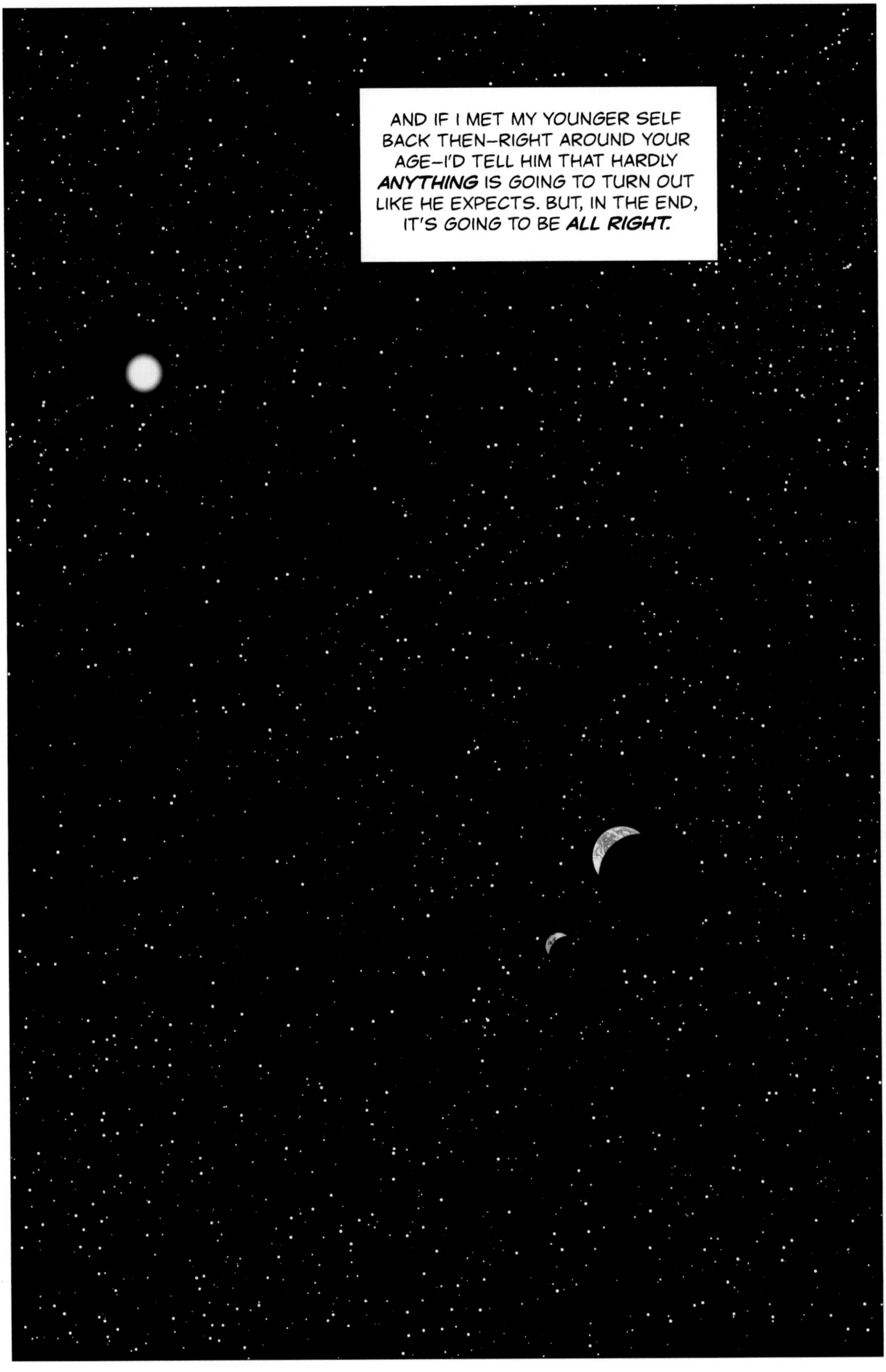
AND IF I MET MY YOUNGER SELF BACK THEN—RIGHT AROUND YOUR AGE—I'D TELL HIM THAT HARDLY ***ANYTHING*** IS GOING TO TURN OUT LIKE HE EXPECTS. BUT, IN THE END, IT'S GOING TO BE ***ALL RIGHT.***

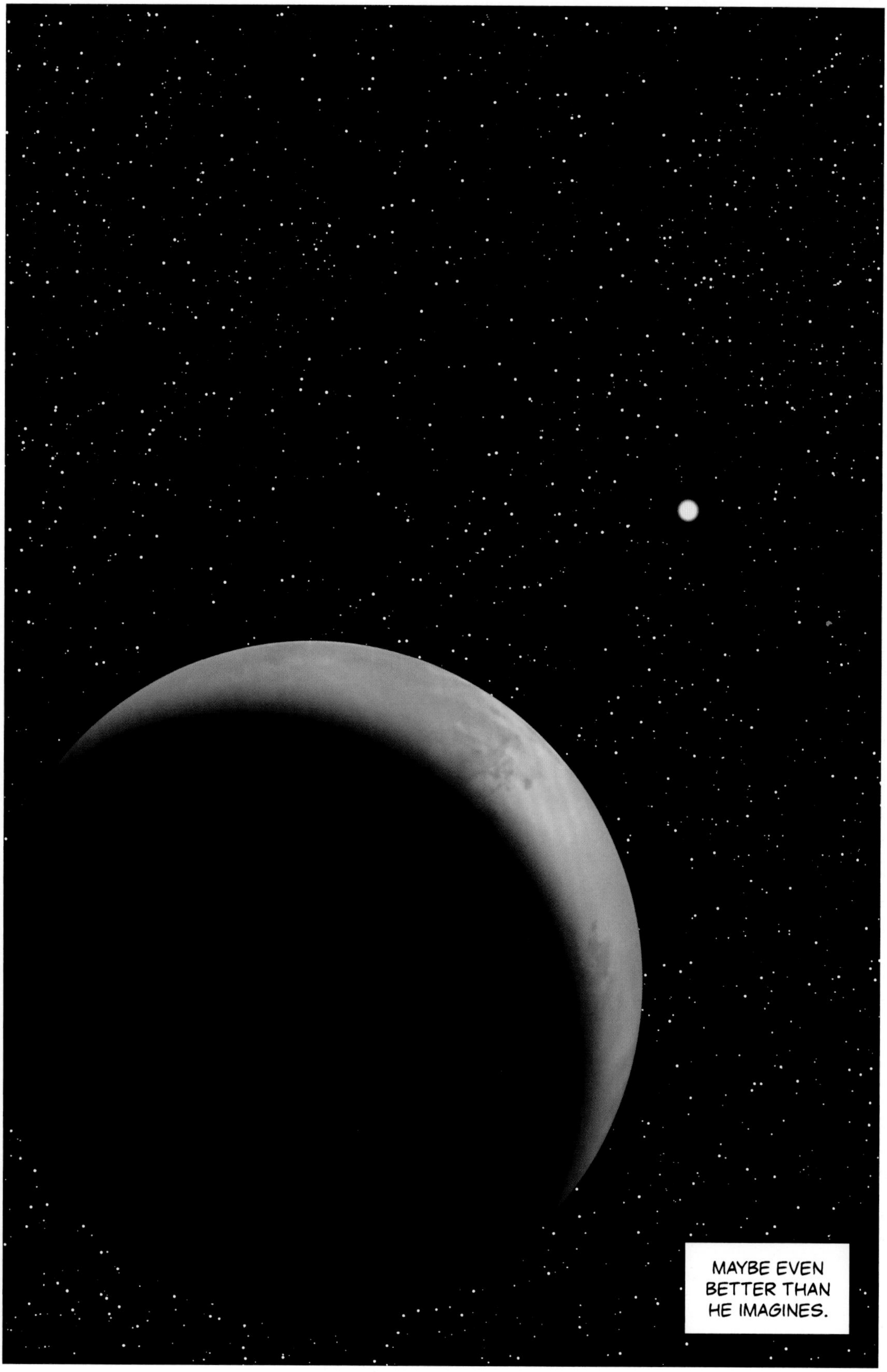
MAYBE EVEN
BETTER THAN
HE IMAGINES.

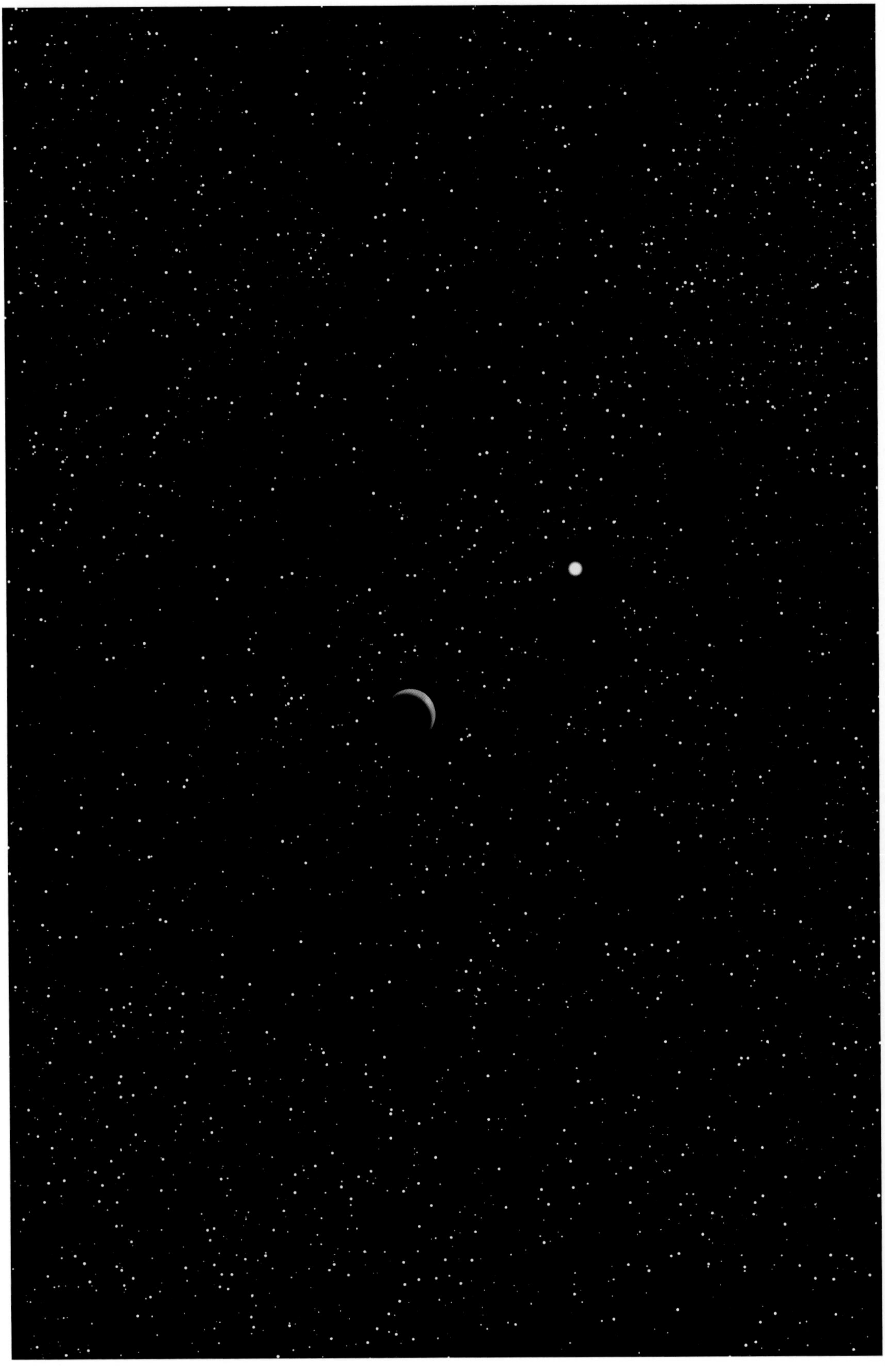

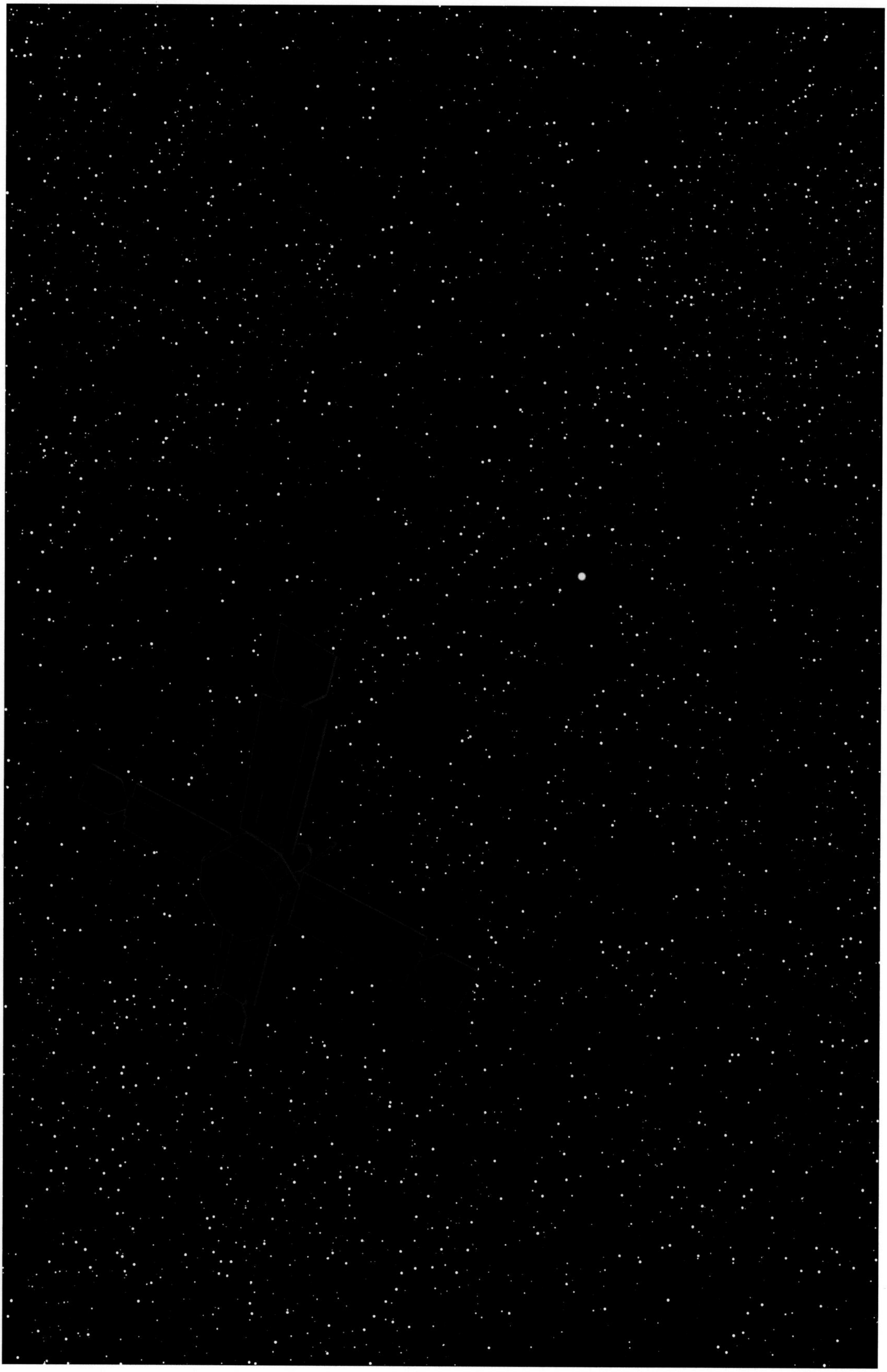

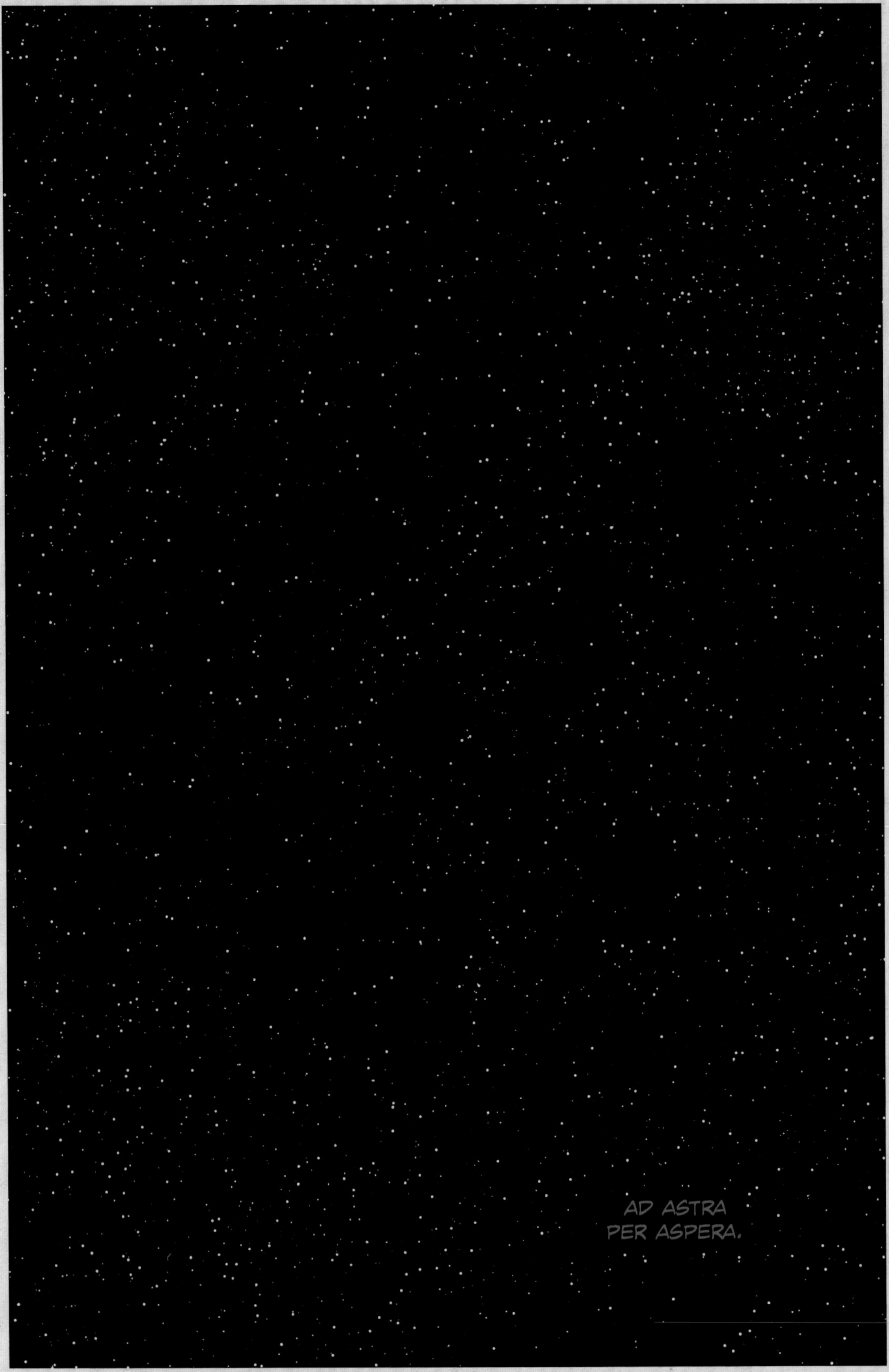

AD ASTRA
PER ASPERA.